CRA

Good

for ease of revision

Examination Guide – Shows how the chapter covers each exam group's syllabus

Subheads break content into manageable units

the *Pattern of Questions* in the exam

Text – the information and facts that you need in digestible form

Exam guidance

- the skills to tackle them

- Targets: What the questions are aiming at

- Questions: How to tackle them

- Activity: Real exam questions

Source material just like you find in the exam

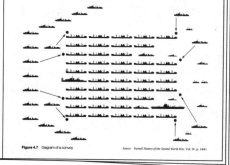

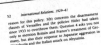

In this book

Success and success

Our book has two main purposes:
- To help you understand many of the major events, ideas and issues which affect you in your everyday lives
- To ensure success when you take the GCSE Modern World History examination papers at the end of your course.

History is relevant to you

Most of the people we have written about are dead and buried, but what they did lives on today. Open a newspaper or listen to the radio or television and you see the direct impact History has upon your life.

An example of what we mean

If in 1914 you had asked History teachers about communism, they would probably not have heard of the word. Today your History teacher will be dealing with communism for much of this course – communists rule about half of the world's people. You can only understand what communism means by looking at how it developed and changed in countries like Russia and China in this century.

Exam coverage

The four main Examining Groups, LEAG (London), MEG (Midland), NEA (Northern) and SEG (Southern) Modern World History syllabuses cover over 100 separate topics. I know, I worked carefully through all the syllabuses and counted them!

So we have picked out the key content common to all four syllabuses. The chapters are arranged in a logical order which reflects the pattern of Modern World History GCSE papers.

Chapter 1   shows how to analyse your own course, how to handle the kinds of questions which you will have to answer, how to interpret sources and how to organise your revision programme.

Chapters 2–6   an outline course on International Relations 1919–1990

Chapters 7–11   the five major topics for study in depth
The First World War – Chapter 7
Russia 1917–1953 –
Chapter 8
Germany 1919–1945 – Chapter 9
America 1919–1941 –
Chapter 10
China 1919–1980 –
Chapter 11

In your own course you will probably have to cover two or three of the topics contained in chapters 7–11. Hopefully the common core in this book will cover at least 80% of what you need for the final examination.

Contents

Topic

Acknowledgements

The authors and publishers wish to thank the following for permission to use copyright material: London East Anglian Group. Midland Examining Group, Northern Examining Association comprising Associated Lancashire Schools Examining Board, Joint Matriculation Board, North Regional Examinations Board, North West Regional Examinations Board and Yorkshire & Humberside Regional Examinations Board, and Southern Examining Group for questions from specimen and past examination papers: Solo Syndication for five cartoons by David Low included in *Years of Wrath. A Cartoon History 1932–1945* by David Low, Gollancz, 1986.

Other acknowledgements for use of figures and tables is as shown within the text.

The authors and publishers also wish to acknowledge the following photograph sources: Bilderdienst Suddeutscher page 180: Camera Press pages 62, 103 bottom right, 125, 213, 218; Chinese National Army Museum page 99; Hulton Picture Company pages 14, 68, 144, 187, 188; By kind permission of the Trustees of the Imperial War Museum pages 70, 81 top, 87 top right, 144; Popperfoto pages 87 top left, 87 bottom, 111, 115, 118, 151, 153; Roger-Viollet pages 75, 157; John Sadovy page 102; Syndication International Ltd page 103 bottom left; Topham Picture Library pages 81 bottom, 103 top, 114, 126, 192; Ullstein Bilderdienst pages 173, 179, 181 right; UNRWA/George Nehmeh page 117; US National Archives page 93; The Wiener Library page 181 left.

Every effort has been made to trace all the copyright holders but if any have been inadvertently overlooked the publishers will be pleased to make the necessary arrangement at the first opportunity.

First published 1990 by

MACMILLAN PRESS LTD
Houndmills, Basingstoke, Hampshire RG21 6XS
and London
Companies and representatives
throughout the world

ISBN 0–333–46875–9

A catalogue record for this book is available from the British Library.

Printed in Hong Kong

10 9   8   7   6   5   4
00 99 98 97 96

Jon Nichol and Sean Lang

Modern World History GCSE

MACMILLAN

What
the exam boards want

Topic	MEG Midland Exam Group	LEAG London Exam Group
2 International Relations 1914–29	The Search for International Order between 1919 and 1929 (Compulsory Element, Paper 1)	E1. The League of Nations and the United Nations (Paper 1) F1. Fascism in Italy and Germany (Paper 1)
3 International Relations 1929–41	The Collapse of International Order in the 1930s (Compulsory Element, Paper 1)	E1. The League of Nations and the United Nations (Paper 1) F1. Fascism in Italy and Germany (Paper 1))
4 The Second World War	World War II is included as element in the optional topic, Germany, 1919–45.	I1. Aspects of the second World War (Paper 1)
5 The Cold War 1945–1962	Tension and Co-operation since 1945 (Compulsory Element, Paper 1)	I2. Super-Power Relations, 1945–75 (Paper 2) C1. Arab-Israeli Relations since 1948 (Paper 1)
6 The Modern World 1962–1990	Tension and Co-operation since 1945 (Compulsory Element, Paper 1)	I2. Super-Power Relations, 1945–75 (Paper 2) C1. Arab-Israeli Relations since 1948 (Paper 1)
7 The First World War	The First World War (Optional Topic, Paper 2)	J1. The Impact of the First World War on British Society (Paper 1)
8 Russia 1917–56	Russia, 1917–41 (Optional Topic, Paper 2)	G1. The Russian Revolution and the Establishment of the Soviet State, 1917–41 (Paper 1)
9 Germany 1919–45	Germany, 1919–45 (Optional Topic, Paper 2)	F1. Fascism in Italy and Germany, 1919–39 (Paper 1)

Topic	MEG Midland Exam Group	LEAG London Exam Group
10 The United States of America, 1919–41	The United States of America, 1919–41 (Optional Topic, Paper 2)	H2. Boom, Depression and New Deal in the United States, 1919–41 (Paper 2)
11 China 1919–80	Communism in China since 1949 (Optional Topic, Paper 2)	A2. The Emergence of a Communist State in China, 1920 to the death of Mao Zedong (Mao Tse Tung) (Paper 2)

	NEA Northern Exam Association	SEG Southern Exam Group
2 International Relations 1914–29	Conflict and Conciliation, Compulsory theme (Paper 1) Peacemaking after the First World War International Co-operation, Optional theme (Paper 2) – The League of Nations	Peace to World War, 1918–41 (Optional Theme, Paper 1)
3 International Relations 1929–41	Conflict and Conciliation, Compulsory theme (Paper 1) – Causes of the Second World War International Co-operation, Optional theme (Paper 2) – The League of Nations – The failure of Collective Security in the 1930s	Peace to World War, 1918–41 (Optional Theme, Paper 1)
4 The Second World War	Conflict and Conciliation, Compulsory theme (Paper 1) – Developing techniques of warfare in the Second World War – The Home Front in Britain – German conquest and occupation in the Second World War	Military Events of the Second World War, 1939–45 (Optional Topic, Paper 2)

Topic	NEA Northern Exam Association	SEG Southern Exam Group
5 The Cold War 1945–1962	Conflict and Conciliation, Compulsory theme (Paper 1) – The Cold War – The Nuclear Arms Race International Co-operation, Optional theme (Paper 2) – The United Nations – Post War Co-operation in Western Europe	The USA and the USSR as World Superpowers since 1945 (Compulsory Theme, Paper 1) The Arab-Israeli conflict, 1945–79 (Optional Topic, Paper 2)
6 The Modern World 1962–1990	Conflict and Conciliation, Compulsory theme (Paper 1) – Guerilla Warfare in Vietnam International Co-operation, Optional theme (Paper 2) – The United Nations – Post War Co-operation in Western Europe	The USA and the USSR as World Superpowers since 1945 (Compulsory Theme, Paper 1) The Arab–Israeli conflict, 1945–79 (Optional Topic, Paper 2)
7 The First World War	Conflict and Conciliation, Compulsory theme (Paper 1) – The reasons why Sarajevo led to war – The Western Front, 1914–18 – The Home Front in Britain	Britain and the Western Front, 1914–18 (Optional Topic, Paper 2)
8 Russia 1917–56	The Russian Revolution: Lenin and Stalin (Optional Topic, Paper 2)	Russia, 1917–41 (Optional Topic, Paper 2)
9 Germany 1919–45	Germany, 1918–39 (Optional Topic, Paper 2)	Germany, 1919–39 (Optional Topic, Paper 2)
10 The United States of America 1919–41	The USA in the 1920s and 1930s (Optional Topic, Paper 2)	Internal Developments in the USA, 1919–41 (Optional Topic, Paper 2)
11 China 1919–80	Communist China	China, 1934–68 Optional Topic, Paper 2)

COURSE AND REVISION PLANNING

1 The Nature of GCSE

In planning out your course and revision, you need to know what GCSE Modern World History is about. The guidelines for your course are laid down in the Examining Group's syllabus, and details of what to do can be worked out from old examination papers. What do the GCSE examiners want from you? Each syllabus has an almost identical set of **Aims** and **Assessment Objectives**. The Aims lay down in general terms what you should get out of the course, while the **Assessment Objectives** give a detailed account of what you will be tested upon. The **Assessment Objectives** are what the examiners have been told to use when drawing up your examination papers. The four **Assessment Objectives** read:

1. To recall, evaluate and select knowledge relevant to the context and to deploy it in a clear and coherent form.
2. To make use of and understand the concepts of cause and consequence, continuity and change, similarity and difference.
3. To show an ability to look at events and issues from the perspective of people in the past.
4. To show the skills necessary to study a wide variety of historical evidence, which should include both primary and secondary written sources, statistical and visual material, artefacts, textbooks and orally transmitted information:
   (i) By comprehending and extracting information from it.
   (ii) By interpreting and evaluating it – distinguishing between fact, opinion and judgement; pointing to deficiencies in the material as evidence, such as gaps and inconsistencies; detecting bias.
   (iii) By comparing various types of historical evidence and reaching conclusions based on this comparison.
   (GCSE National Criteria for History – Assessment Objectives)

What do these words mean? They can be summed up quite simply.

1. *What you know and understand*, the framework of facts, ideas and linked information which you have learned.
2. *Concepts* which give the subject its shape; for example, what causes things to happen and the nature of the changes which occur.
3. *Empathy*, the ability to see things from the viewpoint of people who lived in the past.
4. *Skills* needed to handle historical sources.

2 Your Course – the GCSE Syllabuses

The first thing to do is to find out what your course covers. Your teacher or lecturer will tell you which Examining Group is offering your Modern World History paper. There are two main guides to your course: the syllabus booklet, and the last three years' examination papers. Both of these you should obtain from the Examining Group – they are essential reading.

ACTIVITY 1

Write to your Examining Group for the syllabus and examination papers, using the specimen letter below as a guide.

```
(Your address)
To: The History Section

Dear Sir or Madam,
  Could you please send me your
syllabus for GCSE Modern World
History, and the Modern World History
question papers for the past three
years and specimen papers, if
available. If I need to order the
question papers, could you please send
me an application form.

      Yours faithfully,
      (Your name)
```

The Table on pages 3–5 contains a breakdown of the main elements in the syllabuses of the four main Examining Groups, LEAG, MEG, SEG and NEA. The left-hand column gives the title of *Work Out Modern World History's* chapters, the right-hand columns the main contents of each syllabus.

ACTIVITY 2

Copy out the headings from the Table on pages 3–5 for the topics you will be covering in your own syllabus. Under each heading put in the details of the topics you will have to study. To do this, use the syllabus the Examining Group sent you. The bulk of your course will hopefully be dealt with in the *Work Out Modern World History* chapters in the left-hand column. Don't be put off by posh and complex-sounding titles using long, vague words.

THE CONTENT OF THE EXAMINATION PAPERS

What will you have to cover for the final examination in terms of *content*? We have already looked at the syllabus areas of the four Examining Groups, and seen how this book covers them. Each syllabus is usually made up of two parts: a compulsory element, and topics from which you can choose, as below. All the Examining Groups split their examinations up into two written papers, Paper 1 and Paper 2. Only read the information below which applies to the Examining Group whose syllabus you are following.

Figure 1.1 Examining Groups: papers and times

Examining Group	Paper 1		Paper 2		
	Time hours	% of marks	Time hours	% of marks	Total %
LEAG	2	40	1.5	30	70
MEG	1.75	40	1.5	30	70
NEA	1.5	30	2	40	70
SEG	1.75	40	1.5	30	70

Each group allocates 30% to coursework

London and East Anglian Group (LEAG)

The LEAG syllabus is split up into twenty topics, divided into two lists of ten topics each. List 1 contains topics for Paper 1, List 2 topics for Paper 2. The lists are organised in alphabetical order (see Table 1.1). Paper 1 is in two parts, each of which gets 20% of the marks (40% in total). The paper lasts for 2 hours. Paper 2 gets 30% of the marks and lasts for 1.5 hours. For Paper 1 you have to cover THREE out of the TEN topics in List 1, *Work Out Modern World History* deals with four of these topics in great detail:

> E1, **The League of Nations and the United Nations**
> F1, **Fascism in Italy and Germany, 1919–39**
> G1, **The Russian Revolution and the Establishment of the Soviet State, 1917–41**
> I1, **Aspects of the Second World War**

It provides outline information for:

> C1, **Arab–Israeli Relations since 1948**
> J1, **The Impact of the First World War on British Society**

For Paper 2 you need to know TWO out of TEN topics in detail. We fully cover:

> A2, **The Emergence of a Communist State in China, 1920 to the death of Mao Zedong (Mao Tse Tung)**
> H2, **Boom, Depression and New Deal in the United States, 1919–41**
> I2, **Superpower Relations, 1945–75**

Midland Examining Group (MEG)

MEG has a simpler pattern. Again, the examination is split into two papers: Paper 1 (1¾ hours) and Paper 2 (1½ hours). Paper 1 is for 40% of the marks, and you have to answer three structured questions out of six set. Paper 2 gains 30% of the marks, and is in a single part. There are two structured questions on each of three elements in a core course on **International Relations since the First World War**, although rather oddly it leaves out the Second World War! Table 1.1 gives details. Paper 2 is made up of nine optional topics; you have to answer questions on two of them. We cover five of them in detail:

1. **The First World War**
2. **Russia, 1917–41**
3. **Germany, 1919–45**
4. **The United States of America, 1919–41**
5. **Communism in China since 1949**

Northern Examining Association (NEA)

The NEA has a more complex pattern, with five themes, the first three of which are taught for the final examination:

1. **Conflict and Conciliation**
2. **Governments in Action**
3. **International Co-operation**
4. **Colonialism** (for coursework)
5. **Human Rights** (for coursework)

Work Out Modern World History covers a large amount of

your likely taught course. There are two NEA Papers: Paper 1 (1½ hours) for 30% of the marks, Paper 2 (2 hours) for 40%. You have to study all four sub-sections of **Conflict and Conciliation**, for in Paper 1 the questions on it are compulsory. Theme 1's four sub-sections are:

(a)   **Origins of Conflict**
(b)   **The Changing Nature of Warfare**
(c)   **The Civilian Experience of War**
(d)   **Attempts to Resolve Conflict**

Under each of these sub-sections are listed the syllabus areas; these are indicated in Table 1.1. *Work Out Modern World History* covers all of the areas in the theme **Conflict and Conciliation**. Because the NEA has organised its syllabus in a different way, you must make sure that you work through all the relevant sections in our book, using Table 1.1 to help you. Paper 2 for NEA covers Theme 2, **Governments in Action** and Theme 3, **International Co-operation**. The paper is split into four parts, with THREE questions set on each part, ONE of which will be answered for each part. Theme 2, **Governments in Action**, covers in detail a range of topics identical to that of the other Examining Groups. Theme 2 splits into two sub-sections, A and B, and from each section you have to choose one topic for study, i.e. two in all. The sections' contents are:

Sub-Section A

1.   **The Russian Revolution: Lenin and Stalin**
2.   **Germany, 1918–39**
3.   **Communist China**

Sub-Section B

1.   **The USA in the 1920s and 1930s**
2.   **Britain**

The **International Co-operation** theme is covered in Chapters 2, 3, 5 and 6 of *Work Out Modern World History*, and has THREE questions set on it. The final part of the paper asks you to answer ONE essay-type question from THREE questions covering Themes 2 and 3.

Southern Examining Group (SEG)

The SEG, in its revised syllabus for examination in 1991, reflects very closely the coverage of *Work Out Modern World History*. For Paper 1 (1¾ hours; 40% of the marks), 15% of the total marks are awarded for a compulsory question on Theme 1, **The USA and the USSR as World Superpowers since 1945** (Chapters 5 and 6 of *Work Out*). The remaining 25% will be awarded for two answers, with ten questions being set. One question is on Theme 1 (Chapters 5 and 6 of *Work Out*), and there are nine other questions, three for each of Theme 2, **Peace to World War, 1918–41** (covered in Chapters 2 and 3 of *Work Out*); Theme 3, **Imperialism, Decolonisation and Post-Imperial Relationships**; and Theme 4, **Effects of Technological and Scientific Change since 1914**. *Work Out* provides coverage of four questions for this section.

This means that you can get 27.5% of your marks for studying Theme 1, **The USA and the USSR as World Superpowers since 1945**. Paper 2 allows for study in

detail, with two topics being examined out of seven. *Work Out* covers topics 1–6 of the Paper 2 topics in full (see Figure 1.1) and Topic 7 in outline:

1.   **Britain and the Western Front, 1914–18**
2.   **Russia, 1917–41**
3.   **Internal Developments in the USA, 1919–41**
4.   **Germany, 1919–39**
5.   **China, 1934–68**
6.   **Military Events of the Second World War, 1939–45**
7.   **Arab–Israeli Conflict, 1945–79**

3 Analysing the Examination Papers

Your course will divide into two main areas: work for the final, *written examination* (70% of the marks) and *course-work* (30% of the marks). You do coursework during your course of study, and it is marked by your teacher. This book will deal only with *the final, written examination*.

What will the examination ask of you? Already we have looked at the Assessment Objectives. Each Examining Group lays down the Assessment Objectives it will test in the different parts of the examining; Figure 1.2 contains this information. Again, only look at your own Examining Group. Each Examining Group sets three main kinds of questions: very short answers, paragraph, and short essay questions. All three kinds appear as either free-standing or source-linked questions. Figure 1.3 analyses the number of questions asked for each Group's papers – consult this table, as it will tell you exactly what will be asked of you in your examination.

Very Short Answers

These can be multiple-choice, single-word or sentence answers, which ask you to recall factual information, ideas and concepts. These questions are really a version of Trivial Pursuit, and hopefully will be almost totally missing from the examination you take. *Multiple-choice* questions ask you to ring the correct answer. *Single-word* or *sentence* answers take the form of simple recall. A typical recall question asks:

Who was America's president in 1918?

Paragraph and Short-Essay Questions

Short-paragraph and essay questions ask you to produce an argument to show what you understand about the question. A short-paragraph and an essay question are similar, and are easy to spot. They take the form of asking for a longer piece of writing, e.g.:

'Many felt that the 1919–20 peace treaties would lead to a European War within 20 years.' Why did they feel this way, and how were their fears justified?   (MEG)

Source- or Evidence-Based Questions

These are questions which are tied to historical sources, usually a written extract or a picture. What do we mean

Figure 1.2   Assessment Objectives (see page 10) and the final examination

LEAG

Assessment Objective	Paper 1	Paper 2
1	**Part 1 (20%)	
2	**Part 2 (20%)	
3		
4		**
Total percentage	40	30

**test

MEG

Assessment Objective	Paper 1	Paper 2
1	*	*
2	*	*
3		
4		**
Total percentage	40	30

*important   **very important

NEA

Assessment Objective	Paper 1	Paper 2
1	*	**
2	**	*
3	*	**
4	**	*
Total percentage	30	40

**mainly test   *may also test

SEG

Assessment Objective	Paper 1 Section A	Paper 1 Section B	Paper 2 Section A	Paper 2 Section B
1		5–10	5–10	4–6
2		15–10	10–5	6–4
3				
4	15	5		5
Total percentage	15	25	15	15

Figure 1.3   Breakdown of final examination papers

Key S = Source-based   SH = Short   P = Paragraph   E = Essay   STR = Structured

BOARD	Paper 1	Paper 2
LEAG	TWO HOURS Three questions; for each: 5 S SH/P 2 P/E	ONE & A HALF HOURS Two questions; for each: 6 S SH/P
MEG	ONE & THREE QUARTER HOURS Three questions; for each: 6 S SH/P STR	ONE & A HALF HOURS Two questions; for each: 4 S SH STR 2 S P STR 1 S E STR
NEA	ONE & A HALF HOURS Five questions; for each: 2/4 S P STR 2 S E STR	TWO HOURS Three questions; for each; 6/7 S SH/P STR One question E
SEG	ONE & THREE QUARTER HOURS Section A — One question; 5 S P Section B — Two questions; for each: 4 S P STR	ONE & A QUARTER HOURS Section A — One question; for each: 8 S P STR Section B — One question; for each: 8 S P STR

by a historical source? Historical sources are the raw materials which the historian uses to construct his own view of the past – in other words, to write history. When I wrote this book, I read hundreds of other books to find out about topics like the Russian Revolution. We divide sources up into two main kinds, *primary* and *secondary sources*. Primary sources are the materials which the topic under study generated; things like government reports, letters, photographs, cartoons and newspapers of the time, the clues of history. Secondary sources are what historians or others have later written or said about the subject. This book is a secondary source about Modern World History; it would be a primary source for someone looking at the writing of school books on the subject of Modern World History.

In beginning to work on primary and secondary sources, what steps should you take? Figures 1.4 and 1.5 deal with primary and secondary sources respectively.

Figure 1.4   Handling a primary source

Introduction   How do we go about handling a primary source? Look at Source 1A, and then take these steps:

1.   Is the source primary or secondary?

Source 1A

Source   H. Nicolson, *The Congress of Vienna*, Constable, 1946, endpiece

2. Where is the source taken from – i.e. what is its origin?
3. How complete is the source? Is any of it missing?
4. How authentic is it? Has it been redrawn, rewritten, altered in any way?
5. Did the producer of the source know about what is being commented upon?
6. Did the person producing the source have a reason for trying to push a particular point of view?
7. Does the source show bias, either intended or otherwise?
8. What point of view, values or attitudes does the source put across, either intended or otherwise?
9. What gaps are there in the source?
10. How can the source be checked against other sources?
11. What clues does the source give which you can follow up in other primary or in secondary sources?

Figure 1.5   Handling a secondary source

Introduction   How do we go about judging how much trust we can place upon a secondary source? Follow these steps:

1. Who was the author?
   (a) Was the writer an expert upon the subject, whose word you can trust?
   (b) What do other historians think of him/her; are his/her views sound?
   (c) Do you know of other books the writer has written upon the subject? How good are they?
2. Who is the publisher?
   (a) Is the publisher one which is known to publish sound books, or is it a firm which is unknown or which will even print anything for money?
3. When was the book published?
   (a) A book published a long time ago is less likely to reflect the latest findings and views on the subject.
4. Internal evidence
   (a) How much detail is there inside the passage which suggests that the author knew what s/he was talking about?
   (b) Supporting evidence. Where the writer makes a statement, how does s/he use facts within the passage to back up what s/he says.

5. External evidence
   (a) Do other books support what the passage says?
   (b) Does the passage seem to contain more information than other books?
   (c) How much of the detail ties up with what you already know about the subject?
6. The author's use of language
   (a) Is the passage written using emotional words?
   (b) Does the writer show any bias in what s/he says?

ACTIVITY 3

Take last summer's examination paper. Work out the proportion or percentage of your examination which is directly tied in to the use of sources.

ACTIVITY 4

You should now read carefully through the source-based questions for your Board. This will give you some idea of the problems you will face in tackling such questions.

ACTIVITY 5

Look at Source 1A. It is supposed to show the arrest of Princip, who has just killed Archduke Ferdinand of Austria in Sarajevo (see pages 24–25). The murder sparked off the First World War. What other kinds of sources would you go to to find out about this incident? Draw up your ideas in the form of a spider diagram, with a sources box at the centre. Draw arrows and boxes which you will fill in for the different kinds of sources.

The many forms which source questions take are dealt with below, but fall into the three types described above, ie. short-answer, paragraph or short-essay questions. The marks are shown in parentheses, and suggest how long you should spend on the answer.

A short-answer question using Source 1A might ask:

Name the figure being arrested in the photograph.   **(1)**

A paragraph question might ask:

Why is the figure in the photograph being arrested?   **(5)**

A typical short-essay question tied in to a clutch of sources is:

'On June 30th Hitler's purpose was to put down a second revolution.' Do these sources show this view to be true? Explain your answer fully.   (12) (MEG, November 1988)

ACTIVITY 6

Read through last year's examination papers. Work out the proportion or percentage of short-answer, paragraph and short-essay questions asked for each paper.

	No. of questions	% of total marks
Short-answer		
Paragraph		
Essay		

Warning! Take care not to be fooled by questions on a sources part of the paper which have nothing to do with the sources.

Having briefly begun our work on the kinds of questions which you will find upon your examination papers, and the kinds of demands that they will make upon you, we shall now dig deeper into unravelling the mysteries of coping with the examination.

This book will help you succeed in handling the range of examination questions asked. Work steadily on the next section – it is meant to serve as a guide.

4 Handling Examination Questions

VERY SHORT ANSWERS

We looked at these briefly above. They test the bare, outline factual knowledge which you can remember. How can you remember detail? One good way to master the facts is to produce your own set of very brief notes covering the main details of a topic. These notes can take the form of a list of key facts, or be written out in the form of a spider diagram which shows the links between the different pieces of information. When you revise, for each topic try and get all your notes on to one or two sides of paper.

When you try and remember facts, there are four rules to observe:

1. Always try and link together the facts that you are learning. Facts only mean something in relation to other facts. This is why a spider diagram is such a good idea.
2. Pick out what you think are the key facts, and then tie into them those you feel are less important.
3. When you revise, work out what you think is the best way for you to remember things.
4. Don't learn things you don't understand.

ACTIVITY 7

Read through Chapter 2. List what you think are the six most important facts in the chapter. Turn these facts into questions, e.g.:

Fact   **Question**
World War I ended in 1918.   When did World War I end?

After a one-hour break, ask yourself the questions you have worked out, in any order.

PARAGRAPH AND SHORT-ESSAY QUESTIONS

These two types of questions can be answered in a similar way. The difference between a paragraph and a short-essay answer is that the essay answer should have an argument which connects the paragraphs together. All the Examination Groups will ask you to write answers in the form of a paragraph or a short-essay. The headings or main points of the essay may be given to you. This we call a *structured essay*. There is a standard way of going about writing these answers:

1. **Read through the question with great care.** In particular, note the number of marks which it awards, with the amount of time that you should spend on it.

Look for key words like 'describe', 'explain', 'imagine', 'why'? Think what these words mean, and try and do as they ask. A description is just that – an account of the subject being asked about; while 'imagine' asks you to do something very different, like seeing a situation from the viewpoint of one of the people involved. Does the question give certain key dates or a period (e.g., 1918–29, the Stalinist Era)? You must work out what the examiner will want from you and stick to the point. Thus, if you are asked to describe what life was like for a member of the PLA on the Long March (see Chapter 9), don't talk about Chairman Mao, the Long March's leader.

2. **Make a brief plan.** In your plan, list the main ideas and points which the paragraph or paragraphs will cover. Often single, linked words in a column down the page will do – all they are is trigger words to get your brain and memory working. Cover one main theme per paragraph. The plan can be very short – just a list of the main points.

3. **Writing**
   (a) Think carefully about what you are going to write, and make sure that you stick to the point of the question.
   (b) Include as many relevant facts as you can.
   (c) In examination conditions, only spend the amount of time which the marks for the question suggest.
   (d) Try and write in short, clear sentences – they are much easier to manage.

To give you an idea of how these ideas might work out in practice for both paragraph and essay answers, below is a model answer and an account of how it was written.

Model Answer – Paragraph and Short-Essay Answers

Question

Describe the circumstances in which the League of Nations was established. (10 marks)

Steps to take

In answering such questions, look at the following points in turn:

1. How many marks are allotted to this section, and how much time should you allow? Work this out first, to make sure you put in the right amount of information and spend the correct amount of time in doing your answer.

   In this case there are ten marks, one-tenth of the total for the paper, and you have ten minutes to answer the question.

2. What is the question asking? Look for buzz words, in this case 'describe', 'circumstances' and 'the League of Nations'.

   'Describe' and 'circumstances' are linked together – so the examiner wants a list of things which led to the setting-up of the League of Nations.

   How many things does s/he want you to talk about? In this case at least ten – one mark for each.

3.   What exactly does s/he want you to talk about? The area is very clearly stated – *the setting-up of the League of Nations*. The examiner does not want you to talk about the League of Nations as such, just how it was established.

4.   What form should the answer take?
It is a short essay. It should be a simple piece of prose, written without any frills, flourishes or waffle.

Below is a typical essay question, and an answer which gives you an idea of how you should write simply and clearly, and stick to the point of the question.

Essay question

Describe the circumstances in which the League of Nations was established.   **(10 marks)**

Answer

The League of Nations was set up after the First World War, to deal with the problems which faced the negotiators at the Paris Peace Conference of January 1919, with their hopes and ideals for a better world. The League of Nations was based upon the Fourteen Points of President Wilson of the United States, but other leaders such as Lloyd George had also supported the idea of an international body to secure world peace. During the Paris Peace Conference the negotiators all accepted the need for the League, and its covenant was an element in all five peace treaties.

The League of Nations was designed to make sure that the peace settlement was enforced, and that there would be no future wars. It was also intended to solve other world problems, such as legal disputes between nations, the arms race, the question of refugees, drug-trafficking, plagues and epidemics, colonies and labour relations. In 1919–20 the world was faced with:

the need to avoid another arms race such as led to the First World War and to ensure that Germany remained disarmed;
major refugee problems arising from the flight of people from their homes during the First World War;
a world-wide epidemic of Asian 'flu;
the problem of what to do with the ex-colonies of Germany. League of Nations mandates were a method of supporting President Wilson's belief in the self-determination of people and of handing Germany's colonies over to the Allies.

The circumstances facing the proposed League in 1919–20 presented it with many problems. None of the great powers was willing to give it an independent military force of its own, the idea being that it would rely upon 'collective security' – that is, all the powers acting peacefully together to solve problems. The League also had the problem of enforcing its decisions when two of the world's leading powers, Germany and Russia, were not members.

Commentary

The answer is split into three pieces. It first deals with the background to the League. Note that it mentions details of both President Wilson and the Paris Peace Conference. The second section provides a list of the circumstances the League faced, and how it intended to deal with them. The final part discusses circumstances it failed to deal with. The answer contains about 24 separate factual points.

5 Source-Based Questions

Both primary and secondary sources are of no use to you unless you ask questions about them. Without questions, sources are dumb, lifeless objects. In the examination, questions can take many forms and fall under a number of headings. What kinds of questions will you have to answer? We have sorted them into types in Figure 1.6. The table looks a bit like a pools coupon, and should be as easy to use with a bit of practice.

ACTIVITY 8

Take last year's papers. Put in the year and the paper number. Write the correct question number for the type of question in the question number column, using the source-based question guide (see page 17) to help you.

SOURCE-BASED QUESTION GUIDE

When you are looking at a source-based question, how can you recognise what kind it is? Questions are puzzles, whose meaning is wrapped up in their wording, i.e. how they are asked. Luckily, the question will contain clues about what the examiner wants in the form of key words and phrases. The most common of these are given at the end of each sub-section about the type of questions.

USING THE TABLE IN FIGURE 1.6

The first step in analysing your source-based questions isn't too obvious – you have to see if it is a source-based question or not! Boards often ask questions on the sources' topic which can be answered without reference to the sources. Two questions from the NEA are typical. The first was on a clutch of sources about warfare, the second on a source about Russia's Five-Year Plans of the late 1920s and 1930s:

1. In 1914 Kitchener said the tank was 'a pretty mechanical toy but of limited military value'. Why do you think he thought this?
2. Do you think the Five-Year Plans were successful? Give reasons for your answers.

These are paragraph or short-essay questions, depending upon how long an answer is required. Once you have decided on which questions are genuinely tied in to their sources, we can examine the headings in Figure 1.6.

1. Recall

These require you to remember the meaning of words, phrases, dates, ideas and concepts mentioned or alluded to in the source. Often such questions can be answered without reference to the source, but it is intended to

Figure 1.6 Types of source-based question

Question type	Year	Paper	Question no.
1. Recall **Type 1**			
2. Information linked to EXTERNAL knowledge. Here the source is used to:			
Type 2.1 explain about a situation			
Type 2.2 test an existing opinion or point of view			
Type 2.3 identify in the source a person, place, thing, idea or concept			
Type 2.4 identify in the source a person, place, thing, idea or concept INSIDE another source			
Type 2.5 explain a contradiction or agreement between sources			
3. Use the sources to write a historical account **Type 3**			
4. Analyse the value of the sources to the historian:			
Type 4.1 detect bias			
Type 4.2 assess reliability of sources			
Type 4.3 identify other sources about the subject			
Type 4.4 date the source and put it into context			
Type 4.5 identify the type of source			

serve as a stimulus. A typical recall question is:

(a) What is meant by the following phrase in the source? 'Germany gains the Sudetenland' (SEG)

(b) Name the leader portrayed on the right. (NEA)

2. Information linked to external knowledge

Such questions ask you to link information in the source to what you already know about the topic. This question has FIVE main varieties, Types 2.1–2.5 below:

Type 2.1 These questions ask you to explain either how the source helps show why something happened, what the source is about or what light it throws on the topic, e.g.:

1. With explicit reference to Source 6 and Source 7, explain why Stalin negotiated the Non-Aggression Pact with Hitler in 1939.
2. Explain the cartoon. (NEA)
3. Why has the cartoonist shown a goose and referred to 'a goose step' in Source 5? (MEG)

Key Words/Phrases: 'what clue/evidence suggests', 'evidence to: identify, support, undermine, explain, show why'.

Type 2.2 Questions which test the source against an existing historical opinion, e.g.:

1. Explain, whether or not, in your opinion, the sources support the following statement: 'American economic support for European countries was an act of considerable generosity.' (SEG)
2. 'The Nazis feared little opposition inside Germany in the 1930s.' Is this view supported or contradicted by Sources 2, 3 and 4? Explain your answer. (MEG)
3. 'Russia should not have made the pact with Germany in 1939.' Using the sources, explain how far you agree with this opinion. (NEA)

Key Words/Phrases: 'Sources support', 'contradicted', 'using the sources'. 'Explain'.

Type 2.3 Questions which use evidence inside the source which enables you to identify a person, place,

thing, concept or idea, or which adds to what you already know, e.g.:

1. What evidence is there in Source 2 which helps you to identify:
(a) the speaker
(b) the place?
2. What evidence can be drawn from Sources 3 and 4 to show the difficulties that the partition of Palestine would create for the new Israel? (SEG)
3. Using all the sources, explain the various methods employed by the Nazis to gain political control over Germany in the 1930s? (MEG)

Key Words/Phrases: 'Whether or not', 'how trustworthy', 'evidence from', 'enough evidence', 'Is this view supported or contradicted by the sources?' 'agree with opinion', 'identify', 'show'.

Type 2.4 Evidence inside the source which enables you to identify a person, place, thing, concept or idea *inside another source*, e.g.:

1. How can you use maps 6 and 7 to explain the reference in Source 2 to the treatment of Czechoslovakia?
2. In what ways does the evidence in Sources 1 and 2 support the views advanced in Sources 3 and 4? (SEG)
3. To which two groups listed in Source 3 might the man in Source A have belonged? (MEG)

Key Words/Phrases: 'evidence in Sources . . . support'.

Type 2.5 Questions which ask for the explanation of contradictions and/or agreement between sources, e.g.

1. Is the writer of Source 5's argument undermined by the evidence produced in Sources 3 and 4?
2. How far were Points Four and Five of Source 7 kept to by the clauses of the Treaty of Versailles given in Source 8? (NEA)

3. Source 2 shows British soldiers manning a German trench captured during the Battle of the Somme. This proves that the author of Source 1 is wrong in his judgement. Do you agree with this conclusion? (MEG)

Key Words/Phrases: 'arguments', 'conflicts undermined', 'agree', 'disagree', 'how far', this proves'.

3. Use the sources to write an historical account

The examiner invites you to take part in a genuine historical activity – the writing of your own history, using the sources, e.g.:

Using all the sources, write an account of the part played in the Cultural Revolution by Mao Tse-Tung.   (MEG)

4. Analyse the value of the sources to the historian

A different kind of question is one which asks you to look at the sources in a critical way. You have to judge their value to the historian. Such questions apply a number of tests to the sources. Below are the main types of such questions.

Type 4.1   Questions which ask you to detect bias in the source. 'Bias' is a word mentioned in the GCSE Assessment Objectives, and is something which you should be able to recognise. Bias occurs when one point of view is being put across and other views are being ignored. A typical question is:

What three words and phrases used by the writer of Source 5 show bias?   (SEG)

Key Words/Phrases: 'bias'.

Type 4.2   Assessing the reliability of the source. Such questions ask you to assess how much trust you can put on what the source tells you by looking at the nature of the source, e.g.:

1. What questions would you ask about the reliability of the evidence which the writer of Source 5 uses to support his opinions?   (SEG)
2. How trustworthy is the view given by the cartoon of United States policy towards the Soviet Union?   (SEG)
3. The authors of Sources 1 and 2 promised to take only non-violent action to achieve independence. In Source 4 a British Cabinet minister expressed his view that violence would occur if British rule continued. Does this mean that the authors of Sources 1 and 2 were lying? Explain your answer fully.   (MEG)

Key Words/Phrases: 'reliability', 'trustworthy.'

Type 4.3   Questions which ask you about other sources on the subject, e.g.:

What other sources of information are likely to be available about this conflict?   (NEA)

Key Words/Phrases: 'other sources', 'other types of evidence', 'additional information'.

Type 4.4   Here you are asked to date the source or place it in context, e.g.:

1. What evidence is there in Source 2 which helps you to identify:
(a) the speaker
(b) the place
(c) the occasion on which the speech is occurring?   (SEG)
2. What evidence is there that Source 4 was written in 1940 rather than 1914?   (NEA)

Key Words/Phrases: 'what evidence', 'information'.

Type 4.5   Questions which require you to identify the type of source, e.g.:

Sources 10, 11 and 12 come from either British or Russian sources. Which of the sources do you think are more likely to be British and which are more likely to be Russian? Give reasons for your answers.   (NEA)

Key Words/Phrases: 'primary or secondary sources', 'evidence', 'which of the sources . . . more likely to'.

ACTIVITY 9

Take the papers for the last two years for your syllabus. Sort the source-based questions out into the categories suggested in Figure 1.6.

6 Level of Response Mark Schemes

The Examining Groups will mark your papers using a *Level of Response* mark scheme for each question. This will usually be divided up into from three to five levels, each level showing the quality of thinking expected in the answer, and details of the knowledge/information/facts it should contain. A careful reading of the Level of Response mark schemes (included in this book on pages 19 and 56–7) should give you a clear insight into the examiner's mind. The League of Nations, covered in Chapters 2 and 3, is a favourite area of examination for all Boards. The question below is taken from the SEG specimen paper for their new syllabus, for examination in 1991. Read through Chapters 2 and 3, then do the questions shown below, and mark your answer according to the mark scheme shown after the questions.

7 Revision

At the end of your course you will probably have up to two months for full-time revision. Before this you should have been getting yourself ready. During your course you should have been asked to do a lot of work to prepare yourself for the revision part of the course. Hopefully, you will only have to brush up on what you already have covered and know. Revision tends to be a hard slog, but it should be interesting and give you pleasure, because it is often during revision that you begin to make real sense of much of the material you covered earlier.

REVISION PROGRAMME

Work out a sensible programme for revision, and make sure that you tie it in to the programmes for your other subjects. Base your revision timetable on:

- the chapters in this book
- your notes on paper, cards or in an exercise book and your file of school and college work
- an analysis of the percentage of marks for each section of the course.

The timetable should cover the period March–May. You

Figure 1.7 Sample questions on the League of Nations

Peace to World War, 1918–41

3. **The League of Nations**
Study the Source below and then attempt all parts of Question 3.

As the Covenant clearly shows, the League of Nations was not intended to be a World Federation or Super State. Every important decision had to be by unanimous vote. The League had no power to enforce its decisions; it had power only to suggest and persuade.	1
It was rather like a club. As a club it provided a meeting place for the leaders of every nation. Even non-members sent 'observers'.	5

adapted from *The Post-War World*, (1935) by J. HAMPDEN JACKSON
Question 3

(a) The Covenant (or 'rules') of the League of Nations was included in the peace treaties signed in 1919–20, after the end of the First World War.

Why was the Covenant included in the treaties? **(4 marks)**

(b) In the Source, the author points out some of the weaknesses of the League.

Does this mean that he was opposed to the League of Nations?
Explain your answer. **(7 marks)**

(c) The Source says that the League 'had power only to suggest and persuade'.

Do you agree that this was the case?
Give reasons for your answer. **(5 marks)**

(d) 'Events in the 1930s clearly showed that the League of Nations was unable to keep the peace.'

Explain whether you agree or disagree with this statement.

In your answer you should refer to either Manchuria or Abyssinia or both of them. **(9 marks)**
TOTAL: 25 marks
(SEG, Specimen Paper)

Figure 1.8 Marking scheme specimen

3 (a) L1 Simple statement of causation, e.g. President Wilson insisted on this, the 'rules' were intended to keep the peace. 1–2

L2 Developed contextual statement relates the contemporary situation and/or hopes for the future to recent experience. 3–4

(b) L1 Simplistic deductions based on the extract, e.g. yes, as he sees so many weaknesses; no, he refers to the 'club'. 1–2

L2 Judgements based on the whole extract identify positive as well as negative factors. 3–4

L3 Answers recognise that identification of weaknesses does not necessarily imply opposition and/or vice versa. 5–6

L4 Answers show an awareness of the inadequacy of the extract alone as a basis for judgement, e.g. that it is only an extract and proves nothing about the author's personal view. 7

(c) L1 Simplistic answers agree because the extract says this was the case. 1–2

L2 Answers disagree on the basis of the sanctions available to the League. 3–4

L3 Answers recognise that implementation of the sanctions was dependent on 'persuasion' of the membership. 5

(d) N.B. In this part of the question candidates may discuss either or both of Manchuria and Abyssinia as they choose.

L1 Simplistic answers, e.g. yes, because invasion and conquest occurred regardless of the League; no, because the League did not really try. 1–2

L2 Narrative accounts of what happened and the League's response. 3–5

L3 Answers focus on the League's actions and consider their effectiveness. 6–7

L4 Answers recognise the degree to which the League's effectiveness was dependent on its leading members, especially Britain and France, i.e. the League was only as effective as it was allowed to be. 8–9

should aim to do plenty of revision in the Easter holidays. At the end of the revision programme you should leave two weeks before the examination to work on your weaker points. This will also give you time to go over the topics you have already revised.

March, April, May

After you have worked out the revision programme, spend an average of about 45 minutes a day on revision. For each topic set yourself a 'mini exam', using old papers, questions from *Work Out* or other sources.

The last fortnight

Read carefully through your notes and file for each topic. Continue to work on your examination technique. Check that you know the date of the examination, its time and what subjects are being covered in which paper.

REVISION TECHNIQUES

Here are some tips for revision:

(a) Try and condense the main points of your notes and worksheets down to single headings and statements. You can do this in an exercise book, on paper or on index cards. Put a heading for each topic, and then on a maximum of two sides of an exercise book make brief notes of the main points and facts. Do this in normal note form, or as a spider diagram.

(b) When you have worked through a section, test yourself by attempting under examination conditions old questions on the paper, or in the exercises given you during the course, on the topic. Always time yourself.

ACTIVITY 10

Table 1.1 covers the main sections of *Work Out Modern World History*. Take your examination syllabus (see Activity 1) and the examination papers for the past three years, and work out the percentage of the whole paper which you have covered in your course. In the final column use Table 1.6 to work out the kinds of questions which you will be asked.

INTERNATIONAL RELATIONS, 1919–29

Examination Guide

International Relations, 1919–29 is a major compulsory part in the syllabuses of two of the four Examination Groups, MEG and NEA. It is also a major section of the parts you can choose to do in the LEAG and SEG syllabuses. For MEG, **International Relations, 1919–29** is a laid-down area of study for Paper 1. In the NEA syllabus, it is a major part of one of four sections of the compulsory part of the syllabus, the theme **Conflict and Conciliation** for Paper 1, and also a smaller part of one of three sections of the compulsory part of the syllabus for Paper 2, the theme **International Co-operation**. For LEAG, the area is covered in a range of topics for Paper 1 (see below); while for SEG **International Relations, 1919–29** fall within the topic **Peace to World War, 1918–41**, one of three themes to be chosen from for Paper 1. This is in addition to the compulsory theme, **The USA and the USSR as World Superpowers since 1945**. For SEG, the topic **Peace to World War, 1918–41** is essential background knowledge for studying **The USA and the USSR as World Superpowers since 1945**.

Detailed syllabus coverage for LEAG, MEG, NEA and SEG is as follows.

Syllabus Coverage

LEAG

E1, The League of Nations and the United Nations
F1, Fascism in Italy and Germany, 1919–39
G1, The Russian Revolution and the Establishment of the Soviet State, 1917–41

MEG

The Search for International Order between 1919 and 1932

NEA

Conflict and Conciliation
(d) Attempts to resolve conflict
   (i)   Peacemaking after the First World War
International Co-operation
(a) The League of Nations
   (i)   Foundation, Organisation and Achievements
   (ii) The failure of collective Security in the 1920s and 30s

SEG

Peace to World War, 1918–41
The Paris Peace settlement of 1919–20
Issues arising from the peace settlement
Developments in the 1920s

The Topic Guide on page 22 gives details of this chapter's sections.

ACTIVITY

For a detailed account of the subject content, take your particular Examining Group's syllabus, and the examination papers for the past three years. Each Examining Group examines the syllabus content in different ways. Take the past three years' papers, and work out the pattern of questions for your syllabus, using the breakdown of question types in Chapter 1.

Topic Guide

Figure 2.1   Europe in 1815, after the peace settlement which followed the French Revolutionary and Napoleonic Wars

1 Peace Treaties after the First World War

BACKGROUND

The world you know today did not suddenly appear overnight like a crop of mushrooms. The modern world map is the result of hundreds of years of history, which has involved, among other things, wars, migrations, treaties and international agreements. Until 1914 the political history of the modern world was centred upon Europe, and revolved around the actions of the great powers of Europe who had fought in the Napoleonic wars a hundred years before – England, France, Russia, Prussia (Germany) and Austria–Hungary.

Changes in Europe, 1815–1914

In 1914, the map of Europe had seen some dramatic changes since the Battle of Waterloo in 1815. By 1870 a much bigger and more powerful Prussia had emerged in Northern Europe as the new country of Germany. In the south, Italy, which in 1815 had been a collection of small, independent states, and provinces of Austria–Hungary, had become an independent country by 1870 after a series of wars. All of Europe was also in the grip of an industrial revolution which upset the old balance of power between the five big powers. Not for nothing was it said that Germany was united by 'blood and iron'; the blood of its enemies' soldiers and the iron of its railways, warships, artillery and machine guns. The two maps, Figures 2.1 and 2.2, give you an idea of the main changes.

Figure 2.2 Europe, 1914

Source Harriet Ward, *World Powers in the Twentieth Century*, Heinemann, 1978, p. xvi

The Rise of Japan and America

Outside Europe there had also been some big changes. In the Far East a new power, Japan, had sprung up, and had shown her strength in 1904–5 when she had gone to war with Russia. The Japanese armies managed to smash the Russians' land forces in the Far East. The Russians sailed their fleet around the world to fight the Japanese, only to be humiliated by the Japanese navy, whose broadsides sent the pride of the Russian fleet to the bottom of the Sea of Japan on the afternoon of 27 May 1905.

By 1914 another new power had also emerged, the United States of America. Already she had outstripped the old powers of Europe in terms of heavy industry (see page 185). Figure 2.3 gives an indication of the relative strength of Europe's great powers in 1914.

Africa and Asia

There were other big changes in the rest of the world. Africa, the 'Dark Continent' of 1815, unknown and unexplored, had been carved up between the great powers of Europe. In Asia the old empires who had ruled for centuries, the Ottoman (Turkish), Chinese and Persian, were in a state of decay. Indeed, we can even add to these the Russian and Austro-Hungarian empires (see Figure 2.4). It was to take another war, the First World War, 1914–18, to blow down the international pack of cards. From the shambles the victors created an international settlement which was to lead to the world we know today.

The Communications Revolution

By 1914 the world was beginning to change in another, dramatic way. Man could now fly, by both aeroplane and helicopter, drive motor cars, travel by train and communicate by wireless and telephone. The international age of communications had begun – an age which today can put you into immediate touch with the rest of the world.

Figure 2.3　Strength of the European powers, 1914

Country	Britain	Austria–Hungary	France	Germany	Russia
Population (million)	40.8	50.0	39.6	65.0	159.0
Size of army (million)	0.7	0.8	3.7	4.2	1.2
Size of navy (ships)	388.0	–	207.0	281.0	166.0
Coal output (million tonnes)	292.0	47.0	40.0	277.0	36.0
Steel output (million tonnes)	11.0	5.0	4.6	14.0	3.6

Examination Guidance

Activity 11 introduces one of the kinds of questions you may be asked in the examination upon **International Relations in the 1920s**.

ACTIVITY 11

Targets

Comprehension, recall.

Question Guide

In this case, we look at the use of an outline map of Europe to show what you have understood, aiming at the target skill of *comprehension*. If you were asked to do the exercise using the outlines of the countries involved, without any names, this would also involve the target skill of *recall*.

Activity

Draw an outline of Europe, and mark on it the main changes which occurred between 1815 and 1914. Underneath your map list these changes, with the reasons why they occurred.

THE FIRST WORLD WAR

Sarajevo

The First World War is dealt with as a separate topic in Chapter 7. Here we shall merely look at some of the powers involved, the causes of the war and what were its consequences. The First World War can be seen in many ways as a family quarrel between the five great powers. The ruling families of Austria, Britain, Germany and Russia were indeed very closely related – aunts, uncles and cousins (see Figure 2.5). Indeed, the war was triggered off by a family tragedy in June 1914, when the heir to the Austro–Hungarian throne, Archduke Franz Ferdinand, and his wife, Sophie, went on a visit to Sarajevo in the Austrian province of Bosnia. The Archduke even saw the trip as a family outing for Sophie. Unknown to him, terrorists from neighbouring Serbia were lying in wait for him, terrorists who were as deadly as the IRA. These terrorists, the Black Hand, wanted to unite Bosnia with Serbia in the same way as the IRA want to join Northern Ireland to Eire. As Ferdinand and Sophie drove through Sarajevo, two shots rang out, and within hours they were dead.

Their deaths were to trigger off the crisis which led to the First World War. Why should their murder drag the powers of Europe into a bloody contest?

Figure 2.4　Europe and the world, 1914　　　*Source*　Brian Catchpole, *A Map History of the Modern World*, Heinemann, p. 3

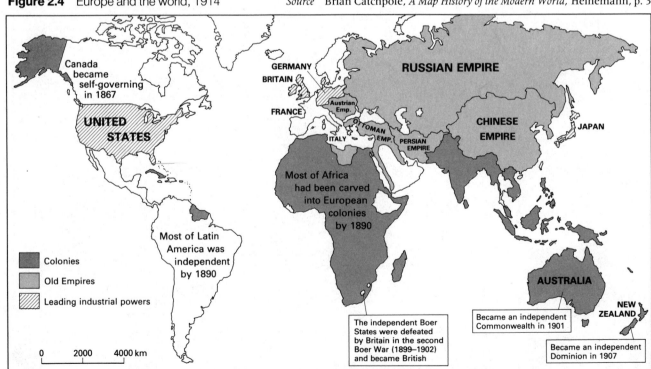

Figure 2.5 The royal families of Europe

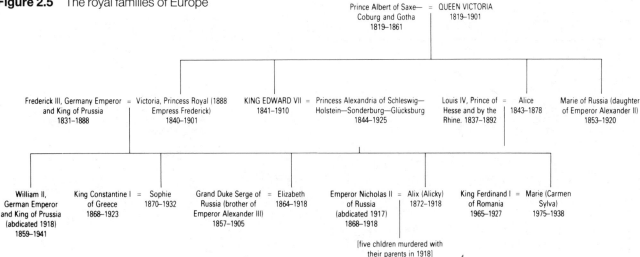

The Alliance System

Historians still argue fiercely over who was to blame for the First World War. Some blame the Germans, others the arms race between the powers, others quarrels over who should gain colonies in Africa. One famous historian, Professor A.J.P. Taylor, even claims that it was the fault of the railway timetables – once the orders had been given to get the rival armies moving, nothing could be done to stop them! By 1914 the countries of Europe were joined together in two rival alliance systems, rather like people handcuffed together in a line. One alliance system was made up of Austria–Hungary and Germany, the other of Serbia, Russia, France and Britain. The members of each alliance promised to help one another in case of attack – a recipe for getting everyone involved in a family quarrel! From July/August 1914, the Alliance System sucked Europe into the whirlpool of war.

Figure 2.6 Europe at war

Source Reader's Digest, *Great Events of the 20th Century*, p. 103

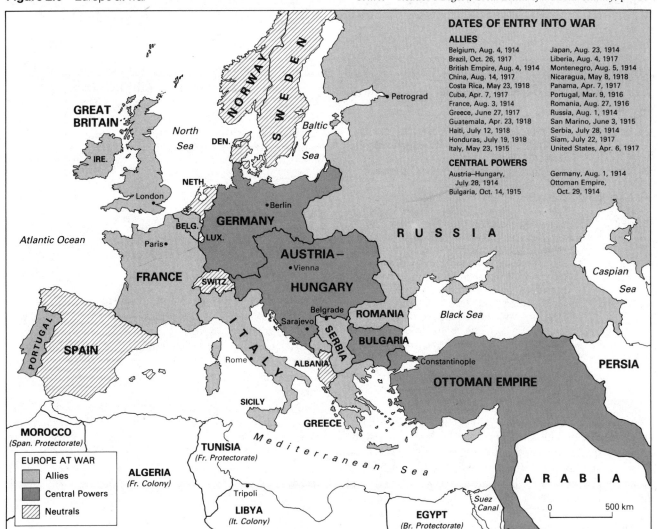

DATES OF ENTRY INTO WAR

ALLIES

Belgium, Aug. 4, 1914	Japan, Aug. 23, 1914
Brazil, Oct. 26, 1917	Liberia, Aug. 4, 1917
British Empire, Aug. 4, 1914	Montenegro, Aug. 5, 1914
China, Aug. 14, 1917	Nicaragua, May 8, 1918
Costa Rica, May 23, 1918	Panama, Apr. 7, 1917
Cuba, Apr. 7, 1917	Portugal, Mar. 9, 1916
France, Aug. 3, 1914	Romania, Aug. 27, 1916
Greece, June 27, 1917	Russia, Aug. 1, 1914
Guatemala, Apr. 23, 1918	San Marino, June 3, 1915
Haiti, July 12, 1918	Serbia, July 28, 1914
Honduras, July 19, 1918	Siam, July 22, 1917
Italy, May 23, 1915	United States, Apr. 6, 1917

CENTRAL POWERS

Austria–Hungary, July 28, 1914	Germany, Aug. 1, 1914
Bulgaria, Oct. 14, 1915	Ottoman Empire, Oct. 29, 1914

EUROPE AT WAR
- Allies
- Central Powers
- Neutrals

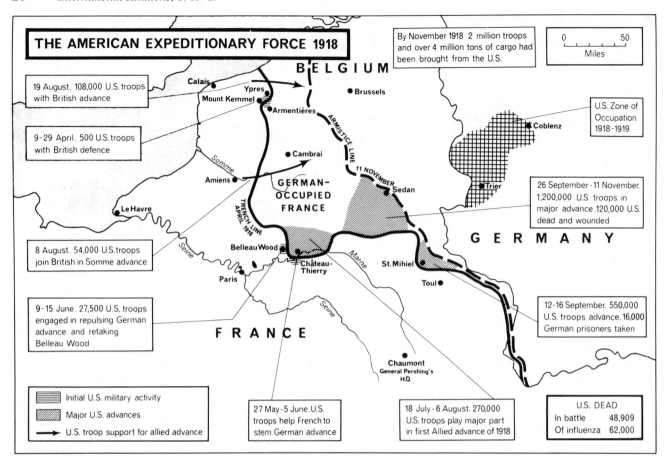

Figure 2.7   The American Expeditionary Force, 1918

Source   M. Gilbert, *American History Atlas*, Weidenfeld & Nicolson, 1968, p. 73

Steps to War

A quick look at what happened can help you see how the war broke out.

28 June	The murder of Archduke Ferdinand. Austria–Hungary demands that Serbia stamp out the terrorists. Serbia refuses.
29 July	Austria shells Belgrade, Serbia's capital. Serbia asks Russia for help.
30 July	Germany demands Russia take no part in the war. Germany gets her army ready for war on both the Eastern and Western fronts. France and Russia are allies, so Germany must be ready to fight them both.
1 August	Russia refuses to accept the German demand; Germany declares war on her, and decides to attack France through Belgium.
4 August	Germany refuses to withdraw forces from Belgium, which Britain has promised to protect. Britain declares war on Germany, and fights with her allies France and Russia.
5 August	All of Europe is at war.

Changes in the Powers Who Fought

Changes occurred among the powers who fought the war (see the table of dates on Figure 2.6). In October 1914 the Germans gained the support of Bulgaria and the Ottoman Empire. In May 1915 the Italians joined the Allies, in return for a promise of large amounts of Austrian land (the Treaty of London). The Allies were greatly strengthened in July 1917 when the United States of America declared war on Germany (see Figure 2.7). Before the war ended, one of the powers had been knocked out of the struggle. In November 1917 the Bolshevik revolution saw the end of the Russian struggle against Austria–Hungary and Germany. So, in March 1918 Russia and Germany signed the peace treaty of Brest–Litovsk. (We examine events in Russia in Chapter 7.)

Examination Guidance

A major part of history examinations involves what you can remember about the topics you have studied. Two kinds of memory are tested: *recall* and *associative memory*. Recall questions ask you what you know without any clues, while associative memory questions give you clues, like documents or maps, to stimulate or trigger off your memory.

The questions below are pure recall ones, in which you are asked to write down the fact you can remember about a topic.

ACTIVITY 12

Target

Recall.

Question Guide

To answer the questions, you need to work through (pages 23–30).

Activity

Write a sentence on each of the following:
(a) the Alliance System
(b) Sarajevo
(c) the Black Hand
(d) the Treaty of London.

BACKGROUND TO PEACE

The Impact of War

All around, you can find signs of the impact of the First World War. In most towns, villages and churches stand silent monuments to the dead. When the war ended in November 1918 over 8 million soldiers had died, many slaughtered in the trench warfare of Western Europe.

Source 2A

If I should die, think only this of me;
That there's some corner of a foreign field
That is forever England. There shall be
In that rich earth a richer dust concealed;
A dust whom England bore, shaped, made aware,
Gave, once, her flowers to love, her ways to roam,
A body of England's breathing English air,
Washed by the rivers, blest by suns of home.
(Rupert Brooke)

The Cost of War

The fearful slaughter in battle was only one of the costs of a war fought on land and sea around the world. Millions died of disease and starvation, and in northern France towns and villages were destroyed. Figure 2.8 sums up the impact of the war. No one knows how many died because of the war – a total of around 20 million dead is often quoted. Once the fighting was over, the victors had to try and make sure of a lasting peace. In January 1919 the triumphant allies met in Paris. What did they all want?

Examination Guidance

This is the first example of a question covering an area of the syllabus which might confront you in the examination room. It is quite a difficult exercise, and it aims to make you think about what the victors were up to during the Paris Conference.

ACTIVITY 13

Targets

Recall, comprehension.

Question Guide

Examiners can ask you to compare two kinds of material, such as tables and a list of points, and then make up your own mind. Make sure that you read through the points carefully, and link your answer in to the information on the table in Figure 2.8.

Activity

Read Chapter 7 and, with reference to Figure 2.8, copy out the list below, and under each point write out the order of importance which Britain, France and the USA might have put upon it **in November 1918**. Explain your reasons for making your choices:

(a) the destruction of the German navy
(b) making Germany pay for war damage
(c) Germany having no future part in European affairs
(d) making sure German armies could never invade neighbouring countries again.

Figure 2.8 The cost of war – rough figures

	Soldiers		Impact on country
	killed	wounded	
Allies			
France	1,400,000	2,500,000	2,000,000 fled from homes 23,000 factories wrecked 300,000 homes destroyed Coal and iron industry destroyed £5,400 million spent on war.
Britain	750,000	1,500,000	Large number of ships sunk by German submarines £9,000 million spent on war
Italy	600,000	1,200,000	North-east Italy ruined.
Russia	170,000	3,000,000	Russian revolutions brought down the government, and led to the Bolshevik seizure of power. Russia surrendered to Germany, and lost richest farming land in the West.
Central powers			
Germany	2,000,000	3,500,000	Germany blockaded at end of war. Widespread hunger and famine. Revolutions break out.
Austria-Hungary	170,000	300,000	Little impact on the empire.
Turkey	375,000	600,000	Little direct impact but fighting in the Middle East provinces.
Bulgaria	100,000	200,000	

For example, if you think point (a) was more important to France than to Britain, and that Britain thought it of more importance than did the USA, the order below point (a) would be: France, Britain, USA.

THE PARIS CONFERENCE

The Five Main Powers – Britain, France, Italy, Japan and the USA

When the Paris Conference opened in January 1919, five powers (the Allies) were in charge: Britain, France, Italy, Japan and the USA. Orlando, the Italian leader, soon stormed out in disgust at the Allies' treatment of Italy's claims to Austrian lands under the 1915 Treaty of London (see Chapter 7). Although the Italians returned, they and the Japanese played a small role. The Japanese were mainly interested in gaining land in the Far East.

It is too easy to see the *Versailles Settlement*, the name given to the five peace treaties of 1919–20, as a logical result of hard bargaining between the three main victors, Britain, France and the USA, led by Lloyd George, Clemenceau and Wilson. The process was much more complex, involving a clash of principles, self-interest, prejudices, public opinion and powerful personalities.

Lloyd George, Clemenceau and Wilson had their own teams of advisers. They also had to listen to the other 29 victorious powers involved in the war, and to two other countries not directly represented at the peace talks – Germany and Russia. We also need to remember that between January and June 1919 both ideas and situations might change. So, we must not think of the Versailles Settlement as a simple list of facts and events, cut and dried, to be put into neat little pigeon-holes and trotted out for GCSE examinations.

In his war memoirs David Lloyd George wrote that the making of the peace covered 'ethnic, territorial and economic affairs in every quarter of the globe,' and it is vital to remember that the Versailles Settlement affected the whole world.

The Goals of Wilson, Lloyd George and Clemenceau

We shall first deal with Woodrow Wilson, President of the USA, because his *Fourteen Points* laid down the guidelines for what followed.

The USA

Woodrow Wilson was a man of ideas and ideals – very clear-minded, determined, even fanatical. He wanted to secure a long-lasting peace settlement based upon ideas of freedom and democracy. In January 1918 he declared his views in what are known as his Fourteen Points:

Source 2B   Wilson's Fourteen Points

1. Open Diplomacy. No secret negotiations and treaties between powers.
2. Freedom of the seas.
3. Free trade.
4. Reduced armaments.
5. Freedom for colonial peoples.
6. Self-determination for Russia.
7. Evacuation of and self-determination for Belgium.

8. Evacuation of French territory, and return of the province of Alsace–Lorraine.
9. Italy to include all Italians.
10 Self-determination for the people of the Austro-Hungarian Empire.
11. Evacuation and self-determination for peoples of Serbia, Romania and Montenegro.
12. Self-determination for the peoples of the Turkish (Ottoman) Empire.
13. Independence (self-determination) for Poland.
14. The setting-up of a League of Nations to keep World Peace.

Note that there is nothing in here about making Germany pay for the cost of the war, or about getting revenge. Some idea of the problems which Wilson's idealism about nations founded on race caused can be seen by studying Figure 2.9. There was no way in which national boundaries could mirror the patchwork quilt of races found on the map.

Figure 2.9   Peoples of the Habsburg Empire

Source   Neil DeMarco, The World This Century, Bell & Hyman, p. 28

Great Britain

David Lloyd George was a shrewd, clever, witty, hard-bargaining politician who was a brilliant negotiator. Two main interests concerned him: the settlement of Europe, and the protection of the interests of the British Empire. What were his aims?

Europe

He favoured leniency towards Germany.

1. *Make Germany pay.* Lloyd George wanted Germany to pay for the costs of the war and the damage caused, but that the payments should not damage German economy. He wanted to build up the economies of, and trade between, the new countries of Eastern Europe and Germany and Russia.
2. *Germany's frontiers.* German-speaking populations of Danzig, Upper Silesia and the Rhineland should remain in Germany.
3. *Germany.* Germany should join the League of Nations. Lloyd George feared that Germany might become a Bolshevik power if treated too harshly.

Germany's armed forces were to be kept at a level which would prevent her from again attacking France.

4. *Russia*. Russia was to be allowed to solve her own internal problems and to join the League of Nations.
5. *Self-determination of peoples*. Lloyd George supported the creation of independent nation states in Eastern Europe, i.e. the Baltic States, Poland, new countries carved mainly from Austria–Hungary, and the enlargement of Serbia.
6. *League of Nations*. He had supported the idea of an international organisation to prevent war.

The British Empire

Britain had gained the backing of all the countries of the Empire during the First World War, and the securing of the Empire was a major concern of Lloyd George.

1. *The Near East*. Britain was to keep mandated territories with their oil supplies.
2. *Africa*. Britain wanted to gain Germany's colonies.
3. *Freedom of the seas*. It was vital for Britain to keep the right to search naval vessels on the high seas.

Textbooks often argue that Lloyd George reacted to public opinion at home which wanted to treat Germany harshly – 'Hang the Kaiser' and 'Make Germany Pay'. But, you should remember that he had just won a general election, and in April 1919 defended his stand at the Paris Conference against an onslaught from papers, *The Times* in particular, who wanted Germany to be heavily punished.

France

Georges Clemenceau was the Prime Minister of France, and his main concerns were with making sure that France was safe from any future German attack, and that Germany should pay for the cost of the war and the damage inflicted upon France. Clemenceau's nickname was 'The Tiger', and he fought tooth and nail to make France secure from any German revenge. In reply to Woodrow Wilson, Clemenceau said:

Source 2C

Mr Wilson, if I accepted what you propose as ample for the security of France, after the millions who have died and the millions who have suffered, I believe – and indeed I hope – that my successor in office would take me by the back of the neck and have me shot before the fortress of Vincennes.

What did Clemenceau want?

1. *Make Germany pay*. Germany should pay for the huge losses which the French had incurred, and the cost of the war to France, including damage to the devastated farming, towns and factories of northern France.
2. *Germany's frontiers*. Germany's frontiers in the West should be such as to prevent any future German invasion of France. This would involve Allied occupation of the Rhineland.
3. *Germany*. Clemenceau was not concerned with German loss of territory or the ceding of German-

speaking areas to other countries. Germany's armed forces were to be kept at a level which would prevent her from again attacking France.

4. *Russia*. Clemenceau wanted to try and prevent the spread of communism.
5. *Self-determination of peoples*. In Eastern Europe, Clemenceau was ready to support Woodrow Wilson, but not when the idea was applied to French colonies.
6. *League of Nations*. Clemenceau backed the idea of a League of Nations.
7. *Empire*. Clemenceau wanted French protectorates in the Middle East, and to preserve the French Empire in Africa.

Examination Guidance

The examination question on the Versailles Settlement may directly or indirectly refer to Wilson's Fourteen Points. You may also need to show an understanding of the differences between the views of Wilson, Lloyd George and Clemenceau. Activity 14 focuses on both these points.

ACTIVITY 14

Targets

Comprehension, recall.

Question Guide

This activity requires considerable skill in selecting the relevant pieces of information from the text in order to make the correct comparisons. To answer it, you will need to read through the accounts above of the views of Lloyd George and Clemenceau.

Activity

Copy out the Fourteen Points, and by the side of each point put in for Britain and France whether their delegations might have backed or opposed Wilson's ideas in January 1919. If you cannot work out the answer, leave the gap blank.

Key   B = back, O = oppose, blank = don't know

Wilson's Fourteen Points	Britain	France
1. Open diplomacy. No secret negotiations and treaties between powers.		
2. Freedom of the seas.		
3. Free trade.		
4. Reduced armaments.		
5. Freedom for colonial peoples.		
6. Self-determination for Russia.		
7. Evacuation of and self-determination for Belgium.		
8. Evacuation of French territory, and return of the province of Alsace–Lorraine.		

9. Italy to include all Italians.
10. Self-determination for the people of the Austro–Hungarian Empire.
11. Evacuation of and self-determination for peoples of Serbia, Romania and Montenegro.
12. Self-determination for the peoples of the Turkish (Ottoman) Empire.
13. Independence (self-determination) for Poland.
14. The setting-up of a League of Nations to keep World Peace.

2 The Versailles Settlement – Germany

The Paris Conference led to five treaties dealing with the defeated countries; one treaty each for Germany, Bulgaria and Turkey, and two treaties for Austria–Hungary (i.e. one for Austria, the other for Hungary).

Each treaty was split into two pieces: the first part was an agreement or **covenant** to establish an international body to preserve peace, The League of Nations; the second contained the terms for dealing with the individual countries.

The *Treaty of Versailles* dealt with Germany. On 28 June 1919 the Germans signed the treaty in the Hall of Mirrors at Versailles – a significant place and date. In 1871 in the Hall of Mirrors William I, King of Prussia, had been proclaimed Germany's Emperor after he had destroyed France's armies in the Franco–Prussian war. Also, 28 June was the anniversary of Sarajevo. Figures 2.10 and 2.11 show the major territorial changes that the Treaty brought about in Europe. Refer to the maps when you read through the main terms of the Treaty.

Germany's Loss of Territory

(a) Alsace–Lorraine returned to France.
(b) Eupen and Malmedy to Belgium.
(c) North Schleswig to Denmark (after a vote or plebiscite).
(d) West Prussia and Posen to Poland.
(e) Danzig, a city of Germans, to be under the rule of the League of Nations.
(f) Memel to Lithuania.
(g) Saar coalfield to be under the League of Nations for 15 years. Plebiscite then to decide who ruled it. The coal-mines meanwhile to be under French control.
(h) Union between Austria and Germany forbidden.
(i) German colonies to be under League of Nations control. Members of the League looked after these 'mandates'.
(j) Estonia, Latvia and Lithuania taken away from Germany, becoming independent states. Germany had seized them from Russia under the terms of the March 1918 Brest–Litovsk treaty.

Figure 2.10   Germany's loss of territory by the Versailles Treaty

Source   B. Catchpole, *A Map History of the Modern World*, Heinemann

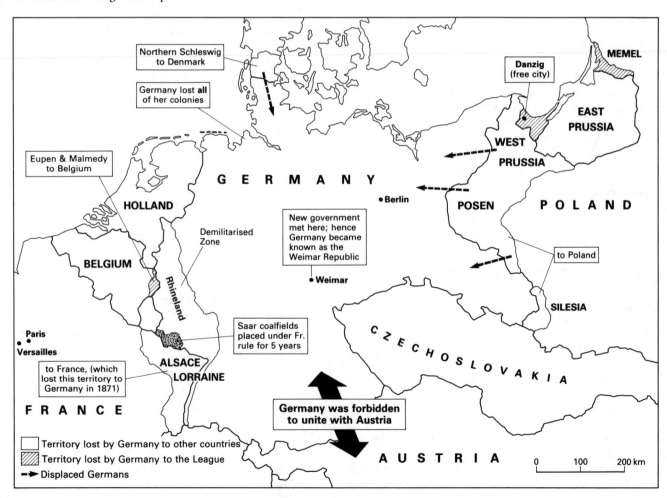

Figure 2.11   The Versailles Settlement, Eastern Europe and the Balkans

Source   N. Lowe, *Mastering Modern World History*, Macmillan, p. 23.

Limitations on German Armed Forces

(k)   Limit of 100,000 for armed forces; no conscription.

(l)   No tanks, armoured cars, military aircraft or submarines.

(m)   Six battleships only.*

(n)   Rhineland – no German troops allowed there. It was *demilitarised*.

---

*The German fleet was handed over to Britain and sailed to the British base at Scapa Flow. The British fleet went on an exercise one day, to come back to find the Germans had literally pulled the plugs out of their ships – they had scuttled them all, and many are still there today! The scuttling was witnessed by a party of children on a local steamer – one of the most amazing things ever seen on a school outing.

The War Guilt Clause

(o)   Germany accepted her guilt for the outbreak of the war.

(p)   The men responsible were to be arrested and tried.

Reparations

(q)   Germany was to pay for the war damage. Most of the money was to go to France. The figure was fixed in 1921 at £6,600 million.

International Peace

(r)   A League of Nations was set up to preserve world peace, and to help improve people's lives. Signers of the Treaty would be the first members, and other powers would join later.

Examination Guidance

The Versailles Settlement is a favourite topic for the examiners, and questions take two main forms – the completion of a blank map and the setting of documentary extracts. A documentary exercise is included below for Activity 15. Activity 15a is a standard map exercise; 15b is aimed to provide a stimulus for thinking about the impact of the Versailles Treaty upon Germany.

ACTIVITY 15a

Targets

Recall, comprehension.

Question Guide

Before you take the examination, make sure that you can do this exercise without reference to your textbook.

Activity

Trace or draw the outline of Figure 2.10, but do not include ANY of the text.

1.   On your outline, mark in and where appropriate name:
    (a)   territories received by France, Belgium, Denmark, Poland, Lithuania
    (b)   territory under the control of the League of Nations
    (c)   territories dealt with in the clause referring to Austria
    (d)   what happened to the Rhine.

2.   List which of these territorial arrangements would fall under the following headings:
    (a)   the self-determination of people/nationalism
    (b)   payment for war damage, reparations
    (c)   the stopping of any future German military advances.

ACTIVITY 15b

Targets

Recall, comprehension, empathy – the ability to look at events and issues from the perspective of people in the past.

Question Guide

Have you or your friends ever been burgled, mugged or robbed? If so, how did you feel – anger, rage, fury, sickness, bitterness, hatred? These were the feelings of many Germans when they heard of the terms of the Versailles Settlement. Their reaction played a big part in the rise of Hitler to power (see Chapter 9). In understanding the impact of Versailles on Germany, you are asked to see things from the viewpoint of the Germans.

Activity 15b takes a specific viewpoint, and asks you to come up with your own ideas, using the information on pages 30–31. It is, in fact, dealing with **Assessment Objective 3** (page 10), summed up in the word 'empathy'.

Activity

If you were able to interview an Austrian corporal in July 1919 how might he react to the terms of the Versailles Treaty? The corporal fought in the German army, was wounded in a gas attack and awarded the Iron Cross for bravery, the German equivalent of the Victoria Cross. What might the corporal say about the following:

(a)   the part the Germans were allowed to play in negotiating the peace

(b)   the way in which the Treaty was linked to Wilson's Fourteen Points, upon whose terms Germany and Austria had agreed to surrender in November 1918, promising fair treatment for nation states

(c)   losses of German territory where Germans were in the majority, both in Europe and abroad, as compared to treatment of other states

(d)   the disarmament clauses

(e)   the war guilt clause

(f)   the payment of reparations, ie. money and goods for war damage

(g)   non-membership of the League of Nations?

3 The Versailles Settlement –Austria–Hungary, Bulgaria and Turkey

Germany's allies, Austria–Hungary, Bulgaria and Turkey, also had peace treaties forced upon them. Before the war ended Austria–Hungary had begun to split up into separate nation-states, for example Austria and Hungary had already declared independence from the Austrian Empire.

Eastern Europe and the Balkans

The Treaties of *Saint-Germain* (Austria) and *Neuilly* (Bulgaria) in 1919 and *Trianon* (Hungary) in 1920 (Figure 2.11) completely changed the map of Eastern Europe and the Balkans. The best way of looking at the changes is to describe the countries which were established or altered, moving from north to south:

(a)   *Poland* was carved out of Russia, Germany and Austria–Hungary. Austria lost Galicia to the new state. The area between Danzig and Germany was known as the *Polish Corridor*.

(b)   *Czechoslovakia* was formed from Austrian lands, but included 3 million Germans living in the Sudetenland.

(c)   *Austria* was a new, small country with the old imperial capital of Vienna at its centre.

(d)   *Hungary* was formed from previous Austrian lands.

(e)   *Romania* expanded to include Austrian lands.

(f)   *Italy* gained the Tyrol, Trentino, Istria and Trieste.

(g)   *Yugoslavia* was formed from an enlarged Serbia, and also included some Bulgarian land.

Clearly the setting-up of a host of new countries, the question of national groups not included in their own countries (see Figure 2.9), the economic chaos caused by breaking up the old Austrian Empire, and the difficulty of recovering from the impact of the First World War all provided major problems for Eastern Europe after 1920.

Turkey

The final treaty, Sèvres (1920), split up the Turkish Empire and sowed seeds of chaos and bitterness which are felt to the present day. Figure 2.12 shows the main territorial terms of the Sèvres Treaty, which involved:

(a)   the loss of lands to Greece

(b)   the handing-over of its Middle Eastern lands as mandates to Britain (Palestine, Iraq and Trans-jordan) and France (Syria).

Examination Guidance

The Versailles Settlement is a favourite of the Examination Boards, so be well prepared to answer questions upon it. Questions fall into two main categories: those directly linked into source-material, and those which require short-answer or essay questions with no reference to the sources. These can appear disguised as stimulus source-based questions, when in fact they can be answered without looking at the source-material, for example:

The Peace Treaties of 1919–20 could have provided the basis for lasting peace. Do you agree? Explain your answer as fully as you can.   (MEG, June 1988)

ACTIVITY 16

Targets

Recall, concepts of similarity and difference, change and cause.

Question Guide

Versailles questions are often tied into the consequences of the peace settlement, and you will need to study Sections 4–7 below (pages 33–40) to answer the Activity. The extract below is typical of those set: you are given a statement about the Versailles Settlement and its consequences, and then asked to use your knowledge and understanding to either agree or disagree with the statement. The marks are shown in brackets.

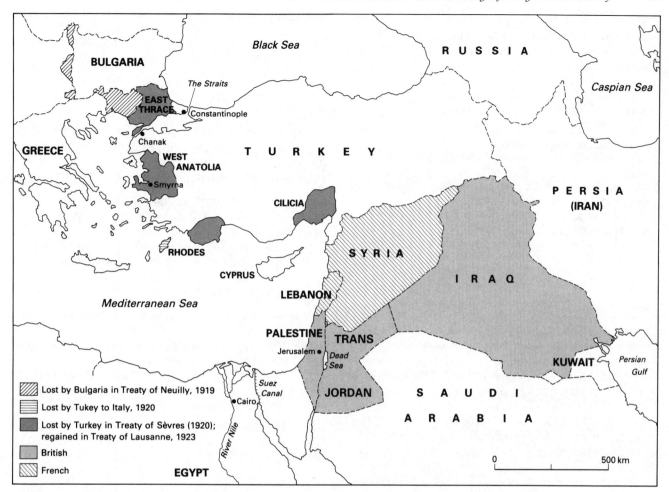

Figure 2.12   The treatment of Turkey at the Treaty of Sèvres, and of Bulgaria at the Treaty of Neuilly

Activity

This extract describes the critics of the Versailles Settlement:

Lloyd George declared in his memoirs that the Treaty had two sets of critics:
'Those who regard it as a cauldron of hatred, revenge and rapacity [greed] . . . who regard President Wilson as the poor dupe [victim] of a couple of expert political gunmen, who alternatively [in turn] bullied and cajoled, hoodwinked and flattered him, until he ultimately [at last] signed on the dotted line'
and
'Those who consider that the Treaty was not a stern enough sentence on the culprits . . . who depict Clemenceau and myself as the converts of an American revivalist [religious preacher]'

(Frank Owen), *Tempestuous Journey – Lloyd George: his Life and Times*, Hutchinson, 1954)

1.   (a) Who were those who thought the treaty was not a 'stern enough sentence on the culprits'?   **(1)**
(b) Who were the 'couple of expert political gunmen'. Explain how the extract enables you to work out your answer.   **(2)**
2.   Who were 'the culprits'. Explain why they were regarded as such, and how this led to their treatment at the Paris Conference.   **(2)**
3.   Explain why some people thought of the Versailles Settlement as 'a cauldron of hatred, revenge and rapacity', and why they thought President Wilson had been deceived by the 'couple of expert political gunmen'.   **(5)**
4.   'Many felt that the 1919–20 peace treaties would lead to a European War within 20 years.' Why did they feel this way, and how were their fears justified?   **(15)**

4 The Versailles Settlement – the League of Nations

When you look at the news on TV today, it may well talk about wars between countries, their quarrels, floods, famines, disease and poverty. These problems were of major concern to the peace-makers at Versailles. Before the First World War, peace depended upon treaties between individual countries, a system which had led to death and destruction in 1914–18. So, in 1919 the Versailles negotiator, under the lead of President Wilson, set up a body, the *League of Nations*, which would help solve disputes between powers. It was hoped that the League would keep the world's peace through **collective security** – that is, all the powers acting together to stop countries from fighting. Collective security is a favourite term which the examiners ask about.

The League of Nations was born in 1920, with its headquarters at Geneva, Switzerland. Figure 2.13 lists the League's aims, while Figure 2.14 shows how it was organised.

Figure 2.13   Aims of the League of Nations

Aims of the League of Nations

1 To keep world peace by settling disputes between nations.
2 To make sure countries kept their independence of countries and did not lose territories.
3 To encourage nations to cut their armies, navies and air forces and reduce their supply of weapons.
4 To improve living and working conditions for all people.

Membership

Countries joining the League had to agree to its aims, set out in the covenant. When the League was formed, it had 42 members, but significantly the most important world power, the USA, was missing. President Wilson did not have the mandate [power] to make America a member. Only the Senate, one of America's Houses of Parliament, could do that – and its members refused, for they had had enough of being sucked into the affairs of Europe and the world, some of them were Wilson's political enemies, and he refused to change any of the League's terms to meet their demands. There were other weaknesses – neither Germany nor Russia was a member, Germany only joining in 1926, while Russia joined in 1934, the year Germany left.

Strengths

The League was also active in the areas of health, labour relations, the settlement of refugees and the stamping-out of drug traffic.

Weaknesses

There were other weaknesses, apart from the USA, Germany and Russia not being members. The main one was the difficulty with which the League could keep the peace. To do this, in the case of a war, it could:

1.   send a commission to find out which power was to blame – the one that had been the attacker, the *aggressor*
2.   pass a motion telling that country to stop fighting
3.   if it refused, ask members not to trade with the countries (*economic sanctions*)
4.   get its members to send troops – the *military sanction*

You can see the problems! If there is a playground fight, who starts it? Who is to blame? How can you find out?

Who stops it if the fighters are the strongest boys and girls in the school, and there are no teachers around?

Another problem was that the League had no troops of its own to send, and could not force member countries to contribute to a peacekeeping force. So, it was a toothless watchdog from the start.

Figure 2.14   Organisation of the League of Nations

Source   K. Shephard, *International Relations*, Basil Blackwell

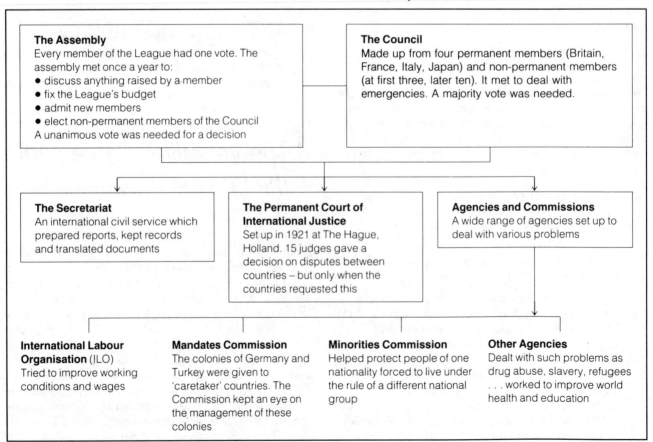

The Assembly
Every member of the League had one vote. The assembly met once a year to:
● discuss anything raised by a member
● fix the League's budget
● admit new members
● elect non-permanent members of the Council
A unanimous vote was needed for a decision

The Council
Made up from four permanent members (Britain, France, Italy, Japan) and non-permanent members (at first three, later ten). It met to deal with emergencies. A majority vote was needed.

The Secretariat
An international civil service which prepared reports, kept records and translated documents

The Permanent Court of International Justice
Set up in 1921 at The Hague, Holland. 15 judges gave a decision on disputes between countries – but only when the countries requested this

Agencies and Commissions
A wide range of agencies set up to deal with various problems

International Labour Organisation (ILO)
Tried to improve working conditions and wages

Mandates Commission
The colonies of Germany and Turkey were given to 'caretaker' countries. The Commission kept an eye on the management of these colonies

Minorities Commission
Helped protect people of one nationality forced to live under the rule of a different national group

Other Agencies
Dealt with such problems as drug abuse, slavery, refugees . . . worked to improve world health and education

Examination Guidance

Questions using sources on the League of Nations can ask you to fill in information about how it was formed, and what was its structure. You may also be asked short-answer questions – an example is given in Activity 17c.

ACTIVITY 17a

Targets

Recall, comprehension.

Question Guide

The question uses a Source to help you show what you understand abut the founding of the League. Some of the answers can be worked out from the cartoon, while others refer to your knowledge.

THE GAP IN THE BRIDGE.

Figure 2.15

Source　*Punch* magazine, 10 December 1919

Activity

Look at the cartoon (Figure 2.15) on the League of Nations, and answer the questions which follow (MEG, June 1988). (How to deal with such questions is dealt with in Chapter 1, pages 16–18.)

1. (a) Who was the US President referred to as the *designer* of the bridge in the cartoon?
(b) What had all the countries named in the cartoon recently had in common?
(c) Which major country, *a founder member of the League*, is not mentioned in the cartoon?
(d) Why does the cartoon show the keystone missing from the bridge?

ACTIVITY 17b

Target

Recall.

Question Guide

This question helps you learn the League's structure, and how it operated.

Activity

Copy the outline of Figure 2.14, leaving the contents of the boxes empty. Fill in the boxes and headings.

ACTIVITY 17c

Targets

Recall, comprehension.

Question Guide

The Activity requires you to write your answers in a paragraph form (see Chapter 1, pages 15–16 for guidance). The section above contains all the information needed to deal with questions 1 and 2, while question 3 is covered in Section 5 below and in Chapter 3, Sections 2 and 3.

Activity

1. Describe the circumstances in which the League of Nations was established.
2. How was the League of Nations organised to carry out its work?
3. Show how the League tried to carry out its work during the 1920s and 1930s.

5 The League in Action – the 1920s

The work of the League in the 1920s needs to be set against the backcloth of the death and desolation caused by the First World War. All those who drew up the terms of the Versailles Settlement had lost friends and relations in the fighting – it was a desire for peace that served as a driving force for many of them. How would you feel if half of the people of your own age had been crippled or had died fighting in the previous four years? It was hoped that the League would keep the peace.

In this, and its other work, was the League of Nations a success or a failure? This section examines the work of the League in the 1920s. To provide a full answer to the question of its failure, you need to look at pages 42–47, which deal with its activities in the 1930s.

To help you work out how successful the League was in the 1920s, consult Figure 2.16, a list of incidents with which it was involved in Europe, and Figure 2.17, a map of where they occurred.

Figure 2.16　Incidents involving the League, the 1920s

1919. Teschen. Poland and Czechoslovakia accepted the League's decision to split the town of Teschen between them.
1919–20. Vilna. The Poles seized Vilna, the old capital of the new country of Lithuania, and refused to give it up. The League was ignored.
1920. Yugoslavia–Albania. The League stopped the Yugoslavs from invading Albania.
1921. Upper Silesia. The League solved the row between Germany and Poland over who should control Upper Silesia.

1921. Aaland Islands. Finland and Sweden accepted the League's decision over who should own the islands.

1920–1. Poland–Russian War. The war was ended without the help of the League of Nations (see page 39).

1923. The Corfu Incident. In the Corfu incident, Mussolini, the ruler of Italy (see pages 45–47), forced Greece to pay Italy a huge fine for the murder of Italian soldiers. The Italian soldiers were part of a League of Nations commission sent to sort out the boundaries between Greece and Albania. Mussolini had ordered the Italian navy to bombard the island of Corfu.

1923. Memel. Lithuania seized Memel, a German port. The League was ignored.

1923. The Ruhr. France marched its troops into the Ruhr to force Germany to pay reparation. The League was not consulted.

1923. Smyrna. The Turks threw the Greeks out of Smyrna; the League was unable to act.

1925. Bulgarian–Greek War. The League of Nations settled a war between Greece and Bulgaria. Greece accepted the League's demand to pay a fine to Bulgaria.

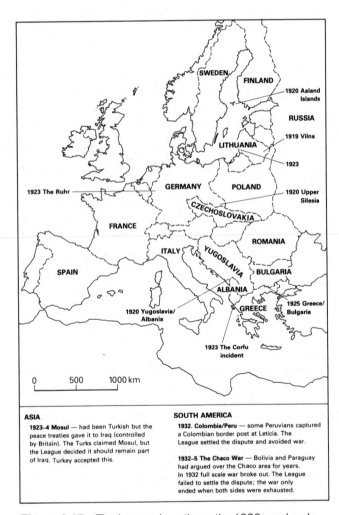

ASIA
1923–4 Mosul — had been Turkish but the peace treaties gave it to Iraq (controlled by Britain). The Turks claimed Mosul, but the League decided it should remain part of Iraq. Turkey accepted this.

SOUTH AMERICA
1932. Colombia/Peru — some Peruvians captured a Colombian border post at Leticia. The League settled the dispute and avoided war.

1932–5 The Chaco War — Bolivia and Paraguay had argued over the Chaco area for years. In 1932 full scale war broke out. The League failed to settle the dispute; the war only ended when both sides were exhausted.

Figure 2.17 The League in action – the 1920s and early 1930s

Work of the League's Agencies

To judge the success or failure of the League of Nations, the work of its agencies needs to be looked at *separately* from its diplomatic work, i.e. its settling of disputes between countries.

The *Health Organisation* took an active part in dealing with the causes of epidemics, in particular the spread of typhoid from Russia.

The *Refugee Organisation* was under the control of Fridtjof Nansen, a famous polar explorer.

An example of the Refugee and Health Organisations work was their help in settling over 1 million Greeks who had fled from Smyrna in Turkey in the early 1920s. Smyrna was part of Turkey handed over to Greece under the terms of the Versailles Settlement; the Turks refused to accept this, re-conquered the area and would have slaughtered the Greeks living there (see pages 32–33). The Health Organisation built farms, villages and towns for the refugees, and gave them the tools, machines and animals to start a new life. The League created work for over half a million Greeks.

The *Mandates Commission* played a limited part in running the territories which were supposed to be under the control of the League, and which would be prepared for independence. But Iran achieved independence in 1932, and in 1935 the Mandates Commission supervised the plebiscite which led to the Saar rejoining Germany. The rest of the Turkish and German colonies remained colonies, in mainly British and French hands.

The *Disarmaments Commission* achieved nothing, although sixty countries attended the 1932 disarmaments conference. Any hopes of disarmament were ended with Hitler's rise to power in Germany (see page 49).

The *International Labour Organisation* (ILO) had some influence in spreading ideas about how workers should be treated. The ILO aimed to get governments to:

- control and improve working conditions
- set a fair length to the working week
- set a level for minimum wages
- bring in benefits for those out of work
- bring in old age pensions.

Examination Guidance

Questions on the League usually ask if it was a success or a failure. So, you need to think about these two questions and a third, more difficult one – to what extent did it succeed or fail?

Questions can take several forms, e.g. the handling of Sources, factual knowledge of the League's organisation and work, the explanation and understanding of its role (as in Activity 18a), and the writing of short answers (as in Activity 17c above).

ACTIVITY 18a

Targets

Recall, evaluate, select knowledge, concepts of similarity and difference.

Question Guide

Here you are asked to think about the role of the League when linked to the nature of the countries it was dealing with.

Activity

For each incident, share out 10 marks between the League and the small and large countries involved, for how well each did in solving the problems listed below; 10 is a high mark, 1 a low one. If the League solved the problem, it gets most of the marks; if it was ignored, they go to the countries which sorted out the problem. A country receives marks for getting its own way. Then add up the marks for incidents involving small, weak countries and the marks for large, strong countries.

What does this suggest to you about how well the League might do in dealing with a major row involving strong countries?

	Small/ weak	Large/ strong	League
1920. Teschen			
1919. Vilna			
1920. Yugoslavia–Albania			
1921. Upper Silesia			
1921. Aaland Islands			
1920–1. Polish–Russian War			
1923. The Corfu Incident			
1923. Memel			
1923. The Ruhr			
1923. Smyrna			
1924. Mosul			
1925. Bulgarian–Greek War			
TOTALS			

ACTIVITY 18b

Targets

Recall, comprehension.

Question Guide

This looks like a simple comprehension exercise, but it has a thinking sting in the tail, i.e. it asks you to think about whether the League succeeded or failed in each case. This raises big questions like what do we mean by a success or a failure?

Activity

Copy the outline of Figure 2.17. By each incident say what it was about. Put a ring around boxes where the League was a success; put a rectangle where it failed.

6 The 1920s – the Search for Peace: Germany

The 1920s were haunted by two fears: first, of another World War, with Germany on the attack once more; secondly, the victors were terrified of the spread of communism or Bolshevism from Russia (see Chapter 8).

So, when we read about the events of the 1920s we need to bear in mind Germany and Russia, two powers who had not even been allowed to join the League of Nations!

Reparations

How would you feel if, after a fight with someone, he sued you and the judge ordered you to pay him huge sums of money in damages? This happened to Germany in May 1921 when the Allies fixed reparations, payments for war damage, at £6,600,000,00. Germany paid some of this money at once, but by 1923 the German government claimed it could not meet the payments.

The Occupation of the Ruhr

If you were unable to obey the judge and pay money or damages to your enemies, the court would send a bailiff to your house to seize your goods. In 1923 the same thing happened to Germany – the French decided to seize the Ruhr (see page 31). The Ruhr produced 80% of Germany's coal, iron and steel. French troops marched into the Ruhr, and the French took over the Germans' industries in the area. The German government was furious, and bitterly protested that the French were breaking the terms of the Versailles Treaty. The German government ordered *passive resistance*, a refusal to obey any French orders, such as orders to load coal on to French trains. The Germans also *printed huge sums of money*. Prices soared, and this inflation wrecked the economy of Germany (see pages 171–173).

Together, the Germans' passive resistance and the massive inflation meant that the French did not receive full reparation payments. At the same time thousands of Germans lost their jobs in the Ruhr's coal-mines and steel-works. So, in September 1923 Stresemann, the new Chancellor of Germany, called off passive resistance as a step in helping sort out a deal with the French and her allies. How was the problem of Germany to be solved – the French to get their money, the Germans control over the Ruhr?

The Dawes Plan, 1924

The Allies set up an international committee under Charles Dawes to look at the problem of reparations. It came up with the *Dawes Plan* (1924) for German payment of reparations, which Germany accepted. The Dawes plan said:

1. Reparations should be paid much more slowly.
2. Germany should have a new, stable currency which would not lose value. This would stop inflation.
3. International loans, mainly American, would be made to help Germany pay their reparations.
4. Loans were also to be used to develop German industry, farming and mining.

At the same time the French agreed to withdraw their troops from the Ruhr.

Once the reparations issue was settled, it was possible to try and establish good relations with the new German government.

The Locarno Pact, 1925

Streseman in Germany and the new French Foreign Minister, Briand, wanted to make sure that France and Germany did not go to war in the future.

A historian, H. Tint, continues the story from the French point of view. When Briand became foreign minister he pressed for an agreement with Germany to guarantee the frontiers of the Versailles Settlement.

Source 2D

. . . in 1925, there seemed to be little hope for such a policy. The Germans had just elected Hindenburg President [a famous First World War German general], and many Frenchmen still thought of him as a war criminal . . . Yet, despite such unpromising beginnings, the ambitious treaty of Locarno was signed within six months of Briand's arrival at the Quai [the French Foreign Office]. This treaty was the result of an initiative by the Germans in which they freely recognised the Rhine frontier and thus endorsed [agreed with] the return to France of Alsace and Lorraine.

Briand had speedily accepted the German suggestion for the treaty, not least because Germany had claimed earlier that the Rhine frontier, like all other provisions [terms] of the Versailles Treaty, had been accepted by her only under duress [when she was forced to do so]. The Locarno Treaty had two further attractions for Briand. First it was underwritten [guaranteed] by both Britain and Italy. Secondly, it had created conditions for Germany's entry into the League of Nations. However, at the same time the French signed a mutual defence treaty with Czechoslovakia.
(H. Tint, *France since 1918*, Batsford, pp 25–6)

The *Locarno Pact* (Source 2E), saw Germany taking an equal role in European affairs, along with Belgium, Britain, France and Italy. Locarno was followed in 1926 by Germany joining the League of Nations.

Source 2E The Locarno Pact

A. Belgium, France and Germany agreed to accept their common borders fixed at Versailles.
B. Britain and Italy guaranteed these frontiers.
C. The Rhineland was to remain demilitarised.
D. France would protect Poland and Czechoslovakia if Germany attacked them.
E. Germany agreed not to use its armed forces against Poland and Czechoslovakia.

The Kellogg–Briand Pact

Source 2F

Finally, the Kellogg-Briand Pact in 1928 for the renunciation [giving-up] of war as an instrument of national policy seemed to all but the most sceptical [doubting] a definite turning point in the history of human endeavour [efforts] and the search for peace. (Harold Macmillan*, *Winds of Change*, p. 202)

What made Harold Macmillan so sure that the world was closer to long-term peace in 1928 than ever before? The signing of the *Kellogg–Briand Pact* seemed to be a huge step. Kellogg and Briand, the American and French foreign ministers, got 65 countries to promise to give up war.

The Young Plan

A second major step was the *Young Plan* (1929) for the repayment of German reparations. It replaced the Dawes Plan with a huge cut in the amount of reparations Germany had to pay, from 6,600 million to 2,000 million pounds. Also, their payment was now spread out over 59 years. The Young Plan had another impact: Briand promised to withdraw French troops from the Rhineland in 1930. The Kellogg–Briand Pact and the Young Plan received widespread support inside Germany.

A referendum or plebiscite in Germany opposing the Young Plan was rejected by a 4:1 majority. In October 1929 Stresemann died. Stresemann's death, and the Wall Street Crash (see pages 192–194), saw an end to the decade which had promised peace.

Examination Guidance

The questions will mainly ask the extent to which the nations of Europe were able to work peacefully together in the 1920s. There could well be a British focus, looking at the role which Britain took in the various complex negotiations of the period.

ACTIVITY 19a

Targets

Recall, evaluate, select knowledge, comprehending and extracting information from a source.

Question Guide

The National Criteria ask you to handle sources, and to understand the information which they contain. In your answer make sure that for each one you mention two separate, but linked, facts.

Activity

With reference to Sources 2D-2F, and your own knowledge, write from one to three sentences on each of (a)–(i).

(a) Who was Briand?
(b) Who was Stresemann?
(c) Who was Hindenburg?
(d) Why would the French think of Hindenburg as a war criminal?
(e) What had happened to Alsace-Lorraine in 1919, and why?
(f) Why did Alsace–Lorraine matter to the French?
(g) What reasons are given in Source 2D for the French being attracted by the Locarno treaty?
(h) Put the reasons in (g) into what you consider to be their order of importance, with your reasons.
(i) What does the French signing of the treaty with Czechoslovakia suggest?

ACTIVITY 19b

Targets

Recall, understanding, concept of cause.

Question Guide

Activity 19b was set by the MEG in June 1988. Note the allocation of marks, so do not spend too much time on sections with only 2 marks.

In question (a), (i) the first extract serves as a trigger. If you cannot remember the names immediately, think of any treaty of the 1920s with two names linked to it – and you are likely to get the right answer! Question (b) expects you to list six points, one for each mark. Answer question (c) after studying Chapter 3.

Activity

Read the following two extracts which concern international agreements reached during the inter-war years and answer the questions which follow.

The nations solemnly declare, in the names of their respective peoples, that they condemn the use of war for the solution of international disputes.

(From the *Pact of Paris*, 1928)

Great Britain has made it possible for the chief nations of Europe to sign, seven years after the greatest war in history, the Locarno Treaty of Peace. It should be a source of pride that British intervention has made peace in Europe something like a real possibility at last.

(From an editorial in *The Times* newspaper, 19 November 1925)

(a) (i) The Pact of Paris is better known by the names of the two statesmen who proposed it. Give their names and the countries they represented. **(2)**

 (ii) Say briefly what Britain had done to make the Locarno Treaty possible. **(2)**

(b) Why were Britain, France and Germany able to cooperate so well in the period 1924–1929? **(6)**

(c) 'Between the wars Britain and France always saw their own interests as more important than any international agreements.' Do you agree? Explain your answer as carefully as you can. **(15)**

7 The 1920s – the Search for Peace: Russia

Source 2G

The years from the ending of the war until 1929 were years in which, in spite of all the loss, all the sorrow, and all the human tragedy, there seemed a good prospect before humanity. We believed in the League of Nations. The phrase 'the war to end war' had not yet become a mockery.
(Harold Macmillan, * *Winds of Change*, Macmillan, 1966, p. 200)

Civil War and Allied Intervention

What led Harold Macmillan to be so hopeful in the 1920s? One of the most serious threats to the peace of Europe came from Russia. In 1917 the communist Bol-

sheviks had seized power in Moscow and Leningrad (see pp. 153–154). Under their leader Lenin they managed to extend their power over Russia in a bitter and bloody civil war (1918–22), between the Bolshevik Reds and the enemy Whites – a civil war in which millions were killed or died from starvation during a terrible famine. During the civil war the war-time Allies, Britain, France, the USA, Italy and Japan, had even sent troops to help the Whites fight the Bolshevik Reds (see p. 156). The Allies feared the spread of communism to Western Europe through the *Comintern* (Communist International) which Lenin had set up to stir up revolution in other countries. By 1921 the Allies' troops had been withdrawn from Russia. Communist victories over the Whites meant the Allied forces were powerless.

Poland

The year 1920 also saw war between Poland and Russia over the disputed new western frontier of Russia. The war ended with the *Treaty of Riga* (March 1921). The defeated Russians were forced to hand over huge areas of land to the Poles (see Figure 2.11).

Rapallo

A weak, isolated, yet communist Russia needed friends. In 1921 she signed treaties with Afghanistan, Mongolia, Persia and Turkey, signed trade agreements with Britain and made a secret agreement with the Germans, the other great leper power of Europe. The Russians allowed German firms to make guns, shells, aeroplanes and submarines in Russia. Later the Germans built tanks, and carried out experiments in gas warfare. This was followed in April 1922 by the *Rapallo Treaty* between Germany and Russia. Rapallo placed their relations on a normal footing:

1. Each side gave up its financial claims on the other.
2. Full diplomatic relations were restarted.

Locarno and the Kellogg–Briand Pact

With Lenin's death in 1924 and Stalin's emergence as Russia's leader, Russia ceased using the Comintern as a tool to bring about communist revolutions. Earlier Lenin had set up the COMmunist INTERNational to spread communism to other countries. Locarno, and Germany's entry into the League of Nations in 1926, placed a strain on relations with Germany. E. H. Carr, [†]a famous historian, tells us about Russia's relations with Britain, China, France and Germany in 1925–9:

Source 2H

For nearly two years after the break with Britain in May 1927 and the collapse of the Chinese revolutionary movement and of the Soviet involvement in China, Soviet foreign relations were in the doldrums. Successive approaches from Moscow were ignominiously rebuffed by the British government. Negotiations with France on debts and credits broke down; though it did not sever diplomatic relations, found a pretext for demanding the recall of Rakovsky, the Soviet Ambassador. Relations with

---

* Harold Macmillan, later Prime Minister of England, was a young MP in the 1920s.

† * E. H. Carr was a lecturer at Cambridge University, and Britain's leading expert on Soviet Russia.

Germany had been temporarily disturbed by her signature of the Locarno treaty and entry into the League of Nations.
(E. H. Carr, *The Russian Revolution*, Macmillan, p. 173)

However, in 1928 Russia took a big step when she signed the Kellogg–Briand Pact (see Section 6 above).

Source 2I

When ratification of the pact by the Western powers was delayed, the Soviet Government proposed to its immediate neighbours to conclude a pact to bring the provisions of the Kellogg pact immediately into force between themselves. This subsidiary [extra] pact was signed in Moscow on February 9, 1929 amid a blaze of publicity, by the USSR, Poland, Latvia, Estonia and Rumania; Lithuania, Turkey and Persia acceded [joined/signed] later.
(E. H. Carr, *The Russian Revolution*, p. 175)

In 1934 Russia was finally accepted as a world power, when she joined the League of Nations.

Examination Guidance

Questions on Russia are likely to be rare in this part of the examination, as on most syllabuses it is a separate examination topic. You should, however, be aware of the details, so you can include them if necessary in your answer on attempts to secure peace in the 1920s.

ACTIVITY 20

Targets

Recall, evaluate, select knowledge, empathy (i.e. looking at events from the perspective of people in the past).

Question Guide

The activity combines the working-out of information from a range of sources with your own knowledge. It serves as a useful revision exercise for the whole chapter. Section (b) of the question looks at a skill usually tested elsewhere, the use of your historical imagination/empathy. It is included here to help you develop your understanding of the topic.

Activity

Using your own knowledge and Sources 2G–I:

(a)   write out the table below with what you can find out about each of the points mentioned.
(b)   under each point put down the reasons why Harold Macmillan might have felt it would have aided world peace.
Refer to the role of the League of Nations.

Points

1.   Allied troops withdraw from Russia
2.   Treaty of Riga
3.   Treaty of Rapallo
4.   Locarno
5.   Russia signs the Kellogg–Briand Pact
6.   Russia's relations with her neighbours by 1930
7.   Russia joins the League of Nations

INTERNATIONAL RELATIONS, 1929–41

Examination Guide

International Relations, 1929–41 is a major compulsory part in the syllabuses of two of the four Examination Groups, MEG and NEA. It is also a major section of the parts you can choose to do in the LEAG and SEG syllabuses. For MEG, **The Collapse of International Order in the 1930s** is a laid-down area of study for Paper 1. In the NEA syllabus, it is a large part of one of four sections of the compulsory part of the syllabus: the theme **Conflict and Conciliation** for Paper 1, dealing with the outbreak of the Second World War. For LEAG, the area is covered in a range of topics for Paper 1 (see below); while for SEG, **International Relations, 1929–41** falls within the topic, **Peace to World War, 1918–41**. **Peace to World War, 1918–41** is one of three themes to be chosen from for Paper 1. This is in addition to the compulsory theme, **The USA and the USSR as World Superpowers since 1945**. For SEG, the topic **Peace to World War, 1918–41** is essential background knowledge for studying **The USA and the USSR as World Superpowers since 1945**.

Detailed syllabus coverage for LEAG, MEG, NEA and SEG is as follows.

Syllabus Coverage

LEAG

Appears directly in two of ten sections, *viz.*:
Topic E1, The League of Nations and the United Nations
Topic I1, Aspects of the Second World War

MEG

The Collapse of International Order in the 1930s

NEA

Conflict and Conciliation
Causes of the Second World War
Hitler's aims and expansionist policies;
Appeasement;
Role of the USSR;
Poland

SEG

Peace to World War
The failure of the League in Manchuria and Abyssinia
Changes to and violations of the Treaty of Versailles
German Expansion after 1935 and the attitudes of Britain, France, Italy and the Soviet Union.

ACTIVITY

Find from past papers all the questions on **International Relations, 1929–41**, and then place them under the headings of the topic guide for this chapter.

Heading in Topic Guide	Year	Paper Date	Number	Question number
Section				

Topic Guide

1 The Great Crash and Depression

Think of setting up small businesses with groups of friends. Each of you makes one thing, like shirts, pencils or shoes. To set up your own business you borrow money from a banker. You trade with your friends, and with other groups who make the same kinds of goods. Then one day the other groups place a tax on all your goods, so you can no longer sell them what you make, and the bank asks for its money back. The result would also be that you would not be able to buy raw materials, equipment and goods from other groups. You would go out of business and lose your job.

Something like this happened on a world-wide scale from 1929 to 1930, with countries taking the role of you and your friends. The story began in October 1929 in America, when the American stock market, Wall Street, crashed (see Chapter 10, Section 3). American banks demanded back the money they had lent European and other foreign countries and businesses in the 1920s. In 1930 America also imposed a stiff tax on imports, the *Smoot Hawley tariffs*. The result was a collapse in world trade, the closing-down of businesses and industries throughout America and Europe. The consequences were drastic. For example, in America 110,000 firms shut between 1929 and 1932, the foreign trade of South America halved, and unemployment in Britain soared

from 1.2 million in 1928 to 2.7 million in 1932 similar to the American pattern (Figure 3.1).

The **Depression** was to be a major background factor in causing the Second World War. It can be seen as being a *long-term cause* of the war. The Depression had different results in different countries. Here are some of them:

Britain

The government slashed spending. It feared expenditure on arms would make the Depression worse. Britain failed to rearm until the late 1930s, and was unable to stand up to Germany.

Germany

The Depression played a big part in helping Hitler and the Nazis come to power. Hitler's foreign policy played a major part in bringing about the Second World War in 1939.

Italy

Italy's leader, Mussolini, was happy to try and conquer Abyssinia as a colony for unemployed Italians, and to take away attention from economic problems at home.

Japan

The conquest of Manchuria was one way of solving Japan's trading problems.

USA

From 1929 America became more and more isolated from Europe, largely because of the cutting of its economic ties. Roosevelt, the American President from 1933, was mainly concerned with trying to solve the problems of the Depression at home, rather than with taking an active part in international affairs (see Chapter 10, Sections 3 and 4).

Examination Guidance

The Great Crash and Depression are likely to be included as an element in a question dealing with the causes of the Second World War, or as a separate topic for a short-notes or single-paragraph answer. Before working through the activities, read the relevant sections on the Depression in the chapters on America and Germany. Activity 21a asks you to match the consequences of the Great Crash with various countries. This kind of question might become much more common. It is widely used in schools and in the most popular textbooks – upon which examiners who set your questions tend to base their questions.

ACTIVITY 21a

Targets

Recall, comprehension, selection.

Question Guide

The activity requires careful thought, because some of

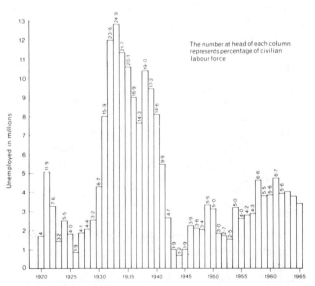

Figure 3.1   The impact of the Depression: unemployment in America, 1920–45

Source Harriet Ward, *World Powers in the Twentieth Century*, Heinemann, 1978, p. 38

the countries are similar, yet responded differently to the Depression. Read through the question, and make the matches between the countries and the outcomes of which you are sure. You can then look at those which are left, and make a good guess on the basis of what you already know.

Activity

Say which is the most likely match between the countries in the left-hand column and the statements in the right-hand column.

Country	Statement
Britain	saw an extreme government come to power dedicated to the overthrowing of the Versailles Settlement
Germany	failed to rearm because it was thought rearmament would make the economy worse
Italy	wanted colonies in China so as to exploit them for economic reasons
Japan	was concerned with sorting out her own economic problems and was not interested in foreign affairs – she followed a policy of isolationism
The USA	decided to conquer part of Africa as a colony for unemployed people at home and so as to distract attention from problems within the country

ACTIVITY 21b

Target

Recall.

Question Guide

Short answers might be required on the following points for either free-standing or source-linked questions. Follow the revision advice in Chapter 1 for memorising detail.

Activity

Write a sentence on each of the following:

(a)   the Wall Street Crash
(b)   Smoot Hawley Tariffs
(c)   the impact of the Depression.

2 Japan, Manchuria and the League of Nations

How do you deal with a school bully? What if he is allowed to get away with it, and builds up a gang of friends who terrorise you? Something like this happened in world affairs in the 1930s. The history of the 1930s is overshadowed by the outbreak of war in September 1939 in Europe, when Germany attacked Poland. The war became world-wide in December 1941, when Japan bombed and torpedoed America's fleet at Pearl Harbour.

The story of the origins of the Second World War is tied up with the failure of the League of Nations as a peace-keeping body. In the 1920s the League had a mixed history, with some successes and some failures (see Chapter 2 Section 5). In the 1930s it was on a downhill path, until by 1939 the League was largely ignored and forgotten, an irrelevance in trying to solve international problems.

The League's first major setback occurred in 1931 in Manchuria, a rich industrial province of China. In 1931 Japan invaded and occupied Manchuria (Figure 3.2).

THE BACKGROUND

Manchuria was a neighbouring province of Korea, already a colony of Japan. By 1905 Japan alrady controlled the Manchurian branch of the Trans-Siberian Railway to Port Arthur. In 1931 China was in a state of Civil War (see Chapter 11, Section 3), and was unable to resist a Japanese attack.

To the generals of the Japanese army in Korea, Manchuria seemed ripe for conquest. The generals were quite capable of acting without orders from the Japanese government. The Japanese government at the time was split between a group who wanted peace, and a group who wanted to occupy China and exploit it as a Japanese colony. The Japanese emperor, Hirohito, may have backed the war party. Source 3A tells of the news of the Japanese attack on Manchuria reaching the Japanese foreign minister:

Source 3A

The morning of 19 September 1931. A reporter was present when the anti-war foreign minister, Shidehara, was told of the Japanese army attack on Manchuria, and tells us Shidehara's 'face turned grey'.

JAPAN'S REASONS

What were the causes of, the reasons for the Japanese attack? Here is a list of possibilities, in no order of importance. Before thinking about them, consult Figure 3.2.

1.   Manchuria was an important area for Japan to acquire vital raw materials – coal, iron, soya-bean oil.
2.   The area was a possible source of markets and raw materials to overcome the economic depression following the Great Crash (see Section 1 above). In 1931, over half of Japan's industry had closed down, and there had been a collapse in the export of its main industrial product, silk.
3.   Manchuria would be an area to settle unemployed Japanese peasants, who had flocked to the cities.
4.   The Japanese generals wanted to fight a war to gain the army prestige, and to build up their own positions. They believed that it was Japan's destiny to conquer Asia.

As a result of the invasion, by early 1932 the Japanese had gained full control over Manchuria.

● In January 1932 the Japanese bombed Shanghai to punish an attack on some Japanese monks.
● In February 1932 the Japanese set up the new puppet

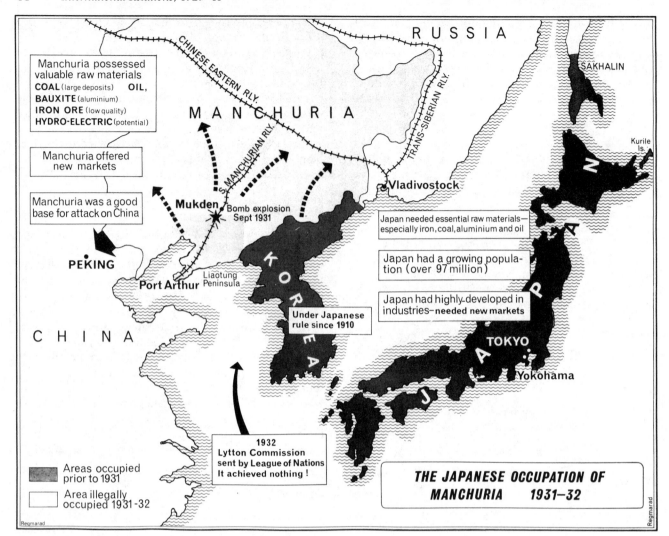

Figure 3.2   The Japanese occupation of Manchuria

Source   B. Catchpole, *A Map History of the Modern World,* Heinemann, p. 53.

state of *Manchukuo*, under Japanese control, to run Manchuria. The puppet head of Manchukuo was the last Chinese emperor, Henry Pu Yi.

The Nationalist government of China (see Chapter 11, Section 3) appealed for help to the League of Nations, using the procedure outlined in Chapter 2, Section 4. The League sent a commission to Manchuria to find out what had gone on. The commission, under *Lord Lytton*, published its report.

- In September/October 1932 the League used the Lytton Commission's findings to condemn the Japanese government.
- In November the League's Council said that Japan and China should hold talks over Manchuria's future.
- In February 1933 the League's Assembly accepted the Lytton report with 42 votes for and Japan against. *Japan walked out of the League.*

Over Japan and Manchuria the principle of collective security had failed in a major test case involving one of the world's great powers. Britain and France had failed to act, for they had not said that the League should use sanctions against Japan.

From 1933 to 1937 the Japanese extended their control over Northern China. In July 1937 they mounted a full-scale attack on Southern China, following a clash between Chinese and Japanese troops at the *Marco Polo*

bridge south of Peking. The Japanese troops bombed and burned the towns and villages of China, and bayoneted, shot, raped and robbed the Chinese, millions of whom fled. The League of Nations was ignored.

Examination Guidance

Japan, Manchuria and the League of Nations is a likely topic within a League of Nations question, but it is also perfect for source-based or short-answer questions in their own right. Activity 22a is based upon MEG and LEAG question patterns. Activity 22b looks at the issue of causation, one of the concepts which is being examined.

ACTIVITY 22a

Targets

Recall, comprehension.

Question Guide

Look carefully at the mark allocations. Note that for questions 1(a) and 1(b) you need to mention a single fact, while for 1(c) you should include two facts. For question (2a) you should link it to the split within the Japanese government and the fact that the Japanese generals in Korea were out of control. Question 2(b) is difficult; it asks you to mention whether the reasons were numbers 1–3 of those listed in the text, or primarily number 4. Note that it is for only 3 marks, so don't write more than three sentences on it. Question 3 is a short-essay answer (follow the guidance given in Chapter 1 on how to deal with such questions.) The question needs a full discussion of the weaknesses in the peace-keeping role of the League of Nations, and then relating that weakness to the situation the League faced in Manchuria. Question 4 asks you to consider the value of the Source to the historian – the word 'trust' indicates this.

Activity

Study Figure 3.2 and Source 3A. Then answer questions 1–3 which follow:

1. (a) What name is usually given to the railway from Russia which passes through Mukden?   **(1)**
    (b) Before 1931, who controlled the area which the Japanese subsequently occupied?   **(1)**
    (c) What happened at the Marco Polo bridge in 1937?   **(2)**
2. (a) Why did Shidehara's face turn grey – Source 3A?   **(3)**
    (b) What does the source suggest about the causes of the Japanese attack on Manchuria in 1931?   **(3)**
3. Comment upon the statement: 'The League of Nations showed its fatal weakness in 1931–2 in its handling of the Manchurian crisis.'   **(12)**
4. How much trust can we place in Source 3A?   **(3)**

ACTIVITY 22b

Targets

Comprehension, causation.

Question Guide

Look carefully at the list of reasons on page 43, and then think about their relative order of importance. You need not worry about whether the order is right; in fact there is no 'correct' answer. The point is that you should be able to defend the answer you have given.

Activity

By one of the headings, **Long-term cause, Short-term cause** or **Immediate cause** put one or more of the causes given on page 43 for Japan's invasion of Manchuria, with reasons for your choice:

Long-term cause	**Reason for choice**
Reason for choice	**Immediate cause**
Short-term cause	**Reason for choice**

3 Italy and Abyssinia

The 1930s and Europe

The 1930s saw the failure of Britain and France both to control the growth of German moves to overthrow the Versailles Settlement, and to stop Italy from supporting Germany after 1936. Britain attempted to keep the peace with Germany by giving in to Germany's demands – a policy known as *appeasement* (see Section 5 below). The League of Nations also became useless as a body for world peace, a situation that became clear during the Manchurian crisis (see Section 2 above). In Europe the emergence of Italy as an ally of Germany and her supporter in the war can be linked to Italy's conquest of Abyssinia in 1935–6. The 1930s ended with the outbreak of the Second World War, which, by mid-1940, saw Germany and Italy fighting Britain and France. In 1941 the struggle spread to include America, Japan and Russia.

Mediterranean Fascism

A major reason for Italy's support of Germany from the mid-1930s was the close similarity between the beliefs and politics of the countries' two leaders, Hitler of Germany and Mussolini of Italy. Hitler is looked at in detail in Chapter 9. What did Mussolini stand for?

Background to Mussolini's beliefs

During the First World War, Italy had been one of the Allies. At the Paris Peace Conference her leaders felt that her demands were not met – in particular she was not given the port of Fiume and the area of Dalmatia, the coastal strip of modern Yugoslavia, a huge area roughly 400 kilometres long by 50 kilometres wide. Within Italy high post-war unemployment and poverty aggravated widespread political chaos and the growth of extreme political parties. One of these parties was the fascist party of Mussolini. What was facism about?

Mussolini's Fascism

Do you know what the National Front stands for? Have you noticed how its enemies often call its members fascists? Next time you read or hear about the National Front, think of these points about Italian facism, and consider which are similar to the views of NF members:

1. *Nationalism.* Pride in the country, and a belief that Italy should be a great power again as it was during the Roman period. The fascist symbol is the *fasces*, a bunch of bound sticks and an axe, the symbol of the Roman Empire (Figure 3.3).

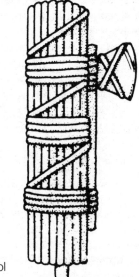

Figure 3.3 The Fascist Symbol

Source Christopher Culpin, *Making History*, Collins Educational, p. 50.

2. *Racism*. Belief in the superiority of the Italian race over other races.
3. *A strong leader*. The party needs to have a strong leader.
4. *A single party*. The fascist party sums up the spirit of the nation. There is no room for opposition parties.
5. *A general loathing of socialism*, and of Bolshevism, the communist regime in Russia, in particular.
6. *Strong police force and armed forces*. These are vital for a powerful state.
7. *The state as the controller of what people say, think and do*. No freedom of the press or broadcasting. Control over education and the family. Even control over religion, but this is difficult in Italy, the home of the Pope. Most Italians are Catholics.
8. *The state as controller of the economy*. The fascist must make sure that industry, commerce and banking are organised to push forward state interests.
9. *Violence*. Support for the use of violence against the state's enemies. Mussolini's backers (the blackshirts) wear uniform and form armed bands which fight vicious street battles against the fascists' opponents.

Mussolini in Power

Mussolini becomes Prime Minister

The Fascists built up their power in the towns and cities of Italy, and had 35 MPs elected to the Italian Parliament in 1921. With Italy in political chaos throughout 1921–2, in October 1922 Mussolini's fascists marched on Rome to seize power. In order to avoid a civil war Mussolini was given the chance to form a government, and he seized his chance with both hands. His part in the March on Rome consisted in arriving in Rome by train – the train had been pointing the other way ready to take him into exile if his bid for power had failed!

Mussolini and Italy

Mussolini changed the law to give the fascists control over parliament. In 1925 fascist thugs murdered Matteoti, the opposition leader. By the end of 1926, opposition parties had been banned and their newspapers closed down, trade unions had been disbanded and Mussolini had been given the power to make laws without asking parliament. Mussolini formed a secret police force to keep control over his enemies.

The economy was placed under the control of a number of *corporations* of bosses, party members and workers' representatives – the *corporate state*. A corporation fixed wages, prices and profits for its own industry, such as mining and iron and steel. In reality businessmen ran industry as they pleased. Schools had to teach what Mussolini told them; history lessons became a farce, showing the glories of fascism.

In foreign affairs Mussolini appeared as a man of peace, despite having shown up the weakness of the League of Nations (see Chapter 2, Section 5, on the Corfu Incident). He played a central part in the international acceptance of the Locarno Treaty in 1925 and the Kellogg–Briand Pact in 1928 (see Chapter 2, Section 8). In the early 1930s Mussolini was a backer of France and Britain against the attempts of Hitler, Germany's new leader, to seize control over Austria in 1934. Mussolini rushed Italian troops to the border to stop any German moves – Hitler backed down. In 1935 at Stresa, Mussolini joined with Britain and France against growing German demands – the *Stresa Front*. Source 3B discusses the Stresa Front, and links it to the growing Abyssinia (Ethiopia) crisis:

Source 3B

On the return of our party to Rome I asked . . . what had happened about Ethiopia [Abyssinia]? It had not been mentioned, he said. I was astounded, and deeply worried. I was in no sense aware of what was happening behind the scenes in London, but I could only conclude that His Majesty's Government had taken some secret decision to let Mussolini go ahead. Otherwise the policy made no sense. There were two alternatives: you could tip Mussolini the wink – which was Laval's policy – or you could tell him that if he violated [broke] the Covenant you would mobilize all your resources against him and even, in the last resort, not shrink from war.
(Lord Gladwyn, * *The Memoirs of Lord Gladwyn*, Weidenfeld & Nicolson, 1972, p. 48)

By the early 1930s Italy was a fascist state, with Mussolini as its dictator. Mussolini had served as a model for Hitler to follow. Mussolini was a backer of force, and happy to use war to make the Italian state a new Rome. The new Rome needed its own empire, and in the mid-1930s Mussolini turned to Africa to bring about his dream. Britain and France had their huge African empires. Why, thought Mussolini, should Italy be left out? Abyssinia was his natural target.

Abyssinia

Abyssinia was an independent African country. Italy had long been involved in Abyssinia, and in 1896 she had suffered the cruel blow of having the Abyssinian Emperor defeat an invading Italian army at the battle of Adowa. Natives who had backed the Italians had their right hands chopped off. Italy had a small, neighbouring colony to Abyssinia, Italian Somaliland, (see Figure 3.4). In 1932 Mussolini saw a report from an Italian general in Abyssinia sketching a plan of conquest. In 1934 there was skirmish at Wal Wal between Italian and Abyssinian troops, and it was clear that Mussolini was itching to seize Abyssinia. Mussolini used Wal Wal as an excuse to revenge the disgrace of Adowa and establish his own empire. In October 1935 Italian forces invaded Abyssinia.

Britain and France

Abyssinia was a member of the League of Nations, and the Italian attack was a clear breach of the covenant, as well as of the Kellogg–Briand Pact. The Emperor of Abyssinia, Haile Selassie, asked for support from the League. The League imposed *limited sanctions* on Italy, which Britain and France backed. Crucial goods for fighting a war, like oil and steel, were left off. The sanctions on goods like cloth and gold had little or no

* Lord Gladwyn was a young British diplomat in Rome in 1935. Here he writes about the Stresa meeting, held at the time of the worsening of the crisis over Abyssinia. Gladwyn discusses the Stresa meeting with a senior diplomat who was at the discussions between the British and Italians over what to do about Germany (see Section 5 below).

Figure 3.4 The position of Abyssinia and the territories of Britain, France and Italy

The Italian conquest of Abyssinia

Italy pressed on with her attack on Abyssinia. An Italian force of some 200,000 men, armed with machine-guns, tanks, flame-throwers, aeroplanes and poison gas routed the native army. In May 1936 the Italians occupied the capital, Addis Ababa, a shanty town of tin shacks and mud huts. Hailie Selassie fled from Abyssinia and at the League of Nations made an impassioned plea for backing. No one listened.

Consequences

1. The outcome of the Abyssinian affair was a split between Mussolini and Britain and France. Mussolini was now ready to move into the camp of Hitler and Germany.
2. The League of Nations was unable to solve a major international problem through collective security. The use of sanctions against Italy had been a pathetic failure.
3. Britain and France had shown they were unwilling to use force against a fascist dictator. This *could* have encouraged Hitler.

Examination Guidance

The Abyssinian crisis ties into two linked topics: the failure of the League of Nations and the causes of the Second World War. You should look at the information from both these viewpoints.

ACTIVITY 23

Targets

Recall, comprehension, handling evidence – extraction of information.

Question Guide

The question is based upon the MEG and NEA patterns, and uses a source to give you extra information in addition to what you find in textbooks.

Activity

Consult Figure 3.4 and Source 3B to answer the following questions:

1. Explain the references to:
    (a) Ethiopia **(1)**
    (b) Mussolini **(1)**
    (c) the Covenant **(1)**
2. Why might Lord Gladwyn have been worried that the impending Italian attack on Abyssinia had not been mentioned during the Stresa negotiations? **(6)**
3. What evidence is there that Laval's policy later received the backing of the British Government, and with what consequence? **(6)**
4. Explain how the fears of Lord Gladwyn were borne out by what happened over Abyssinia in 1935–6, and how his comments throw light upon the move of Italy into Germany's camp in 1936. **(15)**
5. What is the value of Source 3B to the historian, and what are its limitations? **(5)**

impact. In December 1935 Britain and France tried to solve the Abyssinian problem. Britain was in a strong position to act against Italy, and could use her fleet to cut off Italian troops in Abyssinia from support by closing the Suez Canal.

The Hoare–Laval Pact, December 1935

It is said that history tends to repeat itself, the first time as tragedy, the second as farce. The Hoare–Laval Pact was pure farce from the start. The British Foreign Secretary, Hoare, worn-out and ill, went on a skating holiday. His train passed through Paris, so he decided to have a meeting with Laval, the French Foreign Minister, to try and solve the Abyssinian crisis. Over tea and biscuits they came up with the Hoare–Laval Pact. Its main points were:

1. Most of occupied Abyssinia (some two-thirds of the country) was to be handed over to Italy.
2. Abyssinia was to agree to the agreement.

The news of the agreement leaked out – apparently Hoare had been persuaded not to take a strong line against Italy because the Italian fleet might mount a surprise attack and sink the British fleet at the Suez Canal! In Britain there was a howl of protest from the press at the agreement, and in Parliament the government faced a barrage of criticism. So, the Hoare–Laval Pact was scrapped, and Hoare resigned, having returned early from his holiday after a skating accident.

4 The Spanish Civil War

Source 3C

The trip to Rebel Headquarters . . . was on the whole a successful one. In Lisbon, I had already found ample proof of the Portuguese authorities' connivance with [backing of] the insurgents [rebels]. In Seville, evidence of Nazi intervention on Franco's side could literally be had in the streets, in the shape of German airmen, walking about in the white overalls of the Spanish Air Force, but with a small swastika between two wings embroidered on their blouses . . . Finally . . . I obtained an exclusive interview with General Queipo de Llano – the most popular, owing to his radio-speeches, of Franco's Generals – who, believing that I was in sympathy with his side, made some highly indiscreet statements referring to foreign aid. The Civil War had only just entered its second month, and non-intervention was still a carefully maintained fiction; Hitler kept denying that he was sending help to Franco and Franco denied receiving it.

(A. Koestler, *The Invisible Writing – an Autobiography*, Collins, 1954, pp. 319–20)

Today when you go to Spain you can read what you like in newspapers, and people will tell you their views on politics, and even how they vote in elections. Twenty years ago this would have been impossible – for Spain was still a fascist state, which continued under the rule of its dictator, Franco, until his death in 1975. One party, no political debate, prisons stuffed with political prisoners. How can you make sense of Source 3C, which tells of the start of the struggle which led to Franco's dictatorship, and which hints at the role which the powers of Europe played in the Civil War?

THE CIVIL WAR, 1936–9

During the 1920s the army had ruled Spain under the King. Because of the impact of the Depression on Spain (economic collapse leading to massive unemployment and poverty; see Section 1 above), the King abdicated in 1931. Spain became a *republic*. From 1931 to 1936 the right-wing *republican government* faced risings from provinces demanding independence, and strikes and rebellions from left-wing anarchist and socialist groups, which the army crushed.

In January 1936 the parties of the left won a general election, by the summer it seemed that the communists might gain control of the country. A group of generals, along with a new *fascist party* (see Section 3 above) the *Falange*, planned to seize power instead. Fighting broke out in July 1936, when the army in Morocco revolted. The Moroccan army commander, Franco, soon took charge of the rebel or nationalist forces. His rival for the leadership died when his plane crashed, weighed down with trunks stuffed full of uniforms! The Spanish Civil War (1936–9) was fought with cruelty on both sides; prisoners and suspects were slaughtered without mercy. By 1939 Franco's nationalist forces had gained control over the whole of Spain (Figure 3.5). Over half a million died in the fighting – about one in thirty of the population was killed; villages, towns and cities were wrecked; and the country remained a fascist state for the next 35 years.

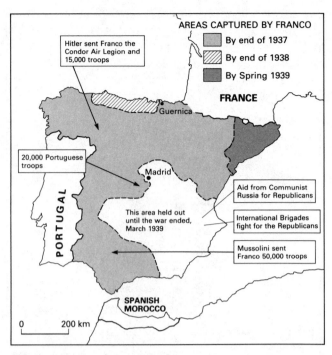

Figure 3.5   The Spanish Civil War, 1936–9

Source   B. Catchpole, *A Map History of the Modern World*, Heinemann

CONSEQUENCES

The Spanish Civil War was important in terms of the outbreak of the Second World War for these reasons:

1.   Hitler and Mussolini came to the aid of Franco and the nationalists (the Falange). They sent troops and airmen as well as arms and equipment to Spain. The Italians had some 50,000 men in the country, the Germans over 15,000. In October 1936 Hitler and Mussolini formed the Rome–Berlin Axis (see Section 6 below).
2.   Britain and France refused to intervene, and claimed they were neutral. They set up a non-intervention committee, of which Italy, Germany and Russia were members (Source 3D). The British

Source 3D   13 January 1937. The figure with the hands tied behind his back represents the British Foreign Minister; by his side is his French colleague.

Source   D. Low, *Years of Wrath*, Gollancz, 1986

and French governments allowed volunteers to go to Spain to fight and join the *International Brigade*, which fought on the side of the republic. The stance of Britain and France suggested that they were unwilling to support a democracy against attacks upon it from the fascists.

3. Russia under Stalin backed the republic. Russia realised she could not rely on Britain or France for support in a struggle against fascism.

4. The war was a testbed for new ways of fighting. The German division of its air force, known as the Condor Legion, bombed towns, the first major use of air power to terrorise civilians. Its destruction of Guernica in 1937 became famous as a major atrocity, immortalised in the painting of Picasso.

Examination Guidance

The Spanish Civil War is not an examination topic in its own right – it appears as an element in **International Relations**, with reference to the outbreak of the Second World War. The main thing is to learn the details so as to be able to answer questions like Activity 24.

ACTIVITY 24

Targets

Recall, comprehension, the concept of cause, evidence – extraction of information, detection of bias.

Question Guide

The activity is based upon the patterns of MEG, LEAG and NEA papers. Use the information above to work out the answers to the questions. For question 1(a), the answers should be clear even if you cannot recognise the figures. Question 2 asks you to list the reasons underlying the roles of the countries portrayed, and also the consequences of their involvement. Question 3 looks at the two sources as historical evidence: 3(a) asks you to concentrate on words and phrases like 'rebel', 'Nazi', 'indiscreet', 'carefully maintained fiction'; 3(b) requires you to link the information in the sources into what you already know about the Spanish Civil War and international relations; 3(c) is a standard question on the value of sources (see pages 16–18).

Activity

Look at Sources 3C and 3D, and then answer the questions.

1. Look at Source 3D and say:
   (a) Who are the three figures seated facing the British and French? **(2)**
   (b) What is the link between them and the planes and warships shown in the background? **(1)**
   (c) What does the figure on the ground represent? **(1)**
   (d) What is the straitjacket? **(1)**
   Look at Source 3C and explain the references to:
   (e) the 'small swastika' **(1)**
   (f) Franco **(1)**
   (g) non-intervention **(1)**

2. Comment upon the situation which Source 3C and the cartoon, Source 3D, show. Explain how it had come about, why the characters in the cartoon are behaving in the ways shown, and what was the outcome of their actions. **(10)**

3. (a) What words and phrases in Source 3C reveal the viewpoint of the author? **(3)**
   (b) How would you use Source 3C and 3D in writing an account of the Spanish Civil War and its impact on international relations? **(5)**
   (c) How useful are either autobiographies or cartoons to the historian? **(4)**

5 Hitler and Europe, 1933–7

In your school or college can you remember what happened when a thug got away with bullying? Did others join the gang? Or did those picked on join up in self-defence? Or did they try and buy off the bully by doing what he wanted? From 1935 to 1938 the powers of Europe were faced with growing threats from a bully – Hitler's Germany. Hitler and the Nazis had come to power in 1933 with a promise to tear up the Versailles Settlement. The Nazis' demands were:

(a) the reoccupation of the Rhineland
(b) the building-up of her armed forces to the level of a major power
(c) the return of German lands in the hands of her neighbours, Poland and Czechoslovakia
(d) the union of Germany and Austria, a country of Germans.

Background

Above we have already said that Hitler had some clear ideas about German foreign policy when he gained office in 1933. The issue is not so clear, for historians argue bitterly about whether Hitler:

1. had a long-term plan to:
- scrap the Versailles settlement,
- win back lost German lands and unite all German people in an expanded Germany or *Reich*
- gain new, rich lands in the east – Poland and Russia, for Germans to settle (*Lebensraum*)
- enslave the non-German people of Europe and set up the Germans as a master race (Aryans) who would rule the world.
  OR
2. seized chances as they arose
- to build up Germany's position,
- to undo the Versailles settlement
- to extend Germany from 1938 to include areas where Germans were a majority; these included territories in the neighbouring countries of Poland, Czechoslovakia and Austria.

Keep in mind these two opposite views as you read through the accounts of Hitler's actions from 1934 to 1939. How did the powers regard Hitler in 1934?

Britain

Britain wanted to avoid any direct clashes with Germany, still trusting to the League of Nations. Her leaders felt many of Germany's demands were justified. This led the British Prime Minister from 1937 to 1939, Chamberlain, to follow a policy of *appeasement*. Appeasement meant giving in to what were seen as the fair demands of Germany. Chamberlain thought that appeasement would avoid any future wars.

France

France had no clear, strong plans for dealing with Hitler. She backed the British policy of appeasement, but also tried to make treaties in Eastern Europe to guard against any German attack.

Both the British and the French governments still saw *the communist threat from Russia as the greatest danger to European peace*. Can you think why?

Italy

Italy wished to make sure that Europe was at peace, and that Germany did not pose a threat to Italy. However, Mussolini shared many of the views of Hitler (see Section 3 above), and they had a lot of common interests.

Japan

Japan was under the control of her generals. Her invasion of Manchuria in 1931 (see Section 1 above) and the views of her leaders meant that she was also a natural ally of Germany.

The USA

America played little or no part in European affairs, being wrapped up with the problems of the Depression (see Chapter 10). In the 1930s America followed a policy of isolation from European affairs.

Russia

Russia's armed forces were weak. In the 1920s and 1930s she had spent little on her army, and in the purges of the mid-1930s Stalin killed off most of his best officers (see Chapter 8, Section 7). Stalin tried to secure Russia from an attack from Germany by making treaties with his neighbours and France.

Rearmament

To carry out his plans, Hitler introduced a major programme of rearmament, building up his army, navy and airforce (see Chapter 9). Versailles had limited the army to 100,000 men. Military expansion meant withdrawing from an international disarmaments conference in 1933 and leaving the League of Nations in 1934. In March 1935 he introduced conscription, a flagrant breach of the Versailles Settlement. The army grew quickly, to some 600,000 men by 1936, and in 1938 his army was 800,000 strong, the airforce had some 2,000 planes and the navy 21 large warships and about 50 submarines or U-boats. Figure 3.7 gives an idea of how quickly German military power grew.

Hitler's Diplomacy

At the same time Hitler tried to appear a man of peace and reason. He claimed that he wanted disarmament, but that all powers should be treated the same. To show that he really meant peace he signed a treaty with Poland in January 1934, in which they agreed not to fight one another. The treaty was a clear signal to Britain that Hitler meant peace. It also freed his hands to move against Austria and Czechoslovakia, as it meant that he had no reason to fear an attack from Poland.

Austria – 1934

The Nazis wished to unite Germany and Austria, the majority of whose people were Germans. In July 1934 the ruler, Dolfuss, the Chancellor of Austria, was murdered, probably by the Nazis. Austria's Nazis seized on the confusion of his death to try and seize power and get Germany's backing. Hitler had not thought of Italy's reaction – a united Austria and Germany would place a powerful neighbour on her borders. Italy had a long history of being invaded and controlled from the German north! So, Mussolini rushed three divisions of tanks to the frontier and warned Hitler that he would not allow a Nazi takeover. Hitler backed down. As a result, Britain, France and Italy formed the anti-German **Stresa Front** in April 1935 (see Section 3 above).

The anti-German front fell apart in 1935–6. First, Hitler cunningly offered Britain an Anglo-German naval treaty in 1935, which seemed to secure British naval supremacy, a major British concern for well over 100 years. This Anglo-German naval agreement allowed Germany a navy 35% the strength of the British one. Britain failed to consult either the French or the Italians about the German offer. The French and Italians were furious, for the naval treaty meant that Germany was now a naval threat to the smaller French and Italian navies. Secondly, both Britain and France fell out with Italy over the Italian invasion of Abyssinia (see Section 3 above).

The Saar – 1935

Under the terms of the Versailles Settlement, in 1935 the people of the Saar voted as to whether they wanted to be reunited with Germany. Nine out of ten said 'yes', so Hitler gained his first German-speaking area for his enlarged Germany, and the rich coal and iron mines of the Saar and its iron and steel works.

The Rhineland – 1936

Hitler's first major territorial move against the Versailles Settlement occurred in 1936. The Rhineland was as German as sauerkraut, but it was also the highway for German armies to the Low Countries and France. So, at Versailles it had been demilitarised – no troops were to be stationed there. The Nazis felt that this was an insult to Germany. By 1936 Hitler wondered whether he should march his troops into the Rhineland. This would be against the wishes of his generals, who knew that if Britain and France decided to fight, Germany would be humiliated and forced to withdraw her soldiers.

In March 1936 Hitler gambled and ordered his forces into the Rhineland, a clear breach of both the Versailles

Settlement (see Chapter 2, Section 2) and the Locarno Pact (see Chapter 2, Section 6).

Consequences

The consequences of the occupation of the Rhineland were profound:

1. It showed that the Versailles Settlement could be torn up.
2. It means that the treaties of the 1920s to secure peace in the West were now worthless scraps of paper.
3. It demonstrated that Hitler was willing to use armed force to gain his ends, not diplomacy.
4. It again showed that the use of force would triumph against the weak Western democracies Britain and France, and that the League of Nations was a dead duck.
5. Hitler's foreign policy of building up a strong, united Germany was not a bluff.
6. It influenced Mussolini to move over to Hitler's side (see Section 6 below).

Examination Guidance

You are unlikely to get a separate question on Hitler and Europe, 1933–6; the subject is likely to be linked to more general questions about:

(a) the failure of the League of Nations
(b) attempts to achieve disarmament from 1919–39

(c) the causes of the Second World War, 1934–9.

The following activity is designed to make you work through the material in a way to prepare you for points (a)–(c) above; it also introduces you to one form of examination – the setting of questions on an extract from a well-known textbook. One day a bit of *Work Out* might pop up on your paper!

ACTIVITY 25

Targets

Recall, comprehension, empathy (i.e. looking at events from the perspective of people in the past), evidence – extraction of information and relating it to existing knowledge.

Question Guide

Question 1 requires you to make two major points about each of (a)–(d). For example, for 1(b), your answer might be: 'The Versailles treaty was the peace treaty which Germany was forced to sign with the Allies in 1919. It placed strict limits on the size of Germany's armed forces.' Question 2 requires you to mention appeasement, and you should also mention two other points, such as that it allowed Germany to build up her armed forces and to unite with Austria. Question 3(a) requires you to mention demilitarisation, and to give a

Figure 3.6 Hitler and Eastern Europe, 1938–9

Source B. Catchpole, *A Map History of the Modern World*, Heinemann, p. 61.

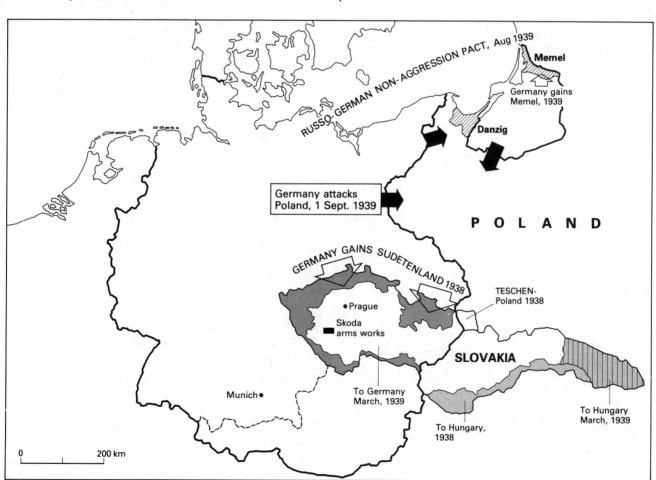

reason for this policy; 3(b) concerns the disarmament clauses of Versailles and the policies Hitler had taken since 1933 to overthrow them. Question 4 asks you not only to mention Britain and France's treatment of Germany, but also their response to Japanese aggression in Manchuria and the Italian attack on Abyssinia.

Activity

Consult Source 3E and 3F and Figures 3.6 and 3.7, and then answer the questions.

Source 3E

In 1936, Hitler made his first real gamble. He sent troops into the Rhineland. This was not only a breach of the Treaty of Versailles, which had been forced on Germany, but also of the Treaty of Locarno, which she had signed of her own free will. The German army was still too weak to fight a war, as Hitler knew full well. He said later, 'The forty-eight hours after the march into the Rhineland were the most nerve-racking in my life.' However, the British took the view that Germany was entitled to send troops into her own territory. As for the French they could have invaded Germany on their own with every chance of success, but apart from sending a few divisions to the frontier, they did nothing. The Rhineland crisis showed how weak Germany's enemies were.
(P. F. Speed, *A Course Book in Modern World History*, Wheaton, 1982, p. 213)

1. Explain the references to:
    (a) Hitler   (2)
    (b) the Versailles Treaty   (2)
    (c) the Treaty of Locarno   (2)
    (d) the Rhineland   (2)
2. What do we normally call the British policy of allowing Germany to 'send troops into her own territory', and what other forms did the policy take?   (2)
3. (a) What had both Versailles and Locarno said about the Rhineland, and why?   (3)
    (b) Why would Germany still be too weak to fight a war, and what had Hitler done to remedy this situation?   (3)
4. The quotation suggests that the occupation of the Rhineland showed the weakness of Britain and France. In what other ways had they shown their weakness by March 1936?   (10)
5. How does the information in Figures 3.5 and 3.6, and Source 9m, p. 179, confirm or contradict the story of German rearmament given in the text?   (5)

6 Steps to War

The period 1936–9 sees the playground bully of European politics, Hitler, getting more and more out of control. The steps he took to include German-speaking areas in a bigger Germany and to overthrow the Versailles Settlement became more and more extreme. Finally his actions led in September 1939 to the outbreak of war against Britain and France. The Second World War had begun.

Figures 3.6 and 3.7 provide a guide to the steps which led to the outbreak of war in 1939.

Source 3F

" Why should we take a stand about someone pushing someone else when it's all so far away .. "

INCREASING PRESSURE

Source   D. Low, *Years of Wrath*, Gollancz, 1986, p. 56

Hitler's foreign policy from 1937 involved the two Western democracies, Britain and France, and his fascist ally, Italy. In 1939 communist Russia also became directly concerned.

APPEASEMENT

The British continued with the policy of appeasement, mentioned in Section 5 above. The British Prime Minister, Chamberlain, backed appeasement, giving in to Germany's demands and avoiding war at all cost, because:

(a) He felt Germany had a just claim to have German land included within Germany.
(b) The Versailles Settlement had been too harsh in its treatment of Germany, e.g. she had a right to her own, large, armed forces; reparations were much too heavy.
(c) Britain was too weak militarily to fight Germany, and needed time to rearm.
(d) The great threat to European peace was from Russian communism, and not Germany.
(e) At all costs the slaughter of another world war must be avoided.

By 1937 appeasement had already led to the collapse of the Stresa Front and the alliance of Hitler and Mussolini, largely because of the fiasco of Britain's Abyssinian policy and her and France's neutrality in the Spanish Civil War (see Sections 3 and 4 above).

MARCH 1938. AUSTRIA – THE ANSCHLUSS (UNION WITH GERMANY)

Hitler's first move was to gain control over Austria. Within Austria the growing Nazi party demanded to have a say in the government. In February 1938 Hitler demanded to see Schuschnigg, Austria's ruler, and at their meeting forced Schuschnigg to give in to his demands to:

(a) make the Nazi leader in Austria, Seyss-Inquart, the Minister of the Interior

(b)   make a second Nazi war minister
(c)   bring about an economic union of Germany and Austria
(d)   lift the ban on the Nazi party
(e)   free all Nazis in jail

In effect, Hitler forced Schuschnigg to hand Austria over to the Nazis. It was straightforward playground bullying – 'Do as I say or I will send in my troops. Britain, France and Italy won't help you.' (see Source 3F.)

Schuschnigg decided to call a referendum to see if the Austrian people wanted union with Germany or not – Austria had always been an independent country. Hitler was furious, for he did not dare risk a vote. So in March the Germans got ready to invade. With the German army poised to strike and Nazis in key positions inside the Austrian police, the plebiscite was called off. Seyss-Inquart had in effect gained control over the government, and Hitler's troops marched in. Union with Germany, the *Anschluss*, had been achieved, Winston Churchill said in Parliament:

Source 3G

Where are we going to be in two years hence, when the German army will certainly be much larger than the French army, and when all the small nations will have fled from Geneva to make up to the ever growing power of the Nazi system, and to make the best terms that they can for themselves?

Figure 3.7   Steps to war

1933   Germany leaves League of Nations
1934   January   German–Polish agreement to settle disputes peacefully – ten-year non-aggression pact. Start of breaking of links between Poland and France, Poland's protector.
1935   German conscription introduced. Build-up of German armed forces.
1936   Hitler occupies the Rhineland. German troops now on French borders.
Fights with Italy in Spanish Civil War.
Rome–Berlin Axis – agreement reached with Mussolini.
Anti-Comintern Pact signed with Japan.
1937   Mussolini joins the Anti-Comintern Pact.
1938   AUSTRIA
Hitler, with Mussolini's backing, now gains control over Austria.
March   Union with Austria – the *Anschluss*.
CZECHOSLOVAKIA
Hitler now mounts a campaign for the union of the German-speaking area of Czechoslovakia, the Sudetenland, with Germany.
September   The Munich agreement. At Munich, Europe's four leading powers, Britain, France, Italy and Germany, agree to Hitler's demands to gain the Sudetenland.
1939   March   Hitler occupies the rest of Czechoslovakia, after having been 'invited' in to restore order.
POLAND
April   Hitler now demands the return of the cities of Danzig, German lands in Poland and rail routes across the Polish Corridor to Danzig.
British support Poles, but fail to sign a treaty with Russia – the only way to back up their opposition to Hitler.
May   Mussolini seizes Albania.

Pact of Steel between Italy and Germany; Mussolini promises to give Hitler full military support in a war.
August   Hitler signs non-aggression pact with Russia, plus a secret deal to split up Poland between them. Before the First World War one-third of Poland had been a Russian province. Britain continues to back Poland.
September   Hitler invades Poland, refuses to withdraw when sent British ultimatum. On 3 September war breaks out.

CZECHOSLOVAKIA – SEPTEMBER 1938, MARCH 1939

Hitler's next move was against Czechoslovakia. The Czechs seemed quite safe – strong western defences, strong army, democracy, treaties with France and Russia against attack, the backing of the Versailles Settlement. But the Czechs were vulnerable to a British and French policy of appeasement, for within Czechoslovakia lived 3 million Germans in the Sudetenland (see Figure 3.6). The Sudetenland was a key area, containing Czechoslovakia's western defences and some 70% of her heavy industry. The Sudetenland stripped away, Czechoslovakia was defenceless.

Hitler couldn't risk an open invasion, and the Czechs under their leader, Benes, would refuse to hand over the Sudetenland. So, Hitler got the Nazis in the Sudetenland to stir up trouble and demand union with Germany. The demands of Hitler and the crisis in the Sudetenland frightened Britain and France so much that they were willing to betray the Czechs and accept the German demands. This was despite the Versailles Settlement and the 1934 French treaty of support for the Czechs.

In September 1938 Chamberlain, Britain's leader, flew to see Hitler three times. After the second meeting, war seemed likely – the Czech army of 2 million got ready to fight, with British backing. Chamberlain was still desperate for peace, and Hitler wanted to avoid war, so Chamberlain flew to Germany a third time. The final meeting was at Munich, and involved the four main West European Powers, Britain, France, Germany and Italy. They agreed to:

1.   Germany taking over the Sudetenland immediately
2.   the Poles and Hungarians gaining Czech lands which contained Poles and Hungarians
3.   Britain and France protecting what was left of Czechoslovakia.

Chamberlain came back in triumph from Munich with one of the most laughable prophecies ever, 'Peace for our time'. The Czechs had been betrayed. As Churchill said, 'We are in the presence of a disaster [the Munich agreement] of the first magnitude [size] which has befallen Great Britain and France.'

In March 1939 Czechoslovakia disintegrated, and Hitler marched in to occupy the rest of the country.

CONSEQUENCES OF THE MUNICH AGREEMENT

(a)   It was clear that Britain and France were unable to stand up to Hitler.
(b)   Hitler felt he could now act with a free hand against Poland (Source 3H).
(c)   The Russians knew they could not rely on the backing of the French against a German attack.

Source 3H

NIGHTMARE WAITING LIST

Source D. Low, *Years of Wrath*, Gollancz, 1986, p. 66

(d)   France's other allies in Eastern Europe – in particular the Poles – knew they could not trust the French.

(e)   The League of Nations was totally discredited.

(f)   The Locarno Treaty, which protected Czechoslovakia, was dead.

(g)   The policy of collective security had broken down.

(h)   Hitler gained powerful new arms works, in particular the Skoda factory, in Czechoslovakia.

Poland

Poland was the next country to go into Hitler's killing bottle. Hitler wanted the German city of Danzig and the German area in between – the *Danzig Corridor*. Germany would then be united with its East Prussian province. Concerning Poland, things were a bit more tricky, for Hitler faced a threat not only from Britain and France, but from Russia as well. Throughout the 1920s Hitler's hatred of communism had led to violent attacks upon communists, and when he was in power they were all murdered or jailed (see Chapter 9). Russia was seen as an arch-enemy, so by 1939 Stalin, Russia's ruler, had good cause to fear Nazi Germany.

Hitler and Russia

In 1935 Stalin had joined with France and Czechoslovakia in a mutual support treaty, but clearly it wasn't worth the paper it was written on.

After Hitler had seized Czechoslovakia, the British government began to prepare for war, but Hitler still thought they would betray Poland as well. In April they promised to back Poland against Hitler. Appeasement still continued, for in July 1939 the British government offered Germany a loan of 1,000 million pounds. Lord Gladwyn tells us in his memoirs:

Source 3I

'The immediate effect of this super-appeasement', I told Cadogan . . . 'has been to arouse all the suspicions of the Bolsheviks, dishearten the Poles . . . and encourage the Germans into thinking that we are prepared to buy peace . . .

I must doubt whether folly can be pushed to a further extreme.'
(Lord Gladwyn, *The Memoirs of Lord Gladwyn*, Weidenfeld & Nicolson, 1972, p. 93)

In the summer the British and French tried to reach agreement with Russia, but the Germans had beaten them to it (Source 3J). In August a stunned world received news of a Soviet–Nazi Pact – the *Molotov–Ribbentrop* agreement. Stalin and Hitler agreed not to declare war on each other and, in a secret part of the treaty, to divide Poland between them.

With Russia on his side, Hitler now had Poland at his mercy. On 1 September he invaded the country, and on 3 September war was declared between Germany and Britain and France.

In 1939–40 Russia and Germany occupied Poland, and Russia took back the territories she had lost after the First World War (Figure 3.8). The year 1940 saw Germany overrun France and Western Europe. Then, in June 1941, Germany attacked Russia.

JAPAN

While Hitler went to war in the West, in the East the Japanese continued their campaign to conquer China. The Americans were opposed to this growth of Japanese power – Japan's control over Asia's Pacific coastline was a threat to American trade. To become a world power Japan needed key raw materials – tin, iron, rubber and oil. These she could gain by taking over the colonies of Britain and France. In 1940 the Japanese, Germany's

Figure 3.8   Germany, Russia and Poland, 1939–41

Source K. Shephard and Jon Nichol, *Russia*, Basil Blackwell, 1986, p. 44

Source 3J

"IF THE BRITISH DON'T, MAYBE WE WILL"

Source D. Low, *Years of Wrath*, Gollancz, 1986, p. 88

allies, occupied French Indo-China, as France's government was now under German control. Japan was now poised to attack Britain's main supply of rubber – her colonies of Burma and Malaya.

Pearl Harbor

In July 1941 Roosevelt, the American President, took steps to curb growing Japanese power and cut off the supply of oil to the country. He demanded that the Japanese should withdraw from both China and Indo-China. The American move to deprive Japan of oil led the Japanese to take the next step – an attack on America. The Japanese decided to wipe out the American fleet, based at Pearl Harbor. On 7 December 1941 Japanese bombers and fighters launched a secret attack on Pearl Harbor. America had entered the war. Churchill's words repay careful reading – they brought tears to my eyes.

Source 3K

No American will think it wrong of me if I proclaim that to have the United States at our side was to me the greatest joy. I could not foretell the course of events. I do not pretend to have measured accurately the martial [military] might of Japan, but now at this very moment I knew the United States was in the war, up to the neck and in to the death. So we had won after all! Yes, after Dunkirk; after the fall of France; after the horrible episode of Oran, after the threat of invasion, when, apart from the Air and the Navy, we were an almost unarmed people; after the deadly struggle of the U-boat war . . . We had won the war. England would live; Britain would live; the Commonwealth of Nations and the Empire would live.

(Winston S. Churchill, *The Second World War*, Vol. III, Cassell & Co., 1950, p. 539)

Examination Guidance

A question upon the origins of the Second World War is very likely from LEAG, MEG, NEA and SEG. LEAG questions can appear in three places: requiring a short single-word or single-sentence answer in the first part of Paper 1, as part of a two- or three-part essay in part two of Paper 1, or as a source-based question in Paper 2. This question will be similar to those asked by MEG on its Paper 1. The MEG question will be based upon an extract or extracts, and directed towards an understanding of both the factual background to the conflict and the reasons for it. NEA will use some four sources to test the same kind of knowledge as MEG, but will also ask questions related to the nature of the evidence used.

ACTIVITY 26a

Targets

Recall, understanding, extract information, explanation (Question 3 (a) (i)–(ii)).

Question Guide

This is Question 3 of the MEG June 1988 paper. Question 3(a) requires recall, but also the ability to extract from the source evidence to support an opinion. For Question 3(b) you should pick up the key word 'Explain', and then you should work out at least six linked points to put into your argument. Question 3(c) requires you *to argue* about the question. Read through the **Model Answer** and then the commentary.

Model Answer to Question (c)

Hitler had made clear his foreign policy aims in *Mein Kampf* and in his campaigns for gaining office and consolidating power in 1930–4. The Nazi party was dedicated to the overthrow of the unjust terms of the Versailles Settlement, the inclusion of all German-speaking peoples within a greater Germany and the gaining of territory in the East, *Lebensraum*, where the expanding German population could live.

With these ideas in mind, it is difficult to see whether war was inevitable after the Nazis gained power in 1933. The question is whether Hitler had a plan to carry out the only policy which would have made war inevitable – the attack on Russia. War involving Russia only became inevitable in 1941, when Hitler decided to pursue a policy of *Lebensraum* and mounted Operation Barbarossa, the invasion of Russia. In summary, war was only inevitable when he turned to the final element in his policy, which involved an attack on Russia.

Commentary

The answer splits into three parts: the outline of the aims of Hitler, then linking those aims to the policy he followed in the 1930s, and finally tying the final aim, *Lebensraum* into the outbreak of war with Russia.

Activity

Read through the following extract on German foreign policy, and answer the questions.

Only a large space on this earth assures a nation of freedom. The National Socialist movement must hold to its aim to secure for the German people the land and soil to which they are entitled. If we speak of soil in Europe today, we can have in mind only Russia and her border states.

The demand for the restoration of the frontiers of 1914 is absurd. The frontiers in 1914 were neither complete, in the sense of including all the people of German nationality, nor sensible in military terms.

(Adapted from *Mein Kampf*, Volume 1, by Adolf Hitler)

(a) (i) What term describes the policy Hitler outlined in the first paragraph? How does the source help you to work out your answer? **(2)**

(ii) Name two of the 'border states' referred to by Hitler in the extract. **(2)**

(b) Explain why Hitler had an aggressive foreign policy. **(6)**

(c) 'Hitler's aims in foreign policy made war inevitable.' Do you agree? Explain your answer as fully as you can. **(15)**

ACTIVITY 26b

Targets

See below.

Question Guide

This activity is from the NEA Specimen Question paper: Both the targets and the guidance as to how to answer the question are contained in the NEA specimen marking scheme, which gives a clear insight into the kind of knowledge the examiner requires. Study the Sources 1–4 on pages 57–58, do questions (a)–(g) on page 58 and then mark your answer using the Levels mark scheme below.

Question 4

(a)   *Target:* recognition of caricatures of major world leaders: – Hitler & Stalin.

(b)   *Target:* comparison of sources and recognition of bias.

3–5

Level 1: simple approach, offering answers based on non historical reasoning: e.g. Source 1 is British because it is written in English. **(1–2)**

Level 2: examines sources closely and independently, reaching a conclusion for each source in general terms e.g.
1 – British because it shows Stalin as a caricature;
2 – Russian – it is a defence of the Pact;
3 – British – critical of Russian leadership. **(3–5)**

6–8

9–11 Level 3: explains reasons why British and Russian views would be seen in this light: e.g. 1 – GB opposed the Pact in 1939, so it is ridiculed by the cartoonist; 2 – an attempt to explain why the Pact was of value to Russia. **(6–8)**

Level 4: a comparison of the wording and ideas of the sources, explaining which is most likely to be Russian or British. Possibly conclude that 3 could be either as it contains criticisms and explanation of Russian policy. Source 4 could be used to justify the conclusion. **(9–11)**

Level 5: as level 4, but concludes that you cannot really decide about 2 and 3 because they were written in 1969, long after the event. **(12–13)**

(c) *Target:* to test the validity of a statement through comprehension and cross referencing of sources.

Level 1: accepts or rejects statement using only one source as evidence. **(1–2)**

Level 2: makes a clear reference to more than one source. **(3–5)**

Level 3: gives a balanced argument in favour and against. **(5–8)**

Level 4: includes cross referencing of all sources to reach a conclusion based on the evidence. **(9–11)**

Reasons expected are:

FOR: Gave time to build up Russia's defences (2); Fear that the Western powers were trying to bring about a German attack on Russia (3 & 4); Afraid of bearing brunt of fighting if they joined West (L);

AGAINST: Hitler's hatred of Russia and Communism (1); Russia's hatred of Fascism (1); Hitler's long term aims (2).

(d) *Target:* to understand the reasoning behind a statement.

Below base line: Hitler was going to conquer the world.

Level 1: Hitler was free to attack Poland; **(1)**

Level 2: shows the significance of the Pact in avoiding a war on two fronts. **(2)**

Level 3: sees levels 1 and 2 as the first steps in Hitler's foreign policy in the context of world conquest in stages. **(3)**

(e) *Target* comprehension and evaluation of a source in the light of a second source.

Level 1: yes or no answer with vague reference to Source 4 as evidence, but shows no clear understanding of the views expressed in sources, e.g. It does not support the view because it says in Source 4 that Russia was not put on a war footing. **(1–2)**

Level 2: shows understanding of the views in Source 2 and refers briefly to Source 4 to prove or disprove it, e.g. Russia expected Hitler to attack and made the Pact to buy time to build up defences, but this is not supported by Source 4 because Russia was not on a war footing. **(3–4)**

Level 3: Builds on level 2, showing full understanding of Source 2 and giving a catalogue of evidence

from 4 to show that Stalin did not use the time to build up Russia's defences e.g.
refused to call up army reserves;
refused to fire on German reconnaissance planes;
industry not on a war footing;
new war machines and weapons not in production;
proven weapons had been withdrawn from service;
armoured units had not been re-organised;
troop training was still on a peace time basis. **(4–8)**

Level 4: uses sources to produce a more balanced answer, e.g.

  (i) makes reference to the awareness of Russian groups that Germany was a danger shown in the suggestion of calling-up reserves.

  (ii) similarly, comments on the fact that Stalin was afraid of attack from Germany, but he wants to delay, presumably because Russia is not ready – would not do anything that might *provoke* war.

In both cases, evidence must be given to show that preparations were not made. **(9–10)**

Level 5: combines both lines of argument given in level 4 and reaches a balanced conclusion based on the evidence. **(11–12)**

(f) *Target:* recognition and explanation of differences between primary and secondary sources.
Award 2 marks for each source if correctly identified and explained. **(4)**

(g) *Target:* to evaluate the reliability of a source.
Answer will depend on the choice of source, but will be marked on the following lines:

Level 1: unqualified acceptance/rejection of evidence e.g. rejected because it is biased. **(1)**

Level 2: view is supported by reference to evidence. **(2–3)**

Level 3: qualified acceptance/rejection either by reference to other sources or by consideration of other factors such as the motives of the author, the one-sided nature of the source or by questioning the meaning of reliability. **(4–8)**

Source 1

The treaty with Germany was a step which the USSR was forced to take in the difficult situation that had come about in the summer of 1939. The Soviet government did not deceive itself regarding Hitler's aims. It understood that the treaty would not bring the USSR lasting peace but only a more or less lengthy breathing-space. When it signed the treaty with Germany the Soviet government undertook the task of using the time thus gained to carry through the political and military measures needed in order to ensure the country's security and strengthen its capacity for defence.
(from 'The Soviet–German Treaty of 1939', an article on it published in 1969)

Source 2   Cartoon from the *Evening Standard*, 1939

Source 3

The Soviet authorities knew that Hitler was preparing to attack the West if he could not frighten them off – and he expected the signing of the Nazi–Soviet Pact to do this. Yet no serious evidence has been produced which would show that British policy was directed to attempting to procure a German attack on the Soviet Union. If the Soviet leadership believed this to be the aim of British policy, they would appear to have been influenced by a major misjudgement.

The real defence of Soviet policy in 1939 is that the British were casting them in a role which if it succeeded in restraining Hitler would be to the credit of Great Britain, whereas if it failed, the Soviet Union would have to bear the burden of fighting on land. Great Britain had no forces available for a major land offensive in Europe and the French saw no point in abandoning their fortifications.
(from 'Directing Hitler Westwards' an article published in 1969)

Source 4

In reply to a question about the military situation in western Europe in the spring of 1940, Stalin said with a smile: 'Daladier's government in France and Chamberlain's government in Britain don't want to get seriously involved in war with Hitler. They are still hoping to push Hitler into war with the Soviet Union.'

In March 1941 the Russian military asked Stalin to agree to the call-up of reserves for re-training. Stalin refused on the grounds that 'it might provide the Germans with an excuse for provoking war'. At this time German reconnaissance planes were making daily flights over Soviet territory and provided the Germans with detailed picture of the Russian defences. Stalin issued strict orders that the planes were not to be fired on.

In the period 1939–1941, Russian industry was not put on to a war footing; many types of new weapons, tanks, and aircraft, which had already been tested and were superior to their German equivalents, were not put into production; some proven weapons, such as the 45-mm. anti-tank gun, were actually withdrawn from service; the reorganisation of armoured units was not carried through; troop training was still on a peacetime basis.
(from 'The Brutal Courtship' by David Floyd, published in 1969)

Study Sources 1, 2, 3 and 4.

(a)   Name Figures A and B in the cartoon (Source 2).
(1 line)   **(2 marks)**

(b)   1, 2 and 3 come from either British or Russian Sources. Which of the Sources do you think are more likely to be British and which are more likely to be Russian? Give reasons for your answer.
(10 lines)   **(13 marks)**

(c)   'Russia should not have made the Pact with Germany in 1939.' Using the Sources, explain how far you agree with this opinion.
(10 lines)   **(11 marks)**

(d)   After this Pact had been signed, the German leader said, 'Now I have the world in my pocket.' What do you think he meant by this?
(3 lines)   **(3 marks)**

(e)   Does the evidence in Source 4 support the views expressed in Source 3? Give reasons for your answer.

(f)   From the Sources, give ONE piece of primary evidence and ONE piece of secondary evidence which tells us about people's views at the time of the Nazi–Soviet Pact. Explain why the examples you have chosen are regarded as being primary or secondary sources.
(3 lines)   **(4 marks)**

(g)   Choose ONE of these Sources and comment on its reliability to the historian.
(5 lines)   **(8 marks)**

THE SECOND WORLD WAR

Examination Guide

This period, from the start of the Second World War in 1939 to the start of the 1950s, was crucially important in shaping the modern world. For that reason, it features in the syllabuses of all the Examining Groups. Take note, though, that only LEAG and SEG look at the Second World War itself in detail; the other groups only look at parts of it. Check just how much of it you will need to know about for the course you are following.

There are parts of this period spread over several of the twenty sections of the LEAG syllabus, e.g. A1 on **India 1918–48** and A2 on **China 1918–76**. The topic is covered in detail in Topic I1, **Aspects of the Second World War**. It is vital background reading for the study of post-1945 topics, in particular Topics F2, **Britain's Changing World Role since 1945**, G2, **The USSR's Relations with Eastern Europe since 1945** and I2, **Superpower Relations, 1945–75**.

Section 3 of the MEG core content includes Allied conferences during the war. Parts of the period also appear in the defined topic **Germany 1919–1945** (Topic C).

For NEA, parts of this period come under the theme **Conflict and Conciliation**, which is compulsory. You will also need to look at it if you are doing the optional theme **International Co-operation**.

The compulsory SEG theme, **The USA and the USSR as World Superpowers since 1945** covers topics dealt with in this chapter. If you are doing the optional topic **Military Events of the Second World War, 1939–45**, you will need to look here in detail.

ACTIVITY

Again, check the past papers of your Examination Group to see which parts of this chapter are likely to be most useful to you.

Topic Guide

1 The European War

The Second World War is a topic more popular with students than with examiners. This is partly because it is such a big topic. It was even more of a world war than the First World War, since massive fighting went on all over the globe. Therefore, we need to break it down into manageable sections.

The longest continuous fighting of the war started in 1931, when the Japanese invaded China, but what is usually considered the starting-point is the German invasion of Poland on September 1939. From then until Pearl Harbor in December 1941 it was really a European war. Germany and Italy fought with Britain and France, and later also with the Soviet Union, fighting first in Europe, and then in North Africa, where Britain, France and Italy all had colonies.

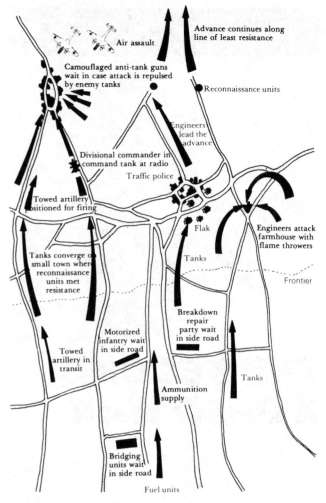

Figure 4.1   How Blitzkrieg worked

Source   Len Deighton, *Blitzkrieg*, Jonathan Cape, 1979, p. 183

BLITZKRIEG IN POLAND

Britain and France declared war on Germany in order to help Poland. In fact they did not help her at all. If you look at a map you can see why. It was too far for either country to get men or supplies there. The French did advance five miles into Germany in the west, but they went back again without causing any damage. The Poles had to fight on their own.

Most people know that the Poles had cavalry, but they also had tanks and aircraft, and they had beaten the Russian army in 1924. But the Poles were not prepared for *Blitzkrieg*.

Blitzkrieg ('lightning war') was a new German plan of attack which had been tested in the Spanish Civil War. In a *Blitzkrieg*, the idea was to take the enemy by surprise and to cause as much panic and confusion as possible. 'Panzer' tanks and dive-bombers would smash through the enemy's defences and spread terror and panic among civilians; the civilians would clog the roads, so their troops could not get to the danger points, and then the German infantry would move in. (The way *Blitzkrieg* worked is shown in Figure 4.1.)

The Polish army collapsed quickly, but the capital, Warsaw, held out. Then, on 17 September 1939, Soviet forces invaded Poland from the east. They linked up with the Germans, and Warsaw surrendered. Poland disappeared from the map.

The Russians had got half of Poland, but they still wanted more land. So they launched an attack against Finland. At first the Finns beat them back, but the Russians counter-attacked, and Finland surrendered in March 1940.

THE 'PHONEY WAR'

The Allies also seemed to have developed a new way of fighting. It was nicknamed *Sitzkrieg*, because all it involved was sitting around not doing anything!

Before you laugh, though, think about what would have been in the minds of the British and French commanders. The French army was far larger than the British, so everything depended on them. They had not forgotten the First World War, which had shown that big attacks against defended positions were suicide. The French had the *Maginot Line* to defend them against a German attack: as long as they stayed behind it, they thought, they were safe.

The Maginot Line was a massive complex of forts and guns, linked by long tunnels underground. It was very strong, but it did not cover the Belgian border, so this sector was guarded by the British.

The French position looked strong, but there were some vital weaknesses:

(a)   The French had plenty of modern tanks and aeroplanes, but they liked to use them in small groups.

These small groupings were no use against a massive German onslaught.

(b) Many French people, particularly soldiers, were convinced that the Germans would win the war. Even worse, they did not see why France should be fighting Germany in the first place: they thought France was only in the war because of the British. This sort of thinking was called *defeatism*, and it was a serious problem.

Now add two more problems: first, the French army had very poor communications – there was not even a radio in the headquarters building in Paris; secondly, many soldiers got tired of waiting for something to happen – and, for the first six months in the West, nothing did – and some began to desert and go home. The French President visited the front, and declared:

Source 4A

I seemed to encounter slackened resolve, relaxed discipline. There one no longer breathed pure and enlivening air of the trenches of 1914–18.
(A. Horne, *To Lose a Battle*, Penguin, 1984 edn, p. 139)

The French army had become lax, unprepared and bored. No wonder people talked about the 'phoney war'.

BLITZKRIEG IN THE WEST

In London, Winston Churchill put forward a plan to end the phoney war. Churchill was First Lord of the Admiralty at this point, and his plan involved the Navy. Germany got iron ore from Sweden, and most of it came through the Norwegian port of Narvik. Churchill planned to attack Narvik and starve the Germans of a vital raw material.

Norway was a neutral country, so Chamberlain, the British Prime Minister, hesitated to attack her. Hitler didn't. On 9 April 1940, the Germans launched another *Blitzkrieg*, swooping down on to Denmark and Norway. An Allied force did manage to take Narvik, but it was soon forced out again. The Allies were beaten and humiliated; Chamberlain resigned.

Churchill became Prime Minister, but on the very day he moved into No. 10 the Germans attacked again. On 10 May 1940 they invaded Belgium, Holland and Luxemburg. This looked like 1914 all over again. The British and French rushed their troops north, expecting another attack through Belgium. Instead, the Germans attacked through the forest of the *Ardennes*, in the centre of the Allied line. They broke through at Sedan, and rushed north. The British and French were trapped between the Germans in Belgium and the Germans

Figure 4.2   German-occupied Europe

Source   David Scott Daniell, *World War II: an Illustrated History*, Ernest Benn Ltd, 1966

coming up from Sedan. The Germans took Calais. What was left of the Allied army was trapped at *Dunkirk*. The British launched *Operation Dynamo* to evacuate the trapped armies. Hundreds of boats, from destroyers to river boats, ferried the men back to England. It worked, though largely because Hitler ordered his Panzers to hold off. Sources 4B and 4C give an idea of the problems which the British faced:

Source 4B

There was no cessation in the fury of the Luftwaffe's attack. Farther down the water the dive bombers were peeling off at 10,000 feet and coming down with a terrifying snarl of their motors to within 3,000 feet of the water . . . Within little more than an hour we had lost three destroyers, a Fleet minesweeper and a gunboat, and four destroyers had been damaged . . . The rate of loss was too heavy. It could not continue. There was no question of goodwill involved: it was a question entirely of ship reserves; we no longer had the ships.
(A. D. Divine, *Dunkirk*, Faber & Faber, 1945, p. 188)

Source 4C

Perfect discipline prevailed ashore and afloat. The sea was calm. To and fro between the shore and the ships plied the little boats, gathering the men from the beaches as they waded out or picking them from the water, with total indifference to the air bombardment, which often claimed its victims. Their numbers alone defied air attack. The Mosquito Armada as a whole was unsinkable.
(Winston S. Churchill, *The Second World War* Vol. II, Cassell, p. 92)

Hitler may have hoped that he could make peace with Britain after Dunkirk. But there was to be no such mercy for the French. The Germans took Paris on 14 June, and France surrendered on 22 June (Source 4D). France was cut in two. The northern half, including the entire Atlantic coastline, was occupied by the Germans (Figure 4.2); the rest was governed by a pro-Nazi government, headed by Marshal Pétain and Pierre Laval and based at Vichy.

Source 4D   Hitler at the scene of the French surrender, 1940

Source   Raymond Cartier, *La Seconde Guerre Mondiale*, Larousse–Paris March, 1965

Examination Guidance

Topics like Dunkirk and the Battle of Britain are popular with examiners: they can find lots of sources like those above upon which to set their questions, and they are easy topics for them to handle, with clear starting- and ending-points, and a limited body of facts for them to test. Activity 27a aims to test your skill in handling historical sources, one of the main Assessment Objectives of GCSE (see page 10 above). Activity 27b has a different goal: empathy, i.e. the ability to see things from the point of view of people who lived in the past.

ACTIVITY 27a

Target

Evaluation of source material.

Question Guide

Examiners like to give you two or three sources to compare. They often choose sources because one contradicts the other. You may be asked if one source is right and one wrong, or if they are biased. Think carefully. Is it possible for two sources to give very different pictures, and yet both be right?

Activity

Read Sources 4B and 4C carefully. They are both about the evacuation from Dunkirk.
1.   How do these accounts give different impressions of Dunkirk?
2.   Which of the writers:
      (a) lived at the same time as Dunkirk?
      (b) was present at Dunkirk?
3.   Make a list of reasons which might explain why these two accounts are different. Which reason is the most likely? Explain why.

ACTIVITY 27b

Target

Empathy (i.e. looking at events from the perspective of people in the past).

Question Guide

Before trying this exercise, look carefully at Source 4D in the text and Source 4E below. Try to get a picture in your mind of how Germans probably felt in the summer of 1940. Then try the questions. Source 4D shows Hitler at the ceremony held to accept the French surrender in 1940. The ceremony took place at the exact spot where the Germans had surrendered to the French in 1918. Look carefully at the photograph. It is a genuine photograph, but it was used a lot by British propaganda. How might the British have found it useful? Source 4E is what Emmi Bonhoeffer said about the reaction in Germany after the fall of France. Emmi Bonhoeffer was a German who opposed Hitler.

Activity

Look closely at Sources 4D and 4E.

Source 4E

Many, many people felt proud when Paris was taken. Because that was our revenge for Versailles.
(Quoted in *Fuhrer: Seduction of a Nation*, Thames TV/Screen Guides, 1989, p. 13)

Then say which of these statements strike you as LIKELY or UNLIKELY:

(a) Hitler and most Germans wanted revenge against France.

(b) Hitler wanted no more territory in Europe.

(c) Hitler had done all he wanted to do in Western Europe.

(d) The German people would have accepted a peace treaty with Britain.

(e) Hitler would have accepted a peace treaty with Britain.

(f) The French would get used to having been beaten by the Germans.

THE AXIS AGAINST THE BRITISH EMPIRE

Many books describe the next stage in the war as 'Britain Alone'. This looks good as a heading, but in fact she had plenty of allies. The British Empire, including the dominions (Canada, Austria, New Zealand and South Africa), had declared war on Germany. Men from the Empire fought in the British forces, and there were plans to carry on the war from Canada if Britain fell. Once war started in the desert, and then later in the Far East, these countries were heavily engaged in fighting.

The United States was officially neutral, but in fact she was very friendly towards Britain. Under the *Cash and Carry* system, British ships could buy war supplies in America and then ship them back to Britain (the Germans could have done the same, but their ships could not get to America). In September 1940, Roosevelt sent fifty First World War destroyers to the Royal Navy, in return for the use of British bases in the Caribbean and Newfoundland. Ordinary Americans could donate food and clothing to the 'Bundles for Britain' appeal during the Blitz. The biggest help of all came in March 1941, when Congress passed the *Lease–Lend Act*. This meant that Britain could buy war materials from America and pay for them later.

Meanwhile, Hitler was planning the invasion of England. The plan was codenamed *Operation Sealion*. An invasion force would cross the Channel in flat-bottomed barges and land along the south coast. Most historians agree that if it had landed, Britain would have fallen.

But the Germans had to control the Channel, and to do that they had to control the sky above it. If the RAF controlled it, their invasion barges could not cross, and the invasion would not happen. It was as simple as that.

Spike Milligan, in his autobiography, a wonderful book which you should all read, and which gives a real insight to what the Second World War meant to a soldier in the army, tells of waiting for Hitler to invade:

Source 4F

SUMMER 1940
Apart from light military training in Bexhill there didn't seem to be a war on at all, it was a wonderful 'shirts off' summer. Around us swept the countryside of Sussex . . . The W.V.S. Forces Corner on the corner of Sea and Cantalupe Road was open for tea, buns, billiards, ping-pong and deserters. The Women's Royal Voluntary Service girls were 'jolly nice', that is, they were undatable. We tried to bait them with Woodbines disguised in a Players packet and trying to walk like John Wayne. The other excitement was watching German planes trying to knock off the radar installations at Pevensey. Bombardier Rossi used to run a book on it. It was ten to one on against the towers being toppled. Weekends saw most officers off home in mufti*. Apparently the same went for the Germans. The phoney war was on.

Source   Spike Milligan, *Adolf Hitler: My Part in his Downfall*, Penguin Books, 1972 edn, p. 33–4.

*mufti = slang for civilian clothes

THE BATTLE OF BRITAIN

You do not need to know every detail of every aircraft in the battle, although you should know that the British used *Spitfire* and *Hurricane* fighters, while the *Luftwaffe* used *Messerschmitt* fighters, and *Junker* and *Heinkel* bombers. It is more important for you to know the five main stages of the battle:

1. *German attacks on shipping convoys in the Channel and on RADAR stations*. The Germans used *Stuka* dive-bombers. Stukas were fairly slow-moving, and easily shot down by the RAF. These attacks soon stopped.

2. *Luftwaffe attacks on RAF airfields*. This was a normal part of *Blitzkrieg*, and it nearly worked. The first big attack was on *Eagle Day*, 13 August 1940. The attack was badly organised, but it still destroyed 47 RAF fighters on the ground. The RAF got warnings from RADAR Radio Detection and Ranging, but the Germans were steadily putting the RAF airfields out of action.

3. *Bombing attacks on London and other cities* (see Figure 4.3). These began by accident, when a German bomber got lost and dropped its bombs over London by mistake. The RAF bombed Berlin the following night, so Hitler ordered the Luftwaffe to hit back. This diverted the Luftwaffe from attacking RAF airfields, and gave the RAF time to recover.

4. *Final battle for control of the sky*. The RAF began to attack in large numbers, while the Luftwaffe launched massive daylight raids. The fiercest fighting was between 7 and 15 September. German losses were too heavy, and Hitler postponed and later cancelled Operation Sealion. This was the end of the Battle of Britain, but there still remained . . .

5. *The Blitz*. The Luftwaffe bombed British cities by night, and the RAF could do very little to stop them. London was bombed for 57 nights in a row, and the centre of Coventry, including the Cathedral, was destroyed in one night. The bombing was supposed to disrupt industry and hit civilian morale. It did not seriously hurt industrial production. Morale did suffer – more than the Government liked to admit – but on the whole the bombs merely strengthened people's determination to fight on.

Figure 4.3   The Battle of Britain

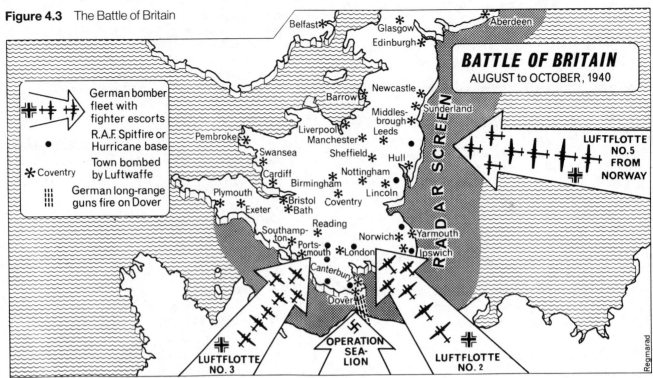

Source   Brian Catchpole, *A Map History of the Modern World* 3rd edn, Heinemann, 1982

WAR IN THE MEDITERRANEAN

After the Battle of Britain, the fighting switched to North Africa. Mussolini had entered the war, and he attacked British possessions there. The British drove the Italians back, taking thousands of prisoners. So Hitler had to send German troops, the *Afrika Korps*, under Field Marshal *Rommel*, to help the Italians. The desert war was a long and bitter campaign, which the British *Eighth Army* (the 'Desert Rats') came close to losing. The port of *Tobruk* changed hands several times, and was finally captured by Rommel in June 1942, with 20,000 British prisoners.

Mussolini also dragged Hitler into war in south-east Europe. In October 1940 the Italians attacked Greece; the Greeks fought back with British help, so Hitler had to come to the rescue once again. Hungary and Romania were already Nazi allies, and Yugoslavia was about to join the Germans as well, when the people rose up and overthrew the government. So, in April 1941 the Germans invaded Yugoslavia, and smashed through to Greece. The British were forced out to the island of *Crete*, but then the Germans launched an airborne attack and forced them off there as well.

Although there were rich oil reserves in North Africa, Hitler never really saw the Mediterranean as a very important campaign. To him it was an annoying distraction from the main aim of the whole war: the invasion of Russia.

Examination Guidance

The Nazi attack on Western Europe and the war in the Mediterranean could both easily appear on the examination paper. Learn the main outline of facts, the key dates and places. Activity 28a helps you build up your own ideas about the meaning of the key concept of causation, i.e. why things occur. Activity 28b asks you to look at the nature of one of the kinds of sources historians use, autobiography.

ACTIVITY 28a

Targets

Recall, concept of causation.

Question Guide

Very few things happen for only one reason. The skill comes in deciding which reasons are important. It often helps to make a list of reasons for any event in history, and then to try to put them into some sort of order. This exercise will help you practise.

Activity

Below are eight reasons why the RAF won the Battle of Britain. Copy them out in what you think is the order of their importance, starting with the most important. All of them are true:

1. The RAF were fighting on their home ground.
2. The British had RADAR.
3. Hitler was determined to attack Russia.
4. The Germans switched from bombing airfields to bombing cities.
5. The Spitfire was faster than the fastest German fighter.
6. The Germans were operating at the limit of their fighters' range.
7. Churchill had said Britain would never surrender.
8. The RAF pilots were very brave.

ACTIVITY 28b

Target

Handling of sources.

Question Guide

An autobiography is the term we give to the story of someone's life if they write it themselves. Spike Milligan was a gunner in the war, and he kept a detailed diary of what happened to him. Later he wrote up these diaries, and also interviewed many of the soldiers he served with. Do not be fooled by knowing that Spike is one of Britain's most famous comics – although his autobiography is very funny, it was written with great care.

Activity

Discuss the value of Source 4F to the historian of the Second World War.

OPERATION BARBAROSSA

Source 4G

If we speak of soil in Europe today, we can primarily have in mind only Russia and her vassal (=slave) border states.
(Adolf Hitler, *Mein Kampf*, quoted in *Führer: Seduction of a Nation*, Thames TV/Screen Guides, 1989, p.13)

Hitler hated Russia because it was the home of communism. Also he said that Slav people, such as Russians, were inferior to Germans. He said Russia should provide *Lebensraum* ('living space') for the Germans. This meant that the Russians were to be forced off their land to make way for Germans.

Even so, the attack took the Russians by surprise. Stalin thought his non-aggression pact with Hitler still held good. Stalin could not afford to fight a war yet, because he had killed so many army officers in his purges in the 1930s (see Figure 4.4). The Red Army was in no state to fight when the German attack started on 22 June 1941. The attack was codenamed *Operation Barbarossa*, after a German mediaeval warrior.

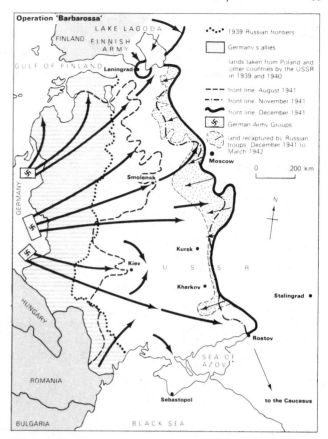

Figure 4.5   Operation Barbarossa

Source   Tony Howarth, *Twentieth Century History*, Longman, 1979

The Germans attacked in three directions: north towards Leningrad, south towards the Ukraine region, and in the centre towards Moscow (see Figure 4.5). The Red Army collapsed, and the Germans pushed ahead fast. They were at Leningrad in seven weeks. In the south, they took Kiev and reached the Black Sea. In the centre, they got to within thirty miles of Moscow. Even worse, as the German army moved forward, special SS squads moved in, rounding up Russian villagers and massacring them. It looked as if Russia would go the way of Poland and France.

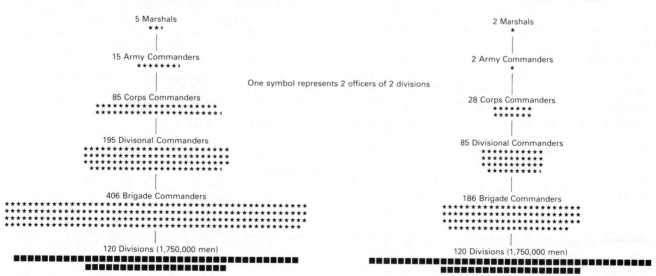

Figure 4.4   The Red Army before and after the Purges

Source   *Purnell History of the Second World War*, Vol. II, p. 656

But already the Germans were running into serious difficulties:

(a)   Russia was so vast that the Russians could usually retreat out of danger. In *Blitzkrieg*, the Germans liked to encircle their enemy, but this was proving impossible in Russia.

(b)   The Russians moved supplies of food and materials, even whole factories, many hundreds of miles beyond the Germans' reach. What they could not move, they destroyed. This meant that the Germans could not live off the land, as they had hoped.

(c)   The way the Germans treated the ordinary people made many Russians join groups of guerrilla fighters, called partisans. Partisans interfered badly with German supply columns.

(d)   Operation Barbarossa had been delayed because of the war in Yugoslavia and Greece. The delay meant that the Germans would not be in Moscow before the Russian winter set in.

The Germans were not equipped to deal with a Russian winter, which brought thick mud first, and then heavy snow. As the winter set in, the German advance stopped, and the Russians fought back.

In the north, Leningrad refused to give in. Hitler ordered that Leningrad, home of the Russian Revolution, should be wiped off the face of the earth, but the city held out for three agonising years, the longest siege in modern history.

In Moscow, the whole population turned out to prepare defences, digging trenches and making tank traps. In December 1941, Marshal Zhukhov counter-attacked with crack Siberian troops. The Germans were driven back in confusion. It was the German army's first major defeat.

Examination Guidance

Operation Barbarossa is quite likely to be an examination topic: it was the turning-point of the war. Activity 29a tests empathy, i.e. the skill of getting inside the minds and feelings of the people who lived at the time – a very difficult thing to do. You must try and make your account tie in closely to what you know actually happened at the time. Activity 29b asks you to think about who was winning the war by 1941. It seems a straightforward question, and the answer might seem easy: Germany was. But, on the other hand, you know that Germany lost the Battle of Britain and was hitting difficulties in Russia. So how can we be so certain that she was winning the war?

ACTIVITY 29a

Target

Empathy (i.e. looking at events from the perspective of people in the past).

Question Guide

We know now that Operation Barbarossa was a disaster for the Germans, but they did not know that then. This exercise will help you to see it as it seemed at the time. Read through pages 60–66 carefully and then try to answer these questions.

Activity

1.   The German generals were very enthusiastic about the plans for Operation Barbarossa. What reasons did they have to be so optimistic? (Look over the German army's record before 1941, and at any other evidence which might be relevant.)

2.   When the Germans attacked, Stalin had a number of choices of action. Which of these strike you as *likely* to appeal to him:
(a)   to order a retreat
(b)   to order his army to stand and fight
(c)   to ask the Germans for peace terms
(d)   to appeal to Britain for help
(e)   to appeal to America for help
(f)   to send agents into the German lines to convert German soldiers to communism
(g)   to destroy all crops and buildings in the Germans' path.

ACTIVITY 29b

Target

Understanding of ideas, facts and information which you think are relevant – the ability to sort out the relevant.

Question Guide

This exercise helps you to make a judgement by looking carefully at how the two sides were doing by 1941. When you have done it, try the same exercise for different stages in the war. (If you want a really tricky year, try 1943.)

Activity

1.   Make a list of the battles mentioned in the text so far. Divide your list into two columns: Allied victories, and Axis victories. (You will need to have a look at Figures 4.2, 4.3 and 4.5 as well.)

2.   Look through the text and the tables for any evidence of:
● outside help for either side.
● numbers of weapons, tanks, etc.
● quality of tactics on either side – i.e. how good their planning was.
● the economic strength of the two sides.

3.   Using all the answers from Questions 1 and 2, write a full answer to each of these questions:
(a)   What were the strengths of the Axis powers by June 1941?
(b)   What were their weaknesses?
(c)   What were the strengths of the Allied powers by June 1941?
(d)   What were their weaknesses?
(e)   On balance, which side (if either) was winning the war?

2 The War against Germany 1942–5

THE BATTLE OF THE ATLANTIC

In the Second World War, war was fought over the whole globe. That meant that men and materials had to be carried over long distances, mostly by sea. So control of the sea was vital.

The British blockaded German ports from the start of the war, so very few German ships were able to get out to sea. In December 1939 the German battleship Graf Spee was trapped in Montevideo harbour by a British force, and her crew sunk her – in shame her captain shot himself. Some German warships managed to put out to sea, like the famous *Bismarck*, but she was hunted down and destroyed by the British. The Germans' main weapon was their fleet of *U-boats*, submarines.

U-boats operated alone or in 'wolf packs'. On the very first day of the war, a U-boat sank the British liner *Athenia*, but the U-boats' main targets were merchant ships carrying supplies between Britain and America (see Figure 4.6). A merchant ship on its own had little chance against a U-boat, so merchant ships began to sail across the Atlantic in *convoys* (see Figure 4.7) with naval protection. One British naval officer described what the battle was like:

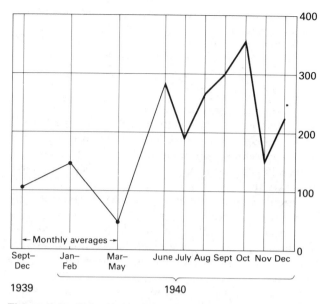

Figure 4.6   Shipping sunk by U-boats in the first year of the war

Source   Purnell History of the Second World War, Vol. I, p. 368

Source 4H

The enemy was planning as well as multiplying. At last, the U-boats were co-ordinating their attack . . . they had long-range aircraft to spot and identify for them, they had numbers, they had training, they had the spur of success . . . The

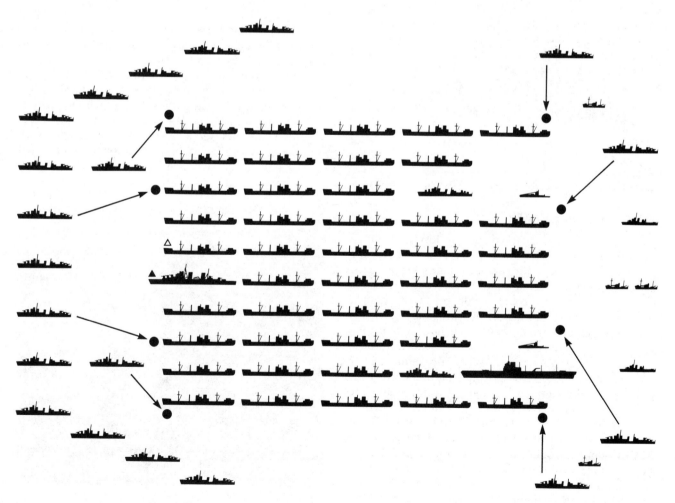

Figure 4.7   Diagram of a convoy

Source   Purnell History of the Second World War, Vol. IV, p. 1441

U-boats gradually extended their operations further westward, until there was no longer, in mid-Atlantic, a safe dispersal-area for the convoys . . . and the escorts themselves were limited in their endurance. So the stain spread, and the ships went down.

(N. Monserrat, *The Cruel Sea*, Penguin, 1970 edn, p.140)

Even when the ships were in convoys, the U-boats could still sink huge numbers of them. The British used *ASDIC* (a sort of underwater RADAR) and depth charges, but ASDIC was not very accurate, and very few U-boats were sunk. For a time it looked as if the U-boats would starve Britain of the supplies she needed from America.

When a ship was hit by a torpedo, the crew had very little chance of escape (and oil-tanker crews had virtually none at all). Even if they got into a lifeboat, their chances of surviving in the icy waters of the Atlantic were very small. Yet, despite this, men still signed on for more crossings.

U-boats attacked American ships too, even though America was neutral in the war. Once they were in the war, the Americans used long-range aircraft to seek out U-boats. Gradually more U-boats were sunk, until in August 1943 there were more U-boats sunk than ships (see Figure 4.8). The Battle of the Atlantic had been won, though at a fearful cost in ships and lives.

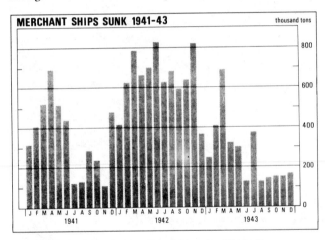

Figure 4.8   Shipping sunk by U-boats, 1941–3

Source   *Purnell History of the Second World War*, Vol. III, p. 993

STALINGRAD AND EL ALAMEIN

In 1942 the Germans attacked again in Russia, this time towards the south. The Russians were not expecting a new German attack, so the Germans made good progress. Hitler told his men to move on to the oilfields in the Caucasus region. Before they could get there, though, they would have to take the city of Stalingrad.

But taking Stalingrad proved far harder than the Germans had expected. The Russians defended it house by house, even room by room. When the Germans blew the buildings up, the Russians fought on in the rubble. It was costing the Germans far too many men, and the German commander, Field Marshal Paulus, wanted to pull out. But Hitler refused to allow it: there would be no retreat and no surrender. So Paulus had to stay put while the Russians surrounded his men and closed in. By January 1943 Paulus had had enough and surrendered. He had started out with 250,000 men; he came out with less than half that number. It was a disaster for the Germans.

Things were changing in North Africa too. The *Afrika Korps* had taken Tobruk, and Rommel was moving on to attack the British bases in Egypt. But that meant he was moving further from his own bases. He was also moving into a trap. The new British commander, *Montgomery*, had prepared a huge tank force, which attacked Rommel's men at *El Alamein* and threw them back. As Rommel retreated, American troops landed behind him, in Morocco and Algeria (*Operation Torch*). Rommel was trapped between Montgomery's men and the Americans. There was more fierce fighting, but the German and Italian forces in North Africa surrendered in May 1943.

BOMBING

Examiners like to ask questions about bombing, because it has caused a lot of argument among historians. If we leave out the atomic bombs, the bombing campaigns in the war fell into four main categories:

1.   *Bombing to back up a ground attack.* This was a standard part of *Blitzkrieg*, and the Allies copied it when they landed in Normandy. The idea was to bomb the enemy's communications, such as bridges and railway lines, and spread terror among civilians. It was mostly done by dive-bombers. These were small planes which could swoop low to drop their bombs, so they could bomb with great accuracy. The German *Stuka* dive-bomber had a siren fitted to its engine to make it appear even more terrifying to people on the ground.

2.   *The Blitz.* The Blitz was the first example of sustained heavy bombing of cities. From September 1940 to March 1941, some 30,000 people died in it and 3½ million homes were damaged or destroyed. The Blitz had two main aims: to hit industrial production, and to make ordinary people give up any hope of winning the war (this is called undermining their morale) by burning their city centres and homes (Source 4I). It did hit industrial production, but not seriously (see Figure 4.9). Civilian morale was affected, more than anyone really cared to admit, especially when ancient cities like Bristol,

Source 4I   The City of London after a bombing raid

Source   A.J.P. Taylor, *The Second World War*, Purnell, p. 72

Figure 4.9   War production in Britain and Germany, 1940–4
Source   Adapted from Max Hastings, *Bomber Command*, Michael Joseph, 1979, p. 370

	1940 Ger	1940 GB	1941 Ger	1941 GB
Military aircraft	10,200	15,000	11,000	20,100
Tanks	1,600	1,400	3,800	4,800
Heavy field guns	4,400	1,000	4,700	3,800

	1942 Ger	1942 GB	1943 Ger	1943 GB
Military aircraft	14,200	23,600	25,200	26,200
Tanks	6,300	8,600	12,100	7,500
Heavy field guns	5,100	4,000	11,700	3,000

	1944 Ger	1944 GB
Military aircraft	39,500	26,500
Tanks	19,000	4,600
Heavy field guns	24,900	2,800

Source 4J

I recall all these raids to show the determined efforts which the Nazis made to break the people's spirit. It had just the reverse effect; it stiffened them and made their determination to resist more resolute than before. 'We can take it' was on everyone's lips . . .
Today we may be forgiven if, when we look up into the sky as, thanks to American help and to those who work in our factories, we see massed 'planes soar over towards the continent, we say in our heart, 'Give it to them good and hard.'
(H. R. Pratt Boorman, *Hell's Corner 1940*, p.87; published by the Kent Messenger, Maidstone, no date)

Cambridge and Exeter were hit. But the overall effect on public opinion was to make people even more determined to fight on, if only to get revenge. When the Germans bombed Buckingham Palace, the King and Queen felt that they were now fighting shoulder to shoulder with the poor Londoners of the East End: they, too, had had their home bombed.

3. *Allied bombing of Germany*. Later in the war, the Allies were able to get their revenge, by bombing Germany even more heavily. Source 4K gives the American air force's official view:

Source 4K

There is one answer to the question so often asked 'Will bombing win the war?' The question is beside the point . . . Whether or not German morale cracks, the work of destroying the enemy's fighting capacity must go on.
(*Target: Germany – the US Army Air Force's Official Story of the VIII Bomber Command's First Year Over Europe*, HMSO, 1944, p. 116)

In one night in 1942, 1,000 planes dropped their bombs over the city of Cologne. The bombing went on around the clock, with the Americans bombing by day and the RAF by night. The aims of the bombing were the same as those of the blitz: to hit industry and to undermine morale, and the results were about the same as well. German industry was only seriously disrupted towards the very end of the war. (See Figure 4.9.) The bombing of Dresden in February 1945 has caused a lot of argument, because it was not a major military target. In one night, some 25,000–40,000 people were killed and the city was virtually destroyed when the bombs started a firestorm. Nothing could live in the streets.

4. *V1 and V2 flying bombs*. These were Hitler's secret weapons. V1s, nicknamed *doodlebugs*, were first launched against London in the summer of 1944. They did a lot of damage, but they could be shot down by fighters. There was no such defence against V2 rockets, of which 1,115 landed on London, killing nearly 3,000 people. If the Germans had had them earlier, the war might have gone very differently. After the war, German scientists who had worked on the V2s helped develop American and Russian nuclear missiles and space rockets.

THE SECOND FRONT

In 1941–3 most of the fighting was going on in Russia. Stalin desperately wanted the British and Americans to open a Second Front in Western Europe to relieve the pressure on his armies. But Churchill and Roosevelt could not do this until the U-boats and the Afrika Korps had both been defeated, and that was not until the middle of 1943. When the British and Americans were ready, they decided to open the Second Front in Italy. They had beaten the Italians so often that they thought invading Italy would be easy. Churchill called Italy 'the soft under-belly of Europe'. He convinced Stalin it was the right place to attack by representing Nazi Europe as a crocodile, with its snout in the channel and its tail flailing around in Russia. Italy was its soft underbelly! In July 1943, Allied forces landed in Sicily.

The Italians were delighted. They greeted the Allies by overthrowing Mussolini and the fascists. The new Italian leader, Marshal Badoglio, then promptly declared war on Germany! But the Germans simply invaded Italy, overthrew Badoglio, replaced Mussolini and stopped the Allied advance. Now the Allies would have to fight their way up the mountainous Italian countryside. It was going to be slow and tough – some soft underbelly! It was not until January 1944 that they landed near Rome, at

Anzio, and they did not take Rome itself until June, only two days before D-Day, the Allied landing in Western Europe.

None of this was any use to Stalin. The Second Front would have to be in France, and that meant landing on the most heavily defended coastline in the world. This would take time to prepare. The Russians were not happy:

Source 4L

The sabotage of the opening of a Second Front [in 1942] and other improper actions of the governments of Britain and the United States showed that in their policies they sought to weaken and bleed white the Soviet Union against which the Nazi Command had concentrated the whole might of the German war machine. Soviet historians have come to the justified conclusion that Britain and the US wanted, at the expense of the USSR, to preserve their own forces and use them at the final stages of the war for pursuing a policy of diktat* after the war.

(Oleg Rzheshevsky, 'Operation Overlord', in *The History of the Second Front*, Novosti Press Agency, 1984, p.24)

D-DAY

Landing an army on an enemy beach is not easy. The Canadians had tried it in 1942 at Dieppe, in northern France, and had been cut to pieces (Source 4M). The Americans had staged landings on Japanese-held islands in the Pacific, and the British and Americans had landed on the coasts of Italy and North Africa. All of these had taught the Allies useful lessons for *Operation Overlord*, the invasion of France.

Source 4M   Victims after the Dieppe Raid, 1942

Source   A.J.P. Taylor, *The Second World War*, Purnell, 1975

The Germans were expecting an attack. They built a huge line of obstacles and fortifications, Hitler's 'Atlantic Wall', all along the coast of France. Rommel was put in command of the defences. He was determined to destroy any invasion force before it could get off the beaches. But the Germans were expecting the attack to be near Calais, where the Channel is very narrow. In fact the Allies were planning to land at the other end of the Channel, in Normandy.

*imposing their will (on the Soviet Union).

Source 4N   D-Day

Source   Imperial War Museum

The Allied commander for Overlord was the American General Eisenhower. Planning Overlord took months. A huge fleet had to be put together to transport the men over the Channel. Huge floating harbours, codenamed *Mulberry*, would cross with them, so that heavy equipment could be unloaded. Oil would come through an underwater pipeline, PLUTO (Pipe Line Under The Ocean). The night before the attack, paratroops would seize key positions such as bridges. The Americans would land on two beaches, codenamed Utah and Omaha, the British and Canadians on three, Gold, Sword and Juno (see Figure 4.10).

The invasion was delayed because of bad weather. Finally, D-Day was fixed for 6 June 1944. A. J. P. Taylor, a famous historian, tells us:

Source 4O

The invasion of France began just before dawn on 6 June. Nearly 200,000 men were engaged that day in naval operations – two-thirds of them British; 14,000 air sorties were flown. In 1940 the Germans invading France had 19 aircraft for each assault division; in 1941, invading Russia, they had 26. On 6 June 1944 the Allies had 260 aircraft per division. Neither the German air force nor the U-boats were able to interfere. By the evening 156,000 men were ashore.

(A. J. P. Taylor, *The Second World War*, Purnell, 1975 edn, p.195)

D-Day was no walk-over. There was fierce fighting on the beaches, especially on Omaha, where for a time the Americans were pinned down. Eventually, though, the Allies broke through the German defences and into the countryside beyond.

But if D-Day was hard, the battle for the Normandy countryside was a bloodbath. The Germans fought for every hedgerow and field, like the Russians in the rubble of Stalingrad. The Allies almost destroyed the ancient city of Caen getting the Germans out of it.

GERMANY COLLAPSES

Once the Allies were out of Normandy, they made speedy progress. The French Resistance seized control of Paris, and the Allies pushed on to the Rhine. But the closer they got to the Rhine, the harder the Germans fought back. The British tried to cross the Rhine in

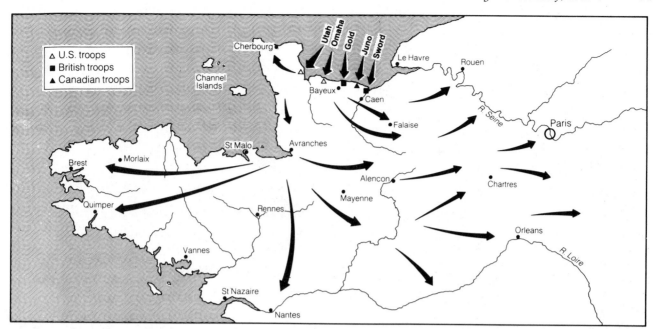

Figure 4.10   The D-Day Landings   *Source*   C. K. Macdonald, *The Second World War*, Basil Blackwell, 1984, p. 39

Holland and were cut to pieces. Then in December 1944 Hitler staged a massive tank attack through the Ardennes. It caught the Americans in the region by surprise, and for a time they were surrounded and cut off. The *Battle of the Bulge* (because of the bulge it made in the Allied front line) only ended when the Germans ran out of fuel.

But the German army was suffering badly. The Russians were crossing the border into Germany itself in the east. Very few German officers now thought they could win the war. In July 1944 a group of them tried to assassinate Hitler with a bomb; they wanted to make peace with the Allies. But the plot failed, and Hitler wanted revenge. The plotters were rounded up and hanged with piano wire from meat hooks, filmed so that Hitler could enjoy their agony. It was clear that many officers had been involved, or had known about the plot. The SS began to arrest army officers and shoot them, even in the battle zones. Many officers thought it would be safer to surrender to the British and Americans than to wait to be taken by the SS or the Russians.

Meanwhile the Americans too had crossed into Germany, and the Russians were in Berlin. In April 1945 American and Russian troops met at Torgau in the middle of Germany. Hitler had retired to an underground bunker, and there, on 30 April, he shot himself. On 7 May Germany surrendered to General Eisenhower, the Allied Supreme Commander.

Examination Guidance

The activities are linked into the following sub-sections of Section 2 above:

Activity 30a – The Battle of the Atlantic; Stalingrad and El Alamein
Activity 30b – Bombing
Activity 30c – The Second Front
Activity 30d – Germany Collapses

All these areas give plenty of scope for showing both what you know and understand about the topic, and the skills you have in handling sources. Again, try and learn up the bare bones of the subject, the important dates and events, and also the geographical details – where the campaigns occurred and the form they took.

ACTIVITY 30a

Target

Selection and deployment of relevant knowledge.

Question Guide

Activity 30a is based on a study of the Battle of the Atlantic and the battles at Stalingrad and El Alamein. It is a hard question, in that it asks you to think about what each side could do before an event, and then what it could do after. First of all sort out in your mind the things which each side could do before the battle. Then think carefully about the event itself and the impact it had. Then put the battles into what you think is the order of their importance, with your reasons for each position.

Activity

Churchill called the Battle of the Atlantic 'the most important battle of the war'. Historians have sometimes said the same about the battles at Stalingrad and El Alamein.

Take each of these three battles, and ask 'What could the Allies do after this battle that they could not do before? What could the Germans not do after this battle that they could do before?' When you have done this, say which battle you think was the most important.

ACTIVITY 30b

Target

Assessment of evidence.

Question Guide

This activity is concerned with bombing and with handling the written, pictorial and statistical sources. In looking for reasons for things happening, think carefully of the meaning of words which will help you answer the question. For example, in Source 4J the final sentence gives the clue about the importance of bombing Germany to the author. In studying the statistics, pay particular care to the separate years, and to the information in the text about the bombing campaigns.

Activity

Look at Source 4I, and read Source 4J and 4K with great care; they were both written during the war, about bombing.

1.   What do Sources 4J and 4K suggest were the reasons behind the Allies' bombing of Germany?
2.   Look at the table of production figures (Figure 4.9). Does it support or contradict the argument in Source 4K?
3.   Suggest a possible date for Source 4J.
4.   Which (if any) of these does Source 4I *prove*? (Be careful):
     ● the German bombing caused extensive damage to London and other British cities.

● German bombing hit British industrial production.
● German bombing hit the morale of the British people.
● German bombing raised the morale of the German people.

5.   Even if you decided that the picture did not *prove* it, which of these statements **could** be supported by the picture?

ACTIVITY 30c

Target

Evaluation of evidence (in this case a secondary source).

Question Guide

In answering this question, look at Figure 1.5 (page 14): it gives you lots of hints for handling the source.

Figure 4.11   Two views of the defeat of Germany

Source   Brian Catchpole, *A Map History of the Modern World*, 3rd edn, Heinemann, 1982

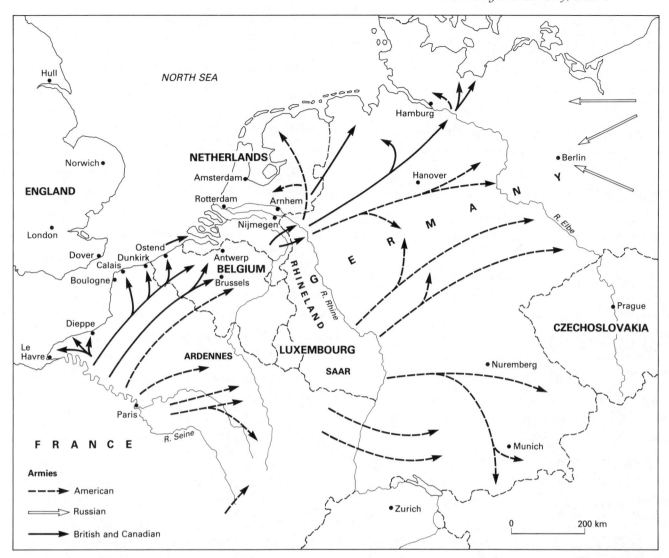

Figure 4.12   Advance into Germany, 1944–5

Source   David Scott Daniell, *World War II: an Illustrated History,*
Ernest Benn Ltd, 1966

Activity

There is more than one way of looking at events in history. Read Source 4L, an account of the Second Front, written by a Soviet Historian.

1. Oleg Rzheshevsky says that Britain and America did not open a Second Front in 1942 because they were waiting until the Germans had bled Russia dry. One way to check this is to see what the Allies were doing in 1942. Look through this chapter for *any evidence you can find* of the situation in 1942 in:
    ● the Atlantic
    ● North Africa
    ● the Pacific
    ● Europe.
    When you have done that, look again at Source 4L. Do you agree with it?
2. A Second Front was opened in 1943, in Italy. What might be Rzheshevsky's view of that?
3. What evidence is there that the Allies knew that D-Day would be difficult and bloody?

ACTIVITY 30d

Target

Assessment of evidence.

Question Guide

Be careful with maps, especially when they have got arrows on them! Look carefully at Figures 4.11 and 4.12. They are based on maps from two very different books, and they are both designed to show the collapse of Germany in 1945.

Activity

1. Which army or armies appear to have defeated Germany in Figure 4.11? Which in Figure 4.12?
2. According to what you already know, which of the two maps would you say is the more accurate?
3. Does that mean that the other map is wrong? (Think very carefully!)

ACTIVITY 30e

Target

Terms and concepts.

Question Guide

A simple revision exercise, which makes you work through this chapter to sort out the key facts: boring but vital. Facts are the clay of history – without them, no bricks.

Activity

Write a sentence to explain what each of these was:

the Maginot Line

Blitzkrieg

Operation Dynamo

lease-lend

Operation Sealion

the Blitz

the Afrika Korps

Operation Barbarossa

partisans

convoys

ASDIC

Operation Torch

stukas

doodlebugs

V2s

the Second Front

Operation Overlord

Mulberry

the Battle of the Bulge.

3 The War against Japan, 1941–5

THE ROAD TO PEARL HARBOR

Make no mistake: the Japanese planes which swooped down on Pearl Harbor in December 1941 were starting a war which the Japanese leaders knew they could not win. So why did they do it?

To understand, we need to look at Japan before the war. She had become a modern country very quickly. Her navy beat the Russians in the war of 1904–5, and she was on the winning side in the First World War.

But in some ways, Japan was still almost a mediaeval country. She still had an emperor who was regarded as a god. But neither the Emperor nor even the Japanese Prime Minister had much say in governing Japan. In practice this was done by the army and the navy, and politicians who did not like it tended to get assassinated.

That sounds like an exaggeration, but it is not. Between 1912 and 1945 *SIX* Prime Ministers were assassinated, along with some generals and other politicians. There were even attempts to kill the Emperor. So politicians really did have to do what the army wanted. And what the army wanted was an empire.

The Japanese felt very resentful after the Treaty of Versailles. All the other Great Powers had colonies in Asia: why shouldn't Japan have some too?

The Japanese thought that if they could get more land in Asia, they would be able to match the British and Americans. The best area to get it seemed to be in China. China was Japan's old enemy, and she was weak and divided. The trouble was that the other powers did not want Japan pushing into China. In particular, the Americans tended to see China as their own special area (there were a large number of American missionaries, and a lot of American money, in China). So, the more Japan pushed into China, the more she came into conflict with Britain and America:

1921–2 *Washington Conference*
Japan agreed that her navy should be no more than three-fifths the size of Britain's or America's. Japan agreed to withdraw her troops from China.

1924 *US Immigration Law*
Huge numbers of Japanese were going to America to look for work. This law said that they could not be made American citizens, so they were not allowed to stay in the country to work.

1929 *The Slump*
America stopped buying Japanese silk. This put many Japanese workers out of work.

1931 *Japan invades Manchuria* (see pages 43–44)
When the League of Nations protested, Japan withdrew from the League. The Japanese Prime Minister protested as well, but he was assassinated.

1936 *Japan signs the Anti-Comintern Pact with Germany*
This meant Japan and Germany would work together to stop communism spreading.

1937 *Marco Polo Bridge Incident* (see page 44)
This started full-scale war between China and Japan. America sent help to the Chinese.

Examination Guidance

Examiners have been known to pick on events involving Japan between the wars for some nasty questions, because they tend to assume that no one bothers to revise them. Activity 31 will give you some practice in empathy, the ability to work out what the people in the past were thinking, or were likely to have thought, while at the same time helping you to get familiar with these events.

ACTIVITY 31

Target

Empathy (i.e. looking at events from the perspective of people in the past).

Question Guide

People will react to events in different ways, depending on who they are and what their point of view is. It's not just a question of saying one lot would approve of something and the other lot wouldn't: sometimes opposing sides will disagree on what actually happened. For example, a football match which went 3–1 might be described as a walk-over by the winning team, or a close match by the losers. Do you get the idea? In this activity, you will have to say what you think the American and Japanese governments would have thought about events between 1921 and 1937.

Activity

Look carefully through the list of events 1921–37 above. For each event, write a sentence giving the Japanese government's version of what happened. Then do the same giving the American government's version.

Japan and China

The Japanese expected to win easily in China. Instead, they got completely bogged down in a war they could not win. They took hold of cities and towns, and they horrified the world when they bombed Shanghai; but they could never control the vast Chinese countryside. Chinese guerrilla groups operated from the hills, and the Japanese could never crush them. Instead of making her rich, the war with China was bleeding Japan dry. She was desperately short of the raw materials she needed to win it, especially oil.

Now, there was plenty of oil close at hand, in southeast Asia and in the Pacific, but it belonged to the Europeans and the Americans. Some Japanese thought it would be wisest to leave these areas well alone and get raw materials by attacking Russia instead.

They changed their minds in 1940, though. Their allies, the Germans, had overrun Europe, and seemed to be about to invade Britain. The Europeans were in no position to defend their colonies in Asia, and, sure enough, the Japanese had no trouble in taking Indo-China from the French in 1941. But if the Europeans were not in a position to fight back, the Americans were.

President Roosevelt told the Japanese to clear out of Indo-China, and to get out of China, and he cut off all oil supplies to Japan until she did. That made the Japanese even more desperate to get hold of the oil in the European colonies. Their thinking went like this:

1. We desperately need oil and other materials to carry on the war in China.
2. We can easily get these from the European colonies in Asia, because the Europeans are in no state to fight back.
3. But if we attack these colonies, the Americans will certainly fight back, and we haven't a hope of beating them.
4. On the other hand, we might be able to arrange a peace treaty with America which would let us keep some of the European colonies, preferably ones which produce oil.
5. But the Americans will only agree to this if (a) we have already captured the areas we want to get hold of; and (b) they have suffered a defeat.
6. So, we must (a) attack the European colonies and capture them VERY fast, so that we have got them secure before any peace talks begin; and (b) get a crippling attack in against the Americans before they are ready to fight.

Japanese intelligence reported that there was a chance to do just that. The American Pacific fleet would be at anchor in *Pearl Harbor* on Sunday 7 December 1941. All the Japanese had to do was to take it by surprise and sink it.

The British had shown how to do it. They had already sunk the Italian fleet, at anchor in the port of Taranto, using torpedo aircraft from aircraft carriers. Now Admiral Yamamoto drew up a plan to do the same thing to the Americans. Early in the morning of 7 December, Japanese Zero fighter bombers took off for Pearl Harbor. They attacked in two waves, sinking four battleships and destroying 120 American aircraft. The next day, America declared war.

Examination Guidance

All the major events of the war are fair game for questions, and Pearl Harbor is as likely to come up as any. The photograph in Source 4P is fairly well known, but it is as open to historical interpretation as any other, and Activity 32a will help you to try your own hand at it. One point to remember: almost anything is useful to historians – they're really very easy to please; the difficulty is in working out HOW a particular source might be useful. Activity 32b was set by SEG in 1988. It's not too difficult, as long as you remember that you ALREADY KNOW the information that you need in order to answer it. With 10 marks going for each section, this sort of question should stand you in good stead.

Source 4P Pearl Harbor

Source in Stewart Ross (ed.) *The Second World War*, Wayland, 1989

ACTIVITY 32a

Target

Evaluation and interpretation of historical evidence.

Question Guide

Photographs may *suggest* any number of ideas to you, but

they only *tell* us exactly what is in them. Look carefully at Source 4P. It shows an American ship after the Japanese attack at Pearl Harbor. The small boat in the foreground is a fire-fighting vessel. Newspapers could use a photograph like this to illustrate any number of stories. Decide in your own mind exactly what story this photograph tells YOU.

Activity

Look carefully at these judgements about Pearl Harbor. Which, if any, of them is supported by the photograph in Source 4P?

- The Japanese attack paralysed the American Pacific fleet.
- The Americans were taken completely by surprise.
- The Americans were able to recover from the attack very quickly.
- The attack gave newspapers in Japan and in America good pictures to stir up their readers.
- Ships in the Second World War were helpless against air attack.
- The Japanese attack was a success.

ACTIVITY 32b

Target

Selection and deployment of relevant knowledge.

Question Guide

This question is asking you to take three events and say how they affected the war. If you like, it is asking you to say how important (or how *significant* – another word examiners like to use) they were. *It is NOT asking you to say what happened.* In fact, the examiners have assumed that you know what happened, otherwise how can you say how each event affected the war? So don't waste time saying how many warnings the Americans had before Pearl Harbor or what types of machine guns the Russians had in Stalingrad (these are both useful to know, but they are not needed here); concentrate on one thing: how did each of these events affect the whole war?

'How do I do that?', you ask. Before you start, take each event in turn and ask yourself two things about it:

(a) Did this event affect the war with Germany, or the war with Japan, or both? (*Not* 'Did it *involve* Germany or Japan?', but 'Did it *affect* Germany or Japan?')

(b) Can we say (however roughly) that one side was winning the war *before* this event, and the other side was winning *after* it? (If you prefer, 'Did this event change anything?')

Activity

The Military Events of the Second World War, 1939–1945
Explain how each of the following events affected the course of the Second World War:

(a) the Japanese attack on Pearl Harbor (December 1941);   **(10 marks)**

(b) the Soviet victory at Stalingrad (December 1942 – January 1943);   **(10 marks)**

(c) the Allied landings in Sicily (July 1943) and in Italy (September 1943).   **(10 marks)**
TOTAL: 30 marks

JAPANESE SUCCESSES

The attack on Pearl Harbor looked impressive in photographs, but it was not as effective as it looked. The ships were sunk in shallow water, so most of them could be repaired and sent back into action. Even more importantly, the American aircraft carriers were not at Pearl Harbor. They were to be crucial in the battles ahead.

For the moment, though, the Japanese seemed to be everywhere at once. They attacked the Americans in the Pacific, at Guam and Wake Island, and in the Philippines. They attacked the British and the Dutch in south-east Asia. They took Hong Kong on Christmas Day 1941, and pressed on through the Malayan jungle towards the British naval base at *Singapore*. Churchill sent two British warships, the *Prince of Wales* and the *Repulse* as a 'vague menace' to scare the Japanese, but the Japanese were not scared, and sank both of them with torpedo aircraft. Reinforcements were rushed to Singapore, but General Perceval surrendered the base in February 1942. Singapore had massive naval guns to defend it, but they were all pointing the wrong way.

Still the Japanese pressed on. They defeated a British and Dutch fleet in the Java Sea, and they invaded Burma. In the Philippines, they trapped a whole American army, under *General MacArthur*, at Bataan. By 1942, they were at the borders of India, and seemed poised to attack Australia (see Figure 4.13). It was an Asian *Blitzkrieg*.

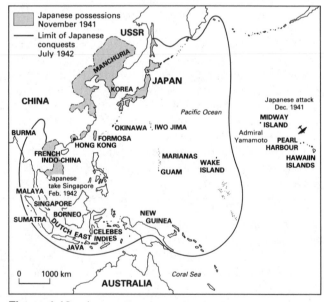

Figure 4.13   Japanese conquests

Source   C. Culpin, *Making History*, Collins Educational, 1984

Why were the Japanese so successful? There is no simple answer, but these are some of the reasons:

- The Allies just were not expecting such a sudden Japanese attack, and were quite unprepared for it.
- The Japanese were well trained for jungle warfare. They had light equipment, often moving forwards on bicycles which could go along the narrow jungle tracks.

The Allies were held up by heavy transport and equipment.

- Japanese soldiers could fight on a small ration of rice, so they were not held up by long supply columns bringing food, as the Allies were.
- The speed with which the Japanese soldiers attacked, and the way they seemed to be able to use the jungle, made many Allied soldiers see them as 'supermen' who could not be beaten.

Things began to change in the summer of 1942. The Americans had broken the Japanese secret radio code, and they were reading the Japanese messages and plans. In May 1942 the Americans attacked a Japanese fleet in the *Coral Sea*, and forced it back. In June, the Japanese sent an invasion fleet to attack the American base on *Midway Island*. The Americans knew the Japanese were coming, and intercepted them. The battle was fought entirely by aircraft from the carriers of the two fleets. The Japanese lost four of their carriers, and some 300 planes. They had to turn back. Two months later, the Americans landed on the Solomon Islands. The counter-attack had begun.

'ISLAND HOPPING' AND BURMA

Many ordinary people in the areas the Japanese had taken over worked against them, just as Resistance fighters in Europe fought against the Germans. The Japanese were disappointed: they had hoped to win people over by setting up the *Eastern Asia Co-Prosperity Sphere*, but in practice this just meant ruthless Japanese exploitation. This was especially true in China, where Chiang Kai-shek led the resistance to the Japanese, with British and American help.

In Burma, a group of British soldiers known as *Chindits* learned how to fight properly in the jungle, and then operated behind the Japanese lines. One of them described a group of Chinese who had escaped from a Japanese labour camp:

Source 4Q

I saw the scars where the Japs had pushed needles beneath their finger-nails and burnt the flesh off their faces and chests with cigarette ends and hot irons. The chief outside worker of this camp had been permanently crippled because the Japs had made him kneel down and had then jumped on the back of his calves; when that failed to make him speak, they had put poles across his shins and, with a man standing on top, had rolled him from knee to ankle.

(F. Spencer Chapman, *The Jungle is Neutral*, Chatto & Windus, 1950, p. 228)

In the Pacific, the Americans had decided on a tactic known as 'island hopping'. Instead of attacking every single island the Japanese held, they concentrated on a few 'stepping stones' which would lead towards Japan. The other islands would then be cut off from their supplies, and would have to surrender.

Island hopping was a deadly business, because the Japanese defended each island fiercely. Not only that, but American commanders in the Pacific could not move as quickly as they wanted to, because most men and materials were reserved for the war in Europe against the Germans. So the Americans were only able to prise the Japanese off these islands very slowly. Not until June

1944 – as other American troops were landing in Normandy – were the Americans able to take the Mariana islands, from where they could launch bombing raids against Japan.

To make things worse, the closer the Americans got to Japan, the fiercer and more fanatical the Japanese defenders became. Now the Japanese launched more attacks at sea. They had lost nearly all that remained of their navy at the Battle of *Leyte Gulf*, but they fought on with *kamikaze* ('divine wind') suicide pilots. Kamikaze pilots crammed their planes full of explosives, and then crashed them on to the decks of American ships.

Kamikaze attacks were spectacular, but, even so, they were a sign that the Japanese were getting desperate. How long could they hold out?

Examination Guidance

Activity 33a is another 'How-useful-is-this-source-to-the-historian?' exercise. Sometimes you will find this sort of question phrased slightly differently, as 'The writer of this source had good reasons for feeling as he did, so therefore he is biased. Does this mean that this source is of no use to the historian?' As you know, it does not mean anything of the sort, but you still need to know how to tackle this sort of question systematically when you meet it. Activity 33b is an examination question set by SEG. It looks like a source-based question, but be careful – the questions are not about the sources at all. This is a common trick – the examiner gives you some source material to focus your attention on the topic, and then asks you questions about the topic rather than about the sources. One last point: it doesn't matter at all if you have never heard of Iwo Jima, or if the examiners choose another island or battle which you have never heard of. The point is that you DO know about the Pacific War, and that is what the question is really about.

ACTIVITY 33a

Target

Evaluation and interpretation of evidence.

Question Guide

The usefulness of sources – you are always being asked 'How useful is this source?' – depends almost entirely on who produced them. In this case, it's a short passage from someone's published memoirs. It's a pretty gruesome incident (DON'T try it at home!), but is it useful evidence? And if so, what is it useful evidence OF? Just as you did with the photograph of Pearl Harbor, look at Source 4Q carefully and ask yourself: 'What does this tell me? What does this NOT tell me?' The important part of the activity is the last one.

Activity

Read the extract from Spencer Chapman's book (Source 4Q) again. What does it tell us about:

- Japanese rule in Burma and China

- the Japanese war economy (think carefully here)
- attitudes of ordinary people towards the Japanese

Is there any other way in which it might be useful evidence?

ACTIVITY 33b

Target

Empathy, i.e. the ability to see things from the point of view of people at the time.

Question Guide

If you look at these questions, you will see that what they are saying, in effect, is: 'This is what the fighting on Iwo Jima was like. Now imagine how the sight of all that would have affected people at the time.' Look particularly carefully at the photograph (if you have covered the First World War, compare this photograph with pictures of the trenches). Before you start answering the questions, remember that Iwo Jima was just one of the Pacific Islands the Americans had to take from the Japanese – and with each island the fighting got tougher.

Activity

(SEG, Summer 1989, Syllabus 2, Paper 2, Question 10)

The Military Events of the Second World War, 1939–1945

Study Photograph 1 and Source 2, and then attempt both parts of the question which follows.

Photograph 1: American forces on the island of Iwo Jima, 600 miles south of Japan.

Source 2

The price of Iwo Jima had been extraordinarily high. Whether the dead were Japanese or American, they had died with the utmost violence. Of the 23 000 men defending Iwo Jima, only 1 083 were ever taken prisoner. As for the Americans, 6 821 soldiers and sailors lost their lives in the struggle for the eight square miles of the island.
(from *The Fight for Iwo Jima*, an article written by D. Yodel in 1968)

(a)   How might the soldiers who fought in the battle for Iwo Jima have explained why they fought so ferociously?
(b)   Explain how the military leaders might have been affected by a battle such as that for Iwo Jima.

TOTAL: 30 marks

THE ATOMIC BOMB

On 1 April 1945, American Marines walked ashore on *Okinawa* Island, the last island before Japan itself. At first, there was hardly any resistance, but further inland they ran into fierce and determined Japanese defenders, well dug in and ready. The Americans suffered 12,500 casualties on Okinawa, their highest loss of the Pacific war. If that was what it cost to take Okinawa, how many men would be killed when they invaded Japan?

The Americans sat down to work it out – like a maths problem. They calculated that if the Japanese defended their own islands as fiercely as they had defended Okinawa – and there was no reason to assume they would not – then the invasion might cost the Allies anything up to 1 million casualties, and the war might drag on until 1947. They would probably have to ask the Russians to help.

Now, remember that this was the summer of 1945. Germany and Italy were beaten, and people had only just celebrated *VE Day* – Victory in Europe. Many people in Britain and America thought the war was as good as over, and they wanted peace as soon as possible. Not only that, but they had very little sympathy for the Japanese. The Allies had started to liberate the inmates of Japanese prisoner-of-war camps, where they found Allied prisoners who had been beaten, starved and tortured. Many people wanted revenge for the way the Japanese had treated their prisoners. The American President, *Harry Truman*, was very interested in any way which would end the war, hurt the Japanese and not cost the Allies a single life. All of this helps explain why the *atom bomb* seemed so attractive in 1945.

The atom bomb had been developed by British and American scientists working at *Los Alamos* in the desert of New Mexico. (The Germans were also working on an atom bomb, but their work was delayed by resistance groups.) In July, the scientists at Los Alamos exploded the world's first atomic bomb. It completely devastated an (uninhabited) area a mile wide. They had two bombs left.

Now, the Allies were already bombing Japan around the clock. In March 1945 a raid on Tokyo set off a firestorm which killed 80,000 people and destroyed a quarter of the city. Was there any need to use the atom bombs? President Truman decided 'Yes'.

American aircraft dropped leaflets on Japanese cities, saying that America had a terrible weapon and that she would use it if the Japanese did not surrender. The Japanese government took no notice. So, on 6 August 1945, a single US bomber, the *Enola Gay*, dropped an atomic bomb nicknamed 'Little Boy' over the Japanese city of *Hiroshima*.

It exploded with a flash and completely destroyed the city. It's difficult to be precise about figures, but it seems likely that it killed 100,000 people and radiated many more.

One of the crew of the *Enola Gay* described what he saw at Hiroshima:

Source 4R

'If you want to describe it as something you are familiar with, a pot of boiling, black oil . . . I thought', said Van Kirk, 'Thank God the war is over and I don't have to get shot at any more. I can go home.'

(L. Giovanitti and F. Freed, *The Decision to Drop the Bomb* (Methuen) p. 26; quoted in James L. Henderson, *Hiroshima*, Longman, 1974, p. 22)

Two days later, the Russians declared war on Japan and attacked Japanese positions in China. The Americans and British wanted Japan to surrender quickly, before the Russians advanced too far. The next day, 9 August, another bomber took off with the second (and last) bomb. It was a very cloudy day, and the pilot could not find his target. So he made for his 'reserve' target, and dropped the bomb there. It exploded over the port of Nagasaki, killing 40,000 people. After the Nagasaki bomb, President Truman broadcast to the American people:

Source 4S

I realise the tragic significance of the atomic bomb . . . We have used it against those who attacked us without warning at Pearl Harbor, against those who have starved and beaten and executed American prisoners of war, against those who have abandoned all pretence of obeying international laws of warfare. We have used it in order to shorten the agony of young Americans. We shall continue to use it until we completely destroy Japan's power to make war. Only a Japanese surrender will stop us.
(Herbert Feiss, *The Atomic Bomb and the End of World War II* (Pt 3) Princeton University Press, 1966, p. 130)

Still the Japanese government could not decide what to do, but for once the Emperor intervened: Japan must surrender. In fact, one historian says that the Emperor had started to persuade his government to consider surrender before either bomb was dropped:

Source 4T

As early as June 22, 1945, the day Okinawa was wrenched from Japanese control, the Emperor took his first cautious step towards undermining those committed to continue the useless struggle. At an Imperial Conference called to discuss the course of events and their implications, he requested the Cabinet or the Supreme Command to consider alternatives to the decision to fight to the end.
(Martin J. Sherwin, *A World Destroyed*, Random House, 1977)

On 2 September 1945, the Japanese government surrendered to General MacArthur aboard the USS *Missouri*, at anchor in Tokyo Bay. The General formally ended the Second World War, saying, 'These proceedings are closed.'

Since then, there has been furious argument about whether or not Truman was right to give the order to drop the bombs. One modern historian points out:

Source 4U

None of the critics of the atomic bomb decisions has been able to demonstrate how the Japanese high command might have been induced to surrender without the combined shock of Russia's entry into the war and the use of two atomic bombs.
(Ronald H. Spector, *Eagle against the Sun*, Penguin 1987, p. 559)

More recently, though, some historians have pointed out that the Japanese were trying to surrender before the bombs were dropped. They say that the Americans *had* to drop the bombs – not to scare the Japanese, but to scare the Russians. (If this doesn't make sense to you, look ahead to page 80 and read about the trouble at the Potsdam Conference.)

Examination Guidance

Was it right to drop the bomb? I'm sorry, but this is one of those arguments that never goes away, and examiners could come up with it at any time. To be fair to them (they're only human, poor things) they may well be interested to hear what you think. Just remember: *there is no one right answer*. However, your answer must be supported by evidence. Activity 34 will get you to look at the various sources quoted above, and will ask you to make your own mind up about them.

ACTIVITY 34

Targets

Evaluation and interpretation of evidence, selection and deployment of relevant knowledge.

Question Guide

Read through Sources 4R–4U carefully. They all throw some light on why the Americans dropped the atom bombs on Japan. Try to decide in your own mind what you think was the most likely reason why Truman decided to drop the bombs – 'hunches' are no good unless you can support them with some evidence! Now try the activity.

Activity

Read these statements carefully. Which of them do you agree with? Explain your reasons fully.
(a) The Americans dropped the bombs to save the lives of their own soldiers.
(b) If both bombs had not been dropped, the Japanese would not have surrendered.
(c) The Americans dropped the bombs to scare the Russians.
(d) Ordinary Americans were glad when the bombs were dropped.
(e) There was no need for the second bomb to be dropped.
(f) There was no need for either bomb.
(g) The Americans only dropped the bomb because they had it, and thought it would be a waste of money not to use it.

You do not have to put these reasons into any particular order. Now write your own answer to 'Why were the atom bombs dropped?'

4 Wartime Conferences

During the war, the Allied leaders met many times to work out how best to beat the Germans and the Japanese. They also discussed what should happen after the war.

At these meetings, Churchill, Stalin and Roosevelt got to know each other well. They did not always get on:

- Stalin had not forgotten that it was Churchill who had sent troops in to Russia to fight against the Revolution.
- Churchill did not trust Stalin. He thought the Russians would try to take over the world after the war, and he was furious with Roosevelt for not seeing this danger.
- Roosevelt did not trust Churchill. He thought Churchill just wanted to expand the British Empire.

At the Potsdam Conference in 1945, Roosevelt was replaced by the new President, *Harry Truman*, and Churchill by the new Prime Minister, *Clement Attlee*.

Unfortunately for you, these conferences are just the sort of thing that examiners like to ask questions about. The two big conferences which you need to know about in detail are *Yalta* and *Potsdam*, both in 1945. With the others, you just need to know what was decided.

The conferences dealt mainly with three topics: Germany, Eastern Europe, and the new *United Nations Organisation*.

CONFERENCES DEALING WITH GERMANY

1943   Casablanca
Germany and her allies would have to surrender *unconditionally* – i.e. on whatever terms the Allies chose.

1943   Teheran
The leaders of Germany would have to stand trial for war crimes after the war.

1944   Quebec
Germany would be divided up into *zones* after the war.

1945   Yalta
The zones of Germany were worked out – one British, one American, one Russian, and one French. Austria was to be divided into four zones, just like Germany. Berlin and Vienna were to be divided into four *sectors*, British, American, Russian and French.

1945   Potsdam
Arrangements were made for the trial of the Nazi leaders at Nuremberg.

CONFERENCES DEALING WITH EASTERN EUROPE

The war had begun in Eastern Europe when Germany invaded Poland. Now Poland and the rest of Eastern Europe were occupied by Russian troops. Stalin wanted to see communist governments set up in these countries, but Churchill and Roosevelt wanted to see free elections.

1943   Teheran
Russia was to be allowed to move into the *Balkans* (i.e. Greece, Romania, Bulgaria, etc.). Russia was also allowed to keep hold of the *Baltic* states, Estonia, Latvia and Lithuania.

1944   Moscow
The Allies agreed on 'spheres of influence' in Europe. In effect, this gave Stalin control over Eastern Europe.

1945   Yalta
The countries in Eastern Europe were to have free elections. Russia could keep the land she had taken from Poland in 1939. All Russians in German uniform taken prisoner by the Allies were to be sent back to Russia (see Chapter 5, Section 2).

1945   Potsdam
Stalin agreed to declare war on Japan. Poland was to get land from Germany between the rivers Oder and Neisse, to make up for the land she lost to Russia under the Yalta agreement.
The Potsdam conference ended in deadlock, because Stalin refused to withdraw his troops from Eastern Europe, and Truman and Attlee refused to give him land in North Africa. Truman took the opportunity to tell Stalin that the Americans had developed the atomic bomb.

CONFERENCES SETTING UP THE UNITED NATIONS ORGANISATION

1941   The Atlantic Charter
Churchill and Roosevelt met on board HMS *Prince of Wales* off Newfoundland. They agreed on a declaration that all nations should live peacefully together. This is usually seen as the birth of the United Nations.

1942   Hyde Park (USA)
This conference coined the phrase 'United Nations' to describe the Allies.

1944   Bretton Woods
The *International Monetary Fund* and the *World Bank* were set up, to lend money to nations which would need it after the war.

1944   Dumbarton Oaks
The details of the new United Nations Organisation were planned.

1945   San Francisco
This conference issued the *Charter* of the United Nations: 'to preserve peace, and encourage social and economic progress throughout the world'.

Examination Guidance

For examination purposes, you need to know about the Atlantic Charter, Yalta and Potsdam in detail. However, you also need to know about the things the other conferences dealt with. For example, what the Allies' plans for Germany were, and how the UN was set up. The first part of this activity is a simple revision exercise to help you get your thoughts in order. The other parts are essay-type questions based on the information – very popular with some examiners. The Target is part of the general objective about knowledge and understanding.

ACTIVITY 35

Target

Deployment of relevant knowledge.

Question Guide

There should not be any real problem here. Just read over the list of conferences and make sure you are clear how the various plans for Germany, Eastern Europe and the UN developed. The first question is easy enough; the others require short-essay answers. Don't say anything you can't back up with evidence, and explain all your answers fully. For example, for Question 3 you might want to say 'No. As far as I can see they were all getting on splendidly'; but you will still need to say WHY you read things that way. Don't forget to take Sources 4V and 4W into account.

Activity

1. Arrange all these conferences by year, putting together all those that took place in 1941, then those that took place in 1942, and so on.
2. To what extent had the Western Allies accepted the idea by 1945 that Russia would rule Eastern Europe after the war?
3. Do the conferences dealing with Germany suggest that differences were brewing between the Russians and the Western Allies?
4. As far as you can tell from these lists and from Sources 4V and 4W, what plans did the Allies have for preventing wars and conflicts once the war was over?

Source 4V   Stalin and Churchill at Yalta

Source   Robert Kee, 1945: *The World We Fought For*, Hamish Hamilton, 1985

Source 4W   Attlee, Truman and Stalin at the Potsdam Conference

Source   Hugh Higgins, *The Cold War*, 2 edn, Heinemann Educational, 1987

5 The United Nations, 1941–50

THE ATLANTIC CHARTER

If you had stopped people in a British street in 1941 and asked them what Britain was fighting against, the answer would have been easy: Hitler. It was much less easy to say what Britain was fighting *for*. If – and in 1941 it was a big 'if' – if Britain won, what would happen? How would she make sure there were no more Hitlers and Mussolinis to start new wars? President Roosevelt was wondering the same thing. In 1941 he and Churchill met on board HMS *Prince of Wales* to try to reach an answer.

They came up with the *Atlantic Charter*. This said that the war was not in order to get more land for Britain or America, but simply to stop the aggressive nations who had started it. Britain and America declared that all nations should work together for peace and security. The was was being fought to make sure they could do so. This was the idea behind the United Nations Organisation.

Setting up the United Nations

These ideals about peace and security were all very well: achieving them proved difficult.

The Atlantic Charter said that all the countries which signed it were not after land for themselves. But what about the Russians? They had seized land in Poland, in Finland and in the Baltic States, and they intended to keep it. Could they do that and still be part of the United Nations?

In 1944, representatives of the Allies met at Dumbarton Oaks to sort out the details of how the United Nations would work. The Russians were not happy because they only had one delegation at the meeting: they wanted sixteen. Finally, the British and Americans agreed to allow them three.

The Russians were not acting without reason. They were the only communist country among all the capitalist countries of the United Nations. Britain had all her Empire and Commonwealth countries, and the USA had the South American countries behind her. So, since the Russians could not have their sixteen delegations, they demanded something else: a *veto*. If a country has a veto, it can stop something from being agreed, however many other countries want it, simply by saying 'No'.

The Charter of the United Nations Organisation was drawn up at the San Francisco Conference in 1945. The Charter said that the UNO would aim to 'save succeeding generations from the scourge of war'. It guaranteed the equal rights of all nations, large and small. It contained a declaration calling on all nations to respect basic human rights. (Ironically, in view of later events, this declaration was written by the Prime Minister of South Africa.)

No one expected the UNO to have an easy time, though. Sure enough, within a few months serious trouble had broken out at the Allied conference at Potsdam.

Trouble at the Potsdam Conference

After Roosevelt died, and Churchill lost the General Election in 1945, the new leaders of the Allies were

Stalin, Truman and Attlee. Stalin and Truman could not stand each other. Even though Attlee was a Labour Prime Minister, he soon showed that he did not trust the Russians any more than Churchill had done.

To make things worse, during the conference Truman received the news that the first atom bomb test in New Mexico had worked. He casually told Stalin that the Americans had the bomb. Stalin seemed pleased, and said he hoped the Americans would soon use it against the Japanese. But everyone realised that the atom bomb made the Americans far more powerful than the Russians.

Stalin carried on with his plans. He wanted to take over the old Italian colony of Tripoli, in North Africa. Truman and Attlee refused to allow it. So Stalin refused to remove his troops from Bulgaria and Romania. The conference broke up in deadlock.

This was the international atmosphere when the United Nations Organisation held its first meeting in London in 1946.

Examination Guidance

The United Nations Organisation is a big topic. You may get a question on how it was set up, and especially on what people expected it to achieve. Basically, people wanted it to do a better job than the League of Nations; but even before it got going, there were reasons for feeling optimistic or pessimistic about its chances. You will need to show that you are aware of this.

ACTIVITY 36

Target

Empathy (i.e. looking at events from the perspective of people in the past).

Question Guide

Look over all the events surrounding the birth of the UN. Check what had been happening at the wartime conferences, and make sure you have got a good grasp of the *general* world situation in 1946. Many people felt optimistic about the UN when it was founded, but were they right? Ask yourself what reasons there were for feeling optimistic or pessimistic about its chances of keeping the peace.

Activity

List reasons people might have had in 1946 for feeling:
(a)   optimistic
(b)   pessimistic
about the chances of the UN keeping world peace. Two reasons have been given below, but there are many more:
Reasons for feeling optimistic
After such a destructive war, none of the nations would want to plunge into another one.
Reasons for feeling pessimistic
There had been increasing evidence of a split between the Western Allies and the Russians, and at the Potsdam Conference they almost came to blows.

THE ORGANISATION OF THE UNITED NATIONS

There was no point in just using the old League of Nations, because that had failed abysmally. The new organisation would have to be different. It would look like this:

Security Council

Trusteeship Council

General Assembly

International
Court of Justice

Secretariat

Economic and Social
Council

UN Agencies

In some ways, this looked like the League. But the UNO was designed so that decisions could be reached and action could be taken – very different from the League!

The Security Council

This meets regularly. If the *General Assembly* is not sitting, the Security Council can take decisions on its own. In 1946 it had five permanent members (Britain, the USA, the USSR, China and France) and six non-permanent members, elected by the General Assembly to sit for two years. In 1965 the number of non-permanent members was increased to ten.

All the five permanent members of the Security Council must agree if it is to reach a decision. So, any one of the five can stop something just by saying 'No'. This is called a *veto*.

The General Assembly

This is the 'parliament' of the UN. Every member state sits in it and has one vote. Most decisions need only a majority, but some important decisions need a two-thirds majority. Decisions of the General Assembly are called *resolutions*, and all member countries are supposed to obey them. This does not always happen in practice.

In 1950 the General Assembly passed a resolution called *Uniting for Peace*. It said that if something had been vetoed by the Security Council, it should be discussed by the General Assembly. If two-thirds of the General Assembly agreed to it, it would become a resolution.

The Secretariat

Anyone can pass resolutions – it's putting them into practice that counts. This is the job of the UN Secretariat, the UN's 'Civil Service'. It is led by the *UN Secretary General*, who often acts as the representative of the UN when disputes arise in the world.

The Secretary General has to put loyalty to the UN above loyalty to his country. This has not prevented some Secretaries General from being accused of bias by some countries.

The Trusteeships Council

This took over the work of the League of Nations Mandates Commission (see pages 34–36). It became less important as the old Mandates started to become independent. Its main problem has been South-West Africa (Namibia). In 1919 this was taken away from Germany and given as a Mandate to South Africa. For a long time, South Africa refused to let go of Namibia, and only did so finally in 1989.

Nowadays, only some islands in the Pacific are looked after by the UN Trusteeships Council.

The International Court of Justice

This sits at The Hague and carries on the work of the old League of Nations Court. It has solved a number of border disputes between member countries.

The Economic and Social Council

This has the huge task of improving the economic and social life of the entire world! It supervises the work of the various *UN agencies*.

UN Agencies

There are many of these. Here are some of the main ones:

- *International Labour Organisation (ILO).* This survived from the League of Nations. It tries to improve working conditions for workers all over the world.
- *World Health Organisation (WHO).* WHO has worked mainly in the Third World, bringing medical help to many poor areas. Thanks to its help, smallpox has disappeared in the world, and cholera and leprosy are limited to very small areas.
- *Food and Agriculture Organisation (FAO).* FAO works in the Third World, helping to improve agriculture and food production.
- *United Nations Educational, Scientific and Cultural Organisation (UNESCO).* UNESCO helps to improve education in poor countries, especially by teaching people to read and write. It also arranges for scientists, artists and writers from all over the world to meet and exchange ideas.
- *United Nations Children's Fund (UNICEF).* This started by helping refugee children after the war. Nowadays it helps children hit by war or famine in all parts of the world.
- *United Nations Relief and Rehabilitation Association (UNRRA).* UNRRA was set up in 1943 to provide help for countries as they were liberated from the Germans, starting in 1943 with Italy. Much of UNRRA's work was with the thousands of refugees stranded all over Europe after the war.
- *United Nations Relief and Works Agency (UNRWA).* This was like UNRRA, but was set up specifically to help Palestinian refugees after the state of Israel was set up in 1948 (see Chapter 6).
- *International Monetary Fund (IMF).* This was set up in 1944 to provide short-term loans to countries in financial difficulty.
- *World Bank.* This is similar to the IMF, but it provides loans for longer periods. It can also invest money in schemes which need support.

Examination Guidance

Activity 37a is perhaps the most popular question about the UN: in what ways was it different from the League of Nations? It's a tricky one, because it means you have to go back and remind yourself about what was good and what was bad about the League. The Target is part of the general objective about knowledge and understanding. Activity 37b is another 'Test Yourself' activity about the terms used in this chapter. Not the most exciting activity, I know, but you need to know what these words mean, and it's fairly easy to get someone to test you.

ACTIVITY 37a

Target

Selection and deployment of relevant knowledge.

Question Guide

This is an essay question. Below you will find some information to help you answer it. You also have all the information in this section. It does not matter if you have not yet looked at what the UN did in action: this is mainly about how the UN was planned. Remember that the UN was based on the League by people who knew the League very well. In other words, they kept what was good about the League, and tried to improve what was bad. So the UN was bound to be like the League in some ways and not in others.

When you have looked at the UN in action, come back to this activity and answer the question again. You may find yourself thinking differently!

Activity

Read each of these points carefully, and then write out your own answer to the question which follows them.

(a) *The UN is a lot bigger than the League.* The League never had more than fifty members; the UN was soon three times as big, as the old European colonies started to join it.

(b) *Both Russia and America were in the UN from the start.* Russia did not join the League until 1934, and America never did. On the other hand, having both Russia and America in the UN has produced difficulties as well as advantages.

(c) *The UN can call on armed support.* If a country in the League committed an act of aggression, the League could only impose sanctions; the UN can send in a *peace-keeping force*, made up of soldiers of many different member states.

(d) *Both the League and the UN have had their biggest successes in the work of their agencies.* In particular, ILO under the League and WHO under the UN have achieved some of the most important work of either organisation.

(e) *The UN can take action more easily than the League.* Most UN decisions only require a simple majority in the General Assembly. On the other hand, the League did not have the problem of the veto held by the permanent members of the Security Council.

(f) *The UN has only had mixed success in stopping wars.* We'll see this in more detail in Chapter 6. However, throughout the 1950s, as the world moved through the period known as the Cold War, the United Nations building in New York tended to be where the two sides' suspicions of each other came out into the open.

Now answer this question:
 How different was the UN from the League?

ACTIVITY 37b

Target

Terms and concepts.

Question Guide

No sweat here. If there are any you don't know, go back and check them in the text. Come back to this test from time to time to see that they have stuck in your mind.

Activity

Write a short sentence about each of the following:

Washington Conference, 1921–2

Manchuria

Pearl Harbor

Singapore

Battle of Midway

'Island Hopping'

kamikaze

Los Alamos

'Little Boy'

Yalta

Potsdam

Atlantic Charter

International Monetary Fund

San Francisco Conference

UN Security Council

veto

UN Secretary General

WHO

UNRRA

UNICEF

5

THE COLD WAR, c. 1945–68

Examination Guide

This is an important topic, and you will need to know your way around it. In particular, you need to know where the various countries in Eastern Europe are. Check on Figure 5.1 *now*! This is now highly relevant to an understanding of the world shattering changes in Eastern Europe since 1989.

For MEG, most of this chapter comes into the third part of the core content, **Tension and Co-operation since 1945**.

NEA's Theme 1, **Conflict and Conciliation**, deals with the Cold War. The United Nations comes into Theme 3, **International Co-operation**.

Parts of this chapter refer to different parts of the LEAG syllabus, according to whereabouts in the world they happened. For example, the Cuban Missile Crisis features in Section D, **Latin America and the Caribbean**. Section G, **The Soviet Union and Eastern Europe**, and Section A, **Asia**, are very relevant here. The United Nations and attempts to reach peace agreements come under Section H, **International Themes**.

This chapter covers roughly the second half of the compulsory SEG Theme 1, **The USA and the USSR as World Superpowers**.

Topic Guide

1 Communism in the World

Before the Second World War, the Soviet Union was the only communist country in the world. But there were plenty of communists active in other countries. In China, for example, the communists were fighting a bitter civil war with the Kuomintang (see Chapter 11). There were also communists in Europe, in Asia and in America.

Trotsky thought Russia should send help to all of these communists, but Stalin said 'No'. He wanted Russia to concentrate on her own problems. When Stalin came to power, he cut off help to Mao Tse-tung and other communist leaders.

The other big new political idea in the world was fascism. When Hitler came to power in Germany, most people assumed he and Stalin would be bitter enemies. In fact, they found they had more in common than they had thought. Stalin allowed the Germans to build armaments inside Russia, and the Russian secret police helped train the Gestapo. In 1939, Stalin signed a non-aggression pact with Hitler, and together they carved up Poland.

This posed a problem for communist leaders elsewhere in the world. They hated the Nazis, and they wanted to fight them; but they would not do anything without orders from Moscow. When war broke out with Nazi Germany in 1939, Stalin told communists not to get involved. He only changed this order when the Germans invaded Russia in 1941.

2 Conflict in the Resistance

Meanwhile, the Germans were taking over most of Europe. In the occupied countries, resistance groups started up. They looked to the communists for help, but the communists were still under orders from Moscow not to get involved. Not surprisingly, the non-communists resented this. When the communists did start to form resistance groups, after the Germans invaded Russia, they kept themselves separate from the other resistance fighters. So, in nearly all the occupied countries, resistance groups were split between communists and non-communists. Often they were bitter enemies, and fought each other as much as they fought the Germans.

Here are some examples of how this happened.

POLAND

When Poland fell in 1939, the Polish government fled to London. The Russians, who had also invaded Poland, set up an alternative government based in the Polish town of Lublin. So there were now three Polish governments:

1.   the original government, now based in London
2.   the official, German government, based in Warsaw
3.   the Russian-backed government, based in Lublin.

The Russians wanted the Lublin government to take over after the war. That meant they had to get rid of Poles who supported the London government. In 1940, the Russians rounded up 15,000 Poles loyal to the London government, mostly army officers, in *Katyn* woods, and shot them. Later they tried to blame the Germans for this massacre.

This killed many Poles loyal to London, but not all. In 1944, as the Russians advanced through Poland, the people of Warsaw rose up against the Germans. The leaders of the rising were loyal to the London government, so, even though they were just outside Warsaw themselves, the Russians did nothing to help them. The Russians waited until the rising had been put down by the SS; then they moved in. Within two years of the end of the war, the communists had taken control of Poland.

FRANCE

The French resistance was organised from London by *General de Gaulle*. There was also a very strong communist resistance movement inside France. The communists did not want de Gaulle to govern France after the war. However, they got no help from the Russians because France was liberated by the British and Americans. The last thing they wanted was a communist government in France. (The second to last thing they wanted was General de Gaulle in control of France, but they didn't have much choice about that!) So, they helped de Gaulle take over France. Even so, there was bitter fighting in France after the war between de Gaulle's supporters and the communists.

YUGOSLAVIA

The Germans never really controlled Yugoslavia because the Yugoslav resistance was so well organised.

There were two resistance groups in Yugoslavia:

1.   the *Chetniks*, led by Mihailovitch, and loyal to the King of Yugoslavia (in exile in England)
2.   the *Partisans*, led by Josip Brosz, known as *Tito*, and loyal to Moscow.

At first the Allies supported the Chetniks. When it seemed that Tito's partisans were doing more harm to the Germans than the Chetniks were, the Allies started supporting Tito instead.

Source 5A shows a picture of Tito. Remember that many photographs, particularly portrait photographs, are designed to give a particular impression to anyone looking at them. What sort of an impression does Source 5A give YOU of Tito?

Yugoslavia was unusual, because it was the only country which really liberated itself. Tito took the capital, Belgrade, in 1944. Then he started massacring his opponents, including the Chetniks. The British and Americans were horrified, and stopped sending supplies to Tito, but by then it was too late.

GREECE

The fighting in Greece was important, because it actually sparked off the Cold War.

When the Germans invaded Greece, the King of Greece fled to England. The Greek communists wanted

Source 5A   Tito – 28th June, 1948

Source   Milovan Djilas, *Tito – the Story from Inside*, Weidenfeld & Nicolson, 1981

Source 5B   Greek partisans

Source   R. Conrad Stein, *Resistance Movements*, Children's Press, 1982

him to stay there, but other Greeks wanted him to come back after the war.

The Greek communist party was called *EAM*. Its resistance fighters were called *ELAS*. Source 5B shows an ELAS patrol.

The royalist resistance fighters – i.e. the ones loyal to the King – were called *EDES*. It's a bit confusing, but keep this handy to check with if you get lost!

As soon as the Germans were gone, ELAS and EDES started fighting each other. It was a particularly nasty civil war. Source 5C shows the body of one man killed by ELAS, with writing on his skin to warn any other

opponents of ELAS that the same would happen to them. ELAS got help from communist countries like Albania, Yugoslavia and Bulgaria, and soon it began to look as if ELAS might win. So Churchill sent British troops to help the royalist EDES to fight back.

Source 5C   How ELAS dealt with its opponents

Source   Robert Kee, *1945: The World We Fought For*, Hamish Hamilton, 1985

By 1947, the British could no longer afford the cost of an army in Greece, and they told the Americans so. President Truman decided to take over, and he sent massive American aid to EDES. ELAS were defeated, and the King of Greece returned.

Remember: **Communists** = EAM (Communist *Party*)
ELAS (Communist *Fighters*)
Non-Communists = EDES

THE SOVIET UNION

Before going on, we ought to mention what happened to the Russian resistance.

Not all Russians were communists. Some had fought against the Revolution in 1917; many more had been appalled by Stalin's reign of terror, and saw no reason to fight for him. Also, many non-Russian people in the Soviet Union wanted to break away and set up their own states. All of these people saw their chance when the Germans invaded Russia in 1941.

None of them had any reason to fight for Stalin, and many had good reason to fight against him. So, many of these Russians offered their services to the Germans, on condition that they should only be used against the Red Army: they had no quarrel with the British and Americans, and did not wish to fight against them. The Germans agreed, and for a time these Russians fought fiercely against the Red Army and the Russian partisans. But after D-Day the Germans were in trouble in the West. They began to transfer some of these Russian units over to the Western front to fight against the British and

Americans. When they got there, the Russians surrendered quickly, rather than fight the Western allies. They were sent to prisoner-of-war camps in England.

Stalin was determined to get his revenge on these people. At the Yalta Conference, he asked the British and Americans to hand them over to him. Churchill and Roosevelt agreed.

The Russians, including many women and children, were forced on to trains and boats and sent back to Russia. Many committed suicide on the journey. Those that got back to Russia were either shot, or sent to concentration camps called *gulags*. The Western allies stopped sending the Russians over in 1946 but by then it was too late for most of them. Not surprisingly, the survivors have remained very bitter about their treatment by the Allies.

Examination Guidance

Examiners could spring resistance movements on you at any time (it gives you an idea of how the Germans felt!). In Activity 38a it's the NEA, in a paper set in 1988. Look at the sources carefully. You have a passage from a textbook, a cartoon and a diary extract. This activity will help you get these sorts of source clear in your mind, ready for when you meet them in the examination room. Visual sources, like photographs, take some getting used to, as it's surprisingly easy to be stumped by an examination question which asks you what a particular picture tells you! Activity 38b will help you get used to those sorts of questions; it is based on the photographs of resistance fighters. Activity 38c is very different. It is asking you to consider some generalised statements about communists in the resistance. Sometimes statements such as these will form part of a structured essay question, leading up to a question about the resistance in general; or you might be asked if the evidence you have looked at supports certain statements, as you are here. Remember that 'evidence' is a very wide term – it includes not just written sources and photographs, but also ANY information you have. Even the text in this *Work Out* book can be used as evidence!

ACTIVITY 38a

Targets

Selection and deployment of relevant knowledge; empathy, i.e. the ability to see things from the viewpoint of people at the time.

Question Guide

The first source is a fairly straightforward passage from a textbook – you often get these in examination papers. (You can normally tell them from the name of the book and the date it was published. You know the sort of thing – '*World History in the Twentieth Century*, published 1985' is probably going to be a school textbook.) Remember that school textbooks are sources too, but who writes them, and who are they written for?

The second source is a cartoon. Try to make sense of it, and you might as well start now. It's called 'The Effectiveness of the Resistance'. Is that what it shows? If so, who is likely to have drawn it? (Why? Who was meant to see it?). If that is NOT what it shows, then the caption must be sarcastic (and in cartoons they often are – you need to be careful of that). But if it is sarcastic, who might have drawn it, and who was supposed to see it?

The third source is short and to the point. 'OK', you might think, 'it says what happened, but it doesn't say much about it. So what?' Well, true it doesn't say much about it, but that is the interesting point. It's from a diary. Why should a diary say so little about this event? (If it happened in your town today, what would your diary entry look like?) What does this extract tell us about how the Germans ruled in Russia, and how ordinary Russians reacted to them?

Activity

(NEA, History Paper 1, Syllabus B, June 1988, Question 2)

Source 1

"Although the armed forces of many countries had been defeated by 1941, underground movements carried on the fight against German military forces. These groups became known as the Resistance movement. The methods that they used included sabotage, distribution of anti-German newspapers and leaflets, helping allied troops to escape from German occupied territory and information gathering.
The resistance movement was also active in Germany. The movement was not very strong because the Nazis arrested all the people they considered to be possible resisters before war was declared in 1939. Hitler was particularly cruel to Germans who tried to depose him. After the failed attempt to assassinate him in 1944, Hitler had the conspirators he caught tortured and hanged with piano wire."
(From 'Contemporary Accounts of the Second World War' by J. Simkin, published 1984)

Source 2

(Cartoon published in 1943)

'THE EFFECTIVENESS OF THE RESISTANCE'

Source 3

"Today, in the public square in the town of Minsk, German soldiers hanged a man and a woman who were members of the resistance."

(From a diary of a Russian, written in 1941)

Study Sources 1, 2 and 3

(a) Using Sources 1 and 2, explain the help that the Resistance gave to the Allies.

(b) Using Sources 1 and 3 and your knowledge of the period, explain in your own words why:
   (i) people **did** join the Resistance movement;
   (ii) people did **not** join the Resistance movement.

ACTIVITY 38b

Target

Evaluation and interpretation of historical evidence.

Question Guide

Look carefully at Sources 5A, 5B and 5C. They are all photographs, and they all show aspects of resistance and partisan fighting. You are seeing them in this *Work Out* book, but where might people have seen them at the time when they were taken? They might very well have seen them in newspapers, or on posters. In other words, they are not just illustrations – they tell us something about the fighting going on at the time. Your task is to try to work out what. To an extent this will depend on your own point of view: for example, you might not think that the picture of Tito from the chest up in Source 5A tells you very much at all. But think for a moment what it would have said to – say – a German soldier, if he had seen it, or to British officials deciding whether to send aid to Tito or to the Chetniks. Now try the activity.

Activity

Look carefully at Sources 5A, 5B and 5C. Make a list of as many things as you can think of that these sources tell us about communist resistance fighters, under these headings:
(a) weapons
(b) organisation
(c) determination

ACTIVITY 38c

Target

Selection and deployment of relevant knowledge.

Question Guide

You have just had information about similar events happening in five very different countries. Historians try to see if they can draw any patterns or generalisations from a lot of examples. This exercise will give you an idea of how it is done.

Activity

Read the details about resistance movements. Now look at these generalised statements. Can any of them be supported by the evidence you have looked at?

(a) The British and Americans resisted communism in every country they could reach.

(b) Communists were only active in countries which the Russians took over.

(c) Wherever communists took over, there was civil war.

(d) The British and Americans were happy to work with communists against the Germans.

You probably found that there was some truth in all of them, but some of the statements had more truth than others. If you listen to people talking about the war (and you'd be surprised how often people do), you will hear them making generalisations – they, too, may have some truth in them, but how much?

Now try to work out a generalisation of your own *which will fit with the evidence about*:

(a) how the British and Americans dealt with Stalin

(b) what communists tried to do in different countries at the end of the war.

3 The Origins of the Cold War

BROAD FRONT? NARROW THRUST?

As the Allies were advancing through France in 1944, Churchill was worrying about what would happen after the war. Would the Russians keep hold of the lands they were liberating? Above all, he was worried about what would happen if the Russians took over all of Germany. At the very least, he thought, the British and Americans ought to try to get to Berlin before the Russians.

The British commander, *Montgomery*, agreed. He wanted a narrow, thrusting attack, straight through to Berlin. The Supreme Allied Commander, *Eisenhower*, disagreed. He thought a narrow, thrusting attack could easily be cut off from its base by a German counter-attack. He preferred to move more slowly, across a broad front.

Still, Eisenhower agreed to let Montgomery have a go. Montgomery wanted to try a sudden airborne attack to seize the bridge over the Rhine at *Arnhem*, in Holland. Then the Allies would be able to race into the heart of Germany, and perhaps beat the Russians to Berlin. However, the attack force landed on top of an SS *Panzer* division, and was cut to pieces. Eisenhower would not allow any more such British adventures. The attack would proceed along a broad front. Eisenhower was in touch with the Russian commander, Marshal Zhukhov, and was quite happy to let the Russians move on and take Berlin.

So, when the war ended, the Russians held Berlin and most of Germany. The Americans only realised too late that they intended to stay there.

YALTA, POTSDAM AND THE BOMB

We have seen how the Allied leaders met many times at conferences during the war. The photographs from these conferences show the leaders smiling and joking (see Source 4W). Churchill and Roosevelt even had a nickname for Stalin, 'Uncle Joe'. But in fact the Allies were growing more and more suspicious of each other.

At *Yalta*, they argued about what should happen to Poland. Churchill wanted free elections; Stalin wanted Poland to become a communist state. Stalin got his way, because he had troops stationed all over Poland.

Instead, Churchill drew up a plan of 'spheres of influence'. These were areas where one side or the other would be allowed a free hand. This plan gave Western Europe and Greece to the British and Americans, and Eastern Europe to Stalin. The land in the middle was Germany.

The leaders met in *Potsdam* to work out what should be done about Germany. They decided to divide the country into four zones. But there were three Western zones against one Russian one, so Stalin demanded something in return. He wanted:

(a)   a base in North Africa, preferably Tripoli
(b)   heavy reparations from Germany.

The British and Americans refused. You don't need to be genius to see why. There was no way they would allow the Russians to have a base in North Africa, from where they could threaten the Mediterranean. Equally, they were not going to start repeating the mistakes they had made at Versailles in 1919 and impose reparations on Germany.

The trouble was that, although they could stop Stalin getting his base in Tripoli, they could not stop him taking reparations payments from Germany. The Russians started dismantling what was left of the Germany industry in their zone, and shipping it back to Russia. They confiscated food, clothing and medical supplies, and shipped those off as well. Soon, there was a serious food shortage in Germany.

Stalin seemed to be getting everything his own way. His troops were all over Eastern Europe, and he was getting reparations out of Germany. Then the Americans dropped the atom bomb on Hiroshima. The Russians had not been expecting the Americans to have it ready so fast, and it seemed to restore the balance between the Americans and the Russians.

Thanks to the bomb, many Americans felt they did not need to worry too much about what Stalin did in Eastern Europe. As long as America had the bomb, no one could touch her. What they did not consider was that the Russians might develop an atom bomb of their own.

'SALAMI TACTICS' AND THE 'IRON CURTAIN'

In the 1930s, when Fascist Parties were growing all over Europe, many European communists fled to Russia. In 1945, they returned to their home countries. Because of their time in Moscow, they were known as *Muscovites*.

The Russians put these Muscovites in charge of the communists in the countries they had conquered. The Muscovites' task was to put the communist party in control of these countries. Stalin had promised Roosevelt and Churchill that there would be free elections in these countries, and there were. But the Russians made sure that a Muscovite was put in charge of the police. Then it was easy for him to have non-communists in the government arrested or murdered. However, the Muscovites did not get rid of all the non-communists at once, as that might raise protests. Instead, they arrested them in batches, or 'slices'. This way of getting rid of non-communists 'slice by slice' was known as *salami tactics*.

Figure 5.1   Cold War Europe

Source   William R. Keylor, *The Twentieth Century World*, Oxford University Press, 1984

By 1946, salami tactics had put communists in control of all of Eastern Europe except Greece, where the Civil War was still going on, and Czechoslovakia. (See Figure 5.1.)

Hungary

Let's look at how salami tactics worked in one country, Hungary.

Hungary fought on the German side in the war, so there was no government in exile, waiting to come back. Hungary was invaded by the Russians, and in 1945 the Allies agreed that Russians troops should stay there. Stalin allowed elections, and the non-communists won a big majority. However, some communists were elected, led by a Hungarian Muscovite called *Rakosi*.

Rakosi now started throwing his weight about. He demanded that this group or that should be banned. If not, he hinted, the Russians would take over the country. Gradually, Rakosi was getting rid of his opponents, 'slice by slice'. Then he got control of the police, and started to arrest his opponents himself. He set up a sinister and brutal secret police unit, the *AVH*. Soon Rakosi had complete control over Hungary.

Rakosi's work was typical of what was happening all over Eastern Europe. Nikita Khrushchev, a leading Russian politician, and later leader of the Soviet Union, recalled in his memoirs:

Source 5D

At the end of the war we had troops stationed in Poland and Hungary. Stalin took an active personal interest in the affairs of these countries, as well as of Czechoslovakia, Bulgaria and Romania . . . One reason for Stalin's obsession with eastern

Europe was that the Cold War had already set in. Churchill had given his famous speech in Fulton urging the imperialistic forces of the world to mobilise against the Soviet Union. Our relations with England, France, the USA and the other countries who had co-operated with us in crushing Hitlerite [i.e Nazi] Germany were, for all intents and purposes, ruined. (S. Talbott (ed.), *Khrushschev Remembers*, Andre Deutsch, 1971, p. 361)

The 'famous speech in Fulton' he mentions took place in March 1946, barely a year after the end of the war. Churchill was speaking in Fulton, Missouri. He said that communist rule had descended on Europe like an '*iron curtain*'. The phrase stuck.

Figure 5.2   War dead, 1939–45

	Military	Civilian
GB	398,000	62,000
USA	292,000	–
Germany	3,500,000	800,000
Italy	330,000	80,000
France	210,671	107,874
USSR	7,500,000	2,500,000
Japan	1,500,000	500,000
China	combined: 2,200,000	

Source   Martin Gilbert, *Recent History Atlas* Weidenfeld & Nicolson, 1966.

Examination Guidance

This period, when the Cold War was getting under way, is the sort of thing examiners dream about. (Candidates might well dream about it too, but not so pleasantly!) The trouble about it is that it *looks* tricky. It's got all the ingredients of panic – East European names, lots of things happening at once, and none of it is as generally familiar as, say, the rise of Hitler or the events leading up to the war. So, Activities 39a and 39b will help you to familiarise yourself with these events. They will also help you to think a little bit more deeply about what was going on. No one is expecting you to say what a good thing it was that the Russians rescued Eastern Europe from the Big Bad Americans, but the examiner will expect you to recognise that there is more than one way of looking at the start of the Cold War. If you get confused and can't quite remember where countries are, check back on Figure 5.1 – that's what it's there for!

ACTIVITY 39a

Target

Empathy (i.e looking at events from the perspective of people in the past).

Question Guide

People always do things for reasons, and their reasons are only rarely simple. We know that the British and the Americans fell out with the Russians very quickly after the end of the war, but do we really know WHY? It can't just be because one lot were communists and the other lot weren't – after all, that had not stopped them all working together during the war. There were many other reasons behind this falling-out of wartime allies. To do this activity, you will need to look at the text of this chapter, and in particular at Source 5D and Figure 5.2. You should also turn back to Chapter 4 and read carefully through the section on the Second Front. When you have looked through all these, try the activity.

Activity

1. List as many ways as you can find in which the Russians and the Western Allies came into conflict between 1944 and 1946.

2. When you have done this, look carefully at Figure 5.2. If the Russians had seen it in 1945, what might they have said it showed about their contribution to the war against Hitler, compared to the Western Allies' contribution?

3. Now take the list that you completed for Question 1. For each event on it, write down what you think a Russian would have said the event showed, and what you think an American might have said.

Model Answer

Event   Stalin demands Tripoli at the Potsdam Conference.

Russian view   This gives the Soviet Union a base in the Mediterranean as compensation for the immense losses she suffered during the war.

American view   This shows that Stalin is not just happy with eastern Europe. He wants to expand his empire even further, into the Mediterranean

Now try it for the other events. Remember, neither side trusted the other!

ACTIVITY 39b

Target

Evaluation and assessment of evidence.

Question Guide

This is a fairly straightforward comprehension exercise based on Source 5D. You know by now that you should treat all sources carefully, but it's still tempting to assume that they are either true or false. (It doesn't help that examiners keep asking daft questions like 'Does this mean Source so-and-so is not true? Explain your answer.') In this case, the thing to do is to make sure you know what Khrushchev was referring to at various points in his speech, and then check it carefully against what you know about what happened. Remember that he is as entitled to his *point of view* as you are to yours: the important thing for you to decide is whether or not what he says *happened* actually did. The question asks you to decide whether his account is reliable. Think carefully: what is the difference between being true and being reliable?

Activity

Read through Source 5D carefully, and answer these questions about it:

1. Khrushchev suggests that there was a reason for Stalin's 'active personal interest in eastern Europe'. What was it?
2. Now compare what Khrushchev says with the events in this chapter. What in his account is:
   (a) true
   (b) untrue
   Now decide: is his account reliable?

4 The Cold War in the 1940s

That was the background to the Cold War. Make sure you have got a general picture of why communists and non-communists were so suspicious of each other so soon after the war, before you look at what they actually did to each other.

TRUMAN DOCTRINE AND MARSHALL AID

Historians usually date the start of the Cold War at 1947. It's a little difficult, because it was not the sort of war that was declared, but 1947 was when the British Foreign Secretary warned the Americans that Britain could no longer afford the war against the communists in Greece. President Truman sent 120 million US dollars aid to the Greek royalists. But he did not stop there. Truman announced that from then on the USA would help ANY country, anywhere in the world, which was resisting communist pressure, either from outside or from within:

Source 5E

It must be the policy of the United States of America to support free peoples who are resisting attempted subjugation by armed minorities, or by outside pressure.
(R. D. Cornwell, *World History in the Twentieth Century*, Longman, new ed, 1980, p. 74)

This policy became known as the *Truman Doctrine*.

No sooner had President Truman announced his doctrine than his Secretary of State, General George Marshall, went even further. Marshall announced a plan to send American aid to any country which was trying to recover from the effects of war. The aid was known as *Marshall Aid*. The Western European countries responded eagerly, and got 13,000 million dollars over the next four years. The Russians were suspicious of the whole plan.

Stalin thought the plan was a trick to create markets for American goods. He called Marshall Aid 'dollar imperialism', and refused to have anything to do with it. He also made sure that the communist countries of Eastern Europe did the same. Even in Czechoslovakia, which was not then a communist country, the Czech communists forced the government to turn down the offer of Marshall Aid.

Mind you, the East Europeans were not happy about it. They were already paying huge sums in reparations to the Russians, and they needed all the help they could get. So, Stalin set up a sort of Russian version of Marshall Aid called *Comecon*. The Russians would put up the money, and Comecon would decide how it should be spent. The trouble was that Russia was too poor herself after the war, and could not put up anything like the sums the Americans were putting into Marshall Aid. So Eastern Europe could only rebuild very slowly after the war, while Western Europe, with Marshall Aid, forged ahead.

THE COMINFORM

Stalin was very worried that communist countries would be tempted by Marshall Aid to join the American side. So in 1947 he set up the *Cominform*, to get the communist countries working closely together, so that none of them would break away. Cominform countries were not allowed to have contracts with non-communist countries.

This immediately caused trouble, because Marshall Tito of Yugoslavia refused to agree to it. He wanted Yugoslavia to trade with the West. Stalin was furious, and expelled Yugoslavia from the Cominform.

Meanwhile, Stalin seized control of the last non-communist country in Eastern Europe, Czechoslovakia. The next elections in Czechoslovakia were due in 1948. The communists looked sure to lose them, because people blamed them for refusing Marshall Aid. So the communists staged an armed coup and seized power by force. The President was forced out of office, and the Foreign Minister was forced out of a window. Then the communists held the elections. Since they were the only party allowed to stand, they won by a large majority.

THE BERLIN AIRLIFT

In 1948, the Western allies joined their three zones of Germany together, and began to draw up a constitution for their half of Germany. A constitution is a set of rules for governing an independent country, so this meant the Allies were planning to make Western Germany into an independent state. The Russians were alarmed. They did not want a strong, rich German state in the West. But the real problem was what should happen to Berlin.

As you can see from Figure 5.3, Berlin is not on the border between East and West: it is right in the heart of Eastern Germany. It was divided into four sectors: British, American, Russian and French. When the Western Allies joined their zones of Germany together, they also joined up their sectors of Berlin. Both western Germany and West Berlin received Marshall Aid. So, West Berlin became very rich, while the Russian zone of Germany all around it remained very poor.

The trouble was that West Berlin was there for everyone in the Russian zone of Germany to see: ordinary Germans could see the difference between life under the Russians and life in the West. This infuriated the Russians.

Things came to a head when the Allies introduced a new currency into Western Germany. All money has to be based on something if it is to be worth anything, and this new money was based on American credit. That made it very strong and valuable. The existing money, which was still in use in the Russian zone, was based on the shattered German economy, which the Russians were busy taking apart as reparations payments. The Germans were very sensitive about the value of their money – many remembered the inflation of 1923 – and they preferred the new, American-backed money.

Figure 5.3 Post-war Germany, 1945–9

Source J. Robert Wegs, *Europe Since 1945*, St Martin's Press, 1977

The Russians managed to keep the new money out of their zone of Germany, but it was difficult to keep it out of East Berlin, because people could still travel freely around all the city. Soon most Berliners, in East and West Berlin, were using the new money. The Russians decided to act. In June 1948 they introduced their own new currency in East Berlin. On the same day, they cut West Berlin off from all contact with the outside world.

Stalin wanted to starve West Berlin into surrender. The Americans thought this was the first part of a military attack on Western Germany. The Western Allies mounted a massive airlift to keep the city supplied, and to defy the Russian blockade.

Hundreds of allied planes flew some 2 million tons of food, clothing and medical supplies into West Berlin, day and night, for ten months. Source 5F shows one of them coming in to land at Tempelhof airport in West Berlin. The planes flew along three routes, into three Berlin airfields (see Figure 5.3). The schedule was so tight that aircraft which overshot the runway could not have another go: they had to return all the way to base. Inevitably, there were accidents. During the Berlin airlift, 79 men and 36 aircraft were lost. But the airlift worked. In May 1949 the Russians lifted the blockade. It was their first setback since the war.

After the airlift, in August 1949, the Allies set their zone of Germany up as the *Federal Republic of Germany*, better known as West Germany, with Konrad Adenauer as its first Chancellor. In October the Russians made their zone into the Democratic Republic of Germany, or East Germany. Germany, like Europe, was split down the middle.

Source 5F   The Berlin airlift

Source   US National Archives

Examination Guidance

The Berlin Airlift is fair game for a question, perhaps using a map. You need to get to recognise the pattern of the three routes taken by the planes towards Berlin during the airlift. Activity 40a is a map activity which will help get the pattern fixed in your mind. As well as maps, examiners like throwing collections of source material at you, to see how you cope. In Activity 40b it's the SEG. If you look at the questions, you will see that they are asking your *opinion*. In other words, there is no 'right' or 'wrong' answer. So, *as long as your opinion is backed up by evidence*, you cannot go far wrong.

ACTIVITY 40a

Target

Recall, selection and deployment of relevant knowledge.

Question Guide

Nothing particularly fancy here: just a quick revision test to help with those short-answer questions. Look at the blank map below, and answer as many of the questions below without checking. When you have done it, turn back to Figure 5.3 to see how well you did. Even if you did well, come back to this test again later and have another go.

Look at this map carefully, and answer these questions:

1. Which countries controlled areas A, B and C?
2. Name countries D and E.
3. What was the area which surrounded city F?
4. Identify areas G, H, I and J.
5. What event does this map show happening?
6. In what year did this event take place?

ACTIVITY 40b

Target

Evaluation and interpretation of evidence.

Question Guide

Remember that for this question, as for any other examination question, you already know more than enough to

Activity

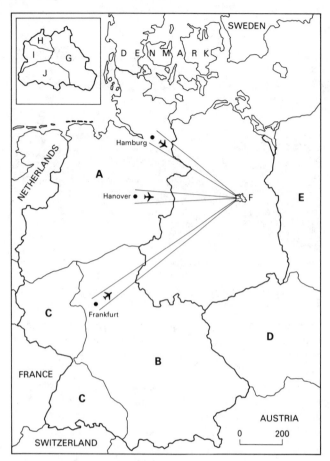

answer the question satisfactorily. Even if you have forgotten about the Berlin blockade, there is more than enough information in the question itself to jog your memory, and you will soon find the details come back to you. The important point in this question is to *explain* your answer carefully. By the way, don't be put off if the examiner suddenly introduces something else that you have never heard of – in this case he has pulled the Siege of Leningrad in out of the blue. *You do not have to know about it in order to answer the question.* It does not even matter if you have never heard of it before. All the information you need about that siege is included in the question.

Activity

(SEG, Summer 1989, Syllabus 2, Paper 1, Section A, Question 1)

The USA and the USSR as World Super-Powers
The Berlin Crisis of 1948–49
Study the Introduction and Sources 1 to 5 and then attempt all parts of the question.
When referring to the Sources in your answers, you should identify them by letter.

(a) What do you think Robert Murphy (Source 1) is suggesting by his description of the blockade?   **(3 marks)**

(b) "Ilya Kremer (Source 2) shows that the Soviet authorities did not intend any harm to the people of West Berlin." Explain whether or not you agree with this statement.   **(4 marks)**

(c) Kremer, the author of Source 2, is a Soviet historian. Nowhere in his article does he mention the Soviet

note referred to by Murphy in Source 1. How do you account for this?   **(5 marks)**

(d) Why does Peter Lane (Source 3) refer to the wartime siege of Leningrad?   **(4 marks)**

(e) "Sources 4 and 5 show that the Western powers had no difficulty in supplying the needs of West Berlin." Explain whether or not you agree with this statement.   **(6 marks)**

(f) "The Russians gained nothing from the blockade in Berlin." Using only the evidence in the Introduction and in Sources 1 to 5, do you agree or disagree with this statement? Give reasons for your answer.
(8 marks)
TOTAL: 30 marks

Introduction: the post-war division of Germany

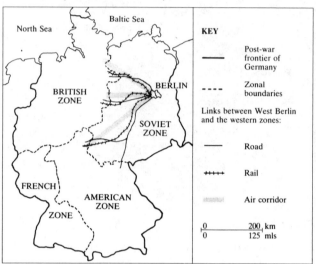

At the end of the Second World War, Germany was divided into four zones of occupation, as shown on the map above. Berlin was also divided into four sectors. Travel to the western sectors of Berlin was by means of three air corridors and certain land links.
The Berlin Crisis of 1948–49 came after the Western powers introduced a new currency in an attempt to deal with the problem of rapidly rising prices. They had been unable to reach an agreement with the Soviet Union over this new currency.

Source 1

All we had about the blockade of Berlin was a note from the Soviet Military Governor saying that the highway would be closed to traffic, because it was in need of repair. Then they put a pole across the road, with just two soldiers – and that was a blockade. It didn't cost them a penny.
(adapted from comments made in an interview in 1971 by ROBERT MURPHY, who had been an American diplomat in the late 1940s)

Source 2

The new currency made necessary the permanent division of Germany. The worthless old marks flooded into the Soviet Zone. The Soviet Military Governor had to take emergency measures to protect eastern Germany. To keep out speculators who were making profits out of the currency situation, some barriers were set up on the lines of communication between Berlin and the western zones. The Soviet authorities were ready to provide food and fuel for the population of the whole of Berlin.
(adapted from *Soviet Foreign Policy*, an article written by Ilya S. Kremer for a British magazine in 1968)

Source 3

The Russians saw a revived western Germany as a threat to eastern Europe, and West Berlin as "a capitalist thorn in the communist side".

On 24 June 1948, Stalin ordered the blockade of all land routes from the West to Berlin. He was sure the Western powers would leave their sectors of Berlin once the 2.4 million people ran short of food and coal. The Russians had had their own bitter experience of blockaded cities. In the War, three million people in Leningrad had been cut off by the German armies. Over a million had died – 632 000 of them from starvation.
(adapted from *Europe Since 1945*, (1985) by Peter Lane)

Source 4

Unloading supplies during the Berlin Airlift
(a photograph taken at the time of the airlift)

Source 5

A minimum of 4000 tons of goods a day were required, using Dakotas (which could carry only 3 tons of goods), Yorks (5 tons) and a few Skymasters (11 tons). Round the clock flying was necessary. Planes arrived at and left Berlin every 30 seconds.

By December 1948, 4500 tons a day were being flown into Berlin. By March 1949, the figure was up to 8000 tons a day. On 9 May 1949, the Russians called off the blockade, leaving the Western powers still in control of their sectors.
(adapted from *A History of the Modern World*, (1981) by R. Poulton)

NATO

It did not take long for the Western allies to form an alliance against the Russians. Britain and France formed an alliance in 1947, and Holland, Belgium and Luxemburg joined the next year. But this alliance could not stand up to the Russians without American help. As American bombers started to return to the bases where they had been stationed during the war, the Americans decided to commit themselves to Western Europe.

In 1949 the USA, Britain, France, Canada and eight other nations formed NATO, the *North Atlantic Treaty Organisation*. If any member was attacked, all the other members would help. The NATO countries set up a joint command of all their forces, with joint exercises and constant co-operation.

Many people in the West felt relieved and safe when NATO was formed. The feeling did not last. In September 1949, scientists in Alaska reported unusually high radiation levels in the air. There was only one explanation: the Russians had tested an atomic bomb. The Cold War was hotting up.

Examination Guidance

Examiners are always throwing collections of source material at you, to see how you cope. In Activity 41 it is the NEA, but they all tend to do it. You just have to put up with it and show that you can cope perfectly well.

ACTIVITY 41

Targets

Evaluation and interpretation of sources; selection and deployment of relevant knowledge.

Question Guide

When you look at these sources, it seems fairly clear what they are all about: the Marshall Plan. On the other hand, Source 4 doesn't mention the Marshall Plan at all – what does it mention instead? Think for a moment and try to remember what you have learned about the Marshall Plan (if you *genuinely* can't remember, go back and check), and about the different ways in which it was viewed in the West and in Eastern Europe. When you have refreshed your memory, have a go at the activity. It's mostly about evaluating sources, but be careful: some of the question are checking up on your knowledge and understanding.

Activity

(NEA, Syllabus A, Paper 2, Question 8, June 1988)

POST WAR CO-OPERATION IN WESTERN EUROPE
Study the sources below and then answer the questions which follow.

Source 1

Marshall Aid – A cartoon published in 1947.

Source 2

"The seeds of communism are nurtured by misery and want. They spread and grow in the evil soil of poverty.

The Marshall Plan will go down in history as one of America's greatest contributions to the peace of the world. Without it, it would have been difficult for Western Europe to remain free from communism."
(From a speech by Harry S. Truman)

Source 3

"The Marshall Plan and N.A.T.O. are all part of the same anti-soviet policy. The first established America's economic control in Western Europe; the second her military domination."
(An historian writing in 1970)

Source 4

A cartoon published in West Germany

(a) What was the Marshall Plan, mentioned in Sources 1, 2 and 3?

(b) What evidence is there in Source 1 to suggest that it was anti-American?

(c) Who was Harry S. Truman, the speaker in Source 2?

(d) According to Source 2, what were the reasons for the growth of communism?

(e) Explain how the Marshall Plan helped "Western Europe to remain free from communism".

(f) Do you think that Source 3 is biased? Give reasons for your answer.

(g) What do the letters N.A.T.O stand for? Explain how it was set up.

(h) Explain clearly the meaning of the cartoon in Source 4.

5 The Korean War

THE BACKGROUND

So far, the Cold War had all been based in Europe. But in 1950 it flared up into a full-scale war at the other end of the world. Most people in Europe had never even heard of the country where it happened: Korea.

In 1947, the Cominform called on the people of colonies all over the world to rise up against their masters. Communist risings began almost immediately all over Asia, in Malaya, Burma, Vietnam and the Philippines. It looked as if Asia was going the same way as Eastern Europe. The Americans were determined to stop that happening.

Two years later, the communists won their greatest victory since 1917, when Mao Tse-Tung took control in China. The Americans were furious and very frightened. It was the same year that the Russians exploded their bomb. It seemed that nothing could stop communism. Then fighting broke out in Korea.

The Japanese had controlled Korea during the war. In 1945 it was divided between the Russians in the north and the Americans in the south. The border between the two zones was the 38th parallel. The United Nations said there should be elections for a new government of all Korea. The Russians said no, because there were more people in the American zone, so the north would be out-voted.

Instead, elections were held just in the south. The south became the Republic of *South Korea*, with its capital at *Seoul*. Its president was *Syngman Rhee*. Syngman Rhee immediately declared himself President of all Korea – including the north.

But the Russians were not to be outdone. They set up the Republic of *North Korea*, with its capital at *Pyongyang* and its own president, *Kim Il Sung*. Kim also claimed to be President of all Korea – including the south. And in 1950, he ordered a full-scale invasion of South Korea.

THE UN GOES TO WAR

The North Korean attack took South Korea completely by surprise. Very quickly, the North Koreans pushed into the South, and took Seoul. Soon the only area in South Korean hands was around the town of Pusan. South Korea appealed to the United Nations. The UN told North Korea to clear out of the South. The North Koreans refused.

At this point, the Americans could have intervened on their own, under the Truman Doctrine. But President Truman did not think that Congress would agree to a war in Korea. So he decided to use the UN instead. He asked the UN to send troops to South Korea. The Russians would certainly stop this with their veto, but they were not actually there: they were boycotting the UN because the Americans would not allow communist China to join. So there was no veto, and the vote was passed. Although all the member states sent troops, the UN army was overwhelmingly American, and its commander was an American hero of World War II, *General Douglas MacArthur*.

THE WAR

The UN troops landed at *Inchon*, well behind the North Korean lines. Very quickly, MacArthur forced the North Koreans back to the 38th parallel (see Figure 5.4). But then Truman ordered MacArthur to cross the border, invade North Korea and reunite the country.

As MacArthur pushed further into North Korea, in China Mao Tse-tung grew worried. He did not want an American army on his border with North Korea. Truman warned MacArthur not to go near the Chinese border, but MacArthur took no notice. So, in October 1950 half a million Chinese troops (the Chinese described them as 'volunteers') poured over the border.

In one famous battle, the British Gloucestershire Regiment held up a massive Chinese attack for three days before giving in. Source 5G shows a soldier of the Gloucesters with two Chinese prisoners.

Figure 5.4   The Korean War

Source   Peter Moss, *Modern World History*, Rupert Hart-Davis, 1979

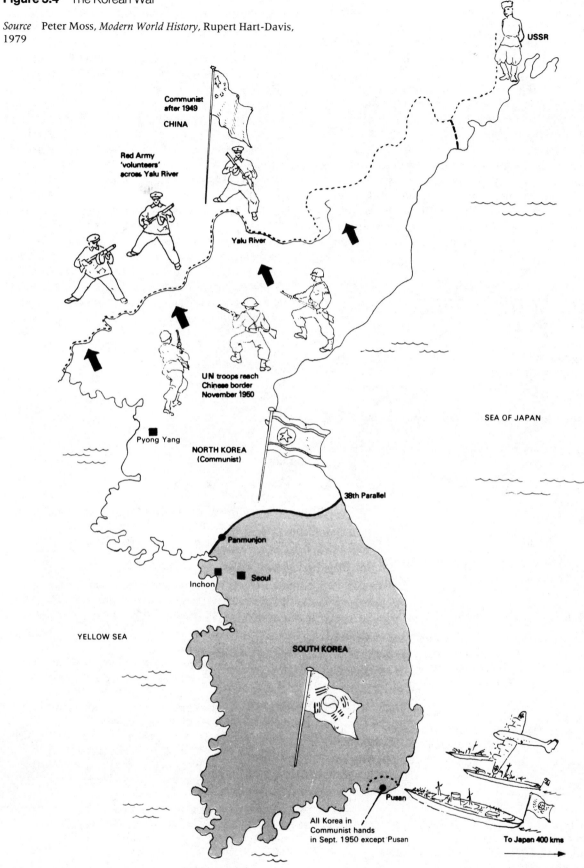

Despite this, by the New Year the Chinese had pushed the UN troops out of North Korea. Then they crossed the 38th parallel and invaded South Korea. Everything MacArthur had won was lost. Truman had only one weapon left: the *atom bomb*.

Truman was considering whether or not to use the

bomb in Korea, but he did not want it discussed in public. But then MacArthur publicly called for a nuclear strike in Korea and an invasion of China. Truman was furious. When MacArthur refused to keep quiet, Truman sacked him.

Meanwhile, the UN forces had recovered and were

pushing the Chinese back, without using nuclear weapons. By June 1951 everyone was back at the 38th parallel again.

They stopped there while peace talks got under way. Finally, in 1953, an agreement was signed which kept the frontier at the 38th parallel.

It is hard to be certain about casualty figures, but as far as we can tell the war cost the Americans 30,000 dead, the Chinese some 500,000 and the Koreans themselves about 1 million. It certainly showed that the UN was tougher than the League of Nations, but it also looked as if the UN was simply fighting America's battles for her. The Americans set up *SEATO* (South East Asia Treaty Organisation) with Britain, France, Australia and New Zealand, to try to keep China surrounded. But it was the Chinese who gained most from the war. They were now, without any doubt, a top-rank world superpower.

Examination Guidance

Korea is a good topic, and in Activity 42a, SEG has followed the standard pattern and given you a collection of sources about it. You do not need a detailed knowledge of every battle in the war – as long as you have read the section on pages 96–98 you will be all right. Activity 42b will give you some practice in comparing similar sources. Don't forget – the normal rules about evaluating evidence still apply: think carefully about how the pictures were taken, and who was likely to see them.

ACTIVITY 42a

Target

Evaluation and interpretation of sources; selection and deployment of relevant knowledge.

Question Guide

Most of these questions can be answered fairly simply from the sources, but the cartoon poses a problem. It is based on a catchphrase which was around at the time, but which you don't hear nowadays. The general idea is clear, though – the people in the cartoon are Russians (you should be able to recognise Stalin among them) claiming to be Koreans. Why should the Russians be in Korea in the first place, and why should they pretend that they weren't? Think carefully before you try the activity.

Activity

(SEG, Syllabus 2, Paper 1, Summer 1988)

The USA and the USSR as World Superpowers

The outbreak of war in Korea in 1950
Study the Introduction and Sources 1 to 5 and then attempt all parts of the question.
When referring to Sources in your answers, you should identify them by letter.
(a) How in Source 1 does General Roberts make it clear that he does not believe South Korea would be able to defend itself in the event of war?   **(2 marks)**

(b) Does Source 1 suggest that General Roberts was genuinely concerned about South Korea? Give reasons for your answer.   **(3 marks)**
(c) (i) North Korea claimed that she had attacked South Korea because of border raids by South Korea. Explain whether or not the United Nations report (Source 2) accepts this North Korean reason.   **(2 marks)**
(ii) Which other Source suggests that this part of the United Nations report was probably accurate and how does it do so?   **(2 marks)**
(d) Why did Pravda (Source 3) consider that 'Syngman Rhee counted in advance on military aid' (line 1)?   **(4 marks)**
(e) The Soviet newspaper Pravda refers to President Truman ordering armed 'support' for South Korea. Why does Pravda place the word 'support' in inverted commas?   **(3 marks)**
(f) (i) Why does the cartoon (Source 4) show several Soviet leaders dressed as Koreans?   **(3 marks)**
(ii) Do Khrushchev's memoirs, as referred to in Source 5, prove that the point made by the cartoonist was correct? Explain your answer.   **(4 marks)**
(g) 'The war in Korea occurred only because the Superpowers allowed it to happen.'
Using only the evidence of the Sources, explain whether you agree or disagree with this statement.   **(7 marks)**
TOTAL: 30 marks

Sources

The outbreak of war in Korea in 1950
Introduction
After the surrender of Japan in 1945, Korea was divided into two along the line of latitude, 38° North. The Soviet Union occupied northern Korea and the United States occupied southern Korea.
By 1950 two separate states had emerged. North Korea was communist and was led by Kim Il Sung. South Korea was pro-Western with Syngman Rhee as President. On 25 June 1950, war broke out between North Korea and South Korea.

Source 1

If South Korea were attacked today by the ground forces of North Korea plus their air force, I feel that South Korea would take a bloody nose. Knowing these people somewhat, I feel they would follow the apparent winner and South Korea would be gobbled up to be added to the rest of Red Asia.
This is a fat nation with warehouses bulging with plenty of rice. It is getting into the position of an excellent prize of war. Strategically, it points right into the heart of Japan and in the hands of an enemy it weakens the Japanese bastion of Western defence.
(from comments by General Roberts, commander of American advisers to the South Korean army, (8 March 1950))

Source 2

The invasion launched by the North Korean forces on 25 June cannot have been the result of a decision taken suddenly in order to repel a mere border attack, or in retaliation for such an attack. Such an invasion, involving seaborne landings and the use of considerable numbers of troops, indicates a well-prepared and well-timed plan.
(from a report (September 1950) by the United Nations Commission which was present in Korea)

Source 3

The clique (ruling group) of Syngman Rhee counted in advance on military aid from their masters across the sea. Truman had given orders to US air and naval forces to give armed 'support' to South Korea.

(from *Pravda*, a Soviet government newspaper, (28 June 1950))

Source 4

From a British newspaper, (28 June 1950)

"NOBODY HERE BUT US KOREANS"

Source 5

Khrushchev's memoirs indicate that Kim Il Sung first proposed the attack and that Stalin agreed. . . .
Kim Il Sung was a strong nationalist, who was proud and had a mission to unite his country.
(from *Origins of the Korean War*, (1982) by P. Lowe)

ACTIVITY 42b

Target

Evaluation and assessment of evidence.

Question Guide

Source 5G shows soldiers in Korea in the act of surrendering; the picture shows Chinese surrendering to the British. Think carefully about the LIKELY circumstances in which this photograph was taken. Was it just by chance that there was a photographer on hand? After all, war correspondents and photographers *do* wander through battle zones looking for good pictures. Or is there more to it than that?

Activity

Look carefully at Source 5G.
1. The picture was shown publicly shortly after it was taken. Why?
2. Look carefully at the people in the photograph. Does the picture look as if it was taken in action, or has it been posed for the camera?
3. There are many ways in which photographs like this can be useful to a historian. List as many of them as you can.

Source 5G

Source Max Hastings, *The Korean War*, Pan Books, 1988,

6 The Cold War in the 1950s

Is there anybody you don't trust? Perhaps more to the point, is there anyone who doesn't trust you? In the 1950s, most of the world's leaders simply did not trust each other. That is no way to have an easy international situation!

Why were they so suspicious of each other?

● The *Western Allies* said:

(a) Russia had forced the people of Eastern Europe to turn communist against their will.
(b) Now Russia was trying to force communism on everyone in the world.
(c) Russia was ruling all of Eastern Europe through fear and terror.
(d) Russia and her allies intended to attack the West.

Think very carefully about what evidence there was for these views by the time the Korean War had ended.

● The *Russians* said:

(a) America was trying to get all the world to depend on her.
(b) America was using NATO as an excuse for occupying Western Europe.
(c) Marshall Aid was a trick to extend American power and influence.
(d) America and her allies intended to attack the communist countries.

How much evidence did the Russians have by 1953 for these fears?

You can probably see that each side had some sort of a case. But it doesn't really matter whether they were right or wrong: what matters is that they *believed* all these things. When people believe that their enemies have a secret plot to destroy them, it is called a *conspiracy theory*. When people believe in a conspiracy theory, they think that anything that happens is part of their enemy's plot. In the 1950s, people on both sides believed very strongly in a conspiracy theory.

ALLIANCES

We have seen how the Western Allies formed NATO in 1949. It soon grew bigger: Greece and Turkey joined it in 1952, and Spain and West Germany joined in 1955. The Russians were furious, especially when the Germans joined it! So in 1955 they formed their own alliance, the *Warsaw Pact* (see Figure 5.5).

NATO only covered Europe. *SEATO* (South East Asia Treaty Organisation) was set up (1945) to cover the Pacific, and *CENTO* (Central Treaty Organisation) was set up (1959) to cover the Middle East. Meanwhile Britain, France and West Germany got together in the *Western European Union* to help defend each other.

So, by the end of the 1950s not just Europe, but the whole world, had been divided up into two armed camps, which did not trust each other.

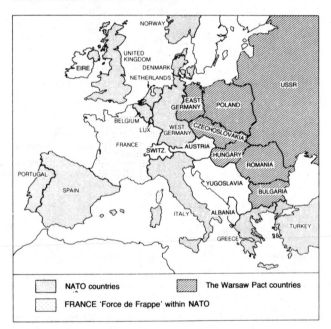

Figure 5.5   NATO and the Warsaw Pact in Europe

Source   Peter Lane, *Europe since 1945*, Batsford, 1985

THE GENEVA TALKS

By 1954, both sides were very frightened. Both had the atom bomb; now both had the even more destructive *hydrogen bomb* as well. The Americans had been badly shaken by the Korean War. The Russians were in all sorts of trouble because Stalin had died in 1953 and they had not yet got a clear leader. Also they were having trouble in Eastern Europe. In 1954, both sides agreed that it would be best to try to talk about their problems at a *summit* conference. They held the summit at Geneva, in neutral Switzerland.

At Geneva, the leaders of the two sides agreed that:

(a)   the French should leave Vietnam, and the country should be divided in two, like Korea

(b)   Russia would *recognise* West Germany (although the West did not recognise East Germany)

(c)   the Russians would pull their remaining troops out of Austria, so that Austria could become a neutral country, like Switzerland

(d)   the leaders of Russia, America, Britain and France would meet at another summit in Geneva in 1955.

People all over the world were delighted. They talked of the 'Geneva Spirit' and the end of the Cold War. It did not last long.

In October 1955, the leaders gathered again in Geneva. This time the talks broke down. The Americans insisted that the Russians should clear out of Eastern Europe, and stop supporting Mao's government in China. The Russians refused. Instead of the 'Geneva Spirit', everyone was now talking about *brinkmanship*: pushing things as far as you dared to the brink of war, without actually declaring it. Both sides went in for it.

RUSSIA'S PROBLEMS

Although she looked very strong, especially to the West, Russia had a lot of problems in the 1950s.

'Titoism'

This was the idea that you could be a communist without following orders from Moscow. It was named after Marshall Tito of Yugoslavia.

Tito had been a communist all his life. He had even been in Russia at the time of the Revolution. We saw in Section 2 above how he took power in Yugoslavia. Once in power, he nationalised industry and started to collectivise agriculture, just as Stalin had done in the 1930s. He helped set up the Cominform, and in his honour its first meeting was due to take place in Belgrade, the Yugoslav capital, in 1948. So how come he fell out so quickly with Stalin?

(a)   The Russians started saying that they, not Tito, had freed the country from the Germans.

(b)   The Russians gave economic aid to Yugoslavia, but they kept any profit it produced for themselves.

(c)   Many Russian officers in Yugoslavia were openly spying and reporting back to Moscow. Tito was furious.

(d)   Tito distrusted Stalin and slowed down the programme of nationalising industry and collectivising agriculture. He allowed people to start up small private companies, and started to get economic help from the West. Now Stalin was angry.

(e)   In 1948 Stalin expelled Yugoslavia from the Cominform.

Tito knew that Stalin would try to get rid of him, so he moved fast. He knew that the Chief of Staff of the Yugoslav army was in Moscow; when he got back, Tito had him shot. Tito also arrested over 14,000 people, in case anyone else tried to overthrow him on Stalin's orders.

For once Stalin was powerless, and could only hurl insults. The very worst insult was to accuse someone of 'Titoism'.

The Struggle for Power

Stalin died in 1953. It took time to appoint a successor. For a time the Prime Minister, *Georgi Malenkov*, and the

Secretary of the Party, *Nikita Khrushchev*, worked together. Then Malenkov resigned and *Bulganin* took his place.

Bulganin and Khrushchev then had a power struggle. In 1958, Khrushchev finally got rid of Bulganin and ruled Russia on his own.

Trouble in East Berlin

Stalin had ruled the countries of Eastern Europe as firmly as Hitler had:

- He would not allow these countries to accept Marshall Aid, so they had to go for Five-Year Plans for industry and collectivisation for agriculture, as Stalin had done in Russia in the 1930s.
- The Russians controlled the press, and set up secret police outfits.
- Even though many of these countries were very religious, the Russians started closing down the churches.

Many people saw their chance to change things when Stalin died. There were demonstrations in Czechoslovakia, but the real trouble was in East Berlin. The East German government announced that the workers must produce more, in longer hours, for a 10% pay cut. The building workers in East Berlin went on strike in protest, and soon all of East Berlin joined in. Crowds filled the streets, and burned down the headquarters of the communist party.

The Russians sent troops in to disperse the crowds. The East German government said that 25 people were killed; Western sources said that between 200 and 400 were killed. Over 25,000 people were arrested, and 42 were executed. Half of the executions were of Russian soldiers who had joined the rising.

After the rising, people carried on leaving East Germany to go and live in the West – 300,000 in 1953 alone.

The Twentieth Party Congress

In 1956 the communist party met in Moscow for its Twentieth Congress. The General Secretary of the Party, Khrushchev, gave a speech. To everyone's amazement, his speech was a fierce attack on Stalin. Up till then, everyone had seen Stalin as a hero and the saviour of his country from the Germans.

Khrushchev said:

- Stalin had been a brutal dictator and murderer.
- Stalin had established a *personality cult*, to get everyone to say how wonderful he was.
- Communists should stop trying to spread communism all over the world.
- The communist countries should *co-exist* peacefully with the West.

To everyone's amazement, in his speech Khrushchev even blamed Stalin for the break with Tito:

Source 5H

Stalin, pointing to a copy of a letter sent by Tito, asked, 'Have you read this?' Not waiting for my reply, he answered, 'I will shake my little finger – and there will be no more Tito. He will fall' . . .
But this did not happen to Tito. No matter how much or how little Stalin shook, not only his little finger but everything else

that he could shake, Tito did not fall. Why? The reason was that, in this case of disagreement with the Yugoslav comrades, Tito had behind him a state and a people who had gone through a severe school of fighting for liberty and independence, a people which gave its support to its leaders.
(*Khrushchev Remembers*, Andre Deutsch, 1971)

Communists all over the world were astounded and confused. If Stalin had been a tyrant, who could they trust to be their leader now? Some of them turned to Mao Tse-tung for leadership. Others looked to Khrushchev. Many people in the West saw his style of leadership, and liked it.

Examination Guidance

If you are looking at Russia after 1945, then the speech to the Twentieth Party Congress is very important, and you need to know what Khrushchev was getting at. Remember that Khrushchev was not a sort of 1950s Mr Gorbachev, and many of Stalin's crimes had to wait until the 1980s to be revealed in Russia. Khrushchev's main aim was to try to reunite the communist world under Russian leadership. There were too many communist leaders, such as Mao and Tito, who seemed to be branching off on their own. His speech, which was in a *secret* session of the Congress (although news of it filtered through fairly quickly to the West), tried to overcome their main objections to Stalin's brand of communism. Activity 43 will help you assess a written source such as Source 5H, and help familiarise you with this important speech.

ACTIVITY 43

Target

Evaluation and interpretation of evidence.

Question Guide

Read Source 5H carefully, then go back and check up on 'Titoism' on page 100. Think carefully about how Stalin saw Tito. Most of the questions are fairly straightforward, but Question 4 requires a bit of thought. Now have a go at the activity.

Activity

Read Source 5H.
1. Whom does Khrushchev blame for the break with Yugoslavia?
2. How does Khrushchev portray Stalin's personality?
3. In what ways does Khrushchev's view of Tito differ from Stalin's view?
4. Bearing in mind all that had happened in the communist world since 1945, why do you think Khrushchev mentioned this point about Tito in his speech?

Trouble in Poland

The Poles were delighted by Khrushchev's speech. They wanted better living conditions, cheaper food and lower taxes. They also wanted the Russians to have less control over Poland. Khrushchev's speech made them think it was safe to demand these things.

At first the Russians were alarmed, but the Polish leader reassured Khrushchev that Poland was still loyal to the Warsaw Pact. Khrushchev agreed to leave Poland alone.

Trouble in Hungary

The Hungarians kept a close eye on what was happening in Poland. We saw in Section 3 how Hungary had been taken over by a ruthless 'Muscovite', Rakosi. Rakosi was loyal to Stalin. He ruled Hungary through the brutal secret police, the AVH. Soon events in Hungary were to erupt into a major crisis – one of the most serious the Russians ever had to face.

When Stalin died, Rakosi, like many Stalinist rulers, resigned. The new ruler of Hungary was *Imre Nagy* (pronounced 'Nodge'). Nagy was very popular with the Hungarians. But Khrushchev did not trust him, and in 1956 he force Nagy to resign. The Hungarians protested at this Russian interference and there were fights between the protesters and the AVH. Nagy came back into power and immediately disbanded the AVH. The AVH did not want to be disbanded, and some AVH men fired on the crowds. The Hungarians were incensed, and some AVH men were lynched. Source 5I shows two AVH men just as they are being lined up against a wall and shot.

Nagy started releasing political prisoners who had been arrested by Rakosi. In November 1956 he told the Russians that he was taking Hungary out of the Warsaw Pact.

Khrushchev was furious. He immediately ordered Russian troops into Hungary. The Hungarians fought back with whatever weapons they had, but the Russians moved tanks into the capital, Budapest. By 14 November they had taken over the country and put a new, pro-Russian leader in power, *Janos Kadar*. Nagy was arrested and later shot.

The West protested furiously at what the Russians had done, and Russia was condemned by the UN. Khrushchev took no notice, and soon politicians were too busy with the Suez Crisis to worry about Hungary.

Examination Guidance

The Hungarian Rising is a well-known event, so you need to know about it. The main question it raises is whether or not it was an *anti-communist* rising. It's not easy to say: Nagy himself was definitely a communist, as was his government, though, like Tito, he wanted to be independent of Moscow. But many of the people Nagy released were very definitely anti-communist. Only recently on the BBC news I heard it referred to as 'the anti-communist rising of 1956'. Activity 44 will show you how different people held very different ideas about this question, often for very different reasons.

ACTIVITY 44

Target

Empathy, (i.e. looking at events from the perspective of people in the past).

Source 5I   AVH members being shot in Hungary, 1956

Source   Peter Lewis, *The Fifties*, Heinemann, 1978

Question Guide

It is quite possible for different people to hold completely different views about the same thing. In this case, different people did hold different views about what the Hungarian Rising was all about, or even if they did agree, they did so for very different reasons. When you have done this activity, ask yourself which view you agree with.

Activity

Below are four views about the events in Hungary in 1956, and four names. Put the views with the people MOST LIKELY to have agreed with them in 1956. (You may find that some names could go with more than one view, or some views with more than one name.)

1.   The events in Hungary in 1956 were an uprising of the people against communism.
2.   The events in Hungary in 1956 were an uprising by a small group of extremists against communism.
3.   The Hungarian rising was not anti-communist; it was only anti-Russian.
4.   Nagy nearly broke up the Warsaw Pact. He had to be stopped.

KHRUSHCHEV
EISENHOWER
NAGY
KADAR

AMERICA'S PROBLEMS

Like Russia, America looked strong, but she had a number of problems in the 1950s.

Spies and Traitors

Most Americans could not believe that the Russians could have made an atom bomb in 1949 without secret information. Soon it began to look as if they were right. In 1946, a British scientist, Dr Alan Nunn May, confessed to having passed secret details about the bomb to the Russians. In 1950 another British scientist, Dr Klaus Fuchs, said he had also been passing atomic secrets to the Russians. What was worse, both men had been cleared by British Intelligence, even though they were both known to be communists.

Source 5J Ethel and Julius Rosenberg under arrest

Source Peter Lewis, *The Fifties*, Heinemann, 1978

Source 5K *Question:* One of these British diplomats is a Russian spy. Which one?
Answer: The man in the white suit, leaning over the desk. He is Donald Maclean.

Source Peter Lewis, *The Cold War*, 2nd edn, Heinemann 1978

It did not stop there. In 1951 two American communists, *Julius* and *Ethel Rosenberg* (Source 5J) were sentenced to death for passing secrets about the hydrogen bomb to the Russians. Then, in the same year, came the most sensational news of all: two officials of the British Foreign Office, *Guy Burgess* and *Donald Maclean* (Source 5K) fled to Moscow. They had been Soviet agents for twenty years. Someone had tipped them off so that they could escape. Who? How many more communist agents were there?

Senator McCarthy

In America, Senator Joseph McCarthy said he knew how many there were. He announced that he had a long list of Soviet agents working inside the American government.

McCarthy forced people to appear before the *Committee on Un-American Activities*. The Committee questioned many Americans: government officials, writers, businessmen, even Hollywood film stars. Some of these people were indeed communists or had been when they were younger, but most were not and never had been. Even so, McCarthy bullied them into admitting that they were communists, and into accusing their friends as well. Some people refused to give evidence, but McCarthy said that that just proved they had something to hide. In any case, it did not much matter whether they said anything or not: the press labelled anyone who appeared before the Committee as a communist.

Even though being a communist was not actually against the law, it was normally enough to lose them their job and their friends. Sometimes they were even forbidden to travel.

At first Americans were delighted: at last someone was doing something about the communists. In 1950 one American wrote to his senator:

Source 5L

If you aren't too busy, please take a moment to tell Joe McCarthy that the plain people of America are grateful to him. (David M. Oshinsky, *A Conspiracy So Immense*, The Free Press (Macmillan), 1985, p. 159)

Source 5M Senator Joseph McCarthy

Source 5M shows McCarthy with some of the letters he received every day, supporting his work to expose communists in America.

But McCarthy got out of hand. He lied and drank heavily and made many enemies in the Senate. His big mistake was to hold hearings on communism in the US army and, what's more, to hold them on television. Thousands of Americans tuned in. Now they could actually see how he treated witnesses, and how ridiculous his accusations were. They just did not believe that the army that was fighting the North Koreans was riddled with communists, as McCarthy said it was. In 1954 the Senate closed down the Un-American Activities Committee, and criticised McCarthy severely.

Examination Guidance

Examiners like to ask you just what a source tells you about something in the past. Most sources will tell you something, but you must be aware that there is a limit to what you can learn from any source. In other words, you can deduce some things, but there are bound to be things that the source does NOT allow you to deduce. Activity 45 helps you to work out just how much you can extract from the small snippets of sources you are likely to get in the examination.

ACTIVITY 45

Target

Evaluation and interpretation of evidence.

Question Guide

What can you, and what can't you, deduce from source material? Look carefully at Sources 5L and 5M. Ask yourself: 'Why has McCarthy had himself pictured with all these letters? What am I supposed to think when I see this photograph?' Is the extract from the letter likely to be typical of what lots of American thought? And if so, what SORT of Americans were likely to think this?

Activity

Look carefully at Sources 5L and 5M
1.   Do these pieces of evidence suggest:
     (a) that many ordinary people in America supported McCarthy
     (b) that all the support McCarthy claimed he had was faked
2.   What, if anything, does this evidence tell us about:
     (a) what ordinary Americans thought about McCarthy
     (b) the use McCarthy made of the support he got
     (c) the truth of McCarthy's charges and claims

Nuclear Weapons

The atom bombs that were dropped on Hiroshima and Nagasaki were carried by *long-range bombers*. Before 1949, only the Americans had both the atom bomb and a bomber to carry it long distances. As we have seen, in 1949 the Russians exploded their own bomb. Immediately, the Americans started building an even bigger bomb, the hydrogen bomb. In 1952, as Britain exploded her first atom bomb, the Americans tested their first H-bomb. It entirely destroyed the Pacific island where it was tested. The Americans could feel safe that they were ahead in the nuclear race.

But it was only a year before the Russians too exploded an H-bomb. By 1955 they also had a long-range bomber to carry it. So the Americans pressed ahead with developing nuclear *missiles*. These did not need a bomber to carry them. Some could be launched from bases in Europe, but ICBMs (*Inter-Continental Ballistic Missiles*) could be launched from America herself.

The Americans wanted to set up bases in Europe for their missiles. Not all the Europeans were happy about this:

● The *French* did not want to see the Germans receiving nuclear missiles, and only agreed to allow West Germany into NATO if she were not allowed them. France formed her own independent nuclear force, the *force de frappe*.

● *Britain* was building up her nuclear forces too. She bought a fleet of *Polaris* submarines from America. These could fire nuclear missiles at targets many miles inland.

But not everyone wanted to see nuclear missiles in Europe at all. The British philosopher Bertrand Russell helped found the *Campaign for Nuclear Disarmament* (CND), which called on all nations to stop making nuclear weapons of all kinds. CND staged marches and got a lot of publicity, but few politicians agreed with it. The British Foreign Secretary said that any country which did not have nuclear weapons was going 'naked into the council chambers of the world'.

The Suez Crisis

By 1956 the British and French had lost large areas of their Empires. India left the British Empire in 1948, and France was forced out of Indo-China in 1954. It was looking as if Britain and France had had their day. But they were both determined to prove they were still powers to be reckoned with.

In 1952 there was a revolution in Egypt. The King was overthrown, and *Colonel Abdel Nasser* took charge. In 1956 Nasser came into conflict with Britain, France and Israel in the *Suez Crisis*. How?

1.   Egypt was a very poor country. Nasser got some economic help from Czechoslovakia, but it was not enough. He decided to build a hydroelectric dam on the River Nile to produce electricity. He also wanted to make use of the fees paid by ships using the Suez Canal.
2.   The trouble was that the Canal did not belong to Egypt: it belonged to the Suez Canal Company. The Company was owned by the British and French, and there were British troops guarding the Canal. Nasser asked the British to withdraw their troops, and in 1954 Britain agreed.
3.   Next Nasser asked the World Bank for a loan to help build the dam on the Nile. The World Bank was dominated by the Americans. They were angry with Nasser, because he had recognised communist China. They refused to lend him the money he needed.
4.   Nasser had to get hold of money somehow. The Nile was no use without the dam, and he couldn't use the Canal because it belonged to Britain and France. He decided to take the Suez Canal over. The fees from the Canal could help finance the dam. On 26 July 1956 he declared the Suez Canal nationalised.

The British and French were annoyed. The British Prime Minister, *Anthony Eden*, said Nasser was like Hitler, and that he must be stopped. Eden asked the Americans to help, but they refused. So Eden turned to France and Israel. On 29 October, the Israelis attacked Egypt. The Americans demanded a cease-fire, but on 5 November the British and French attacked as well. The Americans and the Russians were both furious and called on everyone to pull their troops out of Egypt. The Russians even hinted at a nuclear attack on London. The British and French had to withdraw their troops, and a UN force moved into the Canal zone.

The Suez Crisis showed the world how weak Britain and France had become. It almost split NATO and the Commonwealth.

After Suez, Nasser relied more and more on the Russians, so the Americans had to issue the *Eisenhower Doctrine*: they would resist any attempt to spread communism in the Middle East.

Examination Guidance

The Suez Crisis is a major topic. You will need to know about it for themes on superpower relations, on British or European history, and on the Middle East and the Arab – Israeli conflict. Activity 46a is based on a concept which can catch you off guard if you are not expecting it: *similarity and difference*. Activity 46b has another collection of source material, this time coming to you with love from LEAG. It may sound silly, but when you get a collection of source material like this don't forget to refer to it! You can point to words or passages in the sources that show what you want to say. But at the same time, don't forget that you know more about the topic than you have got here. There is nothing to stop you referring to things about Suez which are not included in these sources.

ACTIVITY 46a

Target

Terms and concepts – similarity and difference.

QUESTION GUIDE

Anthony Eden compared Nasser to Hitler, and was determined not to appease him as Chamberlain had appeased Hitler. But was Eden right to see it this way? Look back at what Hitler did in his foreign policy before 1939 (in Chapter 3). Consider also how the Israelis would have viewed Nasser and Hitler. (You might like to look ahead at the section on the Arab–Israeli Conflict in Chapter 6.)

Activity

1. Write out what Nasser actually did in 1956, before the British and French invasion.
2. For both Hitler and Nasser decide how often each of them used force to get what he wanted and put a ring round the one which most accurately describes each man:
   Hitler. Always   Often
   If there was no choice   Never
   Nasser. Always   Often
   If there was no choice   Never
3. (a) What was Hitler's main aim in the 1930s?
   (b) What was Nasser's main aim in the 1950s?
4. Do you think Eden was right to make his comparison?

ACTIVITY 46b

Target

Evaluation and interpretation of sources.

Question Guide

As with all source questions, make sure you are clear about what each source is saying, and get some idea of why it might say that. Question (b) is about memoirs – think about why people write their memoirs, and who might read them.

Activity

(LEAG, Syllabus A, Paper 2, June 1988)

The Middle East and North Africa

Study Sources 1, 2, 3 and 4, which relate to the Suez crisis of 1956, and then answer questions *(a)* to *(e)* which follow.

Source 1

There may have been mistaken judgments . . . in carrying out our policies, but the test is the motive . . . What were our motives? We had certain objectives which we believed were in the national interest. First, we had a special part to play in preventing a general outbreak of war in the Middle East. Second, Nasser was a menace and must at least be checked. Third, the Canal had to be brought back under some kind of international control.
. . . Right to the end of his life Eden believed that the Government which he had led had done what was right. Because Hitler was not checked, 20 million people had died. Eden was determined to see that it did not happen again.
(from *Suez 1956* by Selwyn Lloyd, published in 1978. Selwyn Lloyd was British Foreign Secretary in 1956)

Source 2

It is tragic that at this very time, when we are on the point of winning an immense victory over Soviet colonialism in Eastern Europe (the Hungarian revolt), we should be forced to choose between following in the footsteps of British and French colonialism in Africa, or splitting our course away from their course. Yet this decision must be made in a mere matter of hours – before five o'clock this afternoon.
(from a statement to a secret U.S. government committee made by J. F. Dulles, the U.S. Secretary of State)

Source 3

This is not a military action to separate the Israel and Egyptian troops. This is a declaration of war against the Egyptian Government in the most brutal terms. It is hard to use moderate language to describe behaviour of that sort. Will the Government stop lying to the House?
(from a statement made by a Labour M.P. in the British House of Commons)

Source 4

The Suez Canal issue was only an excuse for . . . aggressive war against the Arab people, aiming at the liquidation of the national independence of these states.
(from a letter sent by the government of the U.S.S.R. to the British government)

(a) Referring both to Source 1 and to your own knowledge, explain the British government's motives for attacking Egypt in 1956. **(5)**
(b) Source 1 is from a published book of memoirs. What

are the possible disadvantages of this kind of
source?   **(2)**

(c)   Study Source 2. Is Dulles opposed to the British and
French attack on Egypt? Give reasons for your
answer, referring in detail to the source.   **(3)**

(d)   Do Sources 2, 3 and 4 share the same view of the
Suez crisis? Refer in detail to the sources in support
of your answer.   **(6)**

(e)   Which of Sources 2 or 4 is more likely to tell you what
its author really thought? Give reasons for your
answer.   **(2)**

7 The Cold War in the 1960s

As the 1950s closed, East and West seemed to be getting
on better. The British Prime Minister, Harold Macmillan,
visited Moscow, and Khrushchev visited the United
States. Everything seemed very friendly. In fact, the Cold
War was only just entering its most dangerous stage.

THE BERLIN WALL

The Russians and East Germans were very irritated by the
Western Allies' presence in West Berlin. It was a rich and
prosperous city which all of East Germany could see.
Since 1945, 3 million East Germans had fled to the West,
most of them through West Berlin. By 1961 they were
leaving East Germany at the rate of a thousand a day. It
was beginning to harm the East German economy:
something had to be done to stop them.

In 1958 Khrushchev announced that all of Berlin,
including the Western sectors, would become part of East
Germany. When the West protested, he agreed to discuss
the matter at a summit conference, to be held in Paris in
1960. But eleven days before the summit opened, the
Russians announced that they had shot down an American spy plane over Soviet territory. At first the Americans
denied it, but the Russians produced the pilot, *Gary
Powers*. Khrushchev demanded an apology from the
Americans; President Eisenhower refused. The Paris
summit broke up in confusion.

Suddenly, on 13 August 1961, builders and soldiers
appeared on the streets in East Berlin, on the border with
West Berlin. The builders began building a wall right
across the city, separating the two halves. The Wall went
across streets, and even across houses, until West Berlin
was entirely cut off.

The new American president, *John F. Kennedy*, protested furiously, and rushed reinforcements to Berlin.
But although there were tense moments at the Wall,
there was no shooting.

Between 1961 and 1989, hundreds of East Germans
were killed trying to get across the Wall to escape to the
West.

THE CUBAN MISSILE CRISIS

In the 1950s, Cuba had been a sort of rich Americans'
playground: it was dominated by American business and
American money. But in 1959 there was a revolution in
Cuba, and the communists took over, led by *Fidel Castro*.

The Americans were determined to get rid of him. In
1961, they backed a raid by anti-Castro Cubans at the *Bay
of Pigs*. The raid was a disaster.

In Moscow, Khrushchev decided to make use of the
new communist government on Cuba. He had met
Kennedy at a meeting in Vienna and had not been
impressed. Kennedy was a lot younger, and did not have
much experience. Khrushchev may have thought he
could bully him.

The Russians set up eight rocket sites on Cuba, from
where they could launch nuclear missiles against the
USA. The Americans were flying spy planes over Cuba,
and soon discovered what was going on. The first photographs of the missile sites were taken in October 1962.

Kennedy demanded that the Russians should dismantle the missile sites. He also stationed American ships
to blockade the island. But 25 Russian ships were heading towards Cuba (Figure 5.6), presumably carrying
materials or even missiles for the sites. Both sides called
up their troops and put their nuclear forces on full alert.
The world braced itself for a nuclear war.

Figure 5.6   The Cuban missile crisis

Source   Peter Lane, *Europe since 1945*, Batsford, 1985

The Americans had a lot of support. NATO and the
Organisation of American States backed them. They also
took their case to the United Nations, and showed the
world the photographs their planes had taken of the
missile sites. The Russians could not deny the evidence of
the photographs.

Then Kennedy received two letters from Khrushchev.
The first arrived on 26 October: the Russians would
withdraw the missiles if the Americans would agree not
to invade Cuba. It looked as if the crisis was over.

But it wasn't. The next day the second letter arrived.
This time Khrushchev demanded that the Americans
withdraw their own missiles from Turkey, which were
aimed at Russia. Then an American spy plane was shot
down over Cuba, and the pilot was killed. It looked as if
war would break out after all.

At first Kennedy did not know what to do. His brother,
Robert Kennedy, suggested that he should only reply to
Khrushchev's *first* letter and ignore the second letter. So

the Americans accepted Khrushchev's offer to dismantle the missiles, and in return they promised not to invade Cuba. The Russian ships turned round and went home.

At the time, most people saw the crisis as a triumph for Kennedy. Since then, historians have tended to criticise him for taking such enormous risks. The communist world certainly saw it as a humiliating defeat for Khrushchev. He was overthrown soon afterwards, and replaced by *Leonid Brezhnev*.

One result of the crisis was that a direct telephone link was set up between the White House and the Kremlin, so that the leaders of America and Russia could speak to each other without having to send letters. The telephone link was nicknamed the 'hot line'.

Examination Guidance

Activity 47 is a sample examination question about the Cuban Missile Crisis, set by LEAG. Whichever Examination Group you are with, you should have a go at it. Like many examination questions, it gives you a number of short sources, and asks you questions about them.

ACTIVITY 47

Target

Evaluation and interpretation of evidence.

Question Guide

Read the sources through carefully, and check them against the text in the book. Remember that you won't be able to do that in the examination, so you need to make sure you know what happened when it comes to the real thing!

Activity

Latin America and the Caribbean

Study Sources 1, 2, 3 and 4 and then answer questions (a) to (d) which follow:

Source 1

'Then I had the idea of installing missiles in Cuba without letting the United States find out they were there until it was too late to do anything about them. The installation of our missiles would, I thought, restrain the U.S. from hasty military action against Castro's government . . . The Americans had surrounded our country with military bases . . . and now they would learn just what it feels like to have enemy missiles pointing at you.'
(from 'Khrushchev Remembers')

Source 2

'This urgent transformation of Cuba into an important strategic base – by the presence of these large, long-range, and clearly offensive weapons of sudden mass destruction – constitutes an explicit threat to the peace and security of all the Americas . . .
Acting, therefore, in the defence of our own security and of the entire Western Hemisphere . . . I have directed that the following initial steps be taken immediately: . . .'
(from President Kennedy's broadcast of 22 October 1962)

Source 3

'There could be no deal made under this kind of pressure . . . However, I said, President Kennedy had been anxious to remove these missiles from Turkey and Italy for a long period of time . . .'
(adapted from Robert Kennedy's own story of the crisis)

Source 4

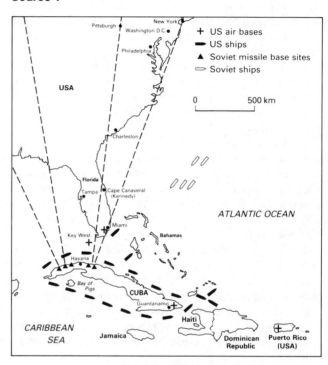

(a) (i) Study Source 1. What does Khrushchev give as his reasons for the installation of missile sites in Cuba? **(2)**
(ii) How justified do you think Khrushchev's claims were? **(2)**

(b) (i) Study Source 2. What does President Kennedy consider to be the aims of Khrushchev and the USSR? **(3)**
(ii) Describe features from Source 4 which would support President Kennedy's view. **(2)**

(c) (i) What does Source 4 show to have been President Kennedy's *initial steps* (line 10) to counteract this threat? **(2)**
(ii) What alternative courses of action were open to President Kennedy and why did he NOT choose them? **(3)**

(d) (i) From Sources 1 and 3 what was the *deal* (line 11) which had been put forward to solve this crisis? **(2)**
(ii) Describe the events which led to the settlement of this crisis. **(4)**

CZECHOSLOVAKIA

For most of the 1960s, Czechoslovakia's economy was in a mess. There were not enough houses for the people, and the transport network was in chaos. The government was an old-style, Stalinist group which did whatever Moscow told it to do. There was strict censorship of the press, and all opponents of the government were arrested.

By 1967 the Czechs had had enough. There were demonstrations against the government, and in 1968 the President resigned. The new leader was *Alexander Dubček*.

Dubček started to change things. He allowed the press to print what it liked, and released a number of political prisoners. Even more importantly, he gave power back to the National Assembly, the Czech parliament, and talked of allowing non-communist parties to sit in it. Dubček described this as 'communism with a human face'. His period in office became known as the *Prague Spring*.

Now, does all this remind you of anything? It should do, if you read about what Imre Nagy did in Hungary in 1956, and what happened there. Dubček was very aware that people would compare him with Nagy, so he was careful to point out the differences. Above all, he stressed that he was not going to take Czechoslovakia out of the Warsaw Pact.

Even so, the new Soviet leader, Brezhnev, did not like what he was hearing from Prague. In May 1968 he moved Russian troops up to the Czech border, and in the summer Warsaw Pact troops held manoeuvres inside Czechoslovakia itself.

In July 1968, Dubček went to meet the Russian leaders, and in August he met leaders from all the Warsaw Pact countries at Bratislava. He assured them that Czechoslovakia would remain a loyal communist country, but he wanted Czechoslovakia to be free to sort out its problems in its own way. For the moment Brezhnev agreed.

But Brezhnev did not want this idea spreading, so he was alarmed when two other communist leaders, Ceaucescu of Romania and Tito, visited Dubček in Prague. Brezhnev decided to stop the changes. On 21 August, Russian troops invaded Czechoslovakia and tanks moved into Prague. Dubček was placed under arrest. Czechoslovakia had gone the way of Hungary after all.

There were huge protests at the Russian invasion. Even communist countries like China, Albania and Yugoslavia protested. The Americans said it was part of the *Brezhnev Doctrine*: the idea that Russia would use force to keep any communist state in line with Moscow.

Examination Guidance

You need to be able to take a long-term view over a period that you have looked at, in order to reach some sort of a judgement about it. In Activity 48a, you need to ask yourself whether one side or the other was winning the Cold War. This is a useful exercise to practise for essay-type questions. Then, to finish up with, Activity 48b is another revision test on those terms which you must be able to recognise and understand.

ACTIVITY 48a

Target

Selection and deployment of relevant knowledge.

Question Guide

Look back over this chapter at the events listed below. Ask yourself what each side was gaining and losing in terms of (a) land or territory; (b) influence or control; (c) money or trade; (d) lives or equipment ; (e) prestige at home or abroad. Bear these categories in mind as you do this exercise.

Activity

Look at each of the crises listed below. Put in the correct columns what, if anything, each side gained or lost from them:

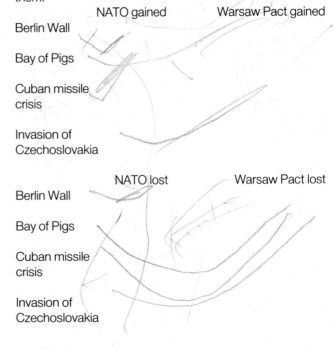

NATO gained   Warsaw Pact gained

Berlin Wall

Bay of Pigs

Cuban missile crisis

Invasion of Czechoslovakia

NATO lost   Warsaw Pact lost

Berlin Wall

Bay of Pigs

Cuban missile crisis

Invasion of Czechoslovakia

ACTIVITY 48b

Target

Terms and concepts.

Question Guide

You need to know what the various terms used in this chapter mean. Test yourself now, and then come back to this list later in your revision.

Activity

Write a sentence to show what each of these were:

Katyn

Partisans

ELAS

Gulags

salami tactics

the Truman Doctrine

Marshall Aid

the Cominform

NATO

the 38th parallel

Pyongyang

SEATO

conspiracy theory

the Warsaw Pact

the Geneva Spirit

brinkmanship

Titoism

the Twentieth Party Congress

the AVH

Burgess and Maclean

Committee on Un-American Activities

ICBMs

CND

the Eisenhower Doctrine

the Bay of Pigs

the 'hot line'

the Prague Spring

the Brezhnev Doctrine

THE MODERN WORLD, 1962–90

I'm sorry about this, but things now get a little less straightforward. The history books start to look at other parts of the world, such as Africa and South America, which they have hardly mentioned up till now. This chapter does not try to cover all these areas. It brings the story of *International Relations* more or less up to date. Don't forget that **International Relations** may well be the core theme for your course.

Examination Guide

This chapter covers parts of Section 3 of the MEG core content on **International Relations**. It also covers part of Topic G, **The Arab–Israeli Conflict since 1945**, Topic H, **The Achievement of Independence in South and South-East Asia**, and Topic 1, **The Achievement of Independence in Africa**.

You will need this chapter for parts of your compulsory NEA Theme 1, **Conflict and Conciliation**, especially for section (d), **Attempts to Resolve Conflict**. It will also be useful for much of Theme 3, **International co-operation**, especially at Section (b), **The United Nations**, and Section (c), **Post War Co-operation in Western Europe**.

For the LEAG syllabus parts of this chapter are relevant for sections:
C1 **Arab-Israeli Relations since 1948,** and E1 **The League of Nations and the United Nations** and for most of the other sections, in particular: E2 **The Population Explosion and Global Resources since 1945**, F2 **Britain's Changing World Role since 1945**, G2 **The USSR's Relations with Eastern Europe since 1945**, I2 **Superpower Relations, 1945–75**, and J2 **The Vietnam War and its impact on Indo-China and the USA.**

For SEG, this chapter will help you with Theme 1, **The Development and Impact of The USA and The USSR as World Superpowers**.

Topic Guide

1 Russia and China: the Sino-Soviet Split

The two communist superpowers, Russia and China, soon fell out with each other. This is called the Sino-Soviet Split (don't be put off by the words: 'Sino-' is just a posh term for Chinese). Why did it happen?

Everything started well enough. Mao Tse-tung made the only trip abroad in his life in 1950, when he travelled to Moscow and visited Stalin. The two leaders signed a treaty of friendship and alliance. The West looked on in horror.

But don't be fooled by smiling photographs like Source 6A. Stalin did not like Mao, and Mao had not forgotten

Source 6A   Mao and Khrushchev in Peking. What might be a possible date for this photograph?

Source   Hugh Higgins, *The Cold War*, 2nd edn, Heinemann Educational, 1987

how Stalin had not helped him when he was fighting the Kuomintang, back in the 1930s (see Chapter 11). Still, for the moment Mao was happy to accept Stalin as the leader of the communist world, while Stalin promised to give China as much economic aid as he could.

This happy state of affairs lasted precisely six years. In 1956 Mao read Khrushchev's speech to the Twentieth Party Congress (see Source 5I). He could not believe what he was reading. Here was Khrushchev – Mao said – going *directly* against the teaching of Marx and Lenin!

In 1969, an American journalist wrote a book called *The Coming War between Russia and China*. In his book, he said this:

Source 6B

When the Russians add up the record the answer is 'no' to the question, Is Mao a Communist? As for Mao, he is equally firm. Moscow is not Communist. The Kremlin, in Mao's view, has abandoned Marx for Wall Street. Neither side sees the other as Communist. Therefore there is no *ideological barrier* for hostility, conflict, war.
(Harrison E. Salisbury, *The Coming War Between Russia and China*, Pan Books 1969, p. 85)

Let's look more closely at where Mao disagreed with Khrushchev, because it's important:

Khrushchev said:	*Mao said:*
● Stalin was a brutal tyrant.	● Stalin was a good, firm leader of the communist world.
● East and West should co-exist peacefully.	● The West was the enemy and could not be trusted.
● There should be no more communist revolutions.	● Communists should work for revolution all over the world.

Mao and Khrushchev disagreed sharply over the events of the 1950s and 1960s:

1.   Mao was worried by the risings in East Berlin, Poland and Hungary (see Chapter 5, Section 6): it was he who insisted that the Hungarian leader, Imre Nagy, should be executed.

2. On the other hand, Khrushchev was worried at the way Mao was challenging the Americans. They were still supporting Chiang Kai-shek, who was now based on the island of *Formosa (Taiwan)*. Khrushchev was afraid that Mao would provoke the Americans into a nuclear war.
3. The Russians were not impressed with Mao's 'Great Leap Forward' (see Chapter 11). They said it would not work, and it didn't. Mao said the Russians just could not understand a communist revolution based on peasants instead of workers.
4. Things got worse as the 1950s ended. Mao criticised Khrushchev for visiting the West, and said Russia was no longer fit to lead the communist world. Other communist countries started to take sides between Moscow and Peking.
5. In 1962 Mao said Khrushchev should not have backed down in the Cuban Missile crisis (see Chapter 5, Section 7).
6. Mao attacked the Test Ban Treaty of 1963 (see Section 5 below).
7. The Russians refused to share their nuclear secrets with the Chinese, and supported India when Mao attacked her in 1962.
8. When Mao launched the Cultural Revolution (see page 217), the Russians attacked it just as much as the West did.
9. Meanwhile China was becoming a superpower independent of Russia. She exploded her own atom bomb in 1964, and an H-bomb three years later.
10. China refused to attend the Twenty-Second Party Congress in Moscow in 1966, and attacked the Russian invasion of Czechoslovakia (see Chapter 5, Section 7).

Worst of all, there were clashes between guards along the 4,500-mile frontier between the two countries. In the worst clash, in 1969, 31 Russian border guards were killed.

The Americans watched all this with interest. Officially, they were strongly against Mao, and still supported Chiang Kai-shek. Not only that, but during the Vietnam War China sent help to the North Vietnamese. But when President Nixon decided to pull America out of Vietnam, he also aimed for better relations with China. In 1971, the Americans agreed to recognise communist China. This meant that Mao's China could enter the UN and take her seat on the Security Council. The next year, Nixon visited Peking and met Mao Tse-tung. This time it was the Russians who looked on in alarm.

Examination Guidance

If you are studying more recent history, from the 1960s onwards, then you need to know about the Sino-Soviet split.

ACTIVITY 49

Target

Evaluation and interpretation of historical evidence.

Question Guide

One big danger that historians always have to guard against is *hindsight*. This is judging things in the past because you know, looking back, what really happened and what didn't. It's a danger, because it makes you forget that people alive at the time didn't know what was going to happen – they didn't have the advantage of hindsight. In fact, they didn't know as much as you do about what they were doing! But that does *not* mean that they were stupid, or that they were entirely wrong. This exercise should help you to understand that.

Read Source 6B carefully. (*Ideological* means to do with political ideas.) Why might people think there would be an *ideological barrier* to war between Russia and China?

Now, there is one small problem: war has not broken out between Russia and China! But this does not mean that the book was *all* wrong, nor does it mean that it is of no use to a historian.

Activity

Read Source 6B and then answer these questions:
1. Check what Harrison E. Salisbury says in this extract against what you already know about Russia and China by 1969. How much of what he says is *right*, and how much is *wrong*?
2. What does he tell us about what these people thought about Russia and China in 1969? (Think carefully about who might have read the book – it was a best seller.)
   (a) the American government
   (b) the Chinese government
   (c) the Russian government
   (d) Western journalists and newspaper readers
3. How is this extract useful to the historian? Explain your answer carefully.

2 The Vietnam War

Forget *Rambo* and *Platoon* for the moment, and any other film you may have seen about Vietnam: they are simply different types of evidence about the way people still remember the Vietnam War. What you will need to know about is what happened in the war itself.

Look at a map. Vietnam is a long, thin country along the coast of Indo-China. It was conquered by the French in the nineteenth century and became a French colony. During the Second World War, it was taken over by the Japanese. The communist resistance was led by *Ho Chi Minh*, and was called the *Vietminh*. In 1945, the Vietminh took control of the north of the country, and set up a capital at *Hanoi*; the south, with its capital at *Saigon*, was given back to the French. War between the Vietminh and the French began almost at once.

THE FRENCH WAR

The French had some help from the Americans, but the Vietminh had massive support from China. In 1954 a French army was cut off and defeated at *Dien Bien Phu*. The French pulled out of Vietnam.

Figure 6.1 Vietnam

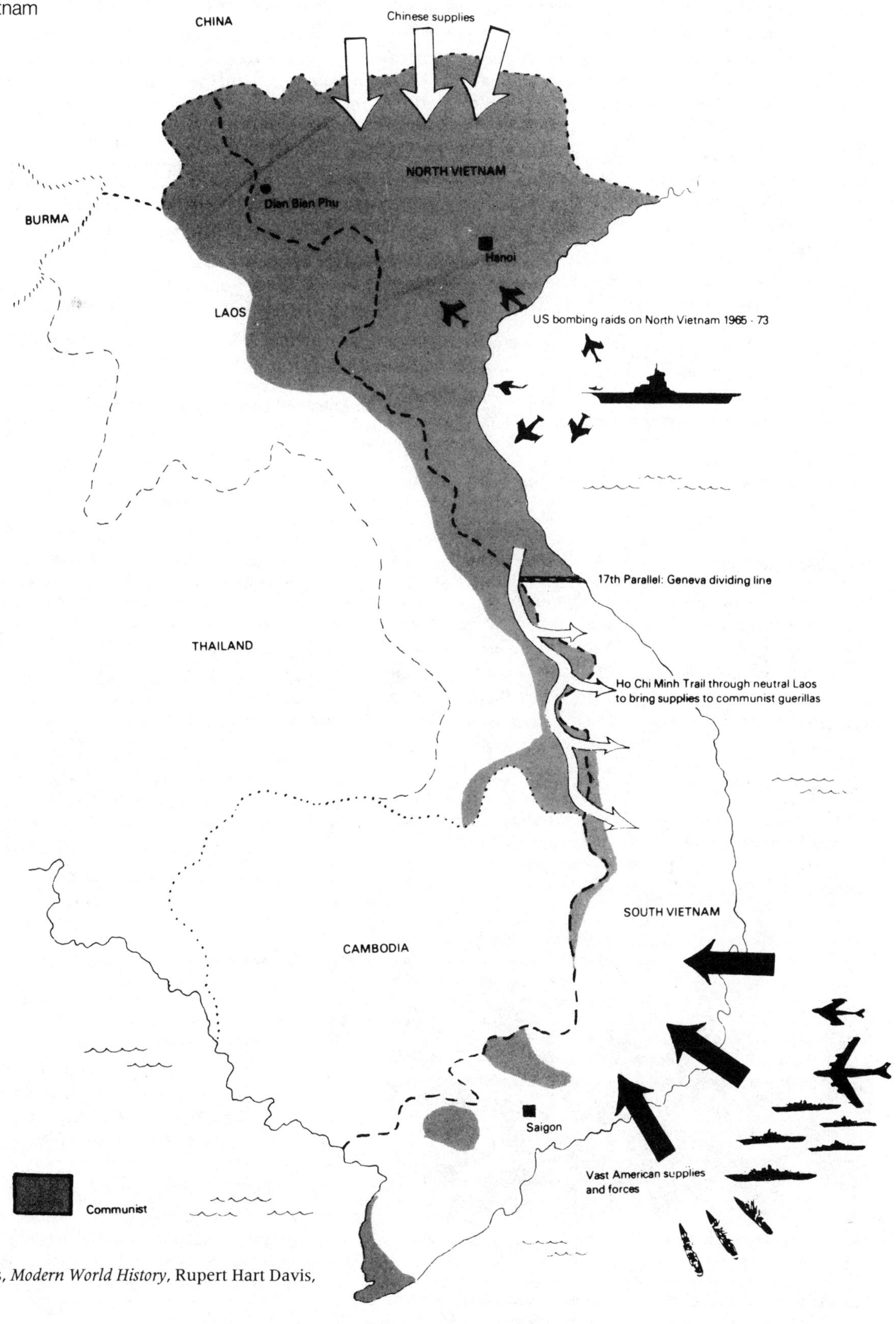

Source Peter Moss, *Modern World History*, Rupert Hart Davis, 1978

Vietnam was discussed at the Geneva Conference in 1954 (see Chapter 5, Section 6). The conference decided that North and South Vietnam should be joined together and the people should elect their own government.

But neither Ho Chi Minh nor the southern leader, *Ngo Dinh Diem*, intended to hold elections. Diem was a tough, harsh leader, and very unpopular with his people. South Vietnamese communists, called *Vietcong*, began to attack Diem's army posts.

The Vietcong had help from North Vietnam. It came down a track hacked out through the jungle in Laos and Cambodia. This track was called the *Ho Chi Minh Trail* (see Figure 6.1).

Diem asked the Americans for help against the Vietcong. President Kennedy sent 2,000 military 'advisers' into South Vietnam. (They were called 'advisers' because the President needed permission from the Senate to send *troops* abroad, but he could send as many *advisers* as he liked.) In fact, these 'advisers' were American troops. By 1964 there were 23,000 of them. But even they could not protect Diem against his own people: in 1963 he was overthrown and killed in a military *coup*.

Meanwhile North Vietnam was getting more and more aggressive. In April 1964 it seems that North Vietnamese gunboats fired on two US destroyers in the *Gulf of Tonkin*. The US Senate immediately passed the *Gulf of Tonkin Resolution*. This said:

Source 6C

Naval units of the Communist regime in Viet Nam . . . have deliberately and repeatedly attacked United States naval vessels lawfully present in international waters . . . These attacks are part of a deliberate and systematic campaign of aggression that the Communist regime in North Viet Nam has been waging against its neighbours.
(M. J. C. Vile (ed.), *The Presidency*, Harrap, 1974, p. 190)

It also allowed President Johnson to send American troops into South Vietnam. The first ones arrived the next year.

THE AMERICAN WAR

The Americans believed that if Vietnam fell to communism, other countries would follow, like a line of dominoes. This idea was called the *Domino Theory*. The Americans said something had to be done to *contain* communism – i.e. to stop it from spreading. Some countries in south-east Asia agreed with this, and Thailand, South Korea, Australia and New Zealand all sent troops to help South Vietnam. But most of America's allies disagreed, and refused to get involved. The UN did not support America either. Even more than Korea, this was to be an American war.

Source 6D   Australian troops in Vietnam

Source   Topham Picture Library

Vietnam became one of the most painful and controversial periods in American history. Poems, songs and films have all been made about it. There are various reasons for this:

- It was the first major war to be fought in front of TV cameras. All wars are terrible, but Vietnam was the first whose horror could be seen each evening in people's homes.
- It happened at the same time as a revolution in attitudes and life-style among young people. Many of the American soldiers who went to Vietnam found

they did not believe in what they were fighting for. Many young Americans drafted into the army fled to Canada rather than fight in Vietnam.
- It was the first war the Americans had ever lost.

The Vietcong fought in small guerilla groups. The Americans under General Westmoreland fought back with heavy bombing to destroy the Vietcong's hideouts: *Operation Rolling Thunder*, launched in March 1965. They also used *napalm*, a chemical acid which kills vegetation and burns people. The bombing did not destroy the Vietcong hideouts, and it turned many more ordinary Vietnamese against the Americans.

There were terrible atrocities on both sides, but American atrocities tended to be more widely reported. The effects of the bombing on ordinary Vietnamese people were shown on TV. When an American patrol massacred some 200–500 South Vietnamese villagers at *My Lai*, world opinion was appalled. One American soldier described My Lai:

Source 6E

It was a sullen, hostile, unpeopled place. We'd go among the My Lai villages and there were never any people: deserted, and yet there were smoldering fires – people obviously lived there. It was a place where men died . . . And in a sense the area of My Lai itself became the enemy, not the people of My Lai, not even the Viet Cong, but the place . . . We took revenge, burning down huts, blowing up tunnels.
(Michael Maclear, *Vietnam: the Ten Thousand Day War*, Thames Methuen, 1986 edn, p. 375)

At the start of 1968, US marines were surrounded by the North Vietnamese Army (*NVA*) at an old French base, *Khe Sanh*. Pictures of the siege were shown on American TV: it was the first most Americans knew that things were not going well. One TV commentator said: 'What the hell is going on? I thought we were winning this war.'

THE TET OFFENSIVE

At the Chinese New Year ('Tet') in 1968, the NVA launched a major attack. This *Tet Offensive* caught the Americans by surprise, because it seemed to be happening everywhere at once, even in places behind the American lines. But when they recovered, they drove the NVA back with heavy losses. North Vietnam had been badly hit, and decided to talk peace. Talks opened in Paris.

The new US president, *Richard Nixon*, had decided to start pulling the Americans out of Vietnam and handing the war over to the South Vietnamese. This was called *Vietnamisation*. But he did not want to abandon South Vietnam altogether. In 1970 he ordered an invasion of *Cambodia*, to destroy the Vietcong bases there. Even though the invasion worked, many Americans were furious at the way Nixon was extending the war – especially as he had actually promised that he would not invade Cambodia.

In 1972 the NVA launched another offensive. Like the Tet Offensive, it ran out of steam, but it reminded the Americans that North Vietnam had not gone away. In 1973 a ceasefire was signed at the Paris peace talks, and the Americans pulled out of Vietnam.

North and South Vietnam remained divided, and the

Vietcong stepped up their attacks. In 1975 North Vietnam invaded, and South Vietnam collapsed. The President fled to Britain, and his capital, Saigon, was renamed Ho Chi Minh City.

Examination Guidance

Vietnam was special. It was THE important event of the 1960s, and many of your teachers and examiners will remember it vividly. In a way, you will find that they *want* you to know about it, because it was a very important time for them. Don't be misled by this, though: you must judge the Vietnam War historically, just like anything else. Activity 50a is familiar territory: assessing a photograph, in this case, one of the most famous photographs to come out of the war. Activity 50b is based on Source 6E in the text, and asks you to try to start to understand what turned ordinary Americans into killers.

It's easy to make a mistake when you look at a question on an examination paper, and say 'That's a question about such-and-such' – as in Activity 50c from MEG. Look at the questions that follow the sources very carefully: are they about the *topic*, or are they about *the way in which it was reported?*

ACTIVITY 50a

Target

Evaluation and interpretation of historical evidence.

Question Guide

Be careful with photographs, even ones which appear to tell a straightforward story. Remember that you are seeing it in a history textbook (or on a hand-out, or on an examination paper, or wherever), but where was it *originally* seen? Why was it taken? Is it designed to appeal to your emotions? If so – and this one is – then you must be extra careful in deciding exactly what it tells you, and – perhaps even more importantly – what it *doesn't*.

Now look carefully at Source 6F, taken in Vietnam in 1972. It shows Vietnamese children fleeing from an American napalm attack. First get clear in your mind what you are looking at. What has happened to the girl's clothes? As it happens, the children are running right into a bunch of news photographers and TV cameramen, and this picture was picked up by news agencies and shown all over the world. This makes it very useful to the historian.

Activity

What, in your opinion does Source 6F tell us about:
(a) how the South Vietnamese viewed the Americans
(b) how the Americans treated the South Vietnamese
(c) how the war was reported in the press and on TV
(d how effective American bombing was
(e) what happened to these children
(f) world opinion about the war

Source 6F   Vietnamese children run from an American napalm raid, 1972

Source   S. M. Harrison, *Warfare and Conflict in the Twentieth Century*, Macmillan, 1988

ACTIVITY 50b

Target

Empathy (i.e. looking at events from the perspective of people in the past).

Question Guide

No one in their right mind is going to say to you: 'Imagine you are an American soldier at My Lai. You have just massacred between 200 and 500 unarmed Vietnamese villagers.' Still, that is what happened, and it is important to try to understand how it could happen (just as it is important to understand how ordinary Germans became SS killers). Read Source 6E very carefully.

Activity

1. In what way, if any, does Source 6E help *explain* the massacre at My Lai?
2. In what way, if any, does it help *excuse* the massacre?

ACTIVITY 50c

Targets

Evaluation and interpretation of sources; selection and deployment of relevant knowledge.

Question Guide

Look carefully at Source 3: it's a very powerful picture, and the most important source in this collection. There's no doubt that this event really happened. There's film of it available, which shows that the man was shot dead seconds after this photo was taken. Examiners get a little bit tired of answers which *always* take the 'How-do-we-know-this-isn't-a-cunning-forgery?' line. (Nine times out of ten, you can rest assured that the sources you are presented with are genuine.) The question is, WHY did it happen? Was the police chief after propaganda – and both sides could make use of a photograph like that – or did he not care about the cameras recording what he was doing? Was he trying to scare the Vietcong? To reassure the South Vietnamese? Or was he not trying to do anything except execute a Vietcong prisoner?

Question 5, which carries most marks, mentions the word 'mistake'. That word should always set alarm bells ringing in your head. One way to work out if someone in the past was making a mistake is to go through a set of questions like these:

1. What did the Vietcong *want* from the Tet Offensive? (To push the Americans back? To scare the Americans? To scare the South Vietnamese? To influence US public opinion? etc.)
2. Did they get what they wanted?
3. Did they gain anything else on top of what they wanted?
4. What did they lose in the offensive?
5. In the *short term*, did they lose more than they gained?
6. In the *long term*, did they lose more than they gained?

When you've thought about that, you are in a better position to decide if the Tet Offensive was a mistake.

Activity

(MEG, Modern World, Paper 2, June 1989, Topic H)

THE ACHIEVEMENT OF INDEPENDENCE IN SOUTH AND SOUTH-EAST ASIA

Look carefully at Sources 1–5. Then answer **all** the questions.

Source 1

A modern historian describes the Tet Offensive in Vietnam.
In September, 1967, the NLF launched a series of attacks on American garrisons. General Westmoreland, the US commander in Vietnam, was delighted. Now at last the NLF was engaging in open combat. At the end of 1967, he was able to report that the NLF had lost 90,000 men. He told President Johnson that the NLF would be unable to replace such numbers and that the end of the war was in sight.
On the evening of 31 January, when it was expected that the NLF would be celebrating the Tet New Year festival, 70,000 of their own men launched a surprise attack on more than a hundred cities and towns in Vietnam.
In this campaign they lost an estimated 37,000 soldiers compared with 2,500 Americans.

Source 2

A US magazine describes the reporting of the Tet Offensive, February 1968.
WAR HITS SAIGON screamed the front page of Washington's 'The News'. But newspapers paled beside television coverage, which that evening projected the offensive into the living rooms of 50 million Americans. There, on colour screens, dead bodies lay amid the rubble and rattle of automatic gunfire as dazed American soldiers and civilians ran back and forth trying to fight off the attackers. Audiences heard the frightened voice of a T.V. correspondent on the spot, doing his best to explain the chaotic situation.

Source 3

A photograph of the execution of a Vietcong prisoner in Saigon by the police chief Nguyen Ngoc Loan. This photograph was published widely, for example on the front page of the London Evening News, 1 February 1968.
(MEG, Modern World, Paper 2, June 1989, Topic H, pp 24–26)

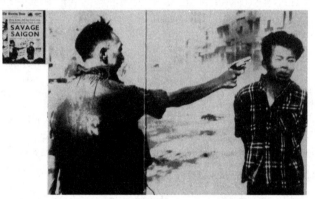

Source 4

Two comments by American military leaders on the US media coverage of the Tet Offensive.
(i) *General Maxwell Taylor.*
The picture of a few houses, presented by a gloomy-voiced television reporter as an example of the destruction caused in Saigon, created the inevitable impression that this was what it was like in all or most of the city.
(ii) *Admiral Grant Sharp.*
The reality of the 1968 Tet Offensive was that Hanoi had taken a big gamble and had lost on the battlefield, but they won a solid psychological victory in the United States because of biased reporting in the media.

Source 5

Graph showing trends in support for the war in Vietnam (as shown in public opinion polls in the USA).

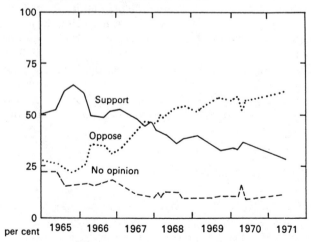

1　Read Source 1.
　　Why was the attack of 31 January 1968 described as 'a surprise attack'? **(2)**

2   Look at Source 5.
    How was the year 1967 important with regard to the attitudes of the American people towards the war in Vietnam?   **(2)**

3   Look at Source 3.
    Is this photograph a record of events or propaganda? Explain your answer fully.   **(6)**

4   Read Sources 2 and 4, and look at Source 3.
    Do these sources prove that the media reports on the war in Vietnam were unreliable? Explain your answer fully.   **(8)**

5   Read all the sources.
    'The Tet Offensive proved to be a serious mistake by the leaders of the Vietcong.' Do these sources show this view to be true? Explain your answer fully.   **(12)**

3 The Middle East

THE ARAB–ISRAELI CONFLICT

The Middle East has been a scene of violence and fighting almost non-stop since the First World War. The causes are very complicated. This has not stopped the Americans and Russians from getting involved, the Americans usually on the side of the Israelis, and the Russians usually on the side of the Arabs.

Formation of the State of Israel, 1948

In 1919 the League of Nations took over Palestine from the Turks and entrusted it to Britain as a Mandate. However, Jews all over the world claimed it as their Promised Land, and began to emigrate there in large numbers. The Palestinian Arabs who lived there protested loudly at this, so the British tried to stop Jews from coming in. However, Jewish terrorist groups hit back by attacking British soldiers. In 1948 Britain withdrew and handed Palestine back to the League's successor, the United Nations. The UN immediately declared the State of Israel.

The Wars of 1948 and 1956

The Arabs were furious, and attacked the new state. Israel beat them off, and took over large areas of Arab lands. Huge numbers of Palestinian Arabs fled from Israel and settled in the neighbouring Arab states (see Source 6G).

In 1956 Israel joined Britain and France in an attack on Egypt. This was the Suez Crisis (see Chapter 5, Section 6). Although Israel did better than her allies, and took some land over from Egypt, she had to hand it back when the war ended.

The Six-Day War, 1967

In 1967, four Arab states, Egypt, Syria, Jordan and Iraq, planned another attack on Israel. The Israelis got wind of the plan, however, and attacked first with devastating force. The Egyptian air force was destroyed in a single day. The Arabs were thrown back, and Israel took over three areas, *Sinai* (including the *Gaza Strip*), the *Golan Heights*, and the *West Bank* of the Jordan (see Figure 6.2).

Source 6G   A Palestinian refugee camp

Source   Robert Wolfson (ed.), *Conflict in the Middle East*, Links Series

Figure 6.2   Israel and the disputed territories

Source   William R. Keylor, *The Twentieth Century World*, Oxford University Press, 1984

Al Fatah and the PLO

The Palestinians had two groups of their own which tried to get rid of Israel: the *Palestine Liberation Organisation*

Source 6H   A British airliner is blown up by Palestinian terrorists, 1970

Source   Popperfoto

(*PLO*), backed by the other Arab states, and the more exreme *Al Fatah*, led by Yasser Arafat. After the 1967 war, Al Fatah took over the PLO and made it much more violent. The PLO launched raids and terrorist attacks across the border into Israel. PLO terrorists hijacked three airliners in 1970, flew them to Jordan and blew them up in front of news cameras (see Source 6H). Two years later, PLO terrorists killed eleven members of the Israeli team at the Munich Olympics.

But the Arab states were worried that the PLO was getting too strong. King Hussein of Jordan was even afraid that the PLO would take over his country. In September 1970 his army attacked the PLO and drove the Palestinians out of Jordan.

The Yom Kippur War, 1973

By 1973 Egypt and Syria were ready to avenge their defeat in 1967. They launched a surprise attack on the Jewish holy day of *Yom Kippur*. The Israelis were driven back at first, but then they recovered and drove the attacks off so successfully that the Russians threatened to intervene. The Americans put their nuclear forces on alert to support Israel, but the Israelis agreed to make peace.

One important result of the Yom Kippur War was the Arab *oil boycott*. The Arab states stopped all exports of oil to countries which had supported Israel, creating an oil crisis throughout the West. At the time, it showed how much the West depended on the Arab states; since then, many Western countries have developed alternative sources of oil.

The Camp David Agreements

After the Yom Kippur War, *President Sadat* of Egypt decided to talk with Israel. He flew to Tel Aviv in 1977 and met the Israeli Prime Minister, *Menachem Begin*. President Carter of the USA then invited them both to meet again at his hunting lodge, *Camp David*. They all met there the next year, and Egypt and Israel agreed to sign a peace treaty (Treaty of Washington, 1979). Israel handed all of Sinai back to Egypt except the Gaza Strip, and Egypt agreed not to help the PLO. The Arabs were furious with Sadat, and in 1981 a group of fanatics assassinated him in front of his wife.

Israel Invades Lebanon, 1982

Lebanon lies to the north of Israel. It is a half-Muslim, half-Christian country, and in the 1970s men of both religions sat in its governments. Many Palestinians had fled to Lebanon. After the PLO was thrown out of Jordan and Egypt, Lebanon became a very important PLO base. This meant that the Israelis launched raids over the border into Lebanon. Although many Lebanese blamed Israel for these raids, others, especially Christians, blamed the Palestinians. In the south, near the border with Israel, the PLO had virtually taken over from the Lebanese government, and the Lebanese resented it. Then the PLO decided to get rid of the Lebanese government, and helped start up a civil war. Many Lebanese now saw the Palestinians as a thorough nuisance, and were delighted when Israel bombarded PLO positions in Beirut. Lebanese Christians, on the Israeli side, massacred Palestinian refugees in two camps, Sabra and Chatila. The PLO were forced to leave Lebanon.

However, the Israelis decided, unwisely, to stay on. The Lebanese had not got rid of one lot of unwelcome foreigners just to swap them for another: inspired by the Islamic revolution in Iran (see page 119), they fought back against the Israelis and forced them out of the country. The country fell into a complex civil war of rival Muslim groups and Christian groups, all fighting for power.

The war in Lebanon has been made even more complicated by the issue of *hostages*. A number of Muslim groups, often claiming backing from Iran, have recently seized Westerners living in Beirut, and have held them hostage. Sometimes they have demanded the release of Arabs held in Israel or in Western countries, but sometimes they have not issued any demands. The most well-known hostage is *Terry Waite*, who had negotiated the release of some hostages before being taken hostage himself in 1987.

To the End of the 1980s

Many problems still remain unsolved:

- Israel refuses to give up the West Bank and the Gaza Strip, which it has held since 1967. Some people see this as a possible area for a Palestinian state, but Israel is filling it with Jewish settlements.

- In December 1987, the Palestinians living in Israel staged a rising called the *Intifada*, which is still going on. The Israelis replied with shootings and beatings, which lost them much support in the world.

- In 1988 Yasser Arafat declared that the PLO was ready to give up violence and talk with Israel. Instead of demanding that Israel be destroyed, it is now prepared to settle for a separate Palestinian homeland. This idea won the support of many world leaders, but Israel still refused to talk to the PLO.

Examination Guidance

This is a major topic, which sometimes stands as a separate special topic at GCSE, and sometimes fits into wider topics. Either way, you need to know your way round it. I'd be fooling you if I said it was a straightforward topic, and I'm afraid it's getting more complicated almost by the month at the moment. However, the basic problem is straightforward: the Israelis and the Palestinians both lay claim to the same land. Activity 51a is about the latest phase of this easy-to-remember (but very-difficult-to-solve) problem. Activity 51b is a structured essay question, set by SEG in 1988. It looks at the wars of 1956 and 1967. It's an exercise in similarity and difference.

ACTIVITY 51a

Target

Terms, concept of cause.

Question Guide

The Middle East is one of those topics where you are sometimes asked to say how the present-day situation arose from events in the past. In fact, this is hard to do here, especially as the Iranian Revolution and the war in Lebanon have both served to make things even more complicated than they were before. However, don't despair: this exercise will help you.

Activity

On 24 July 1989, *The Times* carried this report:

Source 6l

Schools reopen: Primary schools for almost 200,000 Palestinians in the occupied territories reopened on Saturday last after being closed for six months on the orders of the Israeli Army.

No reopening date has yet been set for the higher grades.

('The higher grades' means the higher years – i.e. the secondary schools.)

1. What are 'the occupied territories' referred to?
2. Why might the Israeli army have ordered that Palestinian schools should be closed? (Suggest as many reasons as you can, and then check them, either with your teacher or by looking through newspaper reports in your local library.)
3. What are the *short-term*, and what are the *long-term* reasons behind this piece of news?

ACTIVITY 51b

Targets

Terms and concepts – causation, similarity and difference; selection and deployment of relevant knowledge.

Question Guide

These questions ask you to do three things. First, you have to explain why the 1956 war broke out. That's a question about causation – why things happen. It's just a matter of getting the long-term and short-term causes clear in your mind. Then it asks you to describe the main events. Notice that this carries fewer marks than either of the other two parts. Don't skimp on it, but don't spend too long on it either. You should not need to give any more than you have got on pages 104–105 (but don't copy them out – that really is a waste of time, and the chances are that you won't remember it afterwards). The third question is about similarity and difference: you have to compare the wars of 1956 and 1967. To do that, you have to look at both wars. What were the reasons for the war in 1956? What were the reasons in 1967? Were they the same? . . . and so on. As always in GCSE, you'll do better if you give most thought to *explaining* your answer.

Activity

(SEG, Syllabus 2, Paper 2, Summer 1988, p.4)

The Arab–Israeli Conflict, 1947–1973

(a) Why in 1956 did war break out in the Middle East?   **(10 marks)**

(b) Describe the main events of the war of 1956.   **(8 marks)**

(c) 'War involving Israel and her neighbours occurred once more in 1967. This war began in the same way and took place for the same reasons as the war of 1956.

Do you agree or disagree with this statement? Explain your answer.   **(12 marks)**

TOTAL: 30 marks

THE ISLAMIC REVOLUTION

In the 1970s, the Arab world began to copy many Western ideas and ways of life. Very strict Muslims, called *fundamentalists*, said this was against what Islam said. The fundamentalists were particularly strong in *Iran*. The Shah of Iran was a great admirer of the West and was trying hard to Westernise the country.

In 1979 the fundamentalists in Iran staged a revolution and took over the country. Their leader was the *Ayatollah Khomeini* (an Ayatollah is a Muslim religious leader). Later a crowd of Iranian students forced their way into the American Embassy in Teheran, the capital, and took the staff hostage. The Americans could do nothing to rescue them, and they were only released in 1981.

The Iranians tried to spread their *Islamic Revolution* throughout the Muslim world. Fundamentalists in Egypt assassinated President Sadat, because he had signed a peace treaty with Israel.

Although the Islamic Revolution saw America as its biggest enemy, the Russians have also suffered. In 1979 they invaded *Afghanistan* and set up a communist government. The Afghans fought back fiercely, and groups of fundamentalist guerrillas, called *mujaheddin*, forced the Russians to withdraw in 1989.

When the Gulf War ended in 1988 between Iran and Iraq, see p. 126, many people thought that Iran could mend relations with the West. However, this was prevented by a book. The British author Salman Rushdie, himself an ex-Muslim, wrote a novel called *The Satanic Verses* which was seen by many Muslims as attacking fundamentalists and the Prophet Mohammed. Muslims all over the world were outraged, and the Ayatollah Khomeini called on them to kill Rushdie. Western governments were appalled by this attack on free speech, and relations between Iran and Britain broke down again.

4 International Relations and Human Rights

HUMAN RIGHTS

Believe it or not, you are extremely lucky. No one can arrest you for what you say or think. No one can torture you, and no one can stop you having the vote when you reach 18 (unless you go insane, go to prison or become a member of the House of Lords!). It is easy to forget that this amount of freedom is not normal in most of the world.

Your rights are protected by the law, and by the *United Nations Declaration of Human Rights*. This says:

- All human beings are born free and equal in dignity and rights.
- Everyone has the right to life, freedom and personal security.
- No one should be held in slavery.
- No one should be tortured.
- No one should be arrested, kept in detention, or sent into exile, without a good reason being given.

Even so, these rights are violated all over the world, even by countries which have agreed to uphold them.

There are many examples of this. These are just a few:

The Soviet Union

People who oppose the government, called *dissidents*, have been arrested and sent to concentration camps called *gulags*. Some have even been shut away in mental hospitals. Many Russian Jews who wish to emigrate to Israel have been refused permission. They are known as *refusniks*.

South Africa

Since 1948 the South African government has used the system of *apartheid*. Officially, this just means 'separate development' for black and white people; in fact it means that all the best jobs and houses are kept for the whites, while black people who have protested about this have been arrested without trial and tortured.

Other Countries

There have been many other examples from all over the world. In black Africa, *Idi Amin* of Uganda and *Jean–Bedel Bokassa* of the Central African Republic ruled their countries through terror. In *South America*, military dictatorships have been set up over nearly the whole continent. In the 1970s the Argentinian government arrested thousands of people who have never been seen since – the 'Disappeared'. In Europe, *Spain* and *Greece* were both military dictatorships until the 1970s. But perhaps the worst examples have been in Asia. Hundreds of thousands of *Chinese* were killed after the Revolution, and during the Cultural Revolution in the 1960s. China also murdered thousands of people when she invaded *Tibet* in 1950. In 1989, when Chinese students demonstrated in favour of democracy, the Chinese army moved in and opened fire, massacring hundreds in front of television cameras. In *Cambodia*, some 3 million people were killed on the orders of its communist ruler, *Pol Pot*.

The democratic countries often complain about these violations of human rights. Unfortunately, their own records are not always clean. *France* used torture in its war against the rebels in Algeria. *Britain* has done the same in Northern Ireland. In the *United States*, there was a long and bitter campaign in the 1960s to gain civil rights for black people. When the black leader, *Martin Luther King*, was assassinated in 1968, many people saw it as a sign of how few rights black Americans had.

THE HELSINKI AGREEMENT

In 1975, representatives of 35 countries met in Helsinki and signed an agreement to uphold human rights. This has not stopped some of these countries carrying on as they did before. Some dissidents in Eastern Europe have tried to keep an eye on whether or not their governments are keeping to the Helsinki Agreement. Many of them have ended up in prison, although the events of 1989 saw most released. One, Havel is now the leader of Czechoslovakia.

PRESIDENT CARTER AND HUMAN RIGHTS

Jimmy Carter was elected President of the United States in 1976. He was determined to make other countries respect human rights. He said America would not send any aid to countries which violated human rights.

The trouble was that that was just what the Americans *were* doing! They had allies, like Iran and the Philippines, whose records on human rights were appalling. They were also selling huge mountains of grain to the Russians. If America had kept strictly to President Carter's policy, she would have had hardly anyone to do business with.

5 Detente

Detente is a French word. It means 'relaxing tension'. It was also used to describe the state of relations between East and West in the 1970s.

Detente worked in many ways. One way was through cultural or sporting links between East and West. Another was through tourism, as more and more people from the West began to visit Eastern Europe. But its most important form was in talks to cut down on nuclear weapons.

ARMS AGREEMENTS

After the Cuban Missile Crisis (see Chapter 5, Section 7) Russia and America made a number of agreements to make sure such a crisis did not happen again:

1963 *Nuclear Test Ban Treaty*
America, Russia and Britain agreed not to hold nuclear tests above ground. Tests underground were still allowed. Also, China and France did not sign.

1967 *Outer Space Treaty*
Sixty countries agreed not to use nuclear weapons in space.

1968 *Nuclear Non-Proliferation Treaty*
Russia, America and Britain agreed not to spread nuclear information or equipment. They invited other countries to sign this agreement, and over ninety did. But China, France, Egypt, Israel, Japan and South Africa all refused.

1971 *Seabed Pact*
No underwater nuclear tests were to be held outside a country's twelve-mile territorial waters.

1972 *Biological Warfare Treaty*
This said countries should not produce biological weapons, and that existing stocks should be destroyed.

None of these removed the threat of nuclear weapons entirely:

- Important countries like France and China refused to sign many agreements.
- More countries, like India and Israel, were developing nuclear weapons all the time.
- Even with these agreements, the Russians and Americans still had enough weapons to destroy the world many times over.

SALT 1

In 1969 the Russians and Americans set up the *Strategic Arms Limitations Talks (SALT)*. These talks tried to reduce the number of weapons each side had. It was not easy, because now missiles could carry many warheads and hit many different targets, miles apart.

In 1972 the first agreement, SALT 1, was signed. It was to last five years. It said:

- Neither side was to produce any more land or submarine missiles, or long-range bombers.
- The Russians could have more missiles than the Americans, because the Americans had more multi-target missiles (MIRVs).

- The two sides could only have:

	USA	USSR
ICBMs	1,000	1,600
MIRVs	10,000	4,000
Submarine missiles	650	700

- Each side could have 100 anti-ballistic missiles (missiles to shoot down other missiles), on two sites.
- Each side could use spy satellites in space to check that the other side was keeping the treaty.

Even so, each side kept on developing new weapons. In 1974 President Ford went to the USSR to sign the *Vladivostock Agreement*. This allowed the Russians to have 1,320 MIRVs.

THREE-WAY DETENTE

The SALT agreement was a sign that Russia and America were getting on better. Nixon and Brezhnev both visited each other's country, and the Americans agreed to export large amounts of grain to the Soviet Union. In 1975, Russian and American spacemen linked up in space.

The Americans were also on better terms with China. It started when an American table-tennis team toured China in 1971. In 1972 President Nixon visited Peking and met Mao Tse-tung, and in 1975 President Ford did the same. The Americans had already dropped their veto on China's entry into the United Nations, and in 1979 President Carter finally ended American support for Taiwan.

The Cold War seemed to be over, but things were not entirely straightforward:

America was:
- exhausted after Vietnam, but still wanted to stop communism spreading
- on better terms with China because the Chinese had fallen out with the Russians.

Russia needed:
- a rest from the arms race because it was proving too expensive
- trading links with the West.

China needed:
- a powerful ally after her split with Russia
- trading links with the West.

So there were other reasons behind these agreements as well as a wish for peace.

HELSINKI AND SALT 2

We have already mentioned the Helsinki Agreement of 1975 and its Declaration on Human Rights. The Agreement also said that the 1945 frontiers in Europe were permanent. This meant that the West finally accepted East Germany, and the East finally accepted West Berlin.

Meanwhile, each side was still developing new missiles. Both sides produced a new type of *medium-range missile*, to be based in Europe: the Americans developed the *Cruise* missile, and the Russians produced the *SS20*. The Americans also developed the *neutron bomb*, which could kill people without destroying buildings, and the *MX missile*, which could move along underground tracks. None of these weapons were covered by SALT 1.

So the two sides started talks on SALT 2. These talks were difficult, because President Carter accused the Russians of breaking the terms of the Helsinki Declaration on Human Rights. So, the Russians simply threatened to break off the talks.

SALT 2 was finally signed in 1979, but it was not put into operation, because in December of that year, the Russians invaded Afghanistan (see below pages 129–30).

REAGAN AND GORBACHEV

Ronald Reagan was elected President of the United States in 1980. He was determined to take a tougher line with the Russians than Jimmy Carter had done. He did not believe in detente. He stationed Cruise missiles in Europe, and developed a system of destroying missiles using satellites in space – the *Strategic Defence Initiative*, nicknamed 'Star Wars'. Other Western leaders, like the British Prime Minister, *Margaret Thatcher*, also took a tough line with the Russians.

In 1985 Mikhail Gorbachev took over in Russia. He amazed the world by freeing some political prisoners, and by allowing people in Russia to criticise the government. He called this policy *glasnost* (openness). He also started to reform the political system in Russia. In 1989 the first free elections since 1917 were held. These reforms were called *perestroika* (restructure) (see below page 131).

Reagan found he could talk with Gorbachev, and they held three important meetings:

1. Geneva – 1986
    They talked about arms limitations. There was no actual agreement, but they agreed to meet again soon.
2. Reykjavik – 1987
    When Gorbachev arrived, he announced to the press:

Source 6K

We are ready to seek solutions to the most urgent problems now agitating nations . . . to remove and do away with the threat of nuclear war. We call on the entire world community to eliminate nuclear weapons by the end of the century.
(*Reykjavik: Documents and Materials*, Novosti Press Agency Publishing House, Moscow, 1987, p.5)

Gorbachev startled Reagan by offering to get rid of all his nuclear weapons if Reagan would do the same. Reagan was not prepared for this, and the meeting broke up.

3. Washington – The INF (Intermediate Nuclear Force) Treaty – 1987
    The two sides agreed to cut their nuclear forces down drastically. Both sides withdrew their medium-range missiles from Europe (but see Figure 6.3).

Examination Guide

All examiners use cartoons, though there are signs that they might start to use them less in future. They are a curse (cartoons, I mean, though you could say examiners are too). People tend to assume that they are easy, partly because they think that they are meant to be funny. In fact, cartoons can be very difficult, and often very unfunny. Activity 52a will help you, but don't expect to split your sides laughing at it. Activity 52b has a cartoon and two tricky extracts from politicians' speeches as well. They are not easy either, but don't skip them: if you can handle these, you can handle anything.

Figure 6.3   Nuclear weapons in the world, 1989

Source   Peters Atlas of the World, Longman, 1989

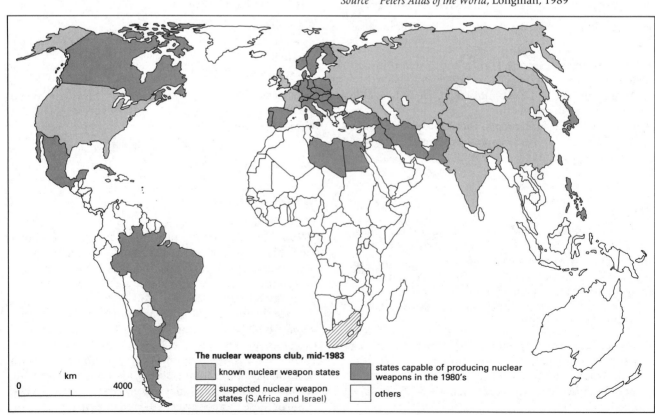

The nuclear weapons club, mid-1983

known nuclear weapon states

suspected nuclear weapon states (S. Africa and Israel)

states capable of producing nuclear weapons in the 1980's

others

km
0   4000

ACTIVITY 52a

Target

Evaluation and interpretation of sources.

Question Guide

Sources 6L and 6M are both cartoons, one Russian and one American. On one of them, the word PENTAGON appears. The Pentagon is the American Ministry of Defence, so called because it is housed in a large, five-sided building. Look at the cartoons carefully, and answer these questions about them.

Source 6L

Source Comager, Leuchtiger and Morris, *A Concise History of the American Republic*

Activity

1. Which is the Russian poster, and which is American?
2. Explain what you think each poster is trying to say.
3. These posters give very different points of view. Does this mean that one of them is right and the other is wrong? Explain your answer carefully.
4. Try to suggest possible or likely dates when these cartoons may have been drawn (they may not necessarily have been drawn at the same time). Explain your choice of dates carefully.

ACTIVITY 52b

Targets

Evaluation and interpretation of sources; selection and deployment of relevant knowledge.

Source 6M

Source Russian poster (from a copy at the Netherhall School, Cambridge)

Question Guide

Before you start, read through Sources 1 and 2 and write down in your own words what they are saying. When you have done that, look carefully at the cartoon. It's quite a full picture, and takes a bit of working out. Brezhnev is tending his 'crop' of missiles, but what is he using for fertiliser? Why are detente and SALT shown as scarecrows? As with all cartoons, this shows the cartoonist's own personal point of view. How likely is it that this reflects the points of view of other people too?

Activity

(SEG, Syllabus 2, Paper 1, Winter 1988)

Sources:
Attitudes towards detente in the1970s
Source 1

Detente is a process of managing relations with a country that could become hostile in order to preserve the peace while maintaining our vital interests.
(From comments by Henry Kissinger, American Secretary of State, (1974))

Source 2

The struggle between the Soviet and American systems in the form of economics, politics and beliefs will be continued. But we shall make sure that this struggle takes place in a way which does not threaten wars, dangerous conflicts and an uncontrolled arms race.

(From comments by Leonid Brezhnev, the Soviet leader, (June 1973))

Source 3

In 1972 President Nixon flew to Moscow on a mission to secure better relations between the USA and the USSR. Both countries had spent three years in their 'Strategic Arms Limitation Talks' (SALT) and, in May 1972, Nixon and Brezhnev signed the agreements known as SALT 1. The agreement, which set limits to defensive missile systems, would last until 3 October 1977. SALT 1 took place in an atmosphere of friendship such as the world had not seen for decades.

(From *A Map History of Our Own Times* by B. Catchpole)

Source 4

Once the first SALT agreement had been signed, Kissinger arranged a series of trade deals with Russia and organised cultural and scientific exchanges between Russia and the USA. He claimed that by promoting Soviet economic development, the USA would help raise living standards, create rising expectations among the Soviet people and produce pressure for reform.

(From *Europe Since 1945* by P. Lane)

Source 5

The main character in this American cartoon of 1974 is Leonid Brezhnev.

The USA and the USSR as World Superpowers
Attitudes towards 'detente', the improvement of the relations between the United States and the Soviet Union, in the 1970s

Study Sources 1 to 5 and then attempt *all* parts of the Question.
When referring to Sources in your answer, you should identify them by number.

1. (a) How, in Source 1, does Henry Kissinger show:
    (i) that he believes detente to be necessary;
    (2 marks)
    (ii) that he does not believe that detente means giving way to the other side?   **(2 marks)**

(b) Does Brezhnev (Source 2) agree with Kissinger's opinion of what detente means? Give reasons for your answer.   **(4 marks)**

(c) Was the SALT 1 agreement, referred to in Source 3, easy to reach? Give reasons for your answer.   **(3 marks)**

(d) How is it suggested in Source 3 that the SALT 1 agreement might be just a first step?   **(2 marks)**

(e) Source 4 describes further contacts with the Soviet Union after SALT 1 had been signed. How would Kissinger expect the United States to benefit from these contacts?   **(3 marks)**

(f) According to the cartoon, Source 5, how is Brezhnev taking advantage of detente?   **(4 marks)**

(g) 'The cartoon, Source 5, proves that American public opinion was opposed to President Nixon's policy of detente.' Do you agree with this statement? Give reasons for your answer.   **(5 marks)**

(h) Do these Sources prove that detente between the Superpowers was successful? Give reasons for your answer.   **(5 marks)**

TOTAL: 30 marks

6 International Organisations

THE UNITED NATIONS

The UN has not managed to stop wars from breaking out, as people hoped when it started. However, it has changed a lot. Look carefully at this table:

Figure 6.4   Membership of the United Nations, 1954–68

	US and allies	USSR and allies	Neutral	Others	Total
1954	41	5	12	2	60
1956	44	9	25	2	80
1968	42	10	71	3	126

Source: John Major, *The Contemporary World: a Historical Introduction*, Methuen, p.197.

By 1980 the UN had 159 members. The new member countries have mostly been countries in Africa or Asia which have become independent of the old colonial powers. They are often called the *non-aligned countries*, because they try to be independent of the Russians and the Americans too.

The Secretary General of the United Nations has always come from a smaller nation, instead of from one of the superpowers.

So far there have been five Secretaries General of the UN:

1. *Trygve Lie* Norway (1946–53)
   The Russians accused Lie of being too pro-American because of the UN's involvement in the Korean War.

2. *Dag Hammarskjöld* Sweden (1953–61)
   Hammarskjöld was also accused of being too pro-American. He was killed in a plane crash while trying to sort out the crisis in the Congo.
3. *U Thant* Burma (1962–71)
   HIs main problem was the American involvement in the Vietnam War, which he was not able to stop.
4. *Kurt Waldheim* Austria (1971–81)
   His biggest problems were the crises in the Middle East. After he resigned he became President of Austria, but he was accused of having been involved in war crimes when he was serving in the German army during the war.
5. *Javier Perez de Cuellar* Peru (1981–)
   Perez de Cuellar was faced almost immediately with the crisis between Argentina and Britain over the Falkland Islands. In his period of office, the UN finally got South Africa to withdraw from Namibia (South-West Africa).

PROBLEMS FOR THE UN

Without a doubt, the biggest success of the UN has been the work of its agencies (this was true of the League as well). It has had mixed success in peacekeeping. This has partly been because the members of the Security Council have always been prepared to veto any action they do not like. They also do not allow the UN to intervene in what they see as their own areas – Central America for the USA, and Eastern Europe for the USSR.

How has the UN dealt with the various crises which have arisen?

The Middle East

Israel was formed by the UN (see Section 3 above), and in 1949 the UN arranged a truce between Israel and her neighbours. The UN also set up UNRWA (United Nationals Relief & Works Agency) to help the Palestinian refugees. In 1956 the UN, with American and Russian support, established a ceasefire in the Suez war. A UN force was sent in to keep the Israelis and Egyptians apart, but the Israelis brushed past it when they attacked Egypt in 1967.

After 1967 the UN passed *Resolution 242*, which called on Israel to return the land she had taken, and on the Palestinians to accept Israel's right to exist. The PLO refused to accept the Resolution until 1988; Israel accepts it in theory, but in practice refuses to hand back the conquered lands.

Both in 1967 and in 1973 the UN called for a ceasefire, but this was ignored. Since then, the UN has condemned Israel for holding on to the West Bank and the Gaza Strip, and has twice invited Yasser Arafat to speak to the General Assembly (see Source 6N).

India and Pakistan

These two countries have sbeen arguing over which of them should own the area of Kashmir ever since they were founded, and they have gone to war over it on three occasions: in 1949, 1965 and 1971. Each time, the UN has arranged a ceasefire.

Source 6N Yasser Arafat speaks to the UN

Source UN Information Centre

The Congo

The Congo was a Belgian colony until 1960. When the Belgians left, the province of *Katanga* tried to break away. Civil war broke out, and the UN sent a peacekeeping force into the country. UN and government troops moved into Katanga and defeated the rebels in a nasty and badly managed campaign. Trouble started again as soon as the UN troops had gone.

Nigeria

This was a similar problem. In 1967, the wealthy province of *Biafra* tried to break away from Nigeria. A fierce civil war broke out, which only ended when the Biafrans were defeated in 1970. The UN was not able to stop the fighting.

Vietnam

During the Vietnam War, the UN criticised the Americans, but it was not able to stop the war.

Cyprus

Cyprus is inhabited by Greeks and Turks, and they hate each other. The UN sent a peacekeeping force in to keep the two communities apart, but it could not stop the Turkish army from invading Cyprus in 1974. The Turks took hold of the northern half of Cyprus and set it up as a separate state, though it is not recognised by the UN.

Rhodesia

In the 1960s, there were 200,000 whites living in Rhodesia, a British colony in southern Africa, and about 4 million blacks. But most of the land, and all political power, belonged to the whites. The British government said this was unfair, and they would only grant Rhodesia her independence if the whites would allow the blacks at least a third of the seats in the Rhodesian parliament. The whites wanted to be independent, but they did not like the British terms. So in 1965, the Rhodesian prime Minister, *Ian Smith*, declared Rhodesia independent, whether Britain liked it or not. This was called *UDI (Unilateral Declaration of Independence)*. Both Britain and the UN condemned UDI, and the UN imposed a complete trade embargo on Rhodesia. But many countries were able to carry on trading with Rhodesia through South Africa.

In the end, the future of Rhodesia was settled by Britain and the Rhodesians in 1979, without involving the UN. Rhodesia got black majority rule, and changed its name to *Zimbabwe*.

South Africa

The UN has often condemned apartheid (see Section 4 above), but has not been able to do anything about it. In 1960, 67 blacks were killed at Sharpeville when police opened fire on a demonstration. In 1976, 200 blacks, including many schoolchildren, were killed by police at *Soweto*. Still the UN could not impose effective sanctions on South Africa.

The UN's main problem with South Africa has been to persuade it to grant independence to Namibia. South Africa finally did this in 1989.

The Falkland Islands

These islands in the South Atlantic are owned by Britain but claimed by Argentina. In 1982 the Argentinians invaded and took them over. The UN passed a resolution, telling the Argentinians to pull their troops out, but they ignored it. The UN could not stop the war which followed, when the British attacked and reconquered the islands. (Source 6O.)

Source 6O The Falklands War at the UN. Britain and the US veto an Argentinian motion.

Source Valerie Adams, *The Falklands Conflict*, Flashpoints Series, Wayland, 1988

Lebanon

The UN could not do anything when Lebanon exploded into a fierce and confusing civil war (see Section 3 above). When Israel and Syria invaded Lebanon in 1978, the UN criticised Israel but not Syria. A UN peacekeeping force was sent to Beirut, but it could not do anything. In 1982 Israel invaded again, and forced the PLO out of Beirut. The UN sent another peacekeeping force, but it could not stop the fighting, which still rages as fiercely as ever.

The Gulf War

When Iraq attacked Iran in 1980, the UN called for a ceasefire, but neither side took any notice. In 1987, however, both sides started attacking neutral ships in the Persian Gulf. There was also evidence that they were using chemical weapons against each other (this is against international law). All five permanent members of the UN Security Council agreed on a tough resolution, which threatened both sides with sanctions if they did not stop fighting. Both Iran and Iraq were exhausted by the war, and agreed to make peace.

Examination Guidance

You need to have some knowledge of the sort of problems the UN has been involved in over the last twenty years. No one is going to expect you to know every detail of every crisis, but you should be familiar with the successes and the failures the UN has had. Activity 53a will help you to tackle the sort of examination question in Activity 53b, from MEG.

ACTIVITY 53a

Target

Selection and deployment of relevant knowledge.

Question Guide

A straightforward task. Look over the list of examples of UN activities, and decide which were 'successes' and which were 'failures' – but think: 'success' and 'failure' *for whom*?

Activity

1. Look over these examples, and sort them into two columns, headed 'Successes for the UN' and 'Failures for the UN'.
2. Do the cases in each column have anything in common?
3. When you have done this, try and answer the question 'Has the UN been a success or a failure since 1955?' Explain your answer carefully.

ACTIVITY 53b

Target

Selection and deployment of relevant knowledge.

Question Guide

The first question is money for old rope, and as long as you bear in mind the circumstances in the world when the UN was set up, so is the second. But keep an eye on the marks each question carries: the third question carries 15. That means that you will be expected to produce a full (and fairly long) answer. Think about all those case studies on pages 125–126. Did they show the UN to be successful, or unsuccessful, or both? Is there anything else that the UN has been successful at? If the UN has not stopped wars, has it at least been able to limit them? When you have thought about those points, try the question.

Activity

(MEG, The Modern World, Paper 1, June 1988)

Read the following extract from the Charter of the United Nations, signed by the representatives of fifty countries in June 1945.

We the people of the United Nations are determined to save succeeding generations from the scourge of war, which twice in our lifetime has brought untold sorrow to mankind, and to reaffirm faith in the fundamental human rights, in the dignity and worth of the human person, in the equal rights of men and women and of nations large and small.

Look at the following plan showing the organisation of the United Nations.

(a) (i) Name the two remaining permanent members of the security council not shown on the plan. **(2)**
(ii) What does the Economic and Social Council do? **(2)**
(b) Why did the Charter stress ideas such as human rights and equality? **(6)**
(c) 'The United Nations has not prevented the "scourge of war" and must therefore be considered a failure.' Do you agree with this statement? Explain your answer is fully as you can. **(15)**

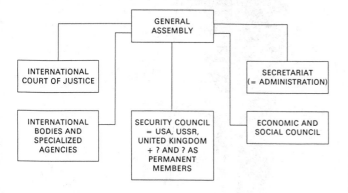

WESTERN EUROPEAN ORGANISATIONS

The Second World War left Europe shattered. Her economy was in ruins as much as her buildings. The world was dominated by the superpowers: Russia, China and America. The Europeans would have to work together if they were to make their mark in future.

The Council of Europe

This was founded in 1949 as a possible first step towards a 'United States of Europe'. Representatives of ten states, including Britain, met at Strasbourg. Since then, it has grown to twenty member states. It can make recommendations, but it has no powers.

European Coal and Steel Community (ECSC), 1951

This was the idea of the French Foreign Minister, *Robert Schuman*. Six countries, France, West Germany, Italy, Belgium, the Netherlands and Luxemburg, agreed to trade freely with each other in coal and steel. It worked very well, with an increase in trade between its members of 170%. So, they decided to extend the idea beyond just coal and steel.

The EEC

The six countries of the ECSC signed the *Treaty of Rome* in 1957, agreeing to trade freely with each other in ALL goods. This meant that they imposed very low tariffs (i.e. customs duties) on each other's goods, or even no tariff at all, but that they all imposed the same, very high tariffs on goods coming in from outside. The scheme was nicknamed the *Common Market*. Its official name was the European Economic Community (EEC). Britain decided not to join, missing the boat as usual.

The EEC has four main bodies:

● the Council of Europe
● the European Commission
● the European Parliament
● the European Court of Human Rights.

Euratom

This was the EEC's organisation for countries to work together to develop atomic energy.

Figure 6.5 Economic unions in Europe, 1960

Source J. Robert Wegs, *Europe Since 1945*, St Martin's Press, 1979

European Free Trade Area (EFTA), 1959

The EEC did so well encouraging trade and industries that other countries were afraid they would be left behind. But they did not want to give up some of their power to the EEC bodies in Brussels and Strasburg. So in 1959, led by Britain, a group of countries formed the *European Free Trade Area, EFTA*. The other countries were Denmark, Norway, Sweden, Switzerland, Austria and Portugal (see Figure 6.5). The EEC was nicknamed the *Six*, and EFTA the *Seven*, which made one British politician remark: 'Europe is all at Sixes and Sevens.'

Britain and the EEC

Britain was the only big European power in EFTA and not in the EEC. She already had strong trading links with her Commonwealth and did not want to give them up. Also, many people in Britain did not want to give up power to the European Parliament. Even so, in 1961 the British Prime Minister, Harold Macmillan, applied to join the EEC. There were a lot of details to work out, particularly the question of whether British colonies and Commonwealth countries would count as part of the EEC (French colonies did), but everything was going well in the talks until 1963. Then President de Gaulle of France broke the talks off and told Britain she could not join the EEC. When Britain tried to join the EEC again in 1967, this time under Harold Wilson, de Gaulle did the same thing (see Source 6P).

De Gaulle said:

- Britain and her Commonwealth would make the EEC poorer, not richer.
- Britain was too closely tied to the USA, and would bring American influence into Europe.
- British farmers would sell their goods more cheaply within the EEC than French farmers, and put the French farmers out of business.

It took another ten years for Britain to get into the EEC. In 1973 she joined under the Conservative Prime Minister, *Edward Heath*. But the next year he was out of office and the Labour Party was in power. Labour had always opposed the EEC. The new Prime Minister, *Harold Wilson*, thought Britain had to pay too much into the EEC's central budget. He got Britain's contribution reduced, and in 1975 he held a referendum on whether Britain should now stay in the EEC. The vote was Yes by 2 to 1.

Problems of the EEC

There have been many problems. The biggest of these has been the fact that the members could not agree on a *Common Agricultural Policy* (CAP). Farmers have produced more food than they can sell, so *butter and grain mountains* have piled up, while much of the world is starving.

This has not been helped by the EEC's bureaucracy, which makes it very difficult for the EEC to take action quickly when this is necessary.

Britain has posed many problems for the EEC since she joined. In 1980, *Margaret Thatcher* demanded that Britain's contribution to the EEC budget, which was still much higher than other countries, should be reduced. More recently, she said that Britain will not support any attempt to set up a united political European state.

Source 6P   De Gaulle blocked Britain's second attempt to join the EEC, in 1967. What does this cartoonist think about it?

Source   Purnell History of the 20th Century, p. 2554

The next big change for Europe will come in 1992, with the creation of the *Single European Market*. This will mean that goods and people can cross frontiers between member states freely. This will bring many benefits, but doubtless many problems too.

Examination Guide

No one is pretending that the story of the EEC is even remotely exciting, but unfortunately it is one of those things that examiners think you *ought* to know about, and they like to set questions on it. Sometimes they choose the early days, ECSC, EFTA and all that (Activity 54a), sometimes they concentrate on Britain's relations with the EEC (Activity 54b). Good luck!

ACTIVITY 54a

Target

Selection and deployment of relevant knowledge.

Question Guide

Although this is based on the map in Figure 6.5, you will need to recall some details from this chapter, and some from Chapter 5 as well.

Activity

Look at Figure 6.5.

1   Were these economic alliances also *political* alliances? Explain your answer carefully.
2   Why do you think the European countries thought there was a need to set up economic alliances after 1945?

ACTIVITY 54b

Target

Evaluation and interpretation of historical evidence.

Question Guide

Another cartoon. Cartoonists loved the idea of de Gaulle telling the British where to get off, and they produced lots of cartoons about it. Try to make sure you can recognise the faces of de Gaulle, Macmillan and Wilson, which normally feature in these cartoons. In this case, it's de Gaulle and Wilson.

Activity

Look at Source 6P.

1.   What does the writing on the ladder refer to?
2.   Whose side do you think the cartoonist is on? Explain your answer.
3.   Why did de Gaulle stop Britain entering the EEC?

THE AMERICAS

The Organisation of American States (OAS)

The OAS was founded in 1948, with backing from the USA. It was supposed to stop communism taking root in North or South America. The OAS supported the USA against Castro in Cuba in 1962. Since then, it has tended to try to be more independent of the USA, and is often opposed to her.

The Organisation of Central American States (OCAS)

OCAS was founded in 1951 with the same aim as OAS. It too started off as very friendly towards the USA, but nowadays it is much less so.

THE THIRD WORLD

It is very difficult to be precise about which countries are in the Third World, and which are not. Roughly speaking, it is made up of countries which used to be colonies of the European powers, and which are now very poor. They have often tried to work together though not always with much success.

The Bandung Conference, 1955

In April 1955, representatives of 25 states, all of them ex-colonies, most of them in Africa and Asia, met at *Bandung* in Indonesia. There they declared that they would try to work together to help each other, and to keep on equal terms with the white powers. Although the Third World countries have many things in common, in fact they have not always lived up to the promises made at Bandung, and they have often gone to war with each other.

The Organisation of African Unity (OAU)

OAU was founded in 1951. It was supposed to act as a sort of United Nations for the African continent. In fact, it has not been able to stop wars between its members.

The Association of South East Asian Nations (ASEAN)

ASEAN was formed in 1967 by Indonesia, Malaysia, Singapore, Thailand and the Philippines. It has tried to stop the spread of communism through south-east Asia, without much success.

7 Problems of the 1980s

AFGHANISTAN

The Islamic Revolution in Iran (Section 3 above) scared the Russians. There are thousands of Muslims in the Soviet Union, and Iran is not far from the border. The country in-between is Afghanistan.

The government of Afghanistan was trying to modernise the country just as the Shah of Iran had done, and the Muslims in the country were up in arms about it. It looked as if the Russians would have a new Islamic Republic on their borders. To stop that, Russian troops invaded Afghanistan in December 1979. They arrested the President and shot him. Then they put a communist government in power, led by *Barbek Karmel*.

The rest of the world was furious. President Carter told the US Senate not to accept the SALT 2 treaty. He stopped all grain exports to Russia, and withdrew America from the 1980 Olympics, which were held in Moscow. Many other countries pulled their athletes out as well. When *Ronald Reagan* was elected in 1980, he sent arms to the Afghan resistance, the *mujaheddin*.

The Chinese also criticised the Russians, and sent arms to help the Afghans. The Russians found they could not beat the *mujaheddin* out of their mountain bases. The war was very expensive for the Russians, and they were not winning it. In 1989, they withdrew. Like the Americans in Vietnam, they had been beaten by small groups of guerrillas.

THE BRANDT REPORT

In 1979 an international commission looked into the problem of poverty and debt in the Third World. It was chaired by a West German politician, *Willi Brandt*. It produced a report which said that the problems of the Third World (which it called the *South*) could only be solved with more of an effort from the rich countries (the *North*). It also pointed out that the problems of the South would ultimately spell disaster for the whole planet, since South and North depend on each other equally.

Since then, not much has been done. There were some moves to help when Ethiopia suffered a terrible famine in 1984; however, much of the famine relief came through the efforts of a single pop singer, *Bob Geldof*, and his relief organisation, *Band Aid*. Governments have still not worked out how best to carry out what the Brandt Report recommended.

SOLIDARITY IN POLAND

Workers in Poland were protesting against sharp rises in prices. They were greatly encouraged when the archbishop of Cracow was elected *Pope John Paul 11* in 1978. In 1980, they formed a free trade union called *Solidarity*. It was led by *Lech Walesa*, and had 10 million members. Solidarity demanded a free press in Poland, and the right to strike. When it looked as if the Polish government might give in to these demands in 1981, the army took over. Its leader, *General Jaruzelski*, banned Solidarity and arrested Lech Walesa. The General had to release him when the Pope visited Poland in 1983, but Solidarity remained banned.

In 1989, however, with *perestroika* and *glasnost* in the USSR, General Jaruzelski lifted the ban on Solidarity and allowed its members to stand in elections. Although the communists won the elections, Solidarity won every seat it was allowed to contest and was allowed to appoint the Prime Minister. The General himself only remained President by one vote!

GLASNOST IN THE SOVIET UNION

In 1985 Mikhail Gorbachev took over in the Soviet Union. He declared a policy of openness (*glasnost* in Russian) and restructure (*perestroika*) of the Soviet system. What this meant, in practice, was that people in Russia were more free to say and write what they like, even if it criticised the government. Communist officials who were not doing their job were sacked. People were allowed to talk openly about Russia's problems, including the massacres and murders of Stalin's period. Most surprisingly of all, a number of political prisoners were released. When Gorbachev called for elections to a new Soviet parliament, some of these ex-prisoners were elected. The world, not to mention the Russians, were amazed.

These changes were very popular both in Russia and abroad. Nevertheless, *glasnost* and *perestroika* have brought problems:

- Some people high up in the communist party do not like these changes and would rather rule Russia in the old, harsh way.
- Other people think the changes are happening too slowly. One communist leader who said so, called Boris Yeltsin, was sacked from the government. However, when the elections were held to the new parliament, he was returned with a large majority.
- The Soviet economy is still very inefficient. Many Russians wonder; 'What is the point of *perestroika* if there is still not enough food in the shops?'
- Some of the non-Russian peoples of the USSR have taken advantage of *glasnost* to demand greater independence. This has been particularly dangerous in two southern republics, Armenia and Azerbaijan, where there have been violent clashes.

THE ENVIRONMENT

Nations are having to work together to work out solutions to problems which threaten the whole planet.

Nuclear Power

Even though it is cheaper and creates many jobs, nuclear energy has produced some major problems. Nuclear waste from the British nuclear reactor at *Sellafield* has leaked into the Irish Sea; there was a major leakage in 1978 at the American reactor on *Three Mile Island;* and in 1986 the Russian nuclear reactor at *Chernobyl* blew up, sending radioactive particles into the air as far away as Norway and Wales. Since Chernobyl, there has been much more international co-operation in developing and controlling nuclear energy.

The Ozone Layer

Chemicals used in ordinary products, like aerosols or refrigerators, wear away the earth's layer of ozone, which protects the earth from the rays of the sun. Too much exposure to these rays can cause serious skin cancer.

1989: Year of Revolutions

Most of this book was written in 1989. As we were putting the finishing touches to it, revolutions suddenly broke out all over eastern Europe. Some parts of this book had suddenly become out of date!

What the people who rose up in 1989 wanted was, for the most part, free elections: that is, elections where anyone could stand – not just the Communist Party. At the moment (January 1990) it looks as if these revolutions have succeeded. However, by the time you read this section, you may know how long this success has lasted. This is how things looked in January 1990:

Hungary

Things started here in 1988, when Janos Kadar (the man who brought the Russian tanks into Hungary in 1956 – (see page 102) was forced to resign. The new leaders of Hungary were very keen on Mr Gorbachev's *glasnost* and *perestroika*. They held free elections to the Hungarian parliament, they closed down the Communist Party, and they tore down the barbed wire along Hungary's border with the west. And in 1989, Imre Nagy (see page 102) was finally given a hero's funeral, with full honours.

Poland

In June 1989 the Polish government was forced to hold free elections. The result was a massive win for Solidarity. General Jaruzelski stayed on as President (see page 130), but the new Polish Prime Minister was a Solidarity journalist, Tadeusz Mazowiecki. Things cannot have been easy for the General – he had once put Mr Mazowiecki in prison! Mr Mazowiecki appealed to the western countries to lend economic help to Poland, to help strengthen her new democratic government.

China

China is not in eastern Europe, of course, but what happened there in 1989 was a very important part of the story. In April, shortly before Mr Gorbachev was due to arrive for a visit, thousands of students occupied the central square in Peking, *Tiananmen Square*, and demanded *perestroika* and democracy for China too. The students were still in control of the square when Mr Gorbachev arrived. The Chinese leaders, *Li Peng* and *Deng Xiaoping*, felt humiliated and embarrassed. As soon as Mr Gorbachev had gone they ordered the army to move into Tiananmen Square and crush the students. The students were massacred, and the democracy movement was crushed; however, the television pictures of the massacre shocked the world. Afterwards the government started telling people that there had been no massacre, and that the only people hurt had been the soldiers.

East Germany

In the summer of 1989, thousands of East Germans went on holiday to Hungary and did not go home. When Hungary opened her borders with the West, these East Germans crossed into the West and made for West Germany. The East German leader, *Erich Honecker*, was furious, and tried to stop anyone from leaving the country. However, big protest movements began in Leipzig and at the *Gethsemane Church* in East Berlin. In October, Honecker resigned, and the new government opened East Germany's borders. On the night of 9 November 1989, the East German government finally opened the Berlin Wall, and began to demolish it.

Soon afterwards, East German television showed pictures of the luxury which the communist leaders had enjoyed, while the people were kept poor. This helped the calls that many East Germans were beginning to make, for *reunification* with West Germany.

Czechoslovakia

At first it looked as if the Czech communist government would survive 1989: when students demonstrated for democracy in November, they were beaten up by the police. But before the end of November, the Czech government too resigned, and in December *Vaclav Havel*, a playwright and a leading opponent of the communist government, became President. The Speaker (Chairman) of the Czech parliament was Alexander Dubček – the Czech leader turned out by the Russians in 1968 (see pages 107–108).

Bulgaria

At first the protests in Bulgaria were about the environment, but when the police beat up the protesters, the protesters turned against the government as well. The government resigned and the new leaders agreed to hold free elections.

Romania

No-one had much time for the leader of Romania, *Nicolae Ceaucescu*, either at home or abroad. He and his wife kept the Romanians desperately poor, while they spent huge sums of money on a vast and ugly complex of palaces and offices in the centre of the capital, Bucharest. They had also started to demolish whole villages in the countryside. Even the Russians had long given up supporting Ceaucescu. The only thing that kept him in power was the huge and fearsome secret police network, the *Securitate*.

In December, troops and *Securitate* forces opened fire on an anti-government demonstration in *Timisoara*, killing hundreds. It seemed as if the opposition was crushed, and just before Christmas, Ceaucescu addressed a large crowd in Bucharest on live television. For the first time, however, the crowd interrupted his speech and began booing him. Soon the whole of Bucharest was in turmoil. The army abandoned Ceaucescu and started fighting the *Securitate*. Ceaucescu and his wife were arrested, and on Christmas Day they were shot. Fierce fighting continued between the army and the *Securitate*, but by the New Year the army had won. The new government promised free elections for 1990.

The Soviet Union

Although there was no revolution in the Soviet Union in 1989, things were looking very unsteady there as the 1990s started. The two main problems were:
1. *Shortages*
   After five years of *perestroika* and *glasnost*, there were still shortages of food and clothing all over the Soviet Union, and people were getting very impatient.
2. *Nationalities*
   The non-Russian people in the USSR saw what was happening in eastern Europe, and decided that they too would like to have free elections, and that they

would like to pull out of the USSR. This feeling was particularly strong in the *Baltic states*, Latvia, Estonia and Lithuania, and in the *Muslim areas* in the south, such as Azerbaijan and Turkestan.

On the international front, Mr Gorbachev met the American President Bush in Malta in December 1989, and declared that *the Cold War was over* – officially.

Examination Guidance

More terms to learn! You should know most of them. No examiner will set you a task quite like this (it's far too easy!), but you cannot do any history examination if you can't cope with this sort of test.

ACTIVITY 55

Target

Terms and concepts.

Question Guide

Get someone to test you. When you have done this test, come back to do it nearer to the examination.

Activity

Write a sentence to say what these were/are:

the Sino-Soviet split

Dien Bien Phu

the Gulf of Tonkin resolution

the domino theory

Khe Sanh

My Lai

Vietnamisation

the Six-Day War

Al Fatah

Camp David

the *Intifada*

The Satanic Verses

the Islamic Revolution

the Helsinki Agreement

detente

SALT

START

perestroika

Resolution 242

UDI

ECSC

the Bandung Conference

Solidarity

the Brandt Report

Chernobyl

THE FIRST WORLD WAR

Examination Guide

The First World War appears on all four of the main Examining Group syllabus in two places: for full details, see pages 3–5.

It plays a part in the coverage of international relations: in relation to the background to the Versailles Settlement, the 1920s and the causes of the Second World War. For NEA, it appears in the compulsory theme for Paper 1, **Conflict and Conciliation**, i.e.

(a) **Origins of Conflict** (one of four sub-sections)
   (i) **The reasons why Sarajevo led to war**
(b) **The Changing Nature of Warfare** (one of four sub-sections)
   (i) **The Western Front, 1914–18**
(c) **The Civilian Experience of War** (one of two sub-sections)
   (i) **The Home Front in Britain**
(d) **Attempts to resolve conflict** (one of three sub-sections)

For LEAG MEG and SEG, it is one of a group of topics or studies in depth which centres have to choose from. The relationship of **The First World War** to other syllabus topics is shown in the table. LEAG offers Topic J1, **The Impact of the First World War on British Society**, dealing with both trench warfare and the impact of the war at home. For MEG, **The First World War** is one of two topics chosen from a list of nine topics for study in detail; for SEG, **Britain and the Western Front** is one of two topics, taken from a list of seven for Paper 2, allowing for the study of topics in depth.

Group	%	Number of topics	The First World War coverage
LEAG	10	1 out of 5 from 20	1914–18
MEG	15	1 out of 2 from 9	1914–18
NEA	7	4 out of 13 sub-sections	1914–18
SEG	15	1 out of 2 from 7	1914–18

Work out from the past papers all the questions asked on The First World War. Questions are very popular on the great battles of the Western Front, and trench warfare in general. Be careful to look at the general sections on international relations, which will often contain specific First World War-linked questions, particularly in relation to the Versailles Settlement.

QUESTION PATTERNS

The question pattern is more fully dealt with on pages 12–19 above. If you cannot get hold of the last three years' examination papers, or the specimen papers, make sure that you are well prepared to cover the topics listed in the **Topic Guide**.

Topic Guide

1 **Beginnings**
2 **World Campaigns and Developments**
3 **The Western and Eastern Fronts**
4 **The War at Sea**
5 **The Home Front**

1 Beginnings

Have you ever watched a wrestling contest on TV, where there are two teams of wrestlers fighting in the same ring? Europe in 1914 was in a similar state, with in the red corner a team made up of the central powers (Austria–Hungary and Germany), and in the blue corner a rival team of the Allies (Britain, France and Russia). Details of events leading to the outbreak of the war are given on page 25.

From 1900 the great powers of Europe had taken part in an arms race, building up their rival armies and navies to make sure that they would be safe in any contest between them and their enemies (see Figure 2.3). Armies and navies are no good by themselves, you need carefully prepared plans for them to swing into action the moment war is declared. All the powers of Europe had such plans in 1914; the most famous was that of the Germans, the *Schlieffen Plan*.

THE SCHLIEFFEN PLAN

The German generals had to deal with the problem of fighting on two fronts – the Western Front, where they faced France, and the Eastern Front, where the Russian steam-roller was their great enemy. So, they came up with a plan whereby they delivered a quick knock-out blow against the French and then turned their forces on the Russians. The French armies were drawn up along the Franco-German border in a deep line of defence. The Germans decided to sweep round them through neutral Belgium, and then swoop on Paris (Figure 7.1). The Schlieffen Plan was a simple, neat idea, but it went badly wrong (see Section 4 below).

THE OUTBREAK OF WAR

The nightmare of World War became a reality on 28 July 1914 when Austrian guns opened fire on Belgrade, the capital of Serbia. The two tag teams of France/Britain/Russia and Germany/Austria–Hungary now swung into action, with declarations of war following thick and fast. Russia, Serbia's ally, got ready for war; so Austria, with her ally, Germany, declared war on Russia. Russia's ally was France, and the German generals knew that success against Russia depended on the Schlieffen Plan knocking out France first. So, they declared war on France on 3 August, and German troops marched into Belgium a day later. Britain, France's ally, had promised to defend Belgium, so she was now sucked into the war as well, on 4 August. Within a week both teams were in the ring, with their forces fully mobilised for action (see page 25 above). A small British army, the British Expeditionary Force, was sent across the Channel to help the Belgians and French – the war on the Western Front had now begun.

2 World Campaigns and Developments

The First World War was fought in a world-wide scale. In 1914 Germany had numerous colonies in Africa, Asia and the Pacific; these quickly fell into British hands (Figure 7.2). With Turkey fighting on Germany's side, and Italy entering the war alongside Britain, France and Russia in 1915, fierce fighting occurred in the Eastern Mediterranean, the Middle East and Mesopotamia and Italy.

The Dardanelles

The easy way to knock Turkey out of the war and to bring help to Russia through its Black Sea ports was to capture Constantinople, Turkey's capital. In March 1915 the British government sent a fleet to achieve this, but the fleet turned back when several ships were struck by mines in the Dardanelles, the narrow passage from the Black Sea to the Mediterranean. Instead the British landed a force of troops at Gallipoli in April 1915 (Figure 7.3). These troops, British, New Zealanders and Australians (Anzacs), faced a hopeless task in trying to defeat the dug-in Turks, who peered down on the British beaches from the heights of Gallipoli. In December the defeated British force was withdrawn – a bitter blow to the Allies. The Turks were undefeated, the Russians had received no help, and Bulgaria was encouraged to join Germany and Austria–Hungary.

Figure 7.1 The Schlieffen Plan

Source Neil DeMarco, *The World This Century*, Bell & Hyman, p. 12.

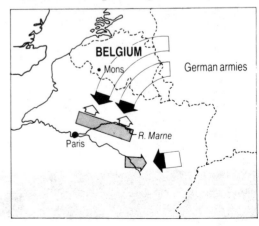

The Schlieffen plan in theory

The Schlieffen plan in practice (1914)

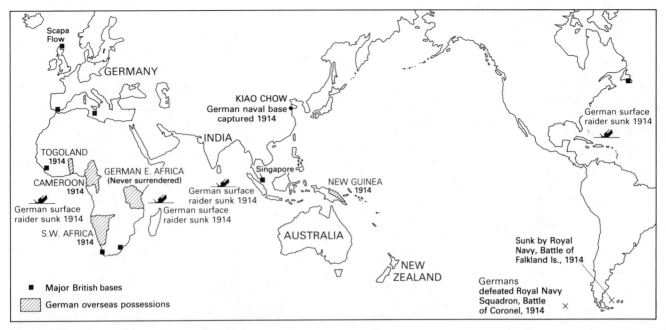

Figure 7.2   The war around the world, 1914

Salonika

In 1915 Serbia was in deep trouble from Austria–Hungary and the Bulgarian threat. So, the British and French sent a joint force to Salonika in neutral Greece, to provide support for the Serbs. The force did little to help, for when Bulgaria joined the central powers in October 1915 the Serbians were quickly overrun.

Mesopotamia

The British had vital oil-wells in Persia, which were under threat from the Turks. So, in 1915 a British army under General Townshend landed in Mesopotamia, Turkey's soft underbelly, with Baghdad as its goal (Figure 7.4). The Turks proved tougher enemies than expected, and the British army became bottled up in Kut-el-Amara in December. The siege lasted until April 1916, when the British army surrendered – a stunning defeat.

Figure 7.3   The battle in the Dardanelles

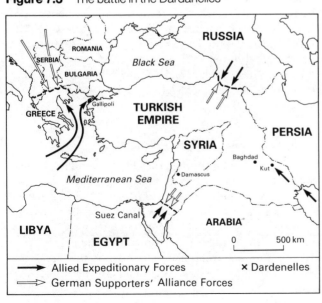

The Desert War

In 1917 and 1918 the British mounted attacks on Turkey's Palestinian and Syrian provinces. Under General Allenby British forces pushed the Turks back in a series of campaigns and captured Damascus. Allenby received help from T. E. Lawrence, 'Lawrence of Arabia', an English officer who worked with the Arab tribes in Arabia to mount a guerrilla war against the Turks (Figure 7.4).

Italy

Fierce fighting occurred in northern Italy between the Austrians and the Italians. In 1917 the Austrians, with German help, routed the Italians at Caporetto. But, the Italians recovered, and in 1918 achieved a major victory over the Austrians.

3 The Western and Eastern Fronts

INTRODUCTION

The bulk of fighting involving British troops in World War I occurred on the Western Front (Figure 7.5), and we tend to concentrate on the details of trench warfare when we study the war in the West.

Figure 7.5   British troops on the Western Front

Date	Number
November 1914	164,000
March 1915	600,000
November 1916	1,500,000
November 1917	2,000,000

A glance at any war monument in any British village, town or city will show why – the list of dead is mostly of

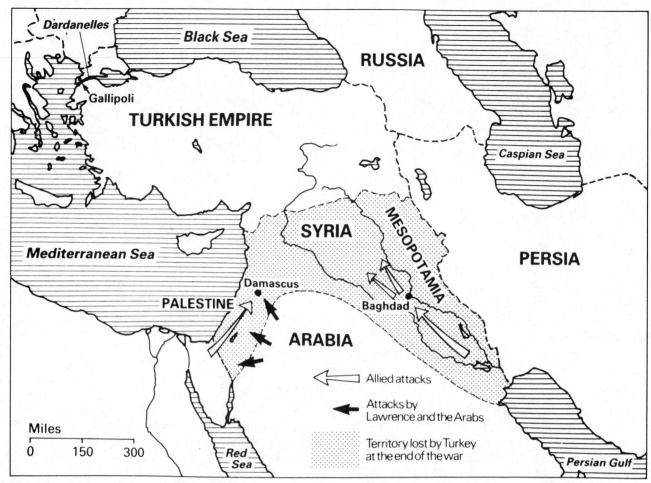

Figure 7.4   The war against the Turks

Source   Christopher Culpin, *Making History*, Collins Educational, p. 22.

those who died in the trenches in 1914–18. However, looking at the details of trench warfare is rather like looking at what goes on inside a rugby scrum while losing sight of the whole game.

THE WESTERN FRONT, 1914–18

The war on the Western Front passed through three phases:

1. **August 1914–September 1914:** the war of mobility
   - the Schlieffen Plan in action
   - the German attack, up to the first Battle of the Marne
2. **August 1914–March 1918:** deadlock in the trenches
   - the Battle of the Marne, to Ludendorff's offensive
3. **March 1918–November 1918:** the war of mobility
   - the German offensive
   - the Allies' counter-attack
   - German defeat

August 1914–September 1914: the war of mobility

Source 7A

A silly German Sausage
Dreamt Napoleon he'd be,
Then he went and broke his promise,
It was made in Germany . . .
But naughty nights at Liege

Quite upset this Dirty Dick,
With his luggage labelled 'England'
And his programme nicely set,
He shouted 'First stop Paris',
But he hasn't got there yet.
For Belgium put the kibosh on the Kaiser,
Europe took a stick and made him sore.

Source 7A gives us a vivid idea of how the war in the West began, with German troops marching into Belgium. The Belgium army put up a fierce resistance at Liege and helped slow the German advance. At the Battle of Mons the British Expeditionary Force (see Section 1 above) also delayed the German advance on Paris (Figure 7.1). The Russian attack in the East also meant that German troops had to be withdrawn to fight on that front. So, by the end of August the Germans had scrapped their original plan to encircle Paris and decided to make a mass attack on Paris from the East.

The Battle of the Marne, 5–11 September 1914

On 5 September began the crucial battle to defend Paris. The French rounded up the taxis of Paris to send fresh troops to key points on the front line – the first use of motorised transport in warfare. The two armies, involving some 2 million soldiers, fought fiercely for a week. By the end of the battle the German attack had petered out, and the German armies had withdrawn to the line of the River Aisne and were beginning to dig defensive trenches.

(Activity 56 (pages 142–143) deals with the first period of the war, August 1914–September 1914.)

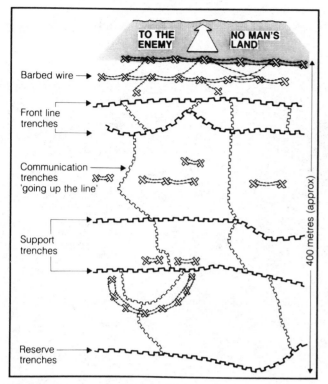

Figure 7.6   Trench warfare

Source   Barry Bates, *The First World War*, Basil Blackwell, p. 14.

The Lines of Trenches

The Battle of the Marne was followed by a race of the armies to the sea, as the Germans tried to outflank the French in the West and break through to Paris. The British Expeditionary Force was fully involved, and at the Battle of Ypres managed to hold off a German attack. Although the Allies had lost the port of Antwerp, they were able to keep hold of the Channel Ports of Dunkirk and Calais, vital for bringing fresh troops and supplies across the Channel. Both sides now dug in, and from their shallow trenches faced each other across a tangled mass of barbed wire (Figure 7.6). The period of trench warfare had begun. Soon the trenches began to develop into complex systems of defences in depth. But we must remember that the trenches also included major established fortifications like that of Verdun, which was at the heart of the French defences against the Germans.

August 1914–March 1918: Deadlock in the Trenches

You will need to know the outline details of the battles listed in Figure 7.7, and also how they relate to what was going on on other fronts (see Figure 7.8).

The Western Front

War on the Western Front was seen rather like a chess game, in which first one side attacks, and then the other, with neither side being able to break through. In-between the attacks and counter-attacks are long periods of relative quiet, while each side gets ready to resume the conflict. What were the main features of trench warfare?

The Trenches

Soldiers lived in networks of trenches like Figure 7.9, a plan of part of the Somme battlefield. A simple, shallow trench was like Figure 7.10, but many trench systems were much more complex, almost like underground villages buried beneath tons of concrete. Each trench network would have kitchens, billets for sleeping, latrines and places for washing. The trenches were organised in a sequence, like Figure 7.6. Behind the immediate front line was a second line of trenches, to support the front line and serve as a line of retreat if the front line was overrun. Communication trenches connected the front line to support and reserve trenches. In front of the trenches lay no man's land, a wilderness of barbed wire and shell holes.

Figure 7.7

Date	Battle	Attacking force	Outcome
1915			
Jan./Mar.	Compiègne	French	Loss of 50,000 men, gain of 500 metres
Mar./May	Neuve Chapelle	British	10,000 men lost, virtually no gain of land
Apr.	Ypres (2nd battle)	German	German use of chlorine gas, German attack fails
May	Vimy	French	French lose 120,000 men – no gains
Sept.	Champagne	French	No gains
Sept.	Loos	British	60,000 British dead, little gain in territory
1916			
Feb./Sept.	Verdun	German	(see page 140)
July/Nov.	Somme	British	(see page 140)
1917			
Mar.	Nivelle offensive	French	No gains, 30,000 killed, French army mutinied
June/Nov.	Ypres (3rd battle)	British	Also known as the battle of Passchendaele. On 7 June British blow up Messines Ridge, with 500,000 kilograms of TNT. Followed by mass attack at Ypres through a battlefield that was a sea of mud. 400,000 British troops killed.
Nov.	Cambrai	British	Tanks broke through the German lines, captured 10,000 soldiers. Attack broke down, Germans regained ground.
1918			
Mar.			German spring offensive ends period of deadlock in the trenches (see pages 140–141).

Figure 7.8   The war in Europe

Source   B. Catchpole, *A Map History of the Modern World*, Heinemann, p. 138.

Trench Warfare

A pattern quickly emerged for trench warfare. Between battles there was spasmodic rifle and machine-gun fire, shelling, mortar attacks and raids across no man's land. Heavy fighting took the form of:

(a) Heavy Shelling – in which a barrage of artillery fire aimed to blast holes in the barbed wire of no man's land and flatten the opposing lines of trenches.

(b) Infantry Attack – with supporting machine and rifle fire, lines of heavily laden soldiers would attack on foot with fixed bayonets, carrying:
  - rifle and bayonet
  - 220 rounds of ammunition
  - pouches and a bandolier
  - water bottle
  - groundsheet and haversack
  - food, bandages, washing bag
  - gas helmet and goggles
  - trenching spade
  - two hand-grenades
  - two empty sandbags

Once they were over the top, hand-to-hand fighting would hopefully lead to the capture of the enemy lines of trenches.

(c) Casualties – most casualties, some six out of ten, were the result of shelling, while only three out of ten deaths arose from rifle or machine-gun fire.

The pattern remained basically unchanged until 1918, with the major changes in fighting being the use of poison gas in 1915 and the introduction of the tank at Cambrai in 1917. Surprise was impossible because of the need to mount a heavy artillery bombardment and attack in mass. Enemy barrage balloons and reconnaissance planes could give early warning of an attack, and reinforcements could be rushed to strengthen weak points in a line.

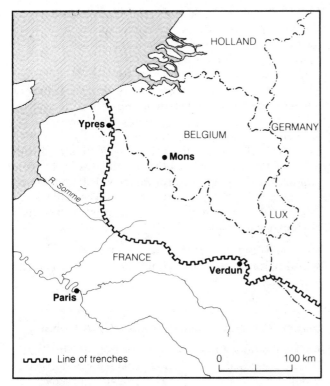

Figure 7.9 The Western Front

Source Barry Bates, *The First World War*, Basil Blackwell, p. 15.

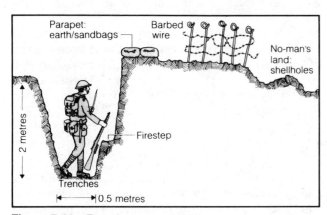

Figure 7.10 Trench cross-section

Source Barry Bates, *The First World War*, Basil Blackwell, p. 14.

The War in the Air

An aspect of warfare on the Western Front was the war in the air, with single combat between pilots flying biplanes – rather like the romantic jousting of knights of old? The reality was a bit different: being trapped in a blazing cockpit, covered in burning petrol without a parachute was not much fun. Soon both sides built up forces of fighter planes and bombers. Dogfights between squadrons of planes were common, and the war saw the emergence of the 'fighter ace' as a popular figure. The most famous was the German Manfred von Richtofen, 'the Red Baron', whose 'flying circus' wreaked havoc among Allied planes.

After the Battle of the Somme both sides used planes increasingly to support their troops, bombing and strafing (machine-gunning) enemy forces. Bombers were also used against civilians: the German airships or *Zeppelins*, (later to be replaced by Gotha bombers) were sent against London, while the British *Handley Page* bombers attacked German towns and cities.

The war in the air was a minor aspect of the war, which was won and lost in huge ground battles between the opposing armies, like those of the Somme and Verdun.

New Weapons

Frankly, I think that learning about things like new weapons isn't really History, which is about what people did. The MEG, SEG and NEA may, however, ask you about new weapons. Here is a list for you to find out about, and how they had an impact on the way the war went:

Barbed Wire

Miles of miles of coiled, rusting barbed wire protected trenches and filled No Man's Land, the area between the two sides' trenches. Barbed wire held up the advance of soldiers, and artillery bombardment could make the tangle an even worse nightmare.

Gas

Poison gas was a horrible new weapon, so foul that the governments of the world have agreed not to use it since 1918. The Germans first used gas in 1915. The green cloud choked to death those who breathed it in; it was just like dying from drowning. Soon a way was found around gas attacks: chemicals soaked in cotton wool or gauze would soak up the gas. These chemical pads were fitted into gas masks, which all troops wore.

Grenades

For hand-to-hand fighting in the trenches, both sides used hand grenades. The Allies' were shaped like pears; the Germans fixed theirs to the ends of sticks.

Heavy Guns or Artillery

The main weapon of the First World War was not the machine-gun – it was the heavy gun. Heavy bombardment of enemy trenches would lead to waves of foot soldiers pouring out of their trenches and across No Man's Land. From 1914 to 1918 these tactics were a failure, because the enemy would climb from their hiding places in deep shelters and use their rifles and machine-guns to mow down the advancing troops. However, by 1918 huge numbers of heavy guns, thousands in action at a time, would punch a hole in a small part of the enemy lines and destroy all their defences. Troops could then storm through these gaps and surround the enemy's forces, trapped in their trenches.

Machine-Guns

Machine-guns were a key weapon in the trenches. A machine-gunner could mow down rows of foot soldiers as they ran or stumbled towards the enemy. In the early battles German machine-gunners cut down the British troops in their thousands.

Tanks

In 1915 a new weapon emerged, an armour-plated tractor carrying a heavy gun and machine-guns – the tank. When first used in battle in 1916 it had little impact. But when ways of attacking with it had been worked out, it became a very powerful weapon in the hands of the Allies in the major offensives of 1918.

Trench Warfare

All of the weapons described above were used in trench warfare, a form of fighting which reached its high point during the First World War on the Western Front.

By themselves these weapons mean little. Think of organising an attack by 1,000 troops on your school and college and organising its defence with the same number. How would you go about both attacking and defending *with* and *without* all the weapons above?

The Battles of Verdun and the Somme

Two battles, both involving the French, and one the British, vividly illustrate the nature of trench warfare:

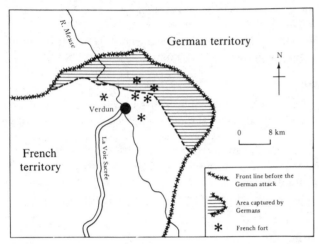

Figure 7.11   The battle of Verdun, 1916

Source   Craig Mair, *Britain at War 1914–1919*, John Murray, p. 48.

1. Verdun, 1916

For the Germans to break through to Paris they had to smash the French army holding the complex of fortifications at Verdun (Figure 7.11). Verdun was one of the great forts the French had built after the 1870 war with Germany, which had been a catastrophic French defeat. In February 1916 the Germans opened a major attack on Verdun, hoping to bleed the French armies dry in their defence of the fortresses. The attack opened with a concentrated artillery attack with about 1,500 heavy guns along a narrow ten-mile front of the River Meuse. The Germans overran the French front-line trenches and captured Fort Douaumont. In the same way as football clubs sack managers when they get bad results, so the French government replaced the commander of Verdun with *General Petain*, who rallied his troops. Petain poured troops and supplies into the area along the only supply road, La Voie Sacrée. The German attack switched to the left flank of Verdun, and in early June they captured Fort Vaux and attacked Souville. In July they broke off their attack, and by winter the French had recaptured their lost forts. The battle of Verdun was over, an horrific killing ground for both sides:

- French dead   380,000
- German dead   340,000

2. The Battle of the Somme, 1 July 1916

The Battle of the Somme helps explain why the Germans

broke off their attack on the French. At the Somme the British attacked the Germans in order to relieve pressure on the French. For weeks before the British had been moving heavy guns, supplies and extra troops to the Somme, so the Germans were well prepared for an attack. They had dug deep concrete protected lines of bunkers where their troops could shelter from an artillery attack. So, when the British commander, *General Haig*, ordered British troops 'over the top' on 1 July 1916, they were faced with lines of fresh German troops armed with rifles and machine-guns. The result was a horrible slaughter, with 20,000 British troops killed, and 35,000 wounded and 2,000 missing or prisoner. The battle lasted for another four months, until 20 November, by which time there were some:

- German dead   650,000
- British dead   500,000 (22,500 officers, 477,500 men)
- French dead   194,000

March 1918–November 1918: the War of Mobility

It is easy to forget that the Germans lost the First World War in a series of battles in 1918 that were as decisive as the Battle of Waterloo. These were battles of attack and counter-attack, and the rapid movement of large numbers of men. By March 1918 the generals had managed to work out a method of breaking the deadlock of trench warfare.

The background to the 1918 campaigns, with Russia out of the war, and the Americans joining in on the side of the Allies, is looked at on page 25. The Schlieffen Plan was almost now working in reverse: with Russia knocked out, the Germans could pour men and resources in to the Western Front.

The Ludendorff Offensive

The German generals worked out a new approach to trench warfare. They would concentrate their artillery and gas attack on a few weak spots in the enemy lines. After a ferocious barrage of concentrated fire, they would then attack with specially trained storm-troopers, using flame-throwers, grenades and light machine-guns. This approach would punch gaping holes through the enemy lines, and the German forces could then encircle the enemy forces and attack them from the rear.

On 21 March Ludendorff attacked, broke through the British and French lines and advanced rapidly to the Marne. The armies of the Allies retreated before the onslaught, defeated but not broken. With the arrival of 50,000 fresh American troops a week, and learning from the German tactics, the Allied armies got ready to counter-attack. Under the single command of the Frenchman *Foch* they aimed to attack the Germans from three sides – from the front and on two flanks, for the German forces had formed a huge bulge into France (Figure 7.12).

The Counter-Attack

In July, the French counter-attacked on the *Marne*, and in early August the British army joined the assault with over 450 tanks. In a series of sweeping victories the Allies routed the German armies, which retreated to a line of fortifications, the *Hindenburg Line*.

Failure of the Ludendorff offensives on the Western Front, 1918

■ Ground captured in Ludendorff's offensives

HOLLAND

British Attacks, September

R. SOMME

Anglo-French attacks, August

R. SEINE

Foch, Allied Commander-in-Chief, began the counter attacks in July

R. MARNE

Paris

Ypres

Apr. attacks

FRONT LINE ON ARMISTICE DAY

A great deal of Belgium was still occupied by the Germans when fighting stopped on November 11th.

OPERATION "MICHAEL" March 21st

May attacks

Verdun

American attacks, Sept.

LUXEM-BOURG

Collapse of Imperial Germany – the Kaiser abdicates and escapes to Holland

▨ Ground captured in Allied offensives July–Nov. 1918

THE DEFEAT OF GERMANY'S PARTNERS 1918

Kiel
BERLIN
☀ **Revolution in GERMANY**
FRANCE
ITALY
AUSTRIA NOV 3rd.
BULGARIA SEP 29th.
Salonika
TURKEY OCT 31st
Aleppo

Regmarad

Figure 7.12   The final battles, 1918   *Source*   B. Catchpole, *A Map History of the Modern World*, Heinemann, p. 25.

Germany's Surrender

At the same time, the war was going badly for Germany's allies. The Italians defeated the Austrians in October at the Battle of Vittorio Veneto, and Austria's other allies, Turkey and Bulgaria, also faced defeat. Inside Germany there was widespread hunger and famine because of the Allied blockade of her ports, and the navy revolted when ordered to sail to fight the British Grand Fleet.

THE EASTERN FRONT

It is easy to forget the Eastern Front, which was just as important as the stagnant war on the Western Front.

While the Schlieffen Plan aimed to knock out the French in the West quickly and turn on the Russians, it was the speed of the Russian attack in the East in 1914 that forced Germany to send troops to that front, thus taking pressure off the French. The Germans were able to halt the Russian attack in two crucial battles, *Tannenberg* and the *Masurian Lakes* in August and September, where they routed the Russian forces. The Russians did far better against the Austrians, whom they defeated. During 1915 and 1916, the Germans continued to push back the Russians, capturing the area of Poland (page 25). However, in June 1916 in the Brusilov offensive the Russians massively defeated the Austrians. Despite success against Austria, Russia faced severe problems at home. Corrupt and inefficient government, and the linking of the Tsar with defeats at Germany's hands, led to revolution in Russia in March 1917 (see Chapter 8, Sections 1 and 2). The communist takeover of November 1917 was followed by the Germans forcing the peace of Brest–Litovsk upon the Russians (Figure 8.5). The Allies later used the harshness of its terms, whereby Russia lost 80% of her industries and some of her richest lands, to justify their own severe treatment of Germany at Versailles.

Examination Guidance

NEA questions will appear in the same form as Activity 56, from the June 1988 paper.

ACTIVITY 56

Targets

Recall; knowledge and understanding; knowledge of sources, and their relationship to general concepts such as causation.

Question Guide

Note the number of marks for each question, and the need to include enough information to 'earn' the marks indicated. For Question 1 (a) one you will need to pick out three or four points for each cartoon to justify why you think that it is either German or British. For example, for Source 7B you would have to explain the meaning of NO THOROUGHFARE, the fact that the little boy has a cap on his head marked 'BELGIUM', his relationship to the man, why the man is carrying a cudgel and the sausages on his belt. Question 1 (b) is asking you to think of the cartoons from the point of view of their drawers, here you are asked to explain *the message* of each cartoonist, i.e. Germany as a bully, Belgium as a little boy sticking up for himself, Britain (Grey) and Serbia (Princip) as guilty prisoners who caused the war, and Britain's role in the system of alliances.

Question 1 (c) is concerned with the causes of the First World War, and what value a cartoon might be in showing what people think. The answer could suggest that Source 7B illustrates the importance of Belgian neutrality to Britain, and the need to stand up against an aggressive, expansionist Germany, while Source 7C indicates the problem of dealing with Serbian nationalism for

Source 7B   Cartoon published in 1914: 'BRAVO BELGIUM'

PUNCH, OR THE LONDON CHARIVARI.—August 12, 1914.

NO THOROUGHFARE

BRAVO, BELGIUM!

Source 7C   Cartoon published in 1914: 'THE GUILTY MEN'

GREY

PRINCIP

the Austrians, particularly when backed by one of the great powers, in this case Britain. The question should also deal with the value of cartoons as such in attempting to write history which looks at events from the vantage-point of governments and politicians. Question 1 (d) asks for a list of at least three sources, with some justification for the choosing of them.

Activity

1. Study Sources 7B and 7C.
    (a) Sources 7B and 7C are drawn by British and German cartoonists. Which cartoon do you think is British and which is German? Give reasons for your answer. **(7)**
    (b) Explain what the cartoonists were trying to show in Sources 7B and 7C. **(6)**
    (c) How useful are these cartoons to an historian writing about the causes of the First World War? **(5)**
    (d) What other sources of information could be useful to an historian writing about the causes of the First World War? **(3)**

4 The War at Sea

Every time you eat a meal it is likely that some of the food on your plate will have been imported from abroad. If an enemy can cut off our food supplies, we will starve. In 1914 it was the same, with a powerful German battlefleet of *Dreadnoughts* stationed across the North Sea waiting to strike, and a growing German fleet of submarines ready to cut British ports off from the world. The British naval commander, Jellicoe was 'the only man on either side who could have lost the war in an afternoon' (Churchill).

The British navy had three jobs, to cut off the Central Powers from supplies from the outside world by mounting a blockade of their ports, to keep open the sea-routes

Figure 7.13 The war at sea

Source B. Catchpole, *A Map History of the Modern World*, Heinemann, p. 21.

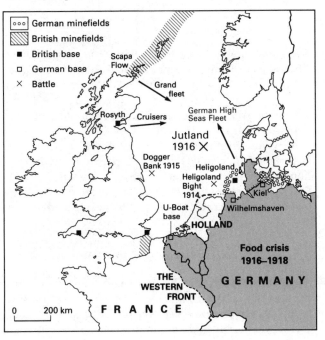

between Britain and the rest of the world, and to transport British troops and supplies across the Channel to Europe.

The World-Wide War

The British navy in 1914 soon rounded up German warships outside Europe. In the Battle of the Falkland Islands German raiders were finally trapped and sunk.

The Blockade of Germany

The British fleet's blockade of Germany caused trouble with neutral powers – the Dutch and Scandinavians, and the Americans. They protested bitterly at the British stopping and searching their ships. The blockade of the Central Powers was effective in causing widespread hunger in Germany. The winter of 1917–18 was called the 'turnip winter' because that was all there was for many to eat, and in 1919 the Germans were forced to accept the Versailles Treaty terms (see page 30), through fear of being starved into submission as the blockade continued.

Submarine Warfare

In 1915 the Germans turned to using mines and submarines as a means of starving Britain into surrender. The most famous victim of the submarines was the American liner *Lusitania*, sunk in May 1915 off Ireland with over 1,000 dead. In 1917 the Germans declared unrestricted submarine warfare, which meant that they would sink without warning any ship which they thought was sailing to a British port. The German gamble on starving Britain into surrender played a big part in getting America to declare war on Germany in April 1917. One million tons of sunk British ships, and severe food shortages and rationing, led the British government to introduce convoys and new means of fighting submarines, in particular depth charges and barrages of mines around the submarines' ports. These methods worked, and the submarine threat was beaten off.

The North Sea – Jutland

The two main fleets of Britain and Germany faced one another across the North Sea. The Germans mounted raids on British towns, and there were skirmishes between the fleets at Heligoland in 1914 and Dogger Bank in 1915. The Battle of Jutland, 31 May 1916, saw a clash between the German and British battle fleets.

The German fleet under *von Scheer* hoped to lure the British fleet into a trap. When the two fleets clashed, it turned into a duel between the battleships and cruisers, with the German gunners proving to be superior. Fourteen British ships were sunk, to eleven German ones. Although the Germans won a points victory, they broke off the battle and steamed back to port. The British fleet returned intact to its bases, and the Germans never sailed again to challenge them. This meant that the British kept control over the North Sea, and the blockade of Germany continued.

5 The Home Front

All over Europe people greeted the outbreak of war with enthusiasm (Source 7D). When war broke out there was an outburst of support for the struggle against Germany and her main ally, Austria–Hungary (see Section 1 above). Young men flocked to join the army, often joining up with their friends and neighbours. Whole battalions were raised from towns and villages, and in many cases they were wiped out *en masse* at battles like the Somme. By 1915 the grim reality of war had sunk in, with it affecting everyone's lives as the country waged a struggle to the death against Germany and Austria–Hungary.

Source 7D   Crowds cheer the outbreak of war

Source   F. Reynoldson, *War in Britain*, Heinemann, p. 7

Source 7E   A First World War poster

Source   F. Reynoldson, *War in Britain*, Heinemann, p. 25

Defence of the Realm Act (DORA)

In August 1914 the government passed DORA, which gave it huge powers over everyone's lives. The government acted to, among many things:

- control what people read in the newspapers and to censor any reports which said that the war was going badly
- close down the pubs in the day time, apart from lunch-time, to stop workers from drinking during working hours
- even stop people from flying kites, ringing church bells and feeding bread to hens and pigeons!

Conscription

In 1914 and 1915 posters urged young men to join the army or navy to fight the hated German enemy (Source 7E). But by 1916 the government could no longer rely on volunteers to provide the soldiers for trench warfare. So, it passed an act ordering all men aged 18–45 to join the forces. The government set up local courts or tribunals to decide whether men who claimed that their work was vital should be allowed to stay at home. Some men, known as *conscientious objectors*, COs or conshies, refused to join the forces on principle – they believed that war was evil. They were often sent to the front line to work as stretcher-bearers, work which almost always led to their injury or death. The pressure on men to fight was intense: if a man was out of uniform, women would approach him and pin a white feather on his jacket – a sign that he was a coward.

THE IMPACT OF WAR

Death

The war brought about huge changes in people's lives. Almost every family had a husband, son or close relative fighting in the trenches. Every day of the war 1,500 men died; no family was spared. In every city, town and village the war memorial is an horrific reminder of those slaughtered in 1914–18.

Also, for the first time for 150 years, death in war became a grim reality for English people living in their homes. In 1914 and 1915 German warships shelled British coastal towns. Airships or Zeppelins, and later planes, bombed London – over 1,000 people died in these raids.

Food

Food was in short supply, and sugar, meat and butter were at last rationed in 1918. The government encouraged the growing of vegetables on small plots or allotments. The problem of food shortage arose from its being imported, for the ships in which it was carried were under attack from German submarines. Food queues became common after 1916; by the end of the year submarines had sunk about 2,500,000 tons of shipping. Another 500,000 tons of shipping were sunk in April 1917, and in December 1917 *The Times* reported:

Source 7F

The following foods have been listed as in short supply: sugar, tea, butter, margarine, lard, dripping, milk, bacon, pork, condensed milk, rice, currants, raisins, spirits, Australian wine.

Women's Role

Figure 7.14   Increase in women workers

Government departments	+ 200,000
Office workers	+ 500,000
Farm workers	+ 250,000
Armed forces	+ 100,000
Nurses	+ 100,000
YMCA	+ 30,000
Engineering industry	+ 800,000
Arms Factories	
July 1914	210,000
July 1915	255,000
July 1916	520,000
July 1917	820,000

The First World War was vital for changing the role of women in British society. The demands of the armed forces for manpower meant a shortage of workers. So, women stepped into the breach, and did many jobs which before had been for men only. Women drove trams, carted coal and flour, took over clerks' jobs in firms and government offices, and played a vital role in heavy industry. In particular, women played a major role in arms factories, like that at Woolwich, whose labour force grew from 14,000 to 100,000 (Figure 7.14 and Source 7G). A writer of the time tells us:

Source 7G

Many of the women did extremely dangerous work, as, for example, when working in TNT [a high explosive] or in shell filling shops. Hours differed in various factories. In some the shifts were nominally 12 hours, in others three shifts of eight hours were worked . . . [During a shift there were few breaks.] Beginning at 7 o'clock they were granted ten minutes at 8 o'clock for a cup of tea. After this break, work went on until 12 o'clock. [After a short lunch the shift continued.]

Middle-class women played their part too. They were no longer fragrant, decorative creatures, but hard-working professionals, men's equals, who even wore trousers.

So vital was the role which women played in the war, that the moment it ended they won the vote for all women aged over thirty.

Examination Guidance

The MEG question will take the standard form below: two simple knowledge-based questions using the source as a stimulus; one question on the value of information inside sources; one question on the nature of sources; and a final question asking you to weave information together.

ACTIVITY 57

Targets

Knowledge and understanding, synthesis, handling of sources.

Question Guide

Questions 1–3 ask you to state two facts that you know about the situation shown, e.g. for Question 1 that they have just heard of the outbreak of war with Germany and Austria–Hungary in August 1914 and are looking forward to fighting on the side of Russia and France against the Germans. Question 4 requires you to do two things: (i) sort out information about both the nature of the sources (i.e. *The Times* newspaper, highly respected and reliable, and a personal diary, a source which is likely to be that of an eyewitness and reliable in terms of showing an individual viewpoint); and (ii) use the information inside the source to suggest whether it is reliable or not (e.g. whether the detail in the diary suggests whether it is or not). The final question invites you to comment upon the information which the sources provide, e.g. the list of occupations in Figure 7.14 and the detailed information on women at work in the munitions industry provides extensive material for you to weave into your answer.

Activity

Look carefully at Sources 7B – 7G and Figure 7.14. Then answer all the questions.

1. Look at Source 7D.
   Why were the people in the picture so happy? **(2)**
2. Look at Sources 7B and 7C
   What message are the cartoons trying to get across? **(2)**
3. (a) In what way can the statistics in Figure 7.14 be useful to the historian of the First World War? **(3)**
   (b) What value is Source 7G to the historian of the First World War? **(3)**
4. Read Sources 7F and 7G
   Which of these two sources is likely to be more trustworthy?
   Explain your answer fully, referring to the sources. **(6)**
5. Using your own knowledge, and information drawn from Figure 7.14 and Sources 7F and 7G, write an account of the impact of the First World War on the role of women. **(14)**

RUSSIA, 1917–56

Examination Guide

Russia appears on all four of the main Examining Group syllabuses, in two places: for full details, see pages 3–5 above.

Firstly, it plays a part in the coverage of **International Relations**: during the 1920s and 1930s in regard to the Versailles Settlement and the relations between the powers in the 1920s, in the 1930s as a major element in the events leading to the outbreak of the Second World War, during the Second World War as a key topic in the struggle against Germany, and after 1945 as one of the two superpowers whose rivalry has dominated international relations.

Russia is also a study in detail in its own right as the world's first communist power. The topic concentrates on the factors which led to the communists seizing power in 1917, the struggle by which they consolidated (made sure of) their control over the country, and the type of society which they created. There are many minor themes as well, such as a study of the meaning of dictatorship in the form of Stalin and the way in which he used the army and secret police to murder his enemies and wipe out all opposition – the Great Terror. Behind a study of Russia lie the questions of what has led to the rise of one of the world's two great superpowers? and what is the nature of its society?

The relationship of Russia to other syllabus topics is shown in the table. For LEAG it is one of three topics chosen from a list of 10 topics for Paper 1. For MEG it is one of two topics chosen from a list of nine topics for study in detail; for NEA one of three topics, chosen from a list of three in Sub-Section A of the Paper 2 theme, **Governments in Action**; for SEG, it is one of two topics taken from a list of seven for Paper 2, allowing for the study of topics in depth.

Group	%	Number of Topics	Russia coverage
LEAG	10	1 of 5 from 20	1917–41
MEG	15	1 out of 2 from 9	1917–41
NEA	10	1 of 1 from 3	1917–56
SEG	15	1 out of 2 from 7	1917–41

Find from past papers all the questions asked on Russia. Be careful to look at the general sections on international relations, which will often contain specific Russia-linked questions, particularly in relation to the outbreak of the Second World War, the Second World War and post-war settlement, and the Cold War and the superpowers' relations, including the period of detente.

QUESTION PATTERNS

The question pattern is more fully dealt with on pages 12–19 above). If you cannot get hold of the last three years' examination papers, or the specimen papers, make sure that you are well prepared to cover the topics listed in the **Topic Guide**.

There has been a tendency to set questions on the Russian Revolution of 1917, and on mainline (almost guaranteed) topics such as Stalin's agricultural and industrial policies. This has been partly to reassure teachers about the form which GCSE is taking, and that it is not a huge break from the old CSE and 'O' levels. Beware – this could well mean that the examiners will change the examination next time! They get fed up setting the same, stock questions, and could well switch to something new. Question-spotting can be dangerous; make sure that you have covered all of the most likely topics.

Topic Guide

1 The Russian Revolution, March 1917

If you had stopped people in the street in January 1917 and asked them about communism, it is very unlikely that they would ever have heard of the word. Today communist regimes rule over half the people in the world, and communist governments control Russia and China and did so in Eastern Europe until 1989. The Russian Revolution of 1917, and the Bolshevik or communist regime which arose from it, directly led to this state of affairs. What were the causes of the Russian Revolution? Historians argue fiercely about both the causes of the Revolution and its nature. The Revolution needs to be set against the background of the state of Russia in 1917, and changes which had happened in the previous fifty years.

CAUSES

Geography

Russia was a huge country, over seventy times the size of Britain. From Vladivostock on the Pacific east coast to St Petersburg in the west on the Baltic Sea, the train journey took well over a week; while from north to south Russia stretched from the icy arctic wastes of Novaya Zemlya to the semi-tropical Iranian borders (Figure 8.1).

The Russian Nation

Russia was an empire which had been expanding for several hundred years. In the nineteenth century it spread both south into Central Asia and east into China. By 1917 around half of its 130 million people were non-Russian.

The Russian People – the Countryside

Russia was a backward country – some 90 million of its people were peasants who had only been free for fifty years from serfdom, a form of slavery. Most peasants were illiterate and lived in villages without any modern water supply, lighting or roads. They paid most of their income to their landlords and the government and lived in a state of poverty. The peasants lived on the huge estates of the nobility, who made up Russia's ruling class.

The Towns

By 1917 Russia was undergoing an industrial revolution, and was a major industrial power, the world's fourth greatest behind America, Britain and Germany. The previous fifty years had seen the rapid growth of towns and cities, and the building of factories which relied on peasant labourers, who flocked to the city to earn a living. Slums grew up in the suburbs of the towns and cities – a rich breeding-ground for the revolutionary ideas of groups like the communists. The largest industrial city was the capital, St Petersburg. A small, educated middle class had grown up to run factories, trade, commerce and the professions, like the law (solicitors) and medicine.

Religion

Russia was a Christian country, with its own Church, the Russian Orthodox Church. Stalin, later Russia's ruler, was trained as an Orthodox priest. The growth of Russia meant that in 1914 it contained some 15 million Muslims. Russia also had around 10 million Catholics and a large Jewish population, mainly in the western area of modern Poland.

The Government

Russia had a single, autocractic ruler, the Tsar. In 1917 Nicholas II (1894–1917) was the Tsar, and he ruled the country with the help of his wife, a German princess, Alexandra. Nicholas and Alexandra ruled Russia with the backing of the landed aristocracy. The Tsar's government relied upon the support of the army, a large, inefficient civil service which ran the governments of the provinces and a secret police.

Opposition – the Revolutionaries

In the hundred years before the 1917 Revolution, Russia had seen the growth of small groups of often violent revolutionaries, dedicated to the overthrow of the Tsar's government. Their most spectacular success was in 1881, when a group blew up the Tsar. One such group of revolutionaries were the followers of a German Jewish thinker *Karl Marx* (1818–83). His followers are known as *Marxists* or *communists*. Karl Marx wrote a book called *Das Kapital* which became, and still is, the Marxists' bible. What did Marx believe?

● History is a struggle between classes for rule.
● History passes through a series of stages as society develops.
● At each stage one class rules. The ruling class is the one which controls the wealth which a society produces. This class will have overthrown the class which ruled in the previous stage.

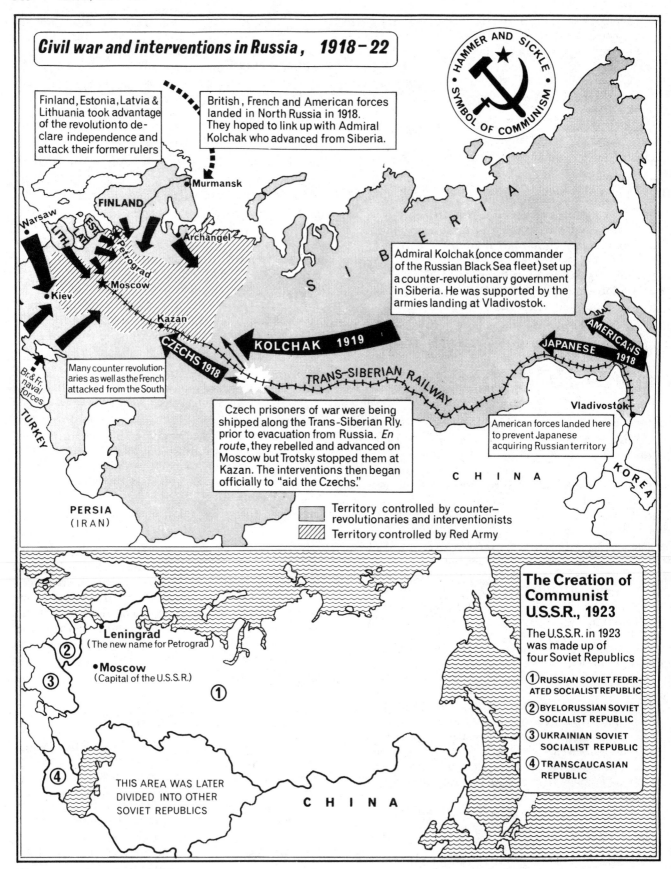

Civil war and interventions in Russia, 1918–22

HAMMER AND SICKLE · SYMBOL OF COMMUNISM

Finland, Estonia, Latvia & Lithuania took advantage of the revolution to declare independence and attack their former rulers

British, French and American forces landed in North Russia in 1918. They hoped to link up with Admiral Kolchak who advanced from Siberia.

Murmansk

FINLAND

Warsaw

EST
LAT
LITH

Petrograd

Archangel

S I B E R I A

Moscow

Kiev

Kazan

Admiral Kolchak (once commander of the Russian Black Sea fleet) set up a counter-revolutionary government in Siberia. He was supported by the armies landing at Vladivostok.

CZECHS 1918

KOLCHAK 1919

TRANS–SIBERIAN RAILWAY

AMERICANS 1918

JAPANESE

Br. & Fr. naval forces

Many counter revolutionaries as well as the French attacked from the South

TURKEY

Czech prisoners of war were being shipped along the Trans-Siberian Rly. prior to evacuation from Russia. *En route*, they rebelled and advanced on Moscow but Trotsky stopped them at Kazan. The interventions then began officially to "aid the Czechs."

American forces landed here to prevent Japanese acquiring Russian territory

Vladivostok

C H I N A

KOREA

PERSIA (IRAN)

Territory controlled by counter–revolutionaries and interventionists

Territory controlled by Red Army

The Creation of Communist U.S.S.R., 1923

The U.S.S.R. in 1923 was made up of four Soviet Republics

Leningrad (The new name for Petrograd)

Moscow (Capital of the U.S.S.R.)

① RUSSIAN SOVIET FEDERATED SOCIALIST REPUBLIC
② BYELORUSSIAN SOVIET SOCIALIST REPUBLIC
③ UKRAINIAN SOVIET SOCIALIST REPUBLIC
④ TRANSCAUCASIAN REPUBLIC

THIS AREA WAS LATER DIVIDED INTO OTHER SOVIET REPUBLICS

C H I N A

Figure 8.1 Russia, 1918–23

Source B. Catchpole, *A Map History of the Modern World*, Heinemann, p. 37.

- The stages are:

Stage	Ruling class	Ruled class/new class
Feudalism	Landowners	Merchants, industrialists (capitalists – middle class)
Capitalism	Middle-class capitalists	Factory workers (proletariat)
Socialism	Proletariat	– All are equal –

- For socialism to be brought about, there will first of all have to be a *dictatorship of the proletariat*. Here the proletariat's leaders have to take the decisions to bring about a society in which the state owns and runs all industry, trade, commerce, land and private property. With no private ownership of wealth, everyone will belong to the same class.

Marxism seemed to fit the pattern of Russian society, which in 1900 appeared to be changing from a state of feudalism to capitalism. The revolutionaries in Russia argued among themselves about the way in which they could bring about a communist or socialist society.

The Russian Revolutionaries

The Russian Marxists were a small group, many of whom lived in exile. A leading Russian Marxist was Vladimir Ilyich Ulanov (1870–1924), known as *Lenin*. Lenin was from a revolutionary background: his brother had been hanged for plotting to blow up the Tsar. When Lenin became a Marxist, the secret police arrested him and sent him into exile in Siberia. On his release Lenin continued to spread Marxist ideas through his newspaper *Iskra* (The Spark), and in 1903 he and other members of his revolutionary party, the Social Democrats, met in London.

When you read the newspaper or listen to the news you will always hear of rows within political parties about the policies they should back. Such rows can sometimes lead to a party splitting up. In 1903 this happened to the Social Democrats. The row is vital to understand, because it played a big part in what happened to Russia from 1917 to 1956.

At the London meeting the Social Democrats split into two groups:

1. *Lenin and the Bolsheviks* (the majority), who backed a small, well-organised party of revolutionaries which would seize power without middle-class (capitalists') support. One of Lenin's backers was a revolutionary called *Stalin*, Russia's ruler from 1927 to 1953.
2. *The Mensheviks* (the minority), who wanted a larger, political party which gained the backing of the middle class in its struggle against the Tsar. A leading Menshevik was *Trotsky*, a key figure in the Russian Revolution and the Russian government from 1917 to 1927.

A third Russian revolutionary group, the *Social Revolutionaries*, believed that a revolution would have to be based on a rising of the peasants, who would be given their land. In 1917 the Social Revolutionaries were the largest revolutionary party. *Kerensky*, Russia's ruler in May–November 1917, was their leader. The Bolsheviks,

Mensheviks and Social Revolutionaries ran Russia from March 1917.

RUSSIA, 1900–17

From 1900 to 1917 a number of events pointed to the outbreak of revolution in 1917.

The Russo-Japanese War, 1904–5

In 1904 Russia went to war with Japan – a quick victory would help take away attention from Russia's problems at home: strikes and demands for the setting up of a parliament. The war was a disaster – the Japanese defeated the Russian army in Manchuria, and at the Battle of Tsushima the Japanese navy sank the Russian battle fleet. The Russians had sailed around the world to fight, sinking British fishing boats in the North Sea on the way! Defeat in the war helped spark off the 1905 Revolution.

The 1905 Revolution

From January to October 1905 the Tsar was faced with a possible revolution: marches, peasant risings, national revolts, a naval mutiny, strikes and, in October, a general strike (Figure 8.2). In St Petersburg and Moscow, the workers elected workers' councils or *soviets* to control their factories and the cities. Under the *October Manifesto* of 1905 the Tsar agreed to call an elected council of *Duma*, a parliament, to help him run the country. The Duma seemed to answer the demands of a middle-class Russian party, the *Cadets*.

The Duma

The first Duma was elected in 1906. It wanted to have control over the government, to appoint and remove ministers, to break up the large estates and to introduce a popularly elected parliament. The Tsar dismissed the Duma within ten weeks, and it soon became clear that the *October Manifesto* was a sham. The Tsar would keep full control over:

- the army
- foreign policy
- taxes and government finances
- the appointment and removal of ministers
- the making of laws.

In 1907 Nicholas changed the rules for choosing a Duma, and from 1907 to 1917 the Duma did as he wanted. But, it was a body through which the Cadet Party could put forward ideas for change, and in 1917 it played a part in the Revolution.

Stolypin

From 1906 until 1911 it seemed that Russia might be able to solve the problem of the new, industrial working class, the poverty of the peasants and the revolutionaries. Peter *Stolypin* was Prime Minister, and he pushed through a number of key reforms:

(a) Peasants no longer had to pay large sums of money for their freedom from serfdom. This made them much better off.

Figure 8.2   The 1905 revolution

Source   B. Catchpole, *A Map History of Russia*, Heinemann, p. 33

(b)   They were helped to buy their own lands. A new group of rich peasants, the *kulaks*, emerged.

(c)   In 1912 a sickness and accident insurance scheme was introduced for workers.

(d)   Over 3,000 revolutionaries were hanged – others were forced into exile.

Stolypin was shot in 1911 by a member of the secret police – Stolypin had enemies in the government, and they may even have plotted his death. But Stolypin's reforms seemed to have brought Russia peace. The year 1913 saw three centuries of rule by the Romanovs, the Tsar's family. There were huge celebrations and popular support for the Tsar – little or no sign of revolution. The industrial revolution was making great progress – in 1913 Russia had the world's fastest-growing economy. There was a growth in the number of unions and thousands of strikes – a sign that in the future the workers might rise against the government.

The First World War, 1914–18

In terms of long-term causes of the Russian Revolutions of 1917, the First World War plays a major part. Russia was an ally of Britain and France, and her armies were soon locked in combat with those of Germany and Austria–Hungary. Although the Germans routed the Russian armies in 1914 at the Battles of Tannenberg and the Masurian Lakes, Russia was able to hold back the Austrian forces and defeat them. The picture of Russia collapsing under the strain of war is a false one; what the

war did was to disrupt the economy and lead to a total collapse of confidence in the Tsar and his government. With major military defeats in 1916 and 1917, this led to the growth of a revolutionary movement in the capital, St Petersburg.

THE RUSSIAN REVOLUTION OF MARCH 1917

Russia had two revolutions in 1917: the first in March saw the Tsar's fall; the second in November led to the communist Bolsheviks' seizure of power. What were the factors which led to the outbreak of revolution in March 1917? Historians have put forward many arguments, here are some of them:

1.   *The Tsar, as commander-in-chief, was linked to the failure of the army against the Germans.* Since 1915 the Tsar had had personal command of the army. The failures against the Germans in General Brusilov's offensive of 1916, and the advances of the Germans during the winter of 1916/17 were blamed directly on the Tsar. Morale among the Russian officers and soldiers was very low because of the continued advance of the Germans.

2.   *The Tsar was blamed for the failure of the government to be efficient and to push the war on successfully.* The government had failed to feed the cities properly: there was widespread hunger in the winter of 1917. Russia was able to grow all the food she needed, and from her growing industry she could make all the guns, bullets and shells she needed. The prob-

lem was in making sure that the food from the farms, and the armaments and supplies, reached the cities and the army.

The roles of the Tsarina, Alexandra, and her chief adviser, Rasputin, were crucial in the collapse of support for the Tsar. The Tsarina, a German ('the German woman') was widely hated – it was even thought that she was a German agent. This seemed the only logical explanation for the moronic way in which she ran the government. Her adviser was a drunken and lecherous monk, Rasputin, who was largely to blame for the sacking of any competent ministers. From August to September 1915 Russia had four prime ministers and three ministers of war. Despite the murder of Rasputin in December 1916, the Tsarina was still blamed for the shambolic state of the government.

3. *Failure of the economy.* Although industry was able to supply the army with all its needs, the collapse of the railway system and the failure of government meant that in the winter of 1917 bread was in short supply and prices soared. Strikes were widespread. The March 1917 Revolution broke out as a bread riot against high prices and food shortages.

4. *The role of the Duma.* The Duma and local Russian councils, the Zemstvos, were ready to help the Tsar fight the war. They wanted him to sack his corrupt ministers and rely on them. The Tsar refused to listen to them. By 1917 they were willing to back any government which would sweep away the corruption of the Tsar's regime and fight the war efficiently.

The March 1917 Revolution was largely a result of the collapse of efficient government. The main Putilov engineering works shut down in early March 1917 because it had run out of coal. The workers called a strike, and in the next few days the strike snowballed. On 8 March, International Women's Day, some 90,000 people joined the march through Petrograd, calling for bread. The capital's transport system collapsed – no trams. By 11 March the government's attempts to use police and troops against the demonstrators had failed (Figure 8.3). The city was in the

Source 8A Soldiers carry a revolutionary banner carrying the slogan 'Liberty, Equality and Fraternity' during the March Revolution

Source Ronald Hingley, *A Concise History of Russia*, Thames & Hudson, 1972, p. 152

grip of a general strike, and soldiers and police had joined the strikers who held mass marches (Source 8A). On 12 March the Law Courts went up in flames, the mob sacked the headquarters of the Secret Police and burned police stations throughout the capital. The chaos in the capital is reflected in the notes of telephone calls a writer received at home on the day the government fell:

Source 8B

(a) The crowds on the Nevskii Street are bigger than ever today.

(b) Workmen of the Putilovskii Factory and of the Vyborg (the workers' quarter) have gone out into the street.

(c) Heavy firing is heard from different sides of the town.

(d) They say the Duma is dissolved.

The Tsar tried to return to the capital, but soldiers stopped his train. Later he heard of the total collapse of his government and the arrest of his ministers. When told that he would have to abdicate, he tried to give the throne to his brother, the Grand Duke Michael, who refused the offer. The reign of the Romanovs was over.

THE NEW GOVERNMENT

The Duma formed a new, provisional government with twelve members. The provisional government was to rule Russia until elections were held for a parliament which would draw up a constitution or new system of government for Russia. At the same time the *Petrograd Soviet*, or council of workers, issued its *Order No. 1*. Each army and navy unit was ordered to set up its own committee, which was to decide whether to obey officers' orders. In other towns and cities revolutionaries formed soviets, which took their lead from the Petrograd Soviet.

Examination Guidance

It is likely that a question on the March Revolution will be combined with one on the November Revolution and the Bolshevik extension of control over Russia from 1917 to 1921. Activity 58 is based on the LEAG, MEG and NEA question patterns.

ACTIVITY 58

Targets

Recall, understanding, concepts cause, evidence – evaluation.

Question Guide

Question 1 is based on recall. Question 2 requires analysis of the source, and linking it to your knowledge of the background to the March Revolution: for example, the fighting would have involved striking workers, demonstrators demanding bread, mutinous soldiers and the city's police and army garrison. Question 3 draws on a range of skills, and forces you to think carefully about the

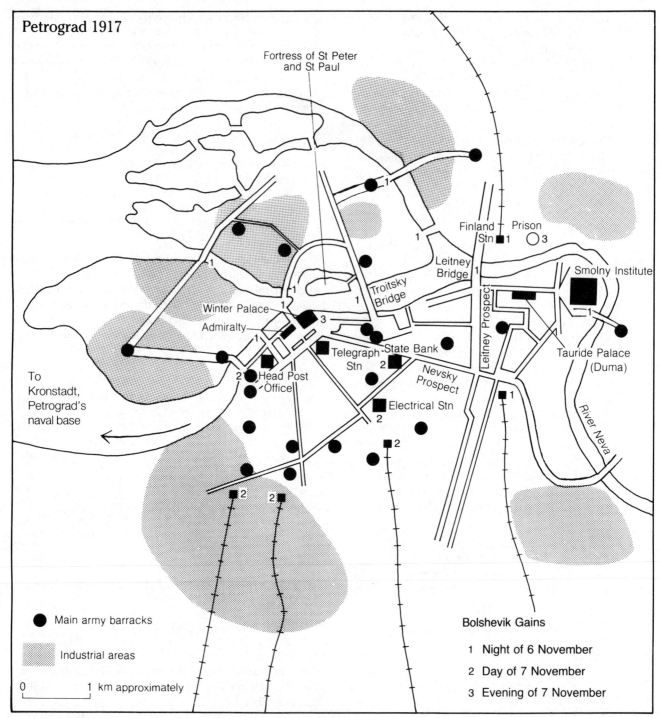

Figure 8.3 Map of Petrograd, November 1917   *Source* J. F. Aylett, *Russia in Revolution*, Edward Arnold, 1981, p. 34

causes of the March Revolution, and link them into the two sources. Question 4 is about the value of different kinds of sources: a photograph, and the record of a person present at the time of the Revolution but receiving news at second hand by telephone.

Activity

Look carefully at Sources 8A and 8B and Figure 8.3. Then answer ALL the questions.

1. (a) Where might the mutinous soldiers have come from? **(1)**
   (b) What was the Duma? **(1)**
   (c) Who had the power to dissolve it? **(1)**

2. (a) Explain what Source 8B means when it says that the workers 'have gone out into the street'. **(2)**
   (b) Who might have been involved in the fighting? **(2)**
   (c) Why might the soldiers have been carrying a banner with the words 'Liberty, Equality and Fraternity' [brotherhood] on them? **(3)**

3. Write an account of the events which led up to the situation illustrated by Sources 8A and 8B. The account should explain what had led to the scenes shown in Source 8A and the telephone comments in Source 8B. **(12)**

4. Discuss the value to the historian of:
   (a) sources like Source 8A **(4)**
   (b) sources like Source 8B **(4)**

2 The November 1917 Revolution

The history of Russia from the Revolutions of March–November 1917 is very complex. We need to lay down the vertebrae of the subject as a backbone for dealing with the detail of the topic. There are two vital things to keep in mind:

1. Russia was still at war with Germany – with the Germans advancing towards the Russian capital and threatening a naval attack.
2. We are mainly talking about what went on in the capital, Petrograd, with special reference to the actions of small groups of revolutionaries who were rivals for power. These were the Social Revolutionaries, the Bolsheviks of Lenin and the Mensheviks. Figure 8.4 lists the main events:

Figure 8.4 Events in Russia, March–October 1917

March 1917
Fall of the Tsar's government. The Duma sets up a provisional government. The Petrograd Soviet of workers formed.

April
Return to Petrograd of the Bolshevik leader, Lenin, from exile. The Germans had sent him back from Switzerland in a 'sealed train' to stir up revolution! Lenin issues his April Theses (Source 8C). The Petrograd Soviet shares power in the government with the Duma.

May
Kerensky, Vice-President of the soviet and leader of the Social Revolutionaries, becomes leader of the government. Backs a policy of fighting the war efficiently. Lenin opposes the war – presses for peace.

June
Bolsheviks win control over the workers' area of Petrograd (Vyborg district). Kerensky mounts summer offensive against the Germans.

July
Failure of the summer offensive. Huge street demonstrations in favour of peace.

The July Rising
Some Bolsheviks, not Lenin and the Bolsheviks' leaders, take to the streets of Petrograd and try and seize power. Government crushes the rising – Bolshevik leaders go into hiding. Lenin flees to Finland.

September
Kornilov Revolt. The army commander, Kornilov, tries to seize control of the government. Rail strike stops his progress. In Petrograd the Soviet organises the workers to resist Kornilov. Collapse of his rising.
The Bolsheviks win control over the Petrograd Soviet. Able to use its Military Revolutionary Committee to seize power.

October
Lenin gets the backing of the Bolshevik party to an attempt to seize power. Lenin fears that Kerensky will try and use the army to crush the Bolsheviks, and that the other revolutionary parties – the Mensheviks and the Social Revolutionaries – will outvote the Bolsheviks in a meeting of soviets from the army, towns and cities of Russia.

HOW THE BOLSHEVIKS SEIZED POWER

The central question asked about the November Revolution is why and how the Bolsheviks seized power. These points need thinking about:

1. The Role of Lenin

Lenin is a key figure in the Bolshevik seizure of power in November 1917. When he returned from exile in April, his April Theses (Source 8C) laid down the main policies the Bolsheviks were to follow in the next six months:

Source 8C   The April Theses of Lenin

1. No support for the provisional government.
2. An immediate end to the war.
3. A republic of peasants and workers Soviets to be formed.
4. The Soviets to control all economic life – the running of industry, transport, farming, trade, commerce and banking.
5. The banks to be government-owned (nationalised).
6. The land to be government-owned (nationalised).
7. The army, police and civil service to be disbanded.
8. The soviets to elect the officials to run a new army, police and civil service.
9. An international body to be formed to spread the Bolshevik revolution around the world.
10. The Bolshevik party to win the workers and peasants round to its views through discussion and argument.

During the summer Lenin pressed for the building up of a small, highly organised Bolshevik party (Source 8D). In October he played the key part in getting the Bolshevik party to agree to an attempt to take over the government without the support of the other revolutionary parties.

Source 8D   Lenin addressing a meeting in Moscow; Trotsky is the man on his left in uniform

Source   R. Hingley, *A Concise History of Russia*, Thames & Hudson, p. 159

2. The Bolsheviks' Organisation

The Bolsheviks were highly organised, with cells within the Petrograd factories, the armed garrison and army units at the front. Within Petrograd, under the lead of the ex-Menshevik Trotsky, they formed their own groups of armed men – the *Red Guards*. They had their own newspaper (*Pravda*); Stalin played a key role in running it. Within the Petrograd Soviet the Bolsheviks played a major role, finally gaining control in September. They were able to get the Soviet's *Military Revolutionary Committee* to back a rising (Source 8E).

Source 8E

Preparations for the insurrection proceeded apace, but along an entirely different channel. The actual master of the capital's garrison, the Military Revolutionary Committee, was seeking an excuse for openly breaking with the government. That pretext was provided on November 4th. by the officer commanding the troops of the district when he refused to let the Committee's commisars control his staff. We had to strike while the iron was hot. The Bureau of the Military Revolutionary Committee, Sverdlov and I participating, decided to recognise the break with the garrison staff as an accomplished fact and to take the offensive. Stalin was not at the conference. It never occurred to anyone to call him . . .

   The Central Committee session [of the Petrograd Soviet] that directly launched the insurrection was held at Smolny [the Smolny Institute – Figure 8.3], now transformed into a fortress, on the morning of November 6th . . . At the very outset a motion of Kamenev's [a Bolshevik leader] was passed. The report of the Military Revolutionary Committee [for a rising] was on the agenda . . . The report states 'Trotsky proposed that two members of the Central Committee be placed at the disposal of the Military Revolutionary Committee to maintain contact with the post and telegraph operators and the railway men; a third member to keep an eye on the Provisional Government . . . Trotsky proposed the establishment of a reserve staff in the Peter and Paul Fortress [the Petrograd army headquarters] and the assignment of one member of the Central Committee there for that purpose.'
(L. Trotsky, *Stalin*, Hollis & Carter, 1947, pp. 233–4)

3. The Bolsheviks' Appeal

The slogan of the Bolsheviks – Bread, Peace, Land and All Power to the Soviets – became of increasing appeal as the summer of 1917 wore on:

- *Bread* – the need to feed the swelling population of Petrograd was a popular cause. It had led to the fall of the Tsar's government in March.
- *Peace* – became a very powerful slogan after the failure of Kerensky's June Offensive, and the threat to Petrograd from a German naval force. Rumours of a German landing were widespread in October 1917.
- *Land* – in the countryside there was a widespread breakdown of law and order as peasants seized control over their land from the aristocratic landlords.
- *All Power to the Soviets* – this would give control of the government to the leaders of the soldiers, factory workers and peasants.

4. The Weakness of Kerensky

Kerensky was a weak leader because he failed after the July days, in which some Bolsheviks attempted to seize power, to wipe out the Bolshevik threat. The failure of the summer offensive meant that his war policy lost popular support. There was a collapse of morale in the army, and the flight of thousands of deserters, many of whom ended up in Petrograd. The Kornilov Rising meant that Kerensky could not rely on the backing of the army. Indeed, he was forced to get the backing of the Bolsheviks in order to stay in power.

THE REVOLUTION

Once Lenin and the Bolsheviks had decided to strike, they moved quickly into action. The Bolsheviks had the backing of the soldiers of the city's garrison and the sailors of the Kronstadt naval base. Lenin used the Red forces to seize control of all the key points in the city. The cruiser *Aurora* sailed up the River Neva to shell the provisional government's base in the Winter Palace. The *Aurora*'s attack led to the flight of the soldiers defending the provisional government. The Bolsheviks broke into the Winter Palace, and arrested most of the members of the provisional government while they were at a meeting to discuss the crisis. Kerensky fled in a motor car. The Bolsheviks also seized control over Moscow, and soon spread their grip to the rest of the country.

Examination Guidance

Questions will take two forms: those linked to sources like Sources 8C and 8D, and essay questions like Activity 59b.

ACTIVITY 59a

Targets

Recall, knowledge and understanding, concepts of cause and consequence, evidence – detection of bias, empathy (i.e. looking at events from the viewpoint of people in the past).

Question Guide

Question 1 is simple recall: you need to write a short sentence containing relevant information about each. Question 2 is the kind of activity which is becoming common in GCSE textbooks, and aims to make you think about the meaning of the April Theses. It could well emerge as a standard examination question – it has already appeared on an LEAG paper. Question 3(a) is aimed at making you tie in the precise points of the April Theses into growing Bolshevik support – you need to work out from the text which points received support. Question 3(b) is rather different: it asks you to take detailed information from the source and tie it into what you already know. Question 4 asks you to mention the reference to Stalin, and that the book was written by Trotsky after Stalin had driven him from Russia.

Activity

Study Sources 8C, 8D and 8E, and then answer the questions.

1. Explain the references to:
   (a) the Provisional Government **(1)**
   (b) Soviets **(1)**
   (c) the Military Revolutionary Committee **(1)**
   (d) Lenin **(1)**
   (e) Trotsky **(1)**
   (f) Bolshevik. **(1)**
2. Using Source 8C and your own knowledge, put a tick in the column which shows the views you think the following people might have held in May 1917 on hearing the April Theses mentioned below. **(14)**

Thesis 2 –

End to the war	Support	No views	Oppose
A poor peasant			
A rich peasant (a kulak)			
An army officer			
An aristocrat			
A soldier on the German front			
A banker			
A Social Revolutionary lawyer			

Thesis 5 –

Government to own banks	Support	No views	Oppose
A poor peasant			
A rich peasant (a kulak)			
An army officer			
An aristocrat			
A soldier on the German front			
A banker			
A Social Revolutionary lawyer			

Thesis 6 –

Land to the peasants	Support	No views	Oppose
A poor peasant			
A rich peasant (a kulak)			
An army officer			
An aristocrat			
A soldier on the German front			
A banker			
A Social Revolutionary lawyer			

Theses 7 & 8

Disband the army	Support	No views	Oppose
A poor peasant			
A rich peasant (a kulak)			
An army officer			
An aristocrat			
A soldier on the German front			
A banker			
A Social Revolutionary lawyer			

3. (a) Explain why the April Theses received increasing backing between April and November 1917. **(3)**
   (b) What light does Source 8D throw on how the November Revolution was organised? **(3)**

4. (a) What does Source 8D suggest about Trotsky's role? **(2)**
   (b) What evidence is there of bias in the writing of Source 8E? **(2)**

ACTIVITY 59b

Targets

Recall, knowledge and understanding, concepts of cause, change and consequence.

Question Guide

Read the question through carefully – have you spotted the two key buzz words, 'How' and 'Why' (see pages 15–16). The question is known as a *structured essay*. When you plan it out, for each of the points given make sure that you have at least two facts to include in your answer. The facts must link into explaining how and why the Bolsheviks gained power.

Activity

How and why did the Bolsheviks seize power in November 1917? You can mention the following in your answer:

- the role of Lenin
- Trotsky and the Red forces
- the Bolsheviks' organisation
- the Petrograd Soviet and the Military Revolutionary Committee
- life in the capital
- the countryside
- the failure of the June Offensive
- the Kornilov Revolt.

3   The Civil War and War Communism

If you had been living in Russia in 1918–22, it is likely that a member of your family would either have died of starvation, lost his or her home, fled into exile or been killed or wounded in fighting. What lay behind these upheavals?

November 1917–January 1918

In November 1917 elections were held for a *Constituent Assembly* to work out a constitution for the rule of Russia. In the elections, the Bolsheviks had only 9 million votes and 175 seats compared to the 21 million votes and 175 seats of the Social Revolutionaries. When the Constituent Assembly met in January 1918, Lenin used Bolshevik troops to break up the meeting.

Peace with Germany

Peace talks opened in December 1918 with the Germans. German advances in the New Year forced Lenin to make

Figure 8.5   The Treaty of Brest–Litovsk

Source   Jos Brooman, *Russia in War and Revolution, 1900–24*, Longman, p. 24

a peace in March 1918, the *Treaty of Brest–Litovsk*. The Treaty stripped Russia of a quarter of her farmland and three-quarters of her coal and iron mines (Figure 8.5).

CIVIL WAR

From January 1918 until 1921 Russia was in a state of civil war. Social Revolutionaries, Mensheviks, backers of

the Tsar and national groups claimed that the Bolsheviks, *the Reds*, had no right to rule. The Bolsheviks' enemies, *the Whites*, gained the backing of British, French, Japanese and American forces, because Russia had signed a peace treaty with Germany in March 1918, taken over the property of foreign firms in Russia and refused to repay the debts of the Tsar's government. The Bolsheviks controlled the central area of Russia (Figure 8.6). They faced four main White Armies – *Admiral Kolchak* in the east, *Generals Deniken* and *Wrangel* in the south and *General Yudenich* in the west. The Bolsheviks built up the Red forces under the able leadership of Trotsky. Trotsky ran the Bolshevik forces on the several war fronts from a special train. The Bolshevik secret police, the *Cheka*, killed many of the Bolshevik enemies. The Whites had no single leadership. In 1920 the Bolsheviks were also at war with the Poles, a war which Poland won. Figure 8.7 lists the main events of the civil war period:

Figure 8.7   The civil war

March 1918
The Treaty of Brest–Litovsk. Russia handed over the Baltic provinces and large areas of Western Russia to the Germans. Attacks of the Czech Legion and the armies of Kolchak. The Czech Legion, some 40,000 Czech prisoners-of-war, had seized control over the Trans-Siberian Railway and towns along its route. The Czechs and Kolchak were defeated by mid-1919.

July
Attempt to murder Lenin leads to the Cheka's 'Red Terror' against known opponents of the regime. Murder of the Tsar and his family at Ekaterinburg.

1918–19
Repulse by November 1919 of attacks in the south from Denikin.

Figure 8.6   Intervention in Russia   *Source*   Jos Brooman, *Russia in War and Revolution*, 1900–24, Longman, p. 28

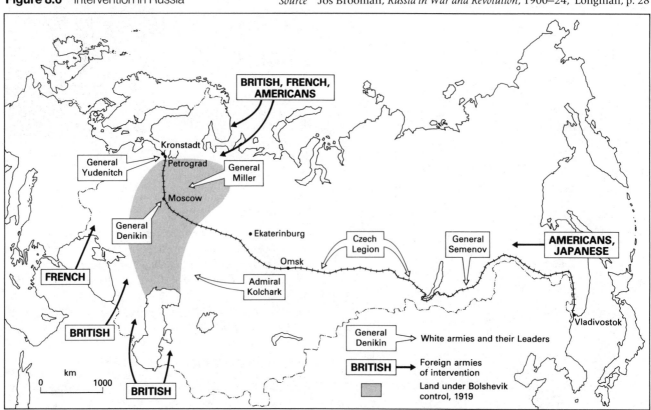

April 1920
Polish attack on Russia.

March 1921
Treaty of Riga. Poland gains claimed lands from Russia.

February
Stalin defeats the Whites in Georgia. (Note: Stalin also organised the defence of Petrograd, and defended Stalingrad so well that it was named after him.)

By the end of 1921 the fighting was over. Why had the Bolsheviks won?
(a) Their policies appealed to both peasants and factory workers.
(b) Their enemies were disunited – with several leaders and no joint command.
(c) The Reds had control over Moscow and Petrograd, Russia's main industrial centres.
(d) The main railway network was based on Moscow–Petrograd; it helped the Bolsheviks meet threats from any quarter.
(e) The Whites received little real help from the British, French and Americans.
(f) The Reds were very well led by Trotsky. He imposed iron discipline on the Red forces, shooting all deserters and those who disobeyed orders.
(g) The Cheka was ruthless in killing opponents of the Bolsheviks.

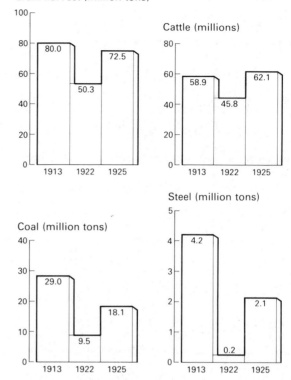

Figure 8.8   Industrial production in Russia, 1913–21

Source   K. Shephard and Jon Nichol, *Russia*, Basil Blackwell, 1988, p. 28

WAR COMMUNISM

To win the war and set up a communist society, Lenin and the Bolsheviks seized control over the economy. This was carried out through a policy known as *War Communism*. War Communism meant:

(a) State ownership of all factories, workshops, mines and the railways. The government decided what each factory should produce. Workers were forced to obey government orders, with a death penalty for strikers.
(b) State control over all trade – private markets were banned. Peasants had to sell their extra food to the government. No profit-making was allowed.
(c) State power to seize grain from the peasants to feed the factory workers and soldiers
(d) State control over banking.
(e) Rationing of food in the towns and cities.

War Communism was a failure. The peasants refused to hand over grain. Villagers ceased to plant their crops, knowing that the Bolsheviks would seize the harvest. In the towns and cities the hand-out of food was a shambles – many people failed to receive enough rations to live on. Output from factories fell sharply (Figure 8.8) – the organisation of industry was chaotic, many of the owners and factory and business managers had fled, workers refused to work for starvation wages.

By the end of the civil war in 1921 a famine had broken out. War Communism, the chaos of the civil war, and the failure of the harvest, meant that millions died (Source 8F).

Source 8F   Victims of famine during the Civil War

Source   K. Shephard and Jon Nichol, *Russia*, Basil Blackwell, 1978, p. 29

Examination Guidance

The Russian civil war and War Communism will often be combined with a question on the 1917 Revolutions and the later period. Questions can take a variety of forms. Activity 60a is taken from the June 1988 SEG paper and requires three short essays; Activity 60b is the MEG specimen paper question, which sets a range of questions on a variety of sources.

ACTIVITY 60a

Targets

Recall, knowledge and understanding.

Question Guide

Spot the buzz word, 'importance', and the limits of the question, 1917–24. Split the time up evenly between the three parts, as you are asked to provide three short essays. Each of these should contain about a dozen separate pieces of linked information tied to the question's specific topic.

Activity

1. The Russian Revolution, Lenin and Stalin, 1917–1941

Study this list of events which happened in Russia within the years 1917–24.

(a) March 1917: The Provisional Government was formed.

.(b) August 1917: General Kornilov's attempt to overthrow the Provisional Government failed.

(c) 1918: The Treaty of Brest–Litovsk with Germany was signed.

(d) 1920: Foreign support for the White forces was finally withdrawn.

(e) 1921: The New Economic Policy was introduced.

Choose three events from the list.

Show the importance of each of your choices in the course of events in Russia from 1917 to 1924.

(3 x 10 marks)
TOTAL: 30 marks

ACTIVITY 60b

Targets

Recall and understanding, concepts of cause, evidence – extraction of information, evaluation, detection of bias or gaps.

Question Guide

Question 1 is simple recall – but note the marks awarded. Question 2 is aimed at recall but does require some conceptual understanding of the causes of what happened.

Question 3 (a) is a pure recall question, while Question 3 (b) requires careful analysis of a source. Make sure that you have found four major reasons. Question 4 requires a fuller treatment of the sources; you will have to look carefully at the other sources to see if you can find evidence to match the key words 'support' and 'contradict'. Be clear in your own mind what these words mean before you start your answer. Question 5 is a standard evaluation-of-sources question, asking you to look for gaps in the evidence and signs of bias. Deal first with the nature of the sources – what they are, who produced them – before looking at what they say in relation to the raising of doubts.

Activity

The Russian Revolution

Look carefully at Sources 1–3. Then answer ALL the questions.

Source 1

These people are unanimous in describing conditions as unbearable, owing to the rule of the Bolsheviks, as well as to the appalling economic conditions brought about by Lenin's regime.

The Russian nation is groaning under the tyranny of the Bolsheviks. Workers and peasants are compelled to work under threat of death. Since only the Red Guards have weapons, a rising of the people is not possible.

Famine is widespread. The peasants refuse to sell food but will only barter it. Unless people have about 1000 roubles [£100] a month they have to starve. It is possible to buy food from the Red Guards who are well fed. Lenin and his colleagues are living in luxury.

(Reports from British refugees on conditions in Russia, October 1918.)

Source 2

1. All Soviets of Workers' and Peasants' Deputies, all committees of the poor and all trade unions are to form detachments.

2. The tasks of the detachments are:
(a) Harvest winter grain in former landlord-owned estates.
(b) Harvest grain in front line areas.
(c) Harvest grain on the land of kulaks or rich people.
(d) Help in harvests everywhere.

3. Grain for the poor must be stored locally, the rest must be sent to grain collection centres.

4. Every food requisition detachment is to consist of not fewer than 75 men and two or three machine-guns.
(Instructions for Harvesting and Grain Requisitioning Detachments, August 1918.)

Source 3

The Economy in 1913 and in 1921

PRODUCTION	1913	1921
Coal (million tons)	29.0	9.0
Oil (million tons)	9.2	3.8
Pig Iron (million tons)	4.2	0.1
Steel (million tons)	4.3	0.2
Bricks (millions)	2.1	0.01
Agriculture (million tons of grain)	80.0	38.0

1. What is meant by
(a) kulaks (Source 2, 2(c)? **(1)**
(b) Soviets (Source 2, 1)? **(1)**

2. What had happened between 1913 and 1921, apart from the Revolutions of 1917, to bring about the state of the Russian economy as revealed in Source 3? Explain your answer briefly. **(4)**

3. (a) Why was the Grain Requisitioning programme, described in Source 2 issued? **(2)**
(b) In what ways does Source 2 indicate that the Bolshevik Government had a number of difficulties in obtaining grain? **(4)**

4. What criticisms of Bolshevik rule are made in Source 1? In what ways do the other sources support or contradict these criticisms? **(10)**

5. What doubts might an historian have about accepting the evidence of
(a) Source 1; **(4)**
(b) Source 3? **(4)**
TOTAL (30)

4 The New Economic Policy

What would England be like if in every city, town and village there had been a state of civil war for three years, with a continuous struggle between rival armies? By early 1921 the Bolsheviks had gained control over most of Russia, but Lenin was confronted with a country facing a mammoth human tragedy. Agriculture, trade and industry were in a state of total collapse (Figure 8.9), and the peasants were on virtual strike against the Red Army, forcing them to hand over their food surpluses. War Communism seemed to have made the crisis worse. The disaster deepened in March 1921 with the huge peasant revolt in the Tambov region to the south-east of Moscow, strikes in Petrograd and the revolt of the sailors of Kronstadt. The backbone of Revolutionary Russia seemed to be crumbling. In 1921–2 a famine meant that some 5 million starved to death (Source 8F). A League of Nations relief programme for Russia, under the control of the explorer *Fridtjof Nansen*, helped solve the crisis.

The Kronstadt Rising

Stalin used Trotsky and the Red Army to crush the revolt of the Kronstadt sailors and the Tambov revolt. The 10,000 rebellious Kronstadt sailors were routed. The Cheka rounded up and shot many of the survivors.

The Tenth Party Congress

In March 1921, at the Tenth Party congress, Lenin banned all opposition inside the party. At the same time he announced the end of War Communism and that the *New Economic Policy* (the *NEP*) would replace it.

What did the NEP mean?

(a) Peasants could sell any spare crops in local markets. No longer would they fear that Bolshevik troops would seize their surpluses.
(b) The more the peasants produced, the less tax they paid.
(c) Private trade was allowed.
(d) Privately owned factories and workshops could be set up with fewer than 20 workers.
(e) Forced labour was ended, bonuses introduced and people were paid in money and not goods.

Impact of the NEP

Small firms were set up, street markets flourished, the peasants were able to sell their produce openly. In towns a new class of businessmen, the *nepmen*, emerged, made rich by the profits of private trade and industry. The economy underwent a quite amazing recovery. Farming recovered very quickly, and wealthy peasants, the kulaks, built up their private farms. But industry took much longer to return to pre-war output levels. The result was an increase in the price of industrial goods in 1923 and a collapse of the income of the peasants – the so-called *Scissors Crisis* (Figure 8.10). However, Figure 8.9 suggests that the NEP was a success. The government, through the new *State Bank* of 1921, solved the problem of massive inflation in 1924. The State Bank issued a new currency (the Soviet rouble) to replace the old, worthless sovznak rouble. The NEP move to allow *kulaks* to employ labourers in 1925 shocked many Bolsheviks. However, the NEP was a short-term policy to pave the way for the bringing-about of communism.

Figure 8.10   The Scissors Crisis

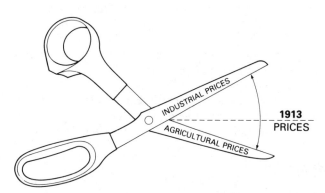

Source   B. Catchpole, *A Map History of Russia*, Heinemann, p. 49.

The 1923 Constitution

In 1923 the Bolsheviks introduced a new constitution which set up the *Union of Soviet Socialist Republics (USSR)*. The country was split up into four separate republics which ran their own internal affairs, such as health and education (p. 148). National concerns, economic planning, defence and foreign affairs stayed firmly in the hands of Lenin and the central government, the *Politburo*.

Source   A. Nove, *An Economic History of the USSR*, Penguin Books, 1969, p. 94

Figure 8.9   Russian economic figures, 1913–26

	1913	1920	1921	1922	1923	1924	1925	1926
Industrial (factory) production (million 1926–7 roubles)	10251	1410	2004	2619	4005	4660	7739	11063
Coal (million tons)*	29.0	8.7	8.9	9.5	13.7	16.1	18.1	27.4
Electricity (million Kwhs)	1945	–	520	775	1146	1562	2925	3508
Pig Iron (thousand tons)	4216	–	116	188	309	755	1535	2441
Steel (thousand tons)	4231	–	183	392	709	1140	2135	3141
Cotton fabrics (million metres)	2582	–	105	349	691	963	1688	2286
Sown area (million ha.)	1.500	–	90.3	77.7	91.7	98.1	104.3	110.3
Grain harvest (million tons)	80.1†	46.1‡	37.6‡	50.3	56.6	51.4	72.5	76.8
Rail freight carried (million tons)	132.4	–	39.4§	39.9§	58.0§	67.5§	83.4§	–

* Excluding lignite.
† This was an extremely favourable year.
‡ These are Gladkov's figures; some other sources are higher (e.g. 42.3 for 1921).
§ For post-war the 'economic year' (i.e. 1920–21, 1921–2, etc).
– not available.

(Sources: *Sotsialisticheskoe stroitel'stvo SSSR* (1934), pp. 2–3; Gladkov, *Sovetskoe narodnoe khozyaistvo (1921–5)* (Moscow, 1964), pp. 151, 316, 357, 383; E. Lokshin *Promyshlennost' SSSR, 1940–63* (Moscow, 1964), p. 32; *Nar. khoz.*, 1932, p. 8.)
Note: There are minor disparities between various sources for most years.

Examination Guidance

The NEP, like the civil war, is more likely to appear linked to questions about the Russian Revolution of 1917 than as a separate examination topic. However, it might be one of a number of short-essay questions. Activity 61 takes a different approach from previous questions; it is based on a modified form of the SEG empathy questions. Working through it should enable you to master the main aspects of the NEP topic.

ACTIVITY 61

Targets

Empathy (i.e. looking at events from the perspective of people in the past).

Question Guide

The question asks you to put forward a view which a particular individual in history *might* have held. Your answers therefore have to be tied into an accurate recall of the main events, and a sense of the possible impact which they had upon the characters involved. It requires a careful reading of the text, and any other accounts you can find of the NEP.

Question 1(a) is a simple attempt to deal with the consequences of War Communism for the groups mentioned. Full marks will be given for pointing out that the civil war could also have caused the situations mentioned. Question 1(b) will require not only an account of the way in which the Red Army and Cheka had been used against the risings, but also an explanation of why they had behaved in this way. Question 1(c) is harder, for it asks you to see things from the viewpoint of a committed Bolshevik who believed in the ideas behind War Communism. Question 1(d) requires an attempt to compare the situation in 1921 with what had happened by 1927, and to point out the good and bad points of the NEP from a Bolshevik's viewpoint.

Activity

It is 1927. You are due to meet a communist party member, at the Putilov Factory in Petrograd, whose brothers had taken part in the Kronstadt and the Tambov peasant risings. What might the party member tell you about:

1. (a) the impact of War Communism upon:
   (i) the peasantry **(2)**
   (ii) the Kronstadt sailors **(2)**
   (iii) the Petrograd workers **(2)**
   (b) how the government had reacted to the Kronstadt rising and the Tambov revolt **(4)**
   (c) his feelings when he heard of the introduction of the NEP's policies **(7)**
   (d) his views on the NEP today in relation to:
   (i) industry **(2)**
   (ii) nepmen **(2)**
   (iii) the kulaks **(2)**
   (iv) street markets **(2)**?

5 The Rise of Stalin

In 1922 the Russian government faced major problems – a peasant agriculture which had to recover from the ravages of the civil war, industry in a state of collapse, threats of risings in the provinces, and the possibilities of invasions from Russia's external enemies. Within the government a continuous debate raged over the way in which they should run Russia. By 1928 Stalin had emerged from this background as Russia's leader. How did he do it?

BACKGROUND

Stalin was the son of a Georgian peasant cobbler. He had been trained as a priest, being expelled from his religious school or seminary in 1899 for spreading his socialist views. In 1904 he became a Bolshevik and backed Lenin. From now on he was a member of the small group of Bolsheviks who ran the party, and in 1912 he became a member of the party's Central Committee. After exile in Siberia, he returned to Petrograd in 1917 and played a role in organising the Revolution, editing the party paper, *Pravda*.

THE CIVIL WAR PERIOD

From 1917 Stalin was a member of the Politburo – the small group which ran the government. During the civil war Stalin had led the Bolsheviks in Georgia, to defeat the Whites in February 1921. Within Georgia he built up his own body of supporters to run the government, and he was ruthless in wiping out all opposition. Inside the central government, in 1917 Stalin was given the post of People's Commissar for Nationalities. From 1920 to 1922 he controlled the Workers' and Peasants' Secretariat, and in 1922 he became General Secretary of the Party. These key posts helped Stalin build up a body of loyal supporters – later they were to back him in his struggles against his rivals for the leadership.

LENIN AND STALIN, 1922–4

The dictatorial way in which Stalin had run Georgia led to bitter protests against his behaviour. Within the party Stalin fell out with Lenin's wife, and Lenin in his will warned against the ruthless way in which Stalin might try and gain power.

STALIN'S RISE TO POWER

In 1924 the government was in the hands of supporters of three men, rivals for power:

1. *Trotsky* – the leader of the Red Army
2. *Zinoviev, Kamenev, Bukharin* – key figures in the Revolution
3. *Stalin* – the Party Secretary

How did Stalin manage to gain power by 1929?

1. *Suspicion of Trotsky*. Trotsky had been a Menshevik until 1917, and the Bolshevik leaders had never accepted him as an equal. They were afraid that he

might be a new Napoleon (Napoleon had become ruler of France after the French Revolution) and use the Red Army to set up a military dictatorship. There were serious rows between Trotsky and the other party leaders. For example, Trotsky wanted to spread communism to other countries and to carry out a 'permanent revolution'.

In 1925 Trotsky was removed from his role in running the Red Army.

2. *Underestimation of Stalin.* The other Politburo members did not think that Stalin would replace Lenin as leader. They thought of him as a dull plodder, who could be given routine jobs like running the administration of the party. He had no ideas of his own. Trotsky tells us in his life of Stalin:

Source 8G

In the spring of 1924 I said to Smirnov [a party leader]: 'Stalin will become the dictator of the U.S.S.R.' Smirnov knew Stalin well. They had shared revolutionary work and exile together for years, and under such conditions people get to know each other best of all.

'Stalin?' he asked me with amazement. 'But he is a mediocrity, a colorless nonentity.'

'Mediocrity yes; nonentity no,' I answered him. 'The dialectics of history have already hooked him and will raise him up. He is needed by all of them – by the tired radicals, by the bureaucrats, by the nepmen, the kulaks, the upstarts, by all the worms that are crawling out of the upturned soil of the manured revolution. He knows how to meet them on their own ground, he speaks their language and he knows how to lead them . . . He has will and daring.'

(L. Trotsky, *Stalin*, Hollis & Carter, 1947, pp. 392–3)

3. *His control over the party.* Stalin used his position as Secretary-General to put his supporters into key positions within the party. He was also able to sack backers of his enemies.

4. *Disagreements over policy.* Stalin was able to use disagreements over policy in order to outvote his rivals for office. There were two stages in this:
   (i)   the removal of Trotsky from office
   (ii) the outvoting of his allies who had attacked Trotsky.

The issue was the form which communism should take in Russia. How was the party to tackle the problems of industry and agriculture? What kinds of society should they try and build up? The issues were very complex, but boiled down to four main points:
   (i)   Should the NEP be allowed to continue, or should the government shut it down and return to communist policies?
   (ii) Should they concentrate on the revolution at home, 'socialism in one country', or try and spread it to other countries, 'permanent revolution'?
   (iii) Should they concentrate on industry or on agriculture?
   (iv) Should they reform agriculture through setting up large state farms or collectives?

Trotsky and his backers wanted to push on with the Revolution and replace the NEP. In 1925 Trotsky had been outvoted and forced out of power. In 1926–7 Stalin turned on Zinoviev and Kamenev, who tried to ally with Trotsky, but Stalin was able to outvote them with his block of party supporters. In 1927 Zinoviev and Kamenev were sacked from the party. Stalin now turned on his last potential rival in the party, Bukharin, over a major row about how to solve the crisis of agriculture. Stalin wanted to attack the kulaks, and shut down the NEP in the countryside. Bukharin opposed him, but he was outvoted in the Politburo in 1929.

5. *Stalin showed great political skill.* In his moves against his enemies Stalin managed to appear reasonable and to take a middle path to sort out bitter party quarrels. He was able to form alliances against common enemies, and when these had been destroyed Stalin would turn on his old allies.

Examination Guidance

Questions on Stalin's rise to power may either be an essay, a short-essay or source-based.

ACTIVITY 62a

Targets

Recall and understanding.

Question Guide

The question is a structured essay (see pages 15–16) aimed at recalling the main features of Stalin's rise to power. The key word is 'describe' – what is required is a list of information, but tied together in a clearly written narrative.

Activity

Describe how Stalin came to power. You can mention the following points in your answer:
- suspicion of Trotsky
- underestimation of Stalin
- his control over the party
- disagreements over policy
- Stalin showed great political skill.

ACTIVITY 62b

Targets

Recall and understanding, evidence – extraction of information, understanding, evaluation.

Question Guide

The question splits up into four sections, each of which refers to Source 8G. Part 1 is a recall question, using trigger words in the test. Part 2 asks you to work out the reasons Trotsky puts forward. You should include all the groups whom he says need Stalin, and explain why. Question 3 asks you to think about the reasons given in the second answer, and tie these reasons in to what you know of how Stalin managed to manoeuvre his way into power in the 1924–9 period. Question 4 is one on analysing the evidence inside a source and assessing its reliability. Refer in detail to Trotsky's use of words such as 'mediocrity' and phrases like 'the tired radicals'.

Activity

With reference to Source 8F and your own knowledge:

1. Explain the meaning of the following:
    - (a) USSR   **(1)**
    - (b) exile   **(1)**
    - (c) bureaucrats   **(1)**
    - (d) nepmen   **(1)**
    - (e) kulaks   **(1)**
2. What reasons does Trotsky advance for thinking that Stalin will become Russia's dictator?   **(5)**
3. How did the events of 1922–9 confirm the views which Trotsky put forward?   **(10)**
4. What words and phrases suggest that Trotsky is biased in his views of Stalin?   **(10)**

6 Agriculture and Industry

BACKGROUND

After four years of bitter in-fighting among Lenin's heirs, by 1928 Stalin had emerged as leader of Russia. The fierce quarrels within the Politburo had largely been over what form communism should take in Russia, and what were the best plans for both industry and agriculture. Stalin had appeared as a moderate who wanted to keep the main features of the NEP and bring about change slowly.

As Russia's leader, Stalin faced two main problems: how to turn the country into a major industrial power and how to modernise agriculture to provide the food, raw materials and money to finance (pay for) the growth of industry. The key figures are those in Figure 8.9, which show that the output of grain had not increased since 1913. In 1928 the First *Five-Year Plan* to turn Russia into a modern industrial nation was under way – how was the countryside going to feed the workers in the expanding towns and cities, and provide the raw materials and capital (money) to pay for the new industries?

AGRICULTURE

Stalin and Collectivisation

Stalin's answer was collectivisation. He announced to the communist party:

Source 8H

What is the way out? The way out is to turn the small and scattered peasant farms into large united farms based on cultivation of the land in common, to go over to collective cultivation of the land on the basis of a new higher technique. The way out is to unite the small and dwarf peasant farms gradually but surely, not by pressure but by example and persuasion, into large farms based on common, cooperative, collective cultivation of the land . . . There is no other way out. (December 1927)

Collectivisation was only an idea – by 1928 less than 1% of villages were collectivised. In 1928 Stalin pressed for the use of force to secure the amount of grain the government wanted. Grain prices were low, so in key areas like the Volga Basin and the Urals, Stalin headed a task-force of police and officials. Stalin closed the free markets, put free traders out of business and ordered the peasants to hand over their grain. This Urals–Siberian method did not solve the long-term problems of modernising farming, so in 1929 Stalin introduced a plan to collectivise all agriculture by 1933.

Reasons for Collectivisation

Inside the party there were fierce debates over what to do with the countryside. Stalin got backing for a switch to a collectivisation policy in 1929 because:

(a) The idea of individual peasant farmers with their own land was not one which a communist could support. Private farming was a basis for the rise of a class of rich, capitalist peasants, the kulaks.

(b) Most communist party members hated the NEP, in which a kulak class had prospered. The time had come for a major change.

(c) Collectivisation was the only way to provide the money, food and raw materials for Russia's Five-Year Plan.

(d) Collectivisation would increase support for Stalin inside the party against his opponents, whom Bukharin led.

The Collectivisation Policy

What were the plans for collectivisation, and what did they mean in practice? In November 1929 the party backed collectivisation. To carry it out:

1. The Politburo sent out an order in December 1929 for state ownership within collectives of:
    - (a)   100% of working animals and cows
    - (b)   80% of pigs
    - (c)   60% of sheep and poultry
2. The Politburo laid down a timetable for the setting-up of collectives throughout the whole country:

Autumn 1930	The lower Volga
1931	Central Black Earth area and the Ukraine
1932	Remainder of central Russia
1933	The north and Siberia

The Kolkhoz

Government officials would help the peasants to set up *kolkhozes*. The kolkhozes were collective farms, in which the state owned the land, the animals, the machinery and the seed. The peasants would only have small, private vegetable plots. Government officials and a committee of peasants would run the kolkhoz or collective. They would have the support of *Motor Tractor Stations (MTS)*. An MTS would contain a pool of tractors which would service a number of kolkhozes. The MTS would hire out its machinery to the kolkhoz.

Figure 8.11   Percentage of peasant households collectivised, 1930

Source   A. Nove, *An Economic History of the USSR*, Penguin Books, 1969, p. 172

	1 March	10 March	1 April	1 May	1 June
USSR *Total*	55.0	57.6	37.3	?	23.6
North Caucasus	76.8	79.3	64.0	61.2	58.1
Middle Volga	56.4	57.2	41.0	25.2	25.2
Ukraine	62.8	64.4	46.2	41.3	38.2
Central Black-Earth region	81.8	81.5	38.0	18.5	15.7
Urals	68.8	70.6	52.6	29.0	26.6
Siberia	46.8	50.8	42.1	25.4	19.8
Kazakhstan	37.1	47.9	56.6	44.4	28.5
Uzbekistan	27.9	45.5	30.8	?	27.5
Moscow province	73.0	58.1	12.3	7.5	7.2
Western region	39.4	37.4	15.0	7.7	6.7
Belorussia	57.9	55.8	44.7	?	11.5

(Source: Bogdenko (citing archive and other materials), p. 31)

Figure 8.12   Progress of collectivisation

Source   A. Nove, *An Economic History of the USSR*, Penguin Books, 1969, p. 174

	1930	1931	1932	1933	1934	1935	1936
Percentage of peasant household collectivised	23.6	52.7	61.5	64.4	71.4	83.2	89.6
Percentage of crop area collectivised	33.6	67.8	77.6	83.1	87.4	94.1	–

(Source: *Sotsialisticheskoe stroitel'stvo SSSR* (1936), p. 278. State farm area and households included.)

The Kulaks

If the peasants were to join collectives, what would happen to the better-off peasants, the kulaks? Stalin's orders were clear – they were to be wiped out: ' . . . *eliminate them as a class . . . When the head is off, one does not mourn for the hair . . . The kulaks are sworn enemies of the collective farm movement.*' This meant that within the villages of Russia the party officials and poor peasant committees seized the kulaks' land, animals and farm machinery and forced them from their homes.

Collectivisation, 1930–6

So far the account of collectivisation appears neat and tidy. In reality, no one was clear what collectivisation really meant, and how it was to be carried out. Making paper plans in Moscow is one thing, carrying them out in Russia's 250,000 villages is a totally different matter. In 1930 the countryside was in total chaos. Figure 8.11 shows the number of peasant households in collectives in 1930 – the government switched its policy in the middle of the year. In 1931 Stalin pressed on with his collectivisation plans, so that by 1936 most of Russia was collectivised (Figure 8.12). What did this mean in reality?

Collectivisation in Reality

We have already noted the attack on the kulaks, which meant that they were wiped out in 1930–1. In 1931–2 the government forced peasants to join the collectives; the result was widespread resistance. Sholokhov, a famous novelist, in his novel *The Soil Upturned*, paints a vivid picture of peasant resistance:

Source 8I

Stock was slaughtered every night in Gremyachy Log. Hardly had dusk fallen when the muffled, short bleats of sheep, the death squeals of pigs, or the lowing of calves could be heard. Both those who had joined the kolkhoz and individual farmers killed their animals. Bulls, sheep, pigs, even cows were slaughtered, as well as cattle for breeding.
(Sholokhoz, *The Soil Upturned*, 1934)

Stalin used the secret police, known by its initials (OGPU) and the army to enforce collectivisation. Hundreds of thousands of kulaks and peasants were murdered, deported to labour camps or forced from their homes and their land. The party officials had no idea of how to run the collective farms; crops were often sown too late or left to rot in the fields at harvest time.

Procurement

In 1932 Stalin in effect declared war on the peasants. The government set high targets for the handing over of grain (*procurement*). The Red Army enforced procurement. This, combined with peasant resistance and the inefficient way some 25,000 government officials from the towns ran the kolkhozes, led to a sharp drop in the amount of food grown. The result was the imprisonment and deportation of some 3 million peasants to the labour camps, and the great famine of 1933.

The 1933 Famine

In 1933 the Russian countryside was in the grip of a famine. No one knows how many people died – the population figures for Russia for 1939 are some 10 million lower than they should be. In 1989 Russian government official figures suggest twice as many might have died – some 20 million in all. Figure 8.13 gives the background figures to the famine.

Figure 8.13   The state seizing of grain, and its export

Source   A. Nove, *An Economic History of the USSR*, Penguin Books, 1969, p. 180

State grain procurements (millions of tons)

1928	1929	1930	1931	1932	1933
10.8	16.1	22.1	22.8	18.5	22.6

(Source: Malafeyev, *Istoriya tsenoobrazovaniya v SSSR* (Moscow, 1964, pp. 175, 177.)

Grain exports (millions of tons)

1927–8	1929	1930	1931	1932	1933
.029	0.18	4.76	5.06	1.73	1.69

(Source: Soviet trade returns.)

The Collective System

By 1936 Russian farming was collectivised, and the Government claimed that there had been a full recovery in the amount of food grown (Figure 8.14). The next major change in Russian farming occurred after Stalin's death in 1953.

Khrushchev and Agriculture

The kolkhoz system had failed to produce a modern, efficient farming industry. Khrushchev, Russia's leader from 1956 tried to reform it by:

(a)   raising food prices to encourage an increase in output
(b)   giving kolkhozes control over their own affairs
(c)   handing over farm machinery from the MTS to the kolkhozes
(d)   allowing peasants greater freedom to sell produce from their private plots.

He also introduced the *Virgin Lands scheme* to plough up the grasslands of Kazhakhstan and Siberia.

Results

The changes led to only a limited increase in farm output. The Virgin Lands scheme turned out to be a disaster – after two successful years, the crops failed, and there was a danger of the ploughed areas turning into a dustbowl.

INDUSTRY

The other side of the economic coin was industry. Stalin stated the choice which faced Russia in 1928:

Figure 8.14   Farming output

Source   A. Nove, *An Economic History of the USSR*, Penguin Books, 1969, p. 186

	1928	1929	1930	1931	1932	1933	1934	1935
Grain harvest, real (million tons)	73.3	71.7	83.5	69.5	69.6	68.4	67.6	75.0
Grain harvest, biological (million tons)	–	–	–	–	–	89.8	89.4	90.1
Cattle (million head)	70.5	67.1	52.5	47.9	40.7	38.4	42.4	49.3
Pigs	26.0	20.4	13.6	14.4	11.6	12.1	17.4	22.6
Sheep and goats	146.7	147.0	108.8	77.7	52.1	50.2	51.9	61.1

(Sources: *Sotsialisticheskoe stroitel'stvo, 1936*, pp. 342–3, 354; Moshkov, *Zernovaya problema v gody sploshnoi kollektivizasii* (Moscow University, 1966), p. 226.)

Source 8J

The history of old Russia shows that she was defeated all the time because she was backward . . . military, cultural, political, industrial and agricultural backwardness . . . We are fifty or one hundred years behind the advanced countries. We must make good this distance in ten years. Either we do so, or we shall go under.

From 1928 to 1941 Russia went through a major industrial change, a change which enabled it to stand up to the onslaught from Germany in 1941. The changes split into two phases: the *First Five-Year Plan* (1928–32) and the *Second Five-Year Plan* (1933–7).

The First Five-Year Plan (1928–32)

This reflected the burning desire of the Politburo to bring about rapid industrial growth. A government planning body, *Gosplan*, set a series of targets for industrial output, targets which were revised upwards. Gosplan also planned out new towns, factories, roads, railways and canals. The planners were faced with a nightmare, for although Russia was already a major industrial power, the plan required huge increases in output. The labour force, mainly peasants, and the sheer problem of building thousands of new factories posed great problems:

Source 8K

The first director of the factory, Ivanov, wrote as follows: 'In the assembly shop I talked to a young man who was grinding sockets. I asked him how he measured and he showed me how he used his fingers. We had no measuring instruments!' Now after fifty glorious years, we must remember all this in detail, remember how the industry was created, which now produces the largest number of tractors in the world, how and in what conditions the first great tractor-works in the country was built in a year and working to full capacity a year later. All this was done in a country where as late as 1910 over two thirds of the ploughs were wooden. (1962)

Progress

The original plan in 1928 aimed to double output in key heavy industries – coal, iron, steel, electricity, chemicals and heavy engineering. Figures were revised upwards in 1929, and a goal was set of completing the plan in four years. The plan aimed massively to expand heavy industry in the old major areas of Leningrad, Moscow and the Donbass. A key element was the build-up of mining and heavy industry in new areas – Magnitogorsk in the Urals, the Kuzbass and Siberia. Factories and mines were also developed in the backward areas of Soviet Central Asia, mining in Kazakhstan and textiles in Georgia. Massive works were carried out – on the Dnieper River the largest hydro-electric scheme in Europe was built. It provided not only vital electric power, but water for farming and a canal to link up north and south Russia. Transport went through major changes – the Turksib railway was built, linking up Siberia and Soviet Central Asia – one line out of the 5,500 kilometres of new railway.

Workers' Targets

To carry out the plan, workers were set targets to which their wages were tied. In 1935 Stakhanov, a miner, was set up as a model for other workers. Stakhanov's team had mined a huge quantity of coal – other workers who achieved similar targets were given medals, and known as Stakhanovites. Workers were punished, and even sent to the labour camps, if the factory managers felt they were failing to produce enough goods.

Private Industry

At the same time private industry was closed down – the age of the nepmen was over. Official figures give a clue to progress made (Figure 8.15), but should be read with great caution.

Figure 8.15 The First Five-Year Plan

Source A. Nove, *An Economic History of the USSR*, Penguin Books, 1969, p. 191

	1927–8 (actual)	1932–3 (plan)	1932 (actual)
National income (1926–7 roubles in 100 m.)	24.4	49.7	45.5
Gross industrial production (1926–7 roubles in 100 m.)	18.3	43.2	43.3
Producers' goods (1926–7 roubles in milliards)	6.0	18.1	23.1
Consumers' goods (1926–7 roubles in milliards)	12.3	25.1	20.2
Gross agricultural production (1926–7 roubles in milliards)	13.1	25.8	16.6
Electricity (100 m. Kwhs)	5.05	22.0	13.4
Hard coal (million tons)	35.4	75	64.3
Oil (million tons)	11.7	22	21.4
Iron ore (million tons)	5.7	19	12.1
Pig iron (million tons)	3.3	10	6.2
Steel (million tons)	4.0	10.4	5.9
Machinery (million 1926–7 roubles)	1822	4688	7362
Superphosphates (million tons)	0.15	3.4	0.61
Wool cloth (million metres)	97	270	93.3
Total employed labour force (millions)	11.3	15.8	22.8

(Sources: 1932 figures from *Sotsialisticheskoe stroitel'stvo* (1934) and the fulfilment report of first five-year plan. For sources of other figures see table on page 146.)

Consumer goods industries also advanced, though, with the exception of footwear, at a pace well below plan. But the modernization of some textile and (especially) food-processing industries made big advances. New bakeries and ice-cream and meat-packing plants opened in many areas.
(A. Nove, *An Economic History of the USSR*, Pelican, 1969, p. 230)

Figure 8.16 gives an idea of what the Second Five-Year Plan achieved.

The Second Five-Year Plan (1933–7)

The new plan paid closer attention to the quality of what was made, and aimed to provide consumer goods for the Russian people. Although the plan had this starting goal, with the rising threat from Hitler's Nazi Germany resources were switched into the making of arms. Russian military spending doubled between 1934 and 1937. The plan's goals were not all fulfilled; some industries did much better than others. Alec Nove, a famous historian of the Russian economy, sums up the Second Five-Year Plan:

Source 8L

The chemical industry grew, but here again the plan was not fulfilled. Branches of special interest to armaments production and synthetic rubber, did a great deal better than did mineral fertilizer. There were inevitable difficulties in expanding this very backward branch of industry: lack of experience among management and labour alike, delays in construction and so forth.

Figure 8.16 Economic output

Source A. Nove, *An Economic History of the USSR*, Penguin Books, 1969, p. 225

	1932 (actual)	1937 (plan)	1937 (actual)
National Income (1926–7 prices) (million roubles)	45,500	100,200	96,300
Gross industrial production (1926–7 prices) (million roubles)	43,300	92,712	95,500
of which: Producers' goods	23,100	45,528	55,200
Consumers' goods	20,200	47,184	40,300
Electricity (milliard Kwhs)	13.4	38.0	36.2
Coal (million tons)	64.3	152.5	128.0
Oil (million tons)	22.3	46.8	28.5
Pig iron (million tons)	6.2	16.0	14.5
Steel (million tons)	5.9	17.0	17.7
Rolling mill products (million tons)	4.3	13.0	13.0
Machine tools (thousands)	15.0	40.0	45.5
Cement (million tons)	3.5	7.5	5.5
Cotton fabrics (million metres)	2,720	5,100	3,448
Wool fabrics (million metres)	94.6	226.6	108.3
Leather footwear (million pairs)	82	180	183
Sugar (thousand tons)	828	2,500	2,421
Tractors (thousands) (15 h.p. units)	51.6	166.7	66.5
Fertilizer (million tons gross)	0.9	9.0*	3.2
Gross agricultural production (million roubles)	13,070	36,160	20,123
Grain harvest (million tons)	69.9	104.8	96.0
Employment, total (millions)†	22.94	28.91	26.99
Employment, industry (millions)	7.97	10.20	10.11
Average money wage (roubles per annum)‡	1,427	1,755	3,047§
Retail price index (1933 = 100)	100	65	180§
Volume of retail trade (1933 = 100)	100	250.7	150§

* Plan specified ten-fold increase over 1932
† Total employed by state institutions and enterprises
‡ Average pay of all employed persons
(Sources: Five year plan documents, and *Promyshlennost' SSSR* (Moscow, 1957). Items marked § from Malafeyev, *Istoriya tsenoobrazo-vaniya v SSSR* (Moscow, 1964), p. 208, 407.)

THE ECONOMY, 1938–56

In the late 1930s the economy was aimed at preparing for war. In 1941–5 Russia had to cope with German occupation of the industrial areas of western Russia. Factories were moved to the east, and Russia was able to build the tanks, guns, planes and other armaments needed to defeat Germany. After 1945 a massive period of rebuilding occurred, with the Russians stripping the factories of occupied Eastern Europe and Japanese-occupied Manchuria for Russia's own industry. The main change in the 1950s from the pattern of the 1930s and early 1940s was the first step in extending Russian economic planning and control to Eastern Europe. In 1949 Russia set up the *Council of Mutual Economic Assistance* (COMECON). COMECON was seen largely as an answer to the Marshall Plan (see page 92) and did little.

Examination Guidance

It is highly likely that there will be a question on either industry or agriculture, or a combined question. Such questions will either be short- or long-essay answers or source-based questions. It is vital to learn up the details of the topics.

ACTIVITY 63a

Targets

Recall, understanding and knowledge, evidence – analysis of statistical information, evaluation, reconciliation of evidence, concepts of cause and change.

Question Guide

The question is from the MEG June 1988 paper, and reflects the kind of questions asked by MEG and LEAG. Question 1 requires recall; Question 2 is basically recall, but asks you to relate your knowledge to the statistics, i.e. you have to mention the difference between output for heavy industry and the consumer goods industry of wool cloth. Question 3 has two elements: the features in the sources which show the official view of the Russian government, and an evaluation of the value of such official sources in relation to the reality. Question 4 is linked to the information about the viewpoints of the two writers, the evidence contained in the other sources and what you know of conditions inside Russia. For example, Source 1 mentions that most of the workers came voluntarily while the rest were forced labour. Question 4 requires you to base your analysis upon the evidence contained in the sources. In analysing the sources, make sure that you deal with the question of the condition of the people. Thus Source 1 suggests that workers were drawn to Magnitogorsk because of poor living conditions elsewhere, Source 4 mentions the attempts of the government to control workers' movements.

Activity

Russia, 1917–1941

Look carefully at Sources 1–5. Then answer all the questions.

Source 1

The history of the construction of Magnitogorsk was fascinating. Brigades of young enthusiasts from all over the Soviet Union came at first. Later groups of local peasants and herdsmen came because of bad conditions in the villages. From 1928 to 1932 nearly three-quarters of a million people came to Magnitogorsk. About three-quarters of these came of their own free will seeking work, bread, better conditions. The rest came because they were forced to.

(An American engineer, John Scott, who worked in Russia, describes industrialization during the first Five Year Plan.)

Source 2

	1927	1932	1937
Electricity (100m kwh)	5.05	13.4	36.2
Coal (million tons)	35.4	64.3	128.0
Oil (million tons)	11.7	22.3	28.5
Steel (million tons)	4.0	6.2	17.7
Wool Cloth (million metres)	97.0	94.6	108.3

(Official Soviet Production Figures, 1927–1937.)

Source 3

(i)   *Hewlett Johnson, 1939. He was Dean of Canterbury Cathedral and an English socialist.*
The Plan removes fear and worry. Nothing strikes the visitor to the Soviet Union more than the absence of fear. No fear of lack of work, no fear of overwork. No fear of wage reductions.

(ii)   *An American economist.*
There is no evidence of more brotherliness among the industrial workers. People have been robbed of freedom. The Soviet regime is founded upon force and fear.

(Two foreign views of the Five Year Plans.)

Source 4

Workers felt very discontented and often left their jobs to look for something better. To stop this movement the government introduced internal passports and dwelling permits in 1932. At the same time absence from work could mean loss of ration card and of home.

(A British historian writing about the Five Year Plans in 1985.)

1.   Look at Source 1.
      (i)   Who was chiefly responsible for the Five Year Plans?   **(1)**
      (ii)   What was Magnitogorsk?   **(1)**
2.   Look at Source 2.
      What do these statistics show were the main aims of the Five Year Plans?   **(2)**
3.   Look at Source 4 which provides two opposite opinions of the Five Year Plans. Which of these opinions is likely to be the more reliable? Explain your answer fully.   **(8)**
4.   Look at all the sources.
      'The achievements of the Five Year Plans were made at the expense of the ordinary Russian people.' Do these sources show this view to be true? Explain your answer fully.   **(12)**
      TOTAL   (24 marks)

ACTIVITY 63b

Targets

Recall and understanding, concepts of change, cause, consequence.

7 Stalin and the Great Terror

Source 8M is a clue about one of the most dreadful series of crimes ever carried out on one man's orders – Stalin's purge of the communist party leaders. It was not only the party leaders who were caught up in the purges; millions of Russians ended up before firing squads or were sentenced to a lingering death in Russia's forced-labour camps. What were the reasons for the purges? How were they carried out, and with what impact?

Source 8M   The October Central Committee

Source   L. Trotsky, *Stalin*, Hollis & Carter, 1947

THE REASONS

Although Stalin was firmly in charge of Russia from 1930, there were still many who would have liked to replace him. Many in the party felt that he should be removed from power for these and other reasons:

(a) the way he had hounded the old Bolshevik leaders out of office, removed them from the communist party and even put them on trial
(b) the disaster of enforced collectivisation
(c) the failure of the First Five-Year Plan to improve living conditions.

Through Stalin's control over the secret police, he was aware of the feelings against him, particularly among the old Bolsheviks who had carried out the Revolution and fought the civil war. A purge of the party would secure him in power and place men loyal to him in office.

ORIGINS OF THE GREAT TERROR

In 1934, at the Seventeenth Party Congress, the leader of the Leningrad Party, *Kirov*, received as much applause as Stalin. Leningrad had always been a rival centre of power to Moscow, and in Kirov Stalin might have scented a deadly rival. Kirov returned to Leningrad, where in December 1934 an assassin killed him. Historians even think Stalin could have had him murdered and used his killing as an excuse to wipe out his enemies. Khrushchev, Russia's leader in 1956, hinted at this when he denounced Stalin to the party.

THE PROGRESS OF THE TERROR

The purges had two sides: the removal of all possible rivals from power, and the arrest of hundreds of thuosands, even millions, of potential opponents of the regime.

PURGING OF THE RIVALS

Massive arrests within the Leningrad party were followed by an attack on the party members who had opposed Stalin in the 1920s. Over the next three years they were all arrested and tried; most were shot. By 1939 Stalin had arrested 1,108 out of 1,966 delegates to the 1934 Party Congress. Out of the party's controlling central committee of 71 members in 1934, only 16 were re-elected in 1939. In 1937 the purge spread to the armed forces – *Tukhashevsky*, the army commander, was shot along with 14 out of 16 army commanders and all 8 admirals. The purge reached down to the lowest ranks of the armed forces' officers.

Stalin even purged the *NKVD*, the secret police. Stalin had murdered its two chiefs, who had carried out the terror against his old colleagues. In 1936 *Yagoda* was removed from office, and then tried and shot. His successor, *Yezhov*, 'the evil dwarf', lost power in 1938 and disappeared. It seems that all their backers in the NKVD were killed. The new secret police chief was *Beria*, a Georgian like Stalin.

THE EXTENT OF THE TERROR

The Terror spread to include millions of Russians. Confessions of the arrested, and any record of opposition to the views of Stalin and his supporters, could mean a knock on the door in the middle of the night. The Terror continued through the 1930s and resumed after the Second World War. Some 2 million returning soldiers were sent to the labour camps. The methods of the secret police, the NKVD, were used in the occupied countries of Eastern Europe. Although the show trials came to an end, in 1953 the arrest of leading Kremlin doctors, accused of a plot to poison the party leaders, could have triggered off a new round of terror. At this point Stalin died.

THE SHOW TRIALS, 1936–8

In 1936 and 1937 Stalin held public show trials of the old leaders of the party, including Kamenev, Zinoviev and Bukharin. They confessed to the most amazing crimes, as an extract from a 1938 Russian textbook suggests:

Source 8N

That revolting enemy of the people, the fascist agent Trotsky, and his revolting friends Rykov and Bukharin, organized in the U.S.S.R. gangs of murderers, wreckers and spies. They foully murdered that ardent Bolshevik, S. Kirov. They plotted to murder other leaders of the proletariat, too. The fascist scoundrels, the Trotskyites and Rykovites caused train collisions in the U.S.S.R., blew up and set fire to mines and factories, wrecked machines, poisoned workers and did all the damage they possibly could. These enemies of the people had a definite programme which was to restore the yoke of the capitalists and landlords in the U.S.S.R., to destroy the collective farms, to surrender the Ukraine to the Germans and the Far East to the Japanese, and to promote the defeat of the U.S.S.R. in the event of war.
(A. V. Shestakov, *A Short History of the USSR*, 1938; quoted in J. Bassett, *Socialism in One Country*, Heinemann, 1978, p. 25)

Why Did They Confess?

The secret police, previously the OGPU but now renamed the NKVD, used these methods:

(a)   mental and physical torture
(b)   continuous interrogation, denying the victims sleep
(c)   blackmail – threats against friends and family members
(d)   signed confessions of other prisoners, providing details of alleged crimes
(e)   promises of lenient treatment if they confessed.

THE IMPACT OF THE TERROR

The Terror had the following results:

(a)   It wiped out most of the old, educated members of the party. It allowed a new, younger generation to take over.
(b)   It placed Stalin's henchmen firmly in power: men like Khrushchev, later Russia's ruler, was the party boss of Moscow in 1935. The courts under Vyshinsky (the chief prosecutor) and the secret police (in the hands of Yagoda, then Yezhov and finally Beria) became tools in Stalin's hands.
(c)   The armed forces were greatly weakened – two-thirds of the officers were executed.
(d)   Art, music, literature were all stifled. A terrible fear spread through the educated classes of Russia – all were at risk from the NKVD.

OTHER DEVELOPMENTS IN RUSSIA

While the Great Terror is the main focus of our attention, we need to remember that throughout the 1930s, 1940s and 1950s great strides were made in improving public services in Russia, in particular *social welfare*, *health* and *education*. By 1939 the Russians had more doctors per 1,000 people than any West European country, and there had been a drop in the illiteracy rate from 50% to 20% of

the adult population. In 1936 a *new constitution* was introduced. On paper it seemed to make Russia more democratic: the people elected a *Supreme Soviet*, which met twice a year for a few days. In reality, with only party members as candidates, democracy was a sham. The Supreme Soviet elected a smaller body, the *Praesidium*, and it in turn chose a *Council of Ministers* or commissars who ran the government with Praesidium members' help. Stalin was secretary of the Council of Ministers, and all-powerful.

HOW SUCCESSFUL WAS STALIN?

It is impossible to provide definite answers to almost all the major questions in history – history is a living subject, in which historians argue all the time about what they think happened in the past, its causes and its consequences. The Stalin question is typical. Here are some things to think about:

(a)   Was Russia able to survive the German attack in 1941 because of the Five-Year Plans?
(b)   Was it necessary to carry out the Five-Year Plans in that way?
(c)   Did Stalin have to introduce collectivisation in order to reform agriculture? Why did agriculture remain backward and inefficient?
(d)   Was it inevitable that Stalin should use force against the peasants?
(e)   What impact did the Terror have on Russia? Did it enable a new generation of leaders to come through who were able to make a success of the Five-Year Plans?
(f)   What credit does Stalin get for changes in health, welfare and education?
(g)   Did Stalin betray the ideas and ideals of Marx and Lenin?

There are no correct answers to these questions – you have to use what you think is the appropriate evidence to support your arguments.

Examination Guidance

The Great Terror is likely to be included as a short-essay question or linked to one or two sources in a more general set of questions on Stalin and Russia. Activity 64 reflects both these approaches.

ACTIVITY 64

Targets

Recall, knowledge and understanding, evidence – extraction of information. and assimilation with existing knowledge, evaluation.

Question Guide

The first question is basically a recall one; Question 2 asks you to be accurate in the way in which you extract evidence from the source, i.e. its mentioning the collision of trains, blowing up of and setting fire to mines and factories, and the poisoning of workers. Question 3 is harder; it requires an examination of the way in which the writer uses language (e.g. words and phrases like 'foully murdered'), arguments and evidence to support his opinions.

Activity

Study Source 8N and answer all the questions.

1.   Explain the references to:
     (a)   Trotsky   **(1)**
     (b)   Kirov   **(1)**
     (c)   Bukharin   **(1)**
     (d)   Bolshevik   **(1)**
     (e)   USSR   **(1)**
     (f)   collectives   **(1)**
     (g)   fascist   **(1)**

2.   (a)   What evidence does Source 8N offer to support its accusations against Trotsky and his backers?   **(3)**
     (b)   What does it claim were the motives behind this behaviour?   **(3)**

3.   What evidence does the piece contain to suggest that the writer is biased?   **(5)**

4.   What arguments and evidence might a supporter of either Trotsky or Bukharin advance to counter the claims put forward in Source 8N?   **(4)**

GERMANY, 1919–45

Examination Guide

Germany appears on all four of the main Examining Groups' syllabuses, in two places; for full details, see pages 3–5 above.

It plays a part in each Group's coverage of international relations, in particular the 1920s and 1930s, the Second World War and, to a lesser extent, post-1945 developments. It also appears as one of a group of topics or studies in depth which centres have to choose from. The relationship of Germany to other syllabus topics is shown in the table. For LEAG, it is part of Topic F1, Fascism in Italy and Germany, 1919–39, one of three topics chosen from a list of ten topics for Paper 1. For MEG, it is one of two topics selected from a list of nine topics for study in detail; for NEA, it is one of three topics, chosen from a list of three given for the Paper 2 theme, **Governments in Action**, Sub-Section A. For SEG, it is one of two topics taken from a list of seven for Paper 2, allowing for the study of topics in depth.

Group	%	Number of topics	coverage
LEAG	10	1 of 5 from 20	1919–45
MEG	15	1 of 2 from 9	1919–45
NEA	10	1 from 3	1918–39
SEG	15	1 of 2 from 7	1919–39

Find from past papers all the questions asked on Germany. Be careful to look at the general sections on international relations, which will often contain specific Germany-linked questions, particularly in relation to the Cold War and the superpowers and the European Community.

QUESTION PATTERNS

The question patterns are more fully covered in pages 12–19 above. Should you be unable to get old papers, make sure that you are well prepared to cover the topics listed in the **Topic Guide**.

The main areas for potential questions are clear:

(a) the establishment of the Weimar Republic,
(b) the Weimar Republic: both the problems it faced and how it overcame them
(c) the rise of Nazism and the early history of the party,
(d) Hitler's gaining and consolidation of power
(e) Hitler in power in the 1930s.

Topic Guide

1 **The Weimar Republic, 1919–29**
   The Founding of the Weimar Republic
   Weimar and Versailles
   Weimar in Crisis, 1923
   Weimar and Stresemann, 1924–29
2 **Hitler and the Nazis, 1919–33**
   The Founding of the Nazi Party, 1919–23
   The Nazi Party, 1924–29
   The Nazi Party's Rise to Power, 1929–33

3   Hitler and Germany, 1933–45
The Nazi Dictatorship
The Use of Nazi Propaganda
Nazi Education and the Hitler Youth Society
The Hitler Youth Movement
Society
Hitler and the Jews

1 The Weimar Republic, 1919–29

THE FOUNDING OF THE WEIMAR REPUBLIC

The guns fell silent in November 1918, but the war was not over for the German people. The Kaiser fled into exile in Holland, and a republic was announced. To make sure that the Germans did not use the ceasefire to prepare for renewed fighting, the Allied navies kept up their blockade of German ports. Cut off from food supplies, the people fell victim to hunger and famine. In January 1919 Germany's voters chose a *National Assembly* to work out a new constitution. In June the National Assembly accepted the peace treaty of Versailles; it knew that Germany would be crushed if it tried to restart the war against the Allied powers. By July 1919 the National Assembly had established the *Weimar Constitution*, under which Germany was ruled until 1933.

From 1919 to 1923 the Weimar government faced threats from both left-wing parties, including communists, and right-wing military groups. Such groups often attacked the local state governments, and threatened to seize power. Typical was the chaos in Berlin, with the murder of the leaders of the communists after they tried to seize power in January 1919, and the attempt of the right wing, the Kapp Putsch, in March 1920 to overthrow the government. Figure 9.1 lists the main events from 1918 to 1921 and gives an idea of the problems which faced any government in Germany. When reading the list, refer to Figure 9.2.

Figure 9.1

1918
November
Armistice – Germany at peace with the Allies.
Revolution breaks out in Kiel, Munich and Berlin.
Abdication of the Kaiser.
The Social Democrats, the largest political party, declare that the country is now a republic.
1919
January
Elections held for a National Assembly to draw up a constitution for the country.
Spartacists, a communist body, seize the main buildings in Berlin and try to form a government. The Defence Minister, Noske, a master butcher by trade, calls in government troops and the Freikorps, a force of right-wing soldiers, to crush the Spartacists. In 'Bloody Week' in Berlin they smash the Spartacists and murder their leaders,Karl Liebnecht and Rosa Luxemburg.
February
The National Assembly meets in the small, peaceful town of Weimar – Berlin is too dangerous.

April
Communist risings in Munich and Bavaria. The army and the Freikorps crush the risings.
June
The National Assembly accepts the terms of the Versailles Treaty.
July
Weimar Constitution announced:
(a)   the vote for all adults over the age of 20
(b)   proportional representation, allowing minority parties to be represented – how many votes a party received determined the number of MPs it had
(c)   voting every four years
(d)   a president in command of the armed forces to be elected every seven years
(e)   total freedom of expression and the right to form any political grouping
1920
March
Right-wing force of ex-soldiers tries to seize power in Berlin – the Kapp Putsch. Government leaders flee, as the army fails to support them. A strike of workers defeats the rising – the government is powerless.

WEIMAR AND VERSAILLES

In June 1919 the German National Assembly agreed to the terms of the Versailles Settlement. This proved to be an albatross around the neck of the Weimar Republic. The Republic was chained to a treaty which two powerful groups of Germans claimed was a betrayal of Germany:

1.   the army and navy commanders and their officers
2.   extremist groups, the most important of which by 1930 was Hitler's Nazi party.

What were the main clauses of the Versailles Settlement?

(a)   *The War Guilt Clause.* Germany and her allies to accept that they were guilty for causing the war, and the destruction and death which followed.
(b)   *Territorial losses.* Alsace–Lorraine to France, Malmedy to Belgium Schleswig to Denmark. The Saar coalfields to be placed in French hands, and the Saar to be under the control of the League of Nations for 15 years. A plebiscite (popular vote) then to decide its future.
        Part of eastern Germany to form part of the new state of Poland. Germany split into two, with free passage of people and goods between the two parts. The League of Nations to run the German city of Danzig. Germany to lose all her colonies. Austria to be an independent country.
(c)   *Military terms.* The German armed forces to be limited to 100,000 men. No air force to be built, no submarines or ships over 10,000 tons. No military fortifications to the west of a line fifty miles from the right bank of the Rhine. Allied troops to occupy the left bank of the Rhine for fifteen years.
(d)   *Reparations.* Germany to pay as much as she could to compensate for the war damage she had caused.

WEIMAR IN CRISIS, 1923

Germany was forced to pay the Allies reparations both in gold and in goods like timber and coal. One thing the government could do to find money for reparations was to print money to pay off its debts at home. The result was a massive fall in the value of money (see Figure 9.3).

Figure 9.2   Germany, 1900–45   *Source*   Robert Gibson and Jon Nichol, *Germany*, Basil Blackwell, front and backpiece

Figure 9.3   The collapse in the Mark, 1919–23

Date	No.*
1919	
Jan.	1
1923	
Jan.	250
July	3500
Sept.	1,500,000
Nov.	200,000,000,000

*i.e. the number of Marks needed in Berlin to buy a loaf.

The Occupation of the Ruhr

The crisis became much worse in the autumn of 1922, when the Weimar Government asked to delay the next payment of reparations, and failed to hand over a shipment of timber to the French. In January 1923 the French response was to send her troops into the indus-trial heartland of Germany – the Ruhr (Source 9A). The factories and mines of the Ruhr produced 80% of Germany's coal and iron. The workers called a general strike, and the Ruhr's industry ground to a halt. The strikers received the backing of the German government, which ordered Germans not to co-operate with the French.

The Great Inflation

The occupation of the Ruhr saw a sharp drop in the German government's income. The Weimar regime's response to how to pay its bills at home was to print more money. The result was a huge increase in prices, *inflation*, as Figure 9.3 shows. Wages became worthless, and people lost the value of all their savings. Money wasn't worth the paper it was printed on – there are photographs of kites made out of money, and washing baskets full of banknotes to pay for things like bread and milk!

Source 9A   A French soldier confronts a German civilian

Source   Purnell History of the 20th Century, p. 1198

Source 9B   Washing baskets full of paper money being loaded on carts

Source   John Ray and James Hagerty, The Twentieth Century World, Heinemann, p. 70

(See Source 9B.) Some people did well out of the great inflation – all those who owed money, or owned property, factories and farms.

Source 9C

The economic crisis ended in November 1923 when the Weimar Republic issued a new kind of currency – the Rentenmark, one Rentenmark being equal to 1,000,000,000 old ones. At the same time the Dawes Plan solved the problem of reparations. From 1924 to 1929 the German economy recovered (Figure 9.4).

The Political Crisis – Socialist Risings and the Beer Hall Putsch

On 26 September the new ruler of Germany, the Chancellor, Gustav Stresemann, announced the end of passive resistance to the French and the resumption of the payment of reparations. Stresemann was faced with revolts from both left- and right-wing groups, who

Output of manufactured goods, 1920–30

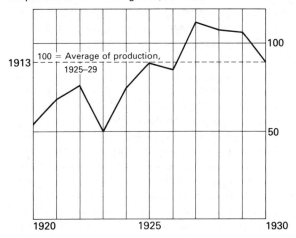

Figure 9.4   The recovery of the German economy, 1923–30

Source   Purnell, History of the 20th Century, p. 1098

loathed his sell-out to the French. To put down these revolts Stresemann had to rely on the army.

Socialist Revolts

The army quickly crushed communist rising in Saxony, Thuringia, Hamburg and the Ruhr. It even removed the pro-communist government of Saxony from power.

The Beerhall Putsch

In Bavaria the army faced a more serious problem. The danger was that the right-wing government would break away and declare independence under the old kings of Bavaria. Hitler (see Section 2 below) had built up his Nazi party in Bavaria's capital, Munich. Hitler hoped that the Bavarian leaders would lead a March on Berlin to overthrow the Weimar Government. On 8 November Hitler kidnapped Bavaria's leaders at a meeting held in a huge beer hall in Munich. The leaders seemed to back Hitler, but managed to escape from the Nazis and call for help. The police and army were used to crush the Nazi rising, and Hitler was jailed.

WEIMAR AND STRESEMANN, 1924–9

From 1924 to 1929 Weimar prospered. A stable currency helped an economic boom, and the number of unemployed fell sharply. Cultural and artistic life flourished, and Weimar was at the centre of a revolution in art and design, the *Bauhaus movement*, which affects all our lives today. In foreign policy Stresemann was hugely successful. Not only did he solve the problem of reparation payments; he also managed to get Germany back on an equal footing with Britain and France (see Chapter 2, Section 6). Stresemann's success was shown in the drop in support for both right- and left-wing extremist groups in elections for the Reichstag, Germany's parliament. In particular the Nazis suffered: they won 32 seats in 1924, and only 12 in 1928.

By October 1929 it seemed that the Weimar Republic would last for ever. Germans were as well-off as before the First World War, and the country had a stable, strong government. The problem of reparation payments (see Chapter 2, Section 6) had been solved, and the relatively small amount of money Germany was now paying was being recycled as loans to help pay for Germany's economic recovery.

All this changed when the Wall Street Crash of October 1929 (see Chapter 3, Section 1) led to a devastating depression in Germany. American demands for the repayment of German loans and the sharp decline in the volume of international trade led to a collapse of German industry. From 1928 to 1930 the number of unemployed doubled from 1.9 to 3.2 million (see Figure 9.5). In the wake of economic disaster the extreme parties prospered. One of these, the Nazis, was to become Germany's new rulers within five years. The 1930 Reichstag election gave the first sign that this might happen, with a huge rise in Nazi support. The Nazis increased their number of seats from 12 to 107.

Figure 9.5

Unemployment –numbers out of work	
1928	1,900,000
1929	2,500,000
1930	3,200,000
1931	4,900,000
1932	6,000,000
Output from mines and factories, 1928 = 100	
1928	100
1933	66
1934	83

Source   Robert Gibson and Jon Nichol, *Germany*, Basil Blackwell, p. 22.

Examination Guidance

Questions for all Examination Groups are likely to involve source material similar to that used in Activity 65, taken from an NEA specimen question.

ACTIVITY 65

Targets

Recall; synthesising information, extraction of evidence from sources, concepts of cause and consequence.

Question Guide

Questions 1(a) and 1(b) require you to work out the simple mathematics involved; Question 1(c) is recall linked into an understanding of the period, while Question 1(d) involves reading through the source and extracting the information it contains, i.e. about the printing presses.

Question 2 tests your understanding of the relationships between causes and their consequences. The listing of the causes as long- and short-term tests ability to recognise the difference between the reparations issue being a long-term cause while the French occupation of the Ruhr was a short-term cause. Section (b) tests whether you can see the linkage between the causes, and point out the way in which inflation was closely linked to the German government's policy on printing money. The

final question asks you to tie in what you know about four major aspects of Weimar history to the general issue of its economic affairs. Guidance on writing answers in short-paragraph form is given on pages 15–16.

Activity

1. (a) If a bar of chocolate costs 5 Marks in November 1918, what would it have cost in February 1922? **(1)**
    (b) If you had borrowed 1 million Marks to build a factory in 1918, to be repaid in November 1923, what would have been the real value of your repayment? **(1)**
    (c) Who or what are the following?
        USA **(1)**
        loans **(1)**
        Allies **(1)**
        reparations payments **(1)**
        war debts **(1)**
    (d) What clue does Source 9B contain as to the cause of the great inflation? **(1)**
3   Below are listed three causes of the great inflation:
    (i) the German government's attempt to get round reparations
    (ii) the government's printing of money
    (iii) the French occupation of the Ruhr.
    With reference to the sources:
    (a) Which are short- and which long-term causes? **(2)**
    (b) Put the causes into your order of importance in terms of causing the crash. Explain your answer. **(4)**
4   Use the sources and your own knowledge to write a short paragraph on each of the following:
    (a) the French occupation of the Ruhr, and its impact **(4)**
    (b) the Munich Putsch **(4)**
    (c) the work of Stresemann after 1924 **(4)**
    (d) the great crash of 1929. **(4)**

2 Hitler and the Nazis, 1919–33

THE FOUNDING OF THE NAZI PARTY, 1919–23

In 1919 in Munich, Bavaria, Hitler joined a small group of right-wing extremists, the German Workers' Party. Its members were dedicated to the overthrow of the Versailles Settlement and the restoration of German greatness. Soon Hitler was organising party meetings, and playing a leading role as an inspired public speaker. The year 1920 saw the German Workers' Party change its name to the National German Workers' Party, the NSDAP, known as the Nazis and lay down a programme of action, its *25 points*. Its most important plans were:

1. a union of all Germans in a greater Germany
2. the equal treatment of Germany as a great power
3. the overthrow of the Versailles Settlement
4. only pure-blooded Germans to be citizens. No Jews would be allowed to be Germans.

5. only citizens to vote and hold government jobs
6. no unearned income to be allowed from bank deposits, stocks and shares
7. workers to share in the profits of industry
8. land to be state-owned
9. death to those who worked against the interests of the state and made excess profits
10. special education for gifted children of poor parents.

In January 1922 Hitler made brutally clear his view of the Nazi party's role:

Source 9D

The new movement aims to provide what the others have not: a nationalist movement with a firm social base, a hold over the broad masses, welded together in an iron-hard organisation, filled with blind obedience and inspired by a brutal will, a party of struggle and actions . . . its aims should be pushed with fanatical will and spirit.

By 1923 Hitler had built up a powerful Nazi party in Bavaria, and early in 1923 he held his first national Nazi rally. Mussolini's March on Rome (see Chapter 3, Section 3) inspired Hitler. Hitler wanted a Nazi march on Berlin, and, with the political crisis of 1923 (see Section 1 above) he mounted the Munich Putsch. Within Bavaria he headed the *Kampfbund*, an alliance of all the nationalist groups who wanted to overthrow the Weimar Government in Berlin. The Kampfbund had strong army support, and Hitler almost gained the backing of Bavaria's ruler, Gustav von Kahr (see Section 1 above). Although von Kahr turned against Hitler and had him arrested and imprisoned, Hitler had shown that the Nazi party could pose a major threat to both the Bavarian and the Weimar Government.

THE NAZI PARTY, 1924–9

From 1924 to 1929 Hitler built up a strong base in Bavaria upon which he would be able to base his bid for power after 1929. While in jail in 1924, he had written *Mein Kampf*, (*My Struggle*), which became the Nazi bible. In it he laid out his aims for a Nazi Germany, including plans for the conquest of lands in the East for German settlement, the wiping-out of both Jews and Marxists and the overthrow of the Versailles Settlement. With the refounding of the Nazi party in 1925, Hitler set up a party which had:

(a) a strong leader, with fanatical personal loyalty from his followers
(b) a single, central base in Munich
(c) party members loyal to the central Nazi party
(d) established a semi-military force of supporters, the SA. The SA were to be a well-trained, strong, non-military mass movement. 'The weapon of the Nazi, and especially of the SA man, is a healthy fist and love for the fatherland in his heart.'
(e) a set of clear policies
(f) used mass public meetings and newspapers to spread its message.

Party Organisation

From its Munich base the party was split up into regions (*Gaue*) and districts with local branches. In 1925 the party had 27,000 members in 23 *Gaue* and 600 local branches. By the end of 1928 these figures had swelled to 109,000 members with 1,380 branches.

Party Popularity

The economic success of Weimar in 1924–9 restored German standards of living to those enjoyed before the First World War. Stresemann's success in removing the threat from France in 1925 by the *Locarno Pact*, and of war in general through the *Young Plan* (1928) (see Chapter 2, Section 6) meant that the Nazis only appealed to fanatics. A ban from 1925 to 1927 on Hitler speaking in public meant that the Nazis could not use his amazing ability as an orator to gain support. The failure of the Nazis to win mass backing was shown in the 1928 Reichstag elections, when the number of Nazi members dropped to twelve.

THE NAZI PARTY'S RISE TO POWER, 1929–33

The Wall Street Crash and the Depression

The Nazi rise to power is closely tied to the economic depression which hit Germany in 1929. The Wall Street Crash of October 1929 led to a collapse of international trade. From 1929 to 1932 output from Germany's factories fell sharply and unemployment soared (Figure 9.5). In the countryside a big drop in the prices of produce like grain, livestock and vegetables forced many farmers and farm-workers on to the breadline or out of work.

The Appeal of the Nazis

The Nazis, with their extensive national organisation and their clever use of mass propaganda – newspapers and public meetings – were in a position to gain massive support from farmers, factory-workers and the middle classes. The Nazis' growing appeal was based upon the following claims:

(a) Germany needed a strong government to solve the crisis. The Weimar system of government was useless.
(b) The Weimar government was ignoring the needs of the people. Its ministers were corrupt and cheating the public.
(c) The Nazis were the heirs of the Kaiser's Germany.
(d) The Nazis would defeat the menace of communism.
(e) The Nazis would look after the needs of the man in the street.
(f) The Nazis would solve all problems which specific government policies had brought about.

The Rise of the Nazis, and the Weimar Government

The Nazis used the ballot box as a means of getting into power. The Depression meant that the government was unable to get the backing it needed from the parties in the Reichstag, so in 1930 the president, *Hindenburg*, began to rule by decree. In effect this swept away the powers of the Reichstag, and gave Hindenburg the power of a dictator. The Chancellor, *Bruning*, with Hindenburg's approval, called an election for September 1930. The election saw a huge increase in the backing for the two main extremist parties – Hitler's Nazis, and the communists (Figure 9.6). The Nazi votes swelled from the 800,000 of 1928 to 6,500,000. The Nazis were now the second largest single party.

Figure 9.6   The 1928, 1930 and 1933 Reichstag Elections

	Nazis	Nationalists	Social Democrats	Centre parties	Communists
1928	12	79	152	148	54
1930	107	41	143	131	77

Source   Robert Gibson and Jon Nichol, *Germany*, Basil Blackwell, p. 23.

The Nazis, 1931–3

Hitler was now in a position to bid for power. He built up his support from great industrialists like the steel baron, *Fritz Thyssen*, who paid huge sums of money to the Nazi party. The worsening of the Depression meant that more and more of the public turned to the Nazis (see Figure 9.6). In the 1932 presidential elections Hitler stood against Hindenburg and received 13 million votes, compared to Hindenburg's 19 million.

Hitler, the Politicians and the Ballot Box

With the massive backing Hitler had gained in the April 1932 Presidential election, it seemed that the Nazis might seize power. The government banned the Nazis' private army (the 400,000 strong SA) and Hitler's bodyguard, the SS. The Nazis struck back, and with the support of the Defence Minister, *Schleicher*, brought down the government of Bruning on 30 May. The new government lifted the ban on the SA and SS, and called a general election.

The July 1932 Elections

The new Chancellor, *Von Papen*, was faced with open street warfare between the SA and their enemies, especially the communists. In particular, law and order broke down in Prussia. Von Papen banned all street demonstrations and took control over the Prussian government:

Source 9E

In Prussia alone between June 1 and 20 there were 461 pitched battles in the streets which cost eighty-two lives and seriously wounded four hundred men. In July, thirty-eight Nazis and thirty communists were listed among the eighty-six persons killed in riots.
(W. L. Shirer, *The Rise and Fall of the Third Reich*, Pan Books, 1964)

In the July elections the Nazis won 230 out of 608 Reichstag seats, and were now by far the largest party. Hitler and the Nazis at once began to manoeuvre for supreme power – but a second general election in November saw a drop in their vote, and their seats reduced to 196.

Plotting for Power, November 1932–January 1933

November, December and January saw plots and counter-plots among the politicians in Berlin. The problem was that no government could survive without Nazi support. In December, Schleicher, who had pulled down Bruning in May, forced Papen out of office and became

Chancellor himself. Schleicher tried everything he could to stay in power, but he failed to win the support of the Nazis' allies, the *National Party*.

In January the President, Hindenburg, finally turned to Hitler and the Nazis to take a leading role in the government. On 30 January Hindenburg named Hitler as Chancellor of Germany. The issue was in doubt to the last minute – in mid-December Hitler had had a furious row with the second-in-command of the Nazi party, *Strasser*, who stormed off in a fury, and the Nazi party had run out of money to pay its printers and local officials.

Hitler as Chancellor, the Reichstag Fire and the March 1933 Reichstag election

Hitler was one of three Nazis in the government – the other eight members of the ruling cabinet belonged to other parties. How did Hitler move from being in a minority to gaining total control?

1. *Hitler called a general election for March 1933.* The Nazis were able to use their position in government to spread the Nazi message.
2. *The Nazi appeal – Nazi propaganda.* The Nazis promised to solve Germany's problems, and not to call any more elections for four years.

Source 9F

Adolf Hitler has said 'Within four years unemployment will be removed' . . . Six million people lie on the streets! What Adolf Hitler promises he keeps to! His will led the NSDAP into government . . . opponents were scornful, but his will overcame all opposition and he became Reich Chancellor . . . Give Hitler four years' time more for reconstruction.
(A Nazi election leaflet, February 1933)

3. *The Nazis promised to smash communism*

Source 9G

Without Hitler we would have Communism. They are trying to burn down villages and destroy everything. Fight and fight again so that Germany becomes free.
(A Nazi speech, 2 March 1933)

4. *Control over Prussia.* Goering, Hitler's cabinet colleague, was appointed as Minister for Prussia. Goering appointed 40,000 SA men as an extra police force – the SA were able to move against the Nazis' enemies and break up their public meetings.
5. *The Reichstag fire.* On the night of 27 February the Reichstag building burned down. The Nazis claimed the communists had caused the blaze, and used it as an excuse for Hindenburg to issue a presidential decree. The decree gave Hitler the power to suppress his opponents' newspapers and arrest them. Over 4,000 communists were jailed.

The March Election

In the election of 5 March the Nazis gained 44% of the vote and 288 seats. With the 52 seats of the right-wing Nationalists, the Nazis now had a majority in the Reichstag. Hitler was now able to form his own Nazi government. Using the powers of the February *presidential decree*, the Nazis appointed their own men to run the governments of the provinces of Germany. The SA attacked their opponents and forced them from office. In Bavaria, the Nazi heartland:

Source 9H

The SA was now swarming along the streets of Munich without any opposition from the city police. Wilhelm Hoegner, the SPD leader, was walking past the editorial office of Der Gerade Weg, the strongly anti-Nazi Catholic weekly, when he noticed SA men wrecking the place. They were doing the same further along the street to the offices of the Social Democractic Münchner Post, where furniture was being thrown out of a fourth-floor window. Copies of the newspaper were being burnt on the street itself . . . During the night, some of the Bavarian ministers had a foretaste of the kind of treatment meted out to opponents of the regime. Stutzel and Schaffer were dragged out of their beds by SA men and taken along to the Brown House. Stutzel was not even allowed to dress, and had to go barefoot and in his nightshirt . . . SA men insulted him and beat him on his head.
(Geoffrey Pridham, *Hitler's Rise to Power: the Nazi Movement in Bavaria, 1923–33*, Rupert Hart-Davis, 1973 pp. 308–9)

Hitler now made sure he would have total control over Germany by getting the Reichstag to pass the *Enabling Laws*.

The Enabling Laws

On 23 March the Reichstag agreed to Hitler's Enabling Laws. They gave the Nazis full control over Germany. For four years:

(a) The cabinet could make laws without passing them through the Reichstag.
(b) The cabinet could make treaties without consulting the Reichstag.
(c) The cabinet could change the German constitution without consulting the Reichstag.
(d) The Chancellor had the power to draw up laws for cabinet approval.
(e) The powers of the President were to remain the same.
(f) The Reichstag was to remain in existence.

The Enabling Laws meant the end of the Weimar Constitution. Germany was now under the complete control of the Nazis. Section 3 below looks at how Hitler used his powers.

Examination Guidance

The rise of the Nazis to power, with reference to the events of the 1920s and early 1930s, is a favourite topic of the examiners. It is almost certain that there will be a question on this period, or on the Nazis' consolidation of power and how they ruled Germany after 1933 (see Section 3 below). Activity 66 mirrors the LEAG, MEG, NEA and SEG question patterns.

ACTIVITY 66

Targets

Recall, concepts of cause, evaluation of sources.

Question Guide

This is a source-based question, which asks you to use the knowledge you have to make sense of the references inside the sources. Question 3 is difficult in that you have to work out from the sources ideas about how the Nazis gained power. For example, Source 9G suggests that Nazi support came from their being seen as a powerful weapon in the struggle against communism. The final question is about the reliability of sources, and you should refer to the detail in the source which might suggest that it is accurate: for example, the naming of an individual and his description of what was happening in a particular street.

Activity

Look carefully at Sources 9E, 9F, 9G and 9H, and, using information from these sources and your own knowledge, answer the questions.
1. What or who was:
    (a) Hitler **(1)**
    (b) communism **(1)**
    (c) the SA **(1)**
    (d) Nazism? **(1)**
2. Explain the reference in the sources to:
    (a) unemployment (Source 9F) **(3)**
    (b) 'Germany becomes Free' (Source 9G) **(3)**
    (c) the behaviour of the SA (Source 9H). **(3)**
3. Use your own knowledge, and information from the sources, to explain how the Nazis gained power in 1932–3. **(12)**
4. What evidence is there in Source 9H to suggest that we can rely upon what it tells us? **(7)**

3 Hitler and Germany, 1933–45

THE NAZI DICTATORSHIP

Source 9I

All hope of an early rising against them [the Nazis] faded as their grip on all aspects of the people's everyday life and affairs tightened to such an extent that life became intolerable for non-Nazis and any possibility of getting together against them seemed out of the question. All organisations, political, religious, cultural or recreational were brought under rigid Nazi control and those few pockets of resistance which had remained were ruthlessly exterminated. This pressure also squeezed the non-conformer out of any chance of earning a living and all freedom of speech was suppressed.
(Fred Lennhof, *My Life*, Shottan Hall)

Fred Lennhof lived in Germany in the early 1930s. Fred was a Jewish factory-owner. In Source 9I he vividly records that the Nazis stamped out all opposition to their rule. How did Hitler do this?

1. *The Nazis' legal powers.* The Nazi victory in the March 1933 Reichstag elections and the Enabling Law (see Section 2 above) gave Hitler all the powers he needed to destroy those who opposed him.

2. *Control over German local government.* In 1933 Germany was made up of states, each of which had its own local government and ran its own affairs. These provincial governments were often in the hands of the Nazis' enemies. So, in April Hitler used the Enabling Law to sweep away the existing pattern of local state government, and to appoint his own Nazi party members as state governors and judges. The Nazi party, through these state governors or *gauliteers*, now had a firm grip on German life. The gauliteers ran their states with a rod of iron.

3. *Control of the trade unions.* In May 1933 the Nazis took over the headquarters of the trade unions, seized their funds and threw their leaders into jail.

4. *The Destruction of opposition political parties – the single-party state.* By March 1933 the communist party had already been banned, and many of its members were in jail. In June Hitler banned the Social Democrats, the only party to vote against the Enabling Law. The Centre party was closed down in July, and in the same month Hitler passed a law which declared that the Nazi party was Germany's only legal political party.

5. *The Nazi party wins army backing – the Night of the Long Knives.* A powerful group of leaders of the SA, the Nazi *stormtroopers* or *brownshirts*, wanted to push the Nazi revolution on further and make sure that the members of the SA were given a large slice of the country's wealth. The SA's 2.5 million members provided the mass, working-class body of party thugs which had terrorised the Nazis' enemies in the 1920s and early 1930s. Under its leader, *Roehm*, the SA even hoped to become the backbone of a new, enlarged German army. The SA were now a major threat to the existing army. Hitler decided to back this small but highly professional force against the SA. On the night of 30 June 1934 Hitler's own private black-shirted bodyguard, the SS, rounded up the leaders of the SA and shot them. These murders, the *Night of the Long Knives*, wiped out opposition inside the Nazi party to Hitler and gained him the backing of the army generals.

HITLER AS FUEHRER

In August 1934 the German President, Field Marshall Hindenburg, died. Hitler became the new President, and took the title of *Fuehrer* or leader. Now Hitler was the armed forces' commander, and all officers and men swore an oath of loyalty to him.

THE BUILDING-UP OF A POLICE STATE

To keep control over Germany, Hitler used his own enlarged private bodyguard, the SS, and a new Nazi secret police force, the *Gestapo*.

The SS

The SS, the Nazis' blackshirts, were Hitler's private bodyguard. In 1929 they were placed under the command of Heinrich Himmler:

Source 9J

. . . a chicken farmer in the village of Waldtrudering, near Munich, a mild-mannered fellow whom people mistook (as did this author when he first met him) for a small-town schoolmaster.
(W. Shirer, *The Rise and Fall of the Third Reich*, Pan Books, 1964)

Figure 9.7   Table of events, 1933–35

1933

March	Enabling Laws passed, giving the Nazis the powers to suppress their enemies.
May	Smashing of all potential opposition, e.g. trade unions.
June–July	Opposition parties banned.

1934

June	Night of the Long Knives. Hitler murders SA leaders.

1934

August	Hitler follows Hindenburg as Germany's President. Germany a police state. Nazis send opponents to prison camps, forerunners of the concentration camps.

1935	The Nuremburg Laws, which ended the right of Jews to be German citizens and to receive the protection of the German law.

Under the control of Himmler the SS acted as the private army of the Nazis' leaders. They arrested the Nazis' enemies after the Reichstag fire and carried out the killing of the SA leaders on the Night of the Long Knives. SS 'Death Head' units set up and ran the *concentration camps* where the Nazis jailed their political opponents and Germans whom they felt were not pure Aryans (Figure 9.7). Within the concentration camps the regime was cruel and sadistic; the guards had freedom to kill and brutalise at will. From 1938 the concentration camps were used to carry out mass murders of non-Aryans, in particular Jews. In 1939 over 65,000 prisoners were killed, about half of the concentration camps' population.

In April 1933 *Goering* set up the *Gestapo* in Prussia, the province he ran, for use against the Nazis' enemies. Himmler became head of the Gestapo in 1934. The Nazi party had sole control over the Gestapo. The *Gestapo Law* of 1936 meant that the Gestapo did not have to have those it arrested tried in the courts. So, members of the Gestapo had complete freedom to torture, kill and imprison at will.

THE USE OF NAZI PROPAGANDA

The Nazi dictatorship extended its control over what people read, thought, heard and saw. *Dr Joseph Goebbels* was the Propaganda Minister from 1933.

Source 9K

On the evening of May 10, 1933 . . . there occurred in Berlin a scene which had not been witnessed in the Western world since the late Middle Ages. At about midnight a torchlight parade of thousands of students ended at a square on Unter den Linden opposite the University of Berlin. Torches were put to a huge pile of books that had been gathered there, and as

the flames enveloped them more books were thrown on the fire until some twenty thousand had been consumed. Similar scenes took place in several other cities.
W. Shirer, *The Rise and Fall of the Third Reich*, Pan Books, 1964)

As well as books and other kinds of literature, Goebbels controlled art, the press, radio, music, the theatre and films. Radio was the main means of getting the Nazi message across – the number of radios increased from around 4 million in 1933 to about 15 million in 1945. Fred Lennhoff, the German Jewish industrialist of Source 9I, gives a vivid idea of the extent of Nazi propaganda:

Source 9L

One evening I went out with a friend to a local restaurant for a meal, a pleasant kind of place, furnished in a homely style with chequered table cloth and vases of flowers. In the middle of dinner the proprietor announced that we would all have to interrupt our meal as Hitler was making one of his speeches over the wireless. In accordance with a government edict, everyone, whether in factories, shops, offices or cafés, had to drop whatever they were doing to listen to what the Führer had to say. At the end of the usual hysterical speech, the radio played what had virtually become the second National Anthem, the 'Horst Wessel' song, composed in memory of a Nazi martyr killed in a riot. Everyone in the restaurant got to their feet and gave the Nazi salute. I stood up out of courtesy, but did not raise my arm. The reaction of the other customers was extremely hostile.
(Fred Lennhof, *My Life*, TS, Shotton Hall)

Source 9M

Source　Purnell History of the 20th Century, p. 1394

The Nazis also staged huge rallies to whip up support. The most famous were at Nuremberg (Sources 9M and 9N).

Source 9N

I watched him on the morning of the next day stride like a conquering emperor down the centre aisle of the great flag-bedecked Uitpold Hall while the band blared forth 'The Basenweiler March' and thirty thousand hands were raised in the Nazi salute. A few moments later he sat proudly in the centre of the vast stage with folded arms and shining eyes . . . 'It is wonderful' he exulted at Nuremberg to the foreign correspondents at the end of the exhausting week of parades, speeches, pagan pageantry and the most frenzied adulation for a public figure this writer had ever seen. Adolf Hitler had come a long way from the gutters of Vienna.
(W. Shirer, *The Rise and Fall of the Third Reich*, Pan Books, 1964)

The supreme example of how Goebbels and the Nazis used propaganda to spread their message was at the 1936 Berlin Olympics. These were supposed to show the world the triumph of Nazi civilisation and Aryan supremacy. 'Aryan' was the name the Nazis gave to the master race; blonde-haired, white-skinned and blue-eyed, descended from the ancient tribes of Germany. Jesse Owens, a negro American athlete, spoiled the party by dominating the mens' events and winning four gold medals.

NAZI EDUCATION AND THE HITLER YOUTH SOCIETY

Schools

The schools were central to the Nazi plans for making sure all Germans held Nazi beliefs. The Nazis were determined to raise a generation of soldiers.

Source 9O

All subjects – German language, History, Geography, Chemistry and Mathematics – must concentrate on military subjects – the glorifications of military service and of German heroes and leaders and the strength of a reborn, strong Germany. Chemistry will teach a knowledge of chemical warfare, explosives, etc., while mathematics will help the young to understand artillery, ballistics, etc.
(Nazi publication, October 1939)

Nazi control over what was taught, the curriculum, led to changes in certain key areas – Physical Training, Biology and History. PT lessons rose in number per week from two to three in 1936, and to five in 1938. In Biology, pupils were taught about race and heredity, and encouraged to measure one another's skulls to see how Aryan they were. An aspect of Biology was stress upon marrying in order to have a large number of children. History lessons were used to justify the rise of Hitler to power as the heir of the Kaiser and to attack the betrayal of Germany in 1918–19. All lessons were used to put across Nazi ideas:

Source 9P

When Klaus got back from school at five o'clock he bullied me into helping him with his homework. Glancing through his school books, I noticed again how different they are from those I had only a few years ago. Here is a maths problem . . .

The iniquitous Treaty of Versailles, imposed by the French and the English, enabled international capitalism to steal Germany's colonies. France herself gained part of Togoland. If Germany's Togoland, for the present under the rule of the French imperialists, covers fifty-six million square kilometres and contains a population of eight hundred thousand people, work out the average living space per inhabitant.

Hitler also set up special schools. The schools for future Nazi leaders, *Napolas*, emphasised Nazi thinking, while the *Adolf Hitler Schools* for officers for the army, navy and airforce stressed physical and military training.

All teachers belonged to the Nazi Teachers' Association, and one-third of them were active party members. By 1938 two-thirds of all teachers had been to Nazi camps, where they spent a month under direct Nazi control.

THE HITLER YOUTH MOVEMENT

By 1936 Hitler had established a youth movement for all six to eighteen year olds. If you had been living in Germany under the Nazis, it is likely that before the age of ten you would have been a *Pimpf*, or little fellow. From ten to fourteen you would have joined either the Young Folk for boys or the Young Girls for girls. Between fourteen and eighteen you would have been a member of the Hitler Youth (boys) or the German Girls' League.

The Hitler Youth Movement prepared German boys for war and German girls for motherhood. Members of the Hitler Youth wore uniforms, learned how to use guns and read maps, and attended camps where they did hard physical training and took part in long marches and army-type exercises. The German Girls' League also went to camp (Source 9Q), took part in physical training but had to have special knowledge of bed-making and house-work. After the age of seventeen, girls could join a 'Faith and Beauty' organisation, which proved popular.

The stress upon the Hitler Youth Movement as the basis for the new, pure, Aryan society had some unexpected outcomes. Of the 100,000 Hitler Youth and Girls' League members who were at the 1936 Nuremberg Rally, 900 girls went home pregnant.

Source 9Q

Source Robert Gibson and Jon Nichol, *Germany*, Basil Blackwell, p. 36

SOCIETY

The Role of Women

The Nazi slogan, *Kinder, Kirche und Kuche*, (Children, Church and Kitchen), summed up the Nazi view of women. They were to support the Nazi state through bearing pure Aryan children, at least four. Hitler gave a clear view of the German woman's role:

Source 9R

Woman has her battlefield too; with each child that she brings into the world for the nation she is fighting her fight on behalf of the nation and supporting her man as loyal housewife.

Each year Hitler gave a medal on his mother's birthday to Germany's most prolific mother. Unmarried women were encouraged to have children by SS fathers. Special homes were set up for these babies. The Nazi party saw the ideal Aryan mother as being large, solid, plain, blue-eyed, blonde and simply dressed. So, the Nazis heavily criticised women who slimmed, wore make-up or tailored trousers, had fashionable hair-styles or who smoked – a daring, modern habit.

The Nazi gaining of power had a disastrous impact upon professional women – married doctors and civil servants were sacked at once. The number of women students at university was cut from one in five in 1933 to one in ten by 1935. By then only one in eight teachers was a woman, and in 1936 women could no longer be judges.

The Role of Men – Work

The Nazis rose to power on the back of unemployment (Figure 9.5). In 1933 the 6 million unemployed were one-third of the work force. The Nazis at once set up a *National Labour Service* (the *RAD*), which provided jobs on public works. The most famous of such works was the building of the motorways or *Autobahns*. Hitler also built up the armaments industry. By 1934 unemployment was halved. The introduction of *conscription* (compulsory military service) in 1935 also slashed unemployment, and by 1939 there was no unemployment. The fall in unemployment was linked to the build-up of the German armed forces and the armaments industry.

The Labour Front

The Nazis replaced the trade unions they had closed down in 1933 with the *German Labour Force*, under *Dr Ley*. The government froze both prices and wages, and the Labour Front enforced these orders. Strikes were banned. Workers were forced to take jobs in key industries. But it proved hard to keep wages down. The boom in industry meant that employers were willing to pay high wages to skilled workers. Firms also provided fringe benefits, like free housing, to attract workers.

Leisure – Strength through Joy

Hitler also set out to control people's leisure. The *Strength through Joy* programme provided cheap holidays for German workers, and even built two cruise-liners for them. In 1938, 180,000 Germans went on cruises, and 10 million enjoyed Strength through Joy holidays. With the doubling of holiday pay, by 1938 one in three workers enjoyed a holiday away from home each year. Sport, theatre, cinemas were all in the hands of the government, who used them to provide mass entertainment for the German people (Sources 9S).

Source 9S   The open-air theatre and memorial at Annaberg, Silesia

Source   R. Grunberger, *A Social History of the Third Reich*, Weidenfeld & Nicolson, p. 297

HITLER AND THE JEWS

Genocide, n. 'Extermination of a race' (*The Concise Oxford Dictionary*). Hitler and the Nazis practised genocide against races they believed were inferior to the pure-blooded Aryan Germans. Gypsies, Jews and the inhabitants of Eastern Europe and Russia (Slavs) fell victim to the Nazi murderers. The best-known case of Nazi genocide is their treatment of the Jews – but we should remember the millions of others the Nazis enslaved and slaughtered, including some 20 million Russians.

Background to the Killing of the Jews

Hitler hated the Jews; he blamed them for Germany's defeat in the First World War and claimed that there was a Jewish plot to conquer the world! When the Nazis gained power in 1933 Hitler pressed for a boycott of all Jewish shops and businesses, and fired Jews from their jobs in the civil service, schools, radio broadcasting and newspapers and magazines.

Life for the Jews became much worse in 1934–5. They were banned from going into many public parks, swimming pools, theatres and cinemas (Source 9T). Jewish

Source 9T   No Jews!

Source   R. Grunberger, *A Social History of the Third Reich*, Weidenfeld & Nicolson, p. 137

shops were marked with a yellow star or a painted sign, *Juden*. Schools taught that the Jews were enemies of Germany and an inferior race. In 1935 Hitler's Nuremberg Laws declared:

(a)   Jews were stripped of German citizenship.
(b)   Jews could not marry German citizens.
(c)   Jews could not have sexual intercourse with German citizens.

These laws are identical to those of the white government of South Africa today towards blacks. No Jew could safely walk the streets, for there was a constant danger that the Nazi SA would beat them up. Jews were banned from many shops, and could find it hard to buy food, meat and medicines. Thousands of Jews fled abroad, but much worse was to come.

In November 1938 a Jew shot a German official at the Paris embassy. At once the Nazis organised a massive attack on Jewish properties – shops, synagogues and homes were burned, looted and wrecked. About 100 Jews died in the SA attacks on what is known as *Kristallnacht* (Night of the Broken Glass). Thousands of Jews were rounded up and sent to German prison camps, where they wore yellow stars and suffered the same terrible treatment as other prisoners – beatings, starvation and killings.

The War and the Jews

The outbreak of the Second World War in September 1939 dramatically changed the position of the Jews.

Instead of being a large, persecuted group inside Germany, the much larger Jewish population which lived in occupied lands, especially Poland, became a target for extermination. Hitler's conquest of lands in the East was part of his programme of obtaining *Lebensraum* (living room), and this policy involved wiping out or enslaving those who lived there already, including the Jews.

In 1939 Himmler ordered the SS to set up special murder squads, *Einsatzgruppen*, to kill any enemies of the Third Reich. The SS would enter a town and village, round up any Jews they could find and shoot them. Other Jews were sent to sealed-off areas of towns or cities, the *ghettoes*, or used as slave labour. The most famous ghetto was the *Warsaw Ghetto*, which in 1945 witnessed a final, desparate rising of the trapped Jews against the Nazis. In the ghettoes the Nazis starved the Jews to death.

The Concentration Camps

The Nazi moves to eliminate the Jews took a new turn in late 1941, when it was decided to set up extermination camps to wipe them out. Jews were rounded up and sent by train to these camps, where they were kept like battery hens in squalid barracks. Starved of food, riddled with disease, brutalised by guards, the prisoners were finally stripped naked and herded into gas chambers, where they were gassed to death. At the most infamous of these camps, *Auschwitz*, over 3 million people, mainly Jews, were murdered. Up to 6 million Jews died all together – no one knows the real number (Figure 9.8).

Figure 9.8   The murder of the Jews

Source   Robert Gibson and Jon Nichol, *Germany*, Basil Blackwell, p. 44

Examination Guidance

The Nazi gaining and consolidation of power is likely to be a central concern of all the Examination Groups setting questions on this topic. The source-based question below is taken from the MEG November 1988 paper, and centres on the Night of the Long Knives.

ACTIVITY 67

Targets

Recall, understanding and explanation, evaluation of evidence, the extraction of information, synthesising information and presenting an argument.

Question Guide

Question 1 is pure recall; Question 2 requires recall and an ability to explain the significance of the terms. For two marks for Question 2(b) you would have to mention the fact that they have both hands raised in surrender and that it might appear that they are saluting Hitler with both hands, whereas the Nazi salute uses one hand. Question 3 asks you to draw upon your memory to link in six separate points about the Nazis relations with the army, but also to argue why historians might find it of value. Question 4 is difficult, in that it does not make clear what it means by 'reliable'. A good answer will comment on the position which the two papers seem to take in regard to Hitler (one for him and the other against him), and then to relate this to how they use their evidence to support their viewpoints. The answer should also comment on the kind of detail used in the articles as an indication of how reliable the source is. Question 5 is a short-essay answer. The answer should deal with the question of the value of all the sources. It should discuss how Sources A and E suggest that Hitler needed army support, while Sources B and C gives an indication of the extent to which the SA was purged, and how the purge had extensive support within Germany.

Germany, 1919–45

Look carefully at Sources 1–5. Then answer all the questions.

Source 1

On this day we should particularly remember the part played by our Army, for we all know well that if the Army had not stood on our side, then we should not be standing here today. We can assure the Army that we shall never forget this.
(Hitler pays tribute to the Reichswehr, 23 September 1933. [Note: Reichswehr = German Army])

Source 2

(i) *The News Chronicle*: By ruthless shooting, Hitler and Goering, aided by the Reichswehr, have quelled what they describe as a 'second revolution' in Germany. In addition to seven Storm Troop leaders shot on Saturday, ten more were executed yesterday.
Apart from the execution of Roehm, yesterday was quiet in Germany after a weekend of ruthless slaughter in which victims included ex-Chancellor von Schleicher and his wife, Herr Klausner and Herr Gregor Strasser, all executed.

In addition Herr von Papen is being kept 'under surveillance' as is Prince August Wilhelm, a son of the ex-Kaiser.

(ii) *The Daily Mail*: Herr Adolf Hitler has saved his country. Swiftly and with relentless severity he has delivered Germany from men who had become a danger to the unity of the German people, and to order in the State.

With lightning rapidity he has caused them to be removed from high office, to be arrested and put to death.

He has acted in the knowledge that the best men in Germany desire to see the country purged of those whose influence was evil.

President von Hindenburg had himself made it plain that stern action must be taken. And in acting Hitler knew that he had the army behind him.

(Two British newspaper reports, both published on 2 July 1934.)

Source 3

It was in the safety of Switzerland that I read of the horrors of the massacre of 30 June 1934.

How closely I myself escaped I only learned a little later. A young Englishman working at the Kaiserhof hotel told me that the S.S. and the Gestapo had ransacked my rooms.

Later still, a German friend who had held an official position where he had seen my Gestapo file, told me: 'They intended to kill you. They had recordings of all your talks with Papen. Then they would have shot the boys who shot you. All an unfortunate mistake, you know.'

(J. Wheeler-Bennett, a British author, recalls the events of June 1934.)

Source 4

A cartoon by Low, a British cartoonist.

They salute with both hands now.

Source 5

I swear by God this sacred oath, that I will render total obedience to Adolf Hitler, the Fuehrer of the German Reich and people, Supreme Commander of the Armed Forces, and will be ready as a brave soldier to risk my life at any time for this oath.

(The oath taken by German soldiers on and after 3 August 1934 (i.e. after the death of President von Hindenburg).)

1. Read Source 3.
   What is the phrase commonly used for 'the massacre of 30 June 1934?' **(1)**

2. Look at Source 4.
   Explain the following:
   (a) 'The Double Cross'; **(1)**
   (b) 'They salute with both hands now'. **(2)**

3. Read Source 5.
   In what ways can this Source be useful to the historian of Nazi Germany? **(6)**

4. Read Source 2.
   Which of these two reports do you consider to be the more reliable? Explain your answer fully, referring to these reports. **(8)**

5. 'On June 30th 1934, Hitler's purpose was to put down a second revolution.' Do these sources show this view to be true? Explain your answer fully. **(12)**

Total marks **(30)**

THE UNITED STATES OF AMERICA, 1919–41

Examination Guide

The United States of America appears on all four of the main Examining Groups' syllabuses in two places: as an element in the study of international relations from 1919 onwards, and as a special subject. This chapter deals with it as a special subject, with reference to changes which occurred within the United States.

The table below shows the relationship of the USA, 1919–41, to other topics in depth on the syllabuses. For LEAG, it is one of two topics to be studied chosen from a list of ten topics for Paper 2. For MEG, it is one of two topics chosen from a list of nine for study in detail; for NEA, one of two topics, chosen from a list of two for sub-section 13 in the Paper 2 theme, **Governments in Action**; for SEG, it is one of two topics taken from a list of seven for Paper 2 allowing for the study of topics in depth. Full details are given on pages 3–5 above.

Group	%	Number of topics	Coverage
LEAG	15	1 of 5 from 20	1919–41
MEG	15	1 of 2 from 9	1919–41
NEA	10	1 of 2 from 2	1919–41
SEG	15	1 of 2 from 7	1919–41

Find from past and specimen papers all the questions asked on the USA, 1919–41. Be careful also to look at the general sections on international relations, which will often contain specific questions linked to America's role in world affairs from 1919 to 1941 (covered in Chapters 2 and 3 above).

QUESTION PATTERNS

The pattern of questions is covered on pages 12–19 above. Should you be unable to get old papers, make sure that you are able to answer questions fully on the topics listed in the **Topic Guide**. The examiners have concentrated on the Great Crash and Depression, and Roosevelt's New Deal. However, be prepared to answer questions specifically on the 1920s; as the years go by examiners look around for new topics upon which to test candidates! Question-spotting is likely to be very dangerous; you MUST be able to answer questions on all the key areas.

Topic Guide

1   Introduction – America in 1919
2   The Roaring '20s
3   The Great Crash and Depression
4   The New Deal

1 Introduction – America in 1919

BACKGROUND

In 1919 America was the world's richest nation (Figure 10.1), and she has remained so to the present day.

Figure 10.1   America and her chief rivals, 1900

The Growing Importance of the United States

	USA	Rival
Coal production (tons)	262 million	219 million (Britain)
Exports (£)	311 million	390 million (Britain)
Pig-iron (tons)	16 million	8 million (Britain)
Steel (tons)	13 million	6 million (Germany)
Railways (miles)	183,000	28,000 (Germany)
Silver (fine oz)	55 million	57 million (Mexico)
Gold (fine oz)	3.8 million	3.3 million (Australia)
Cotton production (bales)	10.6 million	3 million (India)
Petroleum (metric tons)	9.5 million	11.5 million (Russia)
Wheat (bushels)	638 million	552 million (Russia)

America is a country where most people live in towns and cities (Figure 10.2) and make their living from working in factories or service industries. The people of America, apart from the Red Indians, were descended from immigrants or had themselves come to live in America from abroad. They brought with them their beliefs, religions, customs, values and way of life – a vital thing to remember. In 1919 some 15% of Americans had been born in Europe (Figure 10.3). Immigrants arrived in America in the ports on the east coast, but were able to spread inland using the network of railways (Figure 10.4). Our most common image of America in the past is of the Wild West, a land where newcomers could make a fresh start. Immigrants came not only from Europe; for, mainly in the South, there were millions of descendants of African slaves, freed some sixty years earlier in 1865 following the American Civil War. Despite this, through the *'Jim Crow' laws*, whereby blacks were kept apart from whites, the black was in effect denied any real political rights or any chance of social equality.

Figure 10.2   Population of the American urban centres and the countryside

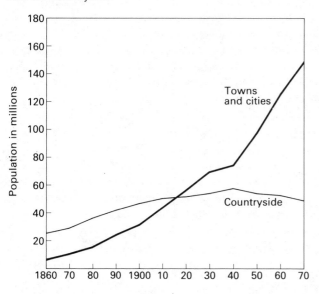

America was a land of big and small businesses, in which there were a few huge, rich companies and hundreds of thousands of smaller firms. The work ethic – work hard and get rich – is something most Americans believe in. Workers in mines and factories worked long hours for little pay. By 1919 bitter struggles between

Figure 10.3   Immigration into the USA

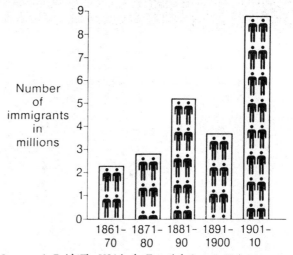

Source: A. Reid, *The USA in the Twentieth Century*, Heinemann, p.4.

huge companies, the *trusts* and unions were common, with strikes, lockouts and even killings. Also, the *trusts* were so strong that they were able to deny many individual Americans the freedom to found their own businesses and control their own lives.

The key to understanding America is its history. In 1776, America, a British colony, declared its independence from Britain and the right of each of its citizens to freedom. Individual freedom and liberty has since been a central plank of American life. At first these rights only applied to white, adult males, but since 1920s it has been seized upon by other groups in society denied their rights, in particular women and negroes. Because America is a country made up from thousands of different races, religions and creeds, small groups with strong views have used freedom and liberty to push their own views to try and get the rest of society to accept them. In the 1920s this led to *Prohibition*, the banning of alcohol.

What do freedom and liberty mean in practice? We have already talked about the growth of business and industry, the economic freedom for every man to make his own living. *Political freedom* saw America emerge as a *democracy*, with two main features: the rule of law, and local and national politicians voted into power. The *rule of law* means that America has a system of judges and courts free (on paper) from the control of politicians. The chief American court is known as the *Supreme Court*. It has the power to declare that laws which the politicians make might be unconstitutional, that is illegal. This occurs if a law breaks the rules for making laws as laid down by the *American Constitution* of 1787. This became a major issue in the mid 1930s, when the Supreme Court said that many of the measures of the New Deal were illegal.

As members of a democracy, American voters choose politicians to run their local district (town) and county (country) affairs, the business of their individual *states*, and the national or *federal* government. The national or federal government is based in Washington, and runs America's foreign and economic affairs, the army, navy and air force, and it plays a key role in domestic politics, such as civil rights. As a democracy, every four years Americans choose a *President* to head the government. They also elect members of two bodies who pass laws and agree to the President's budget. These bodies, *Congress* and the *Senate*, have a similar job to that of our Parliament.

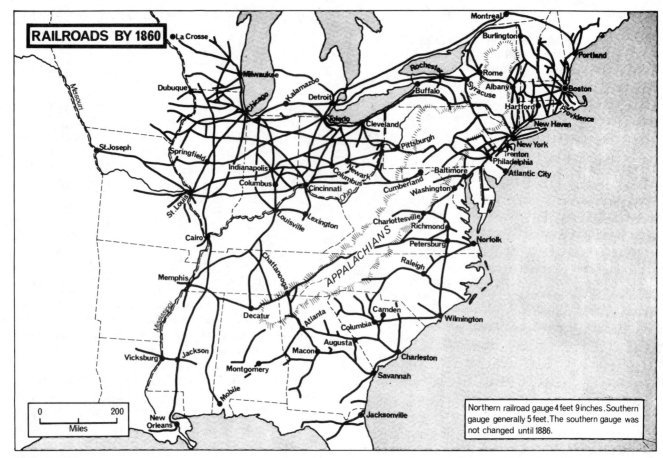

Figure 10.4

Source Martin Gilbert, *American History Atlas*, Weidenfeld & Nicolson, p. 48.

THE FIRST WORLD WAR

In 1914 *Woodrow Wilson* was America's President. He believed in trying to break up the huge industrial trusts, and got Congress to pass laws to limit their powers. (Later, during the New Deal (1933–41) this gave Roosevelt a counter with which to bargain with big industry when he wanted changes in how they dealt with their workers; see Section 4 below). President Wilson also backed *free trade*, and America's 100-year-old policy of keeping its nose out of the political and diplomatic affairs of Europe. This policy of *isolation* meant that when the First World War (1914–18) broke out America refused to take a part. In 1916 Wilson was re-elected after campaigning on a policy of American neutrality in the First World War. However, with German submarines sinking American shipping and even appearing to plot with Mexico, America's hostile neighbour, to attack America, in April 1917 America declared war on Germany. By 1918 American troops were beginning to flood into Europe in large quantities, and they played a crucial role in the crushing defeat of Germany in the summer of 1918. Wilson laid down a peace plan, his *Fourteen Points* (see pages 29–30 above), and he played a leading part in the Versailles Settlement (see Chapter 2, Section 2). When he returned, Congress refused to agree to the Versailles Settlement and refused to allow America to join the League of Nations.

Examination Guidance

It is most unlikely that there will be questions on America in 1919. The questions below are to give you practice in answering the kinds of questions you will encounter, and to familiarise you with the background to the following Sections. Questions 1–3 are based on a LEAG pattern; Questions 4 and 5 are typical of all the Examining Groups.

ACTIVITY 68

Targets

Recall, concepts of change, deployment of sources and drawing conclusions from them.

Question Guide

Questions 1–3 are based on recall; Question 4 asks you to draw conclusions from the figures, for example, Figure 10.1 suggests that America was the world's leading economic power because she had outstripped her main rivals in the key industries of coal, iron and steel, and was an equal of the world's major powers in other areas, such as the growth of wheat and mining of precious metals. Question 5 is about the relative value of sources such as tables, graphs and maps.

Activity

1. Write a sentence giving one reason why the Prohibition laws might have encouraged lawlessness in the USA. **(2)**
2. Write a sentence describing relations between the trusts and the unions in America in 1919. **(2)**
3. Write a short paragraph showing what were the roles of the President, Congress, the Senate and the Supreme Court in America in 1919. **(8)**
4. Use Figures 10.1, 10.2, 10.3 and 10.4 to show:
    (a) how important America was as a world power in 1900 **(3)**
    (b) what was the role of the town and city in America **(3)**
    (c) the impact of immigration on America. **(6)**
    or
    Use Figures 10.1–10.4 to help write an account of how American society changed from 1860 to 1919. **(16)**
5. Discuss the value to the historian of information presented in the form of Figures 10.1–10.4.

2 The Roaring '20s

The 1920s have left me with fleeting impressions – jazz, Charlie Chaplin and silent movies, women's first taste of freedom (Source 10A), with them publicly smoking cigarettes and dancing in short skirts (the 'flappers'), widespread ownership of cars and the Great Crash and Depression, leading to ten years of mass unemployment and misery, the rise of Nazism in Europe and of Japanese fascism in Asia followed by the Second World War.

Source 10A Fashions for motor-cyclists, 1925

Source Harriet Ward, *World Powers in the Twentieth Century*, Heinemann, 1978, p. 15

THE ECONOMY

To fight the First World War, Britain and France relied upon American industry for vital guns and machines, and upon American farmers for food for their people. America loaned huge sums of money to the Allied governments (over 10 billion dollars) to pay for their war effort. After the war America also lent money to Germany to pay off her war debts, the Germans in turn paid money to the Allies, Britain and France, to help their industries. From 1919 the American economy boomed to help rebuild shattered Europe, and from 1919 to 1920 American industry grew quickly as output doubled. Industrialists built new electrified factories with stream-lined production lines making new, mass-produced goods like refrigerators, radios and cookers. In 1921 5,000 fridges were made, in 1929, 900,000; and radio output soared from about 50,000 to 10,000,000 in the same period.

Not everyone was well off. Small-scale farmers saw their real incomes cut. They faced fierce, price-cutting competition from the farmers of Europe and, at home, from large farmers who used new machinery like combine harvesters and powerful tractors to increase their output and cut their costs. The blacks, many of whom worked in poor farming areas in the southern states, also did badly. Huge numbers left the land and went to live in the cities of the north, where they took the worst-paid jobs which no one else would do.

America was going through rapid change; this frightened many people, who felt that their old ideas, values, beliefs and ways of life were under threat. Reaction to change took many forms, three of these were *the Red Scare*, the *Ku Klux Klan* and *Prohibition and crime*.

THE RED SCARE

Russia had fallen under communist control in 1917 (see Chapter 8). Terror of communism has been a driving force in world affairs ever since, and in America in the 1920s an effort was made to get rid of any immigrants whom it was thought might spread communist ideas. Thousands of suspects were deported. Following a Wall Street bomb blast, the 'Red Scare' led to the arrest of two Italian immigrants, *Sacco* and *Vanzetti*. They were accused of having murdered a postmaster. Sacco and Vanzetti were members of an extreme group, the anarchists, and had links with communists. Their trial was a farce, with the judge making clear his belief that they were guilty, despite the inconclusive evidence. The judge sentenced Sacco and Vanzetti to death, and public demonstrations against their sentence swept the world. Despite a review of their case, in 1927 Sacco and Vanzetti were electro-cuted, victims of Red Scare hysteria. Vanzetti's last words plead his case:

Source 10B

I am not guilty of these crimes, but I never commit a crime in my life. I have never steal and I have never kill and I have never spilt blood . . . I would not wish to a dog or to a snake, to the most low and misfortunate creature on the earth. I would not wish to any of them what I have had to suffer for things that I am not guilty of.
But my conviction is that I have suffered for things that I am guilty of. I am suffering because I am a radical, and indeed I am a radical. I have suffered because I was an Italian, and indeed I am an Italian; I have suffered more for my family and for my beloved than for myself but I am so convinced to be right that if you could execute me two times, and if I could be reborn two other times, I would live again to do what I have done already.

CINEMA

One new industry was cinema – in the 1920s the need to mass produce films led the dawning age of *Hollywood*. Nine out of ten films in the world were made in America, and the introduction of talking films in the late 1920s spurred on the film-making boom. In 1927, 60 million Americans a week went to the cinema, in 1929 over 100 million. Cinemas were built in every town, and stars like Buster Keaton, Charlie Chaplin, Mary Pickford and Gloria Swanson became household names.

INDUSTRY

America was booming, and the 1920s saw the mushrooming of skyscrapers in her towns and cities, including that symbol of the age, New York's *Empire State Building*. Although workers' income rose by 50% in the 1920s, the bulk of profits went into the pockets of the industrialists and bankers. Huge monopolies flourished: for example, US Steel ran the steel industry – in steel towns the company was the only major employer, and, because it had banned unions, it could fix wages at a low level. Employers were willing to use police and troops to smash strikes, and protect 'blackleg' workers called in to replace the strikers.

The motor car industry was at the heart of economic growth – think of all the industries which rely upon the making of a motor car and you can understand why. *Henry Ford* led the way, with his Model T Fords. At his Detroit factory he set up an assembly line with each person doing a single job. In the 1920s Ford built over a million Model Ts a year. Mass production meant prices fell sharply. By 1926 the price of a Model T had halved since 1914, making cheap cars available for all. The mid-1920s saw the birth of two other motoring giants, *General Motors* and the *Chrysler Corporation*. Soon their models rivalled Fords, and the shape of the motor industry, with its three "ugly sisters", has remained the same since. By 1929, America had some 27 million vehicles, enough to squeeze in the whole population of the country! The motor car changed for ever how and where people lived, worked and played. A network of roads was built, garages, hotels and restaurants mushroomed and the motor car meant that suburbs spread out from the towns and cities to areas within an hour's drive of the city or town centre.

THE KU KLUX KLAN

A cross, figures in white robes wearing long pointed hats, flaming torches and an Imperial Wizard – a children's television cartoon? No, a procession of members of the Ku Klux Klan (Source 10C), intent mainly on burning the homes and shops of, or beating up and killing, blacks, although they also attacked Jews and Roman Catholics. The Ku Klux Klan was a violent American movement of mainly poor whites, protesting at the changes in the role of the blacks by the 1920s. The move of blacks into North American cities, with them taking over housing in many poor areas, had led to widespread rioting. The Klan had major appeal in the 1920s; it claimed some 5 million members in mid-decade. Support for it collapsed when its leader was jailed for kidnapping a girl who took poison because of the way he had treated her.

Source 10C   Inducting a new member, 1915

Source   Chris MacDonald, *Modern America*, Basil Blackwell, 1987

Source 10D   Has she a fair chance?

The OVERSHADOWING CURSE
THE LEGALIZED SALOON

HAS SHE A FAIR CHANCE ?

"Our religion demands that every child should have a fair chance for citizenship in the coming Kingdom. Our patriotism demands a saloonless country and a stainless flag."---P. A. Baker. General Superintendent Anti-Saloon League of America.

Source   Scott Harrison, *The USA*, Oxford University Press, p. 7

PROHIBITION AND CRIME

The demon drink does the work of the devil (Source 10D). Extremism takes many forms, and in the 1920s hundreds of American religious organisations believed that alcohol was at the root of many of America's social problems – violence, the breakdown of marriage, broken families and hooliganism as well as drunkenness. So, in 1919 bodies like the Women's Christian Temperance (anti-drink) League got Congress, the American Parliament, to pass the *18th Amendment* to the American Constitution and a law to ban the making and sale of alcohol. This law, the *Volstead Act*, came into force in 1920. America was now 'dry' – with amazing results.

Many Americans wanted to go on drinking, and to supply their needs *bootleggers* either made alcohol illegally in factories or smuggled it across the Mexican or Canadian borders. Liquor was sold in 'bootleg' stores or drunk in secret bars or *speakeasies*. In 1919 there were around 15,000 legal bars in New York, by 1930 some 30,000 illegal speakeasies had replaced them. The Volstead Act was tailor-made for the criminals of Chicago and New York, as a huge demand for an illegal product led to vast profits. Big crime boomed during the 1920s; gangsters like *Al Capone* ran the factories, the smuggling operations and the speakeasies (Source 10E).

Source 10E

We had one speakeasy in the basement of the Board of Education building, believe it or not, a real posh place owned by Mr Capone. You used to go down a dark hall and rap on a steel door. There was a certain signal . . . a peephole would open and a guy identify you. Inside was a beautiful Gay Nineties Bar. The bourbon was good, the scotch was excellent and the prices were right, 75c a drink.

Prohibition gave big crime a boost in other areas like prostitution, gambling, lending money and drug-dealing. Men like Capone and *Bugs Moran* ran rival gangs, who would control towns and cities through bribing politicians and policemen, and even rigging local elections. In Chicago, Capone had the mayor, Bill Thompson, in his pocket, and he even had full control over the local town of Cicero, where his followers forced the voters to support the gangster's candidates. *Gang warfare* was rife, the most famous killings occurring in Chicago on 14 February 1929, when Capone is suspected of having had murdered six members of Moran's rival gang in the *St Valentine's Day Massacre*. No one was ever arrested; Capone threw a party on the same day on a visit to Miami, saying that perhaps Moran was to blame!

GOVERNMENT: HOME AND ABROAD

Home

Woodrow Wilson's Democratic Party Presidency came to an end in 1920. America's new President, *Warren Harding*, was a Republican, and the Republicans were in power until 1933. *Republicanism* was the party of big business, a party of balanced budgets, economic freedom and the minimum of government interference in the economy. Typically, Harding placed *Andrew Mellon* in charge of the government's finances. Mellon was America's second richest man, with a fortune based on aluminium and oil. Mellon did little, apart from cut taxes, which helped increase sales (Source 10F). Government income soared from the Fordney–McCumber trade tariff of 1922, which placed high taxes on imports.

The government did two important things in the 1920s. It cut the right of immigration by the *1921 Immigration Act*, so that by 1929 the numbers of immi-

Source 10F   Cartoon, 1920s

Source   Purnell History of the 20th Century, p. 1237

grants had been cut to 150,000 a year from the 850,000 a year in 1907–14. Harding also put into reverse Wilson's policy of free trade. America feared competition from the expanding industry of Europe, and in 1922 the *Fordney–McCumber Tariff Act* placed high tariffs on foreign imports. A trade war began with European countries, a war which made worse the Great Depression which began in 1929. More seriously, the Fordney-McCumber Tariff Act cut off Japan from its main foreign market, and led an economically depressed Japan down the path which led to Pearl Harbor.

Harding's Presidency was marked by government inactivity and private scandal. Harding dished out government jobs to his mates from his home state of Ohio. Soon they were up to their necks in scandals, as they dipped their greedy paws into the 'pork barrel' of government funds, bribes and contracts. The most famous scandal involved the receipt of loans (bribes) from an oil speculator hoping to buy the lease on a probable oilfield, the Teapot Dome in Wyoming, (Source 10G). When Harding died, his Vice-President, *Calvin Coolidge* (1923–9), took over. A man of few words, Silent Cal said little and did less, apart from cutting income tax on the wealthy. When he died the famous wit Dorothy Parker asked the question, 'How could they tell?'

Abroad

The end of Wilson's Presidency was marked by Congress's refusal to accept the Versailles Settlement and the League of Nations. American government in the 1920s was marked by a conscious move to cut off America from the rest of the world (see Section 4 below) and to give government as small a role as possible in finance and industry. The *Washington Naval Conference* of 1921–2 led to Britain, Japan and America agreeing to end a naval arms race in the Pacific. All sides agreed to scrap large parts of their navies. The agreement was not followed up;

Source 10G   A view of the Presidency

Source   Purnell History of the 20th Century, p. 1235

soon it was a dead letter. In Europe, America was involved in sorting out the financial problems of Germany: the *Dawes Plan* of 1924 (see Chapter 2, Section 6) laid the foundations for the great German economic recovery of the 1920s. The 1928 Kellogg–Briand Pact was the last major international agreement not to use force to solve problems between rival powers. It, too, was not worth the paper it was written on (see Chapter 2, Section 6). The Young Plan of 1929 seemed to wrap up the problem of Germany's reparations, but optimism was short-lived. Soon the cold wind of the Great Depression blew down the financial house of cards.

Examination Guidance

Questions will probably concentrate on a single element of the 1920s, such as economic recovery or gangsterism.

ACTIVITY 69a

Targets

Recall, sources – evaluation, including the detection of bias.

Question Guide

Question 1 requires simple one-word or one-sentence answers which provide an accurate, factual response: for example, the answer to Question 1(a) is 'anarchists', to Question 1(b) 'Christianity' and 'the American flag'. Question 2 asks you to look inside the source to find the relevant information: for the first part the way in which

Vanzetti protests his innocence, for the second the way in which he says he would willingly die for his beliefs. Question 3(a) requires you to link the information in the cartoon with your knowledge of the period, while 3(b) forces you to comment on the style of the cartoon. Question 4 is a standard one on the nature of photographic sources, in this instance a close examination of whether the picture is posed or not. Question 5 asks you to relate the sources to your knowledge of the period. Be sure to link each source in to the specific knowledge you have: for example, Source 10D should be tied in to the passing of the Volstead Act.

Activity

1. (a) Read Source 10B. Which radical group did Vanzetti belong to?   **(1)**
    (b) Look at Source 10C. Name two things which the photograph suggests the Ku Klux Klan members believed in.   **(2)**
    (c) Look at Source 10F. Who was Mellon?   **(1)**
    (d) Look at Source 10G. Name one case of crime or a scandal in the 1920s which the cartoon might refer to.   **(1)**
2. Read Source 10B.
    (a) What does the source suggest about Vanzetti's guilt?   **(1)**
    (b) What does the source suggest about his radical beliefs?   **(2)**
3. Study Sources 10F and 10G.
    (a) What message is the cartoonist of Source 10F trying to get across?   **(3)**
    (b) What evidence is there that the cartoonist of Source 10G is biased?   **(3)**
4. What problems does Source 10A pose for the historian?   **(4)**
5. Study Sources 10A–G. Do they give a good impression of America in the 1920s. If so, why?   **(12)**

ACTIVITY 69b

Targets

Recall, sources – evaluation, including the detection of bias.

Question Guide

This question is taken from the June 1989 MEG paper and is an excellent illustration of the ways in which a clutch of sources is used to test your understanding of the period. Question 1 is a simple recall one, although 1(b) asks for knowledge linked to the movement cutting down on the number of immigrants in the 1920s. Question 2 asks you to look inside the source for the evidence required, in this case that the customers were drinking illegally. A good answer to Question 3 will comment on both the imagery in the picture, with the contrasts between the figure at the bar and the bartender on the one hand and the inset picture of a downtrodden young woman and her impoverished family on the other, and on the emotive language used in the caption, in particular the idea that drinking leads men into slavery. Question 4 will require a comment first upon the nature of the statistics, in that they were produced by an association against Prohibition, and then upon how they might have been compiled, i.e. their accuracy. In analysing the figures, you should emphasise the contrast between the price of drink before Prohibition and that after, the total amount being spent in the two periods on drink, and the change in the pattern of drinking from spirits and beer to mainly spirits.

Activity

The United States of America, 1919–41

Look carefully at Sources 1–5. Then answer all the questions.

Source 1

A poster in favour of Prohibition, published by the Anti-Saloon League in 1919. (The label attached to the bag of money says: WEEKS WAGES. Above the drawing of the woman and child, the caption says: THE SALOON IS WELL NAMED 'THE POOR MAN'S CLUB' IT KEEPS ITS MEMBERS AND THEIR FAMILIES ALWAYS POOR.)

SLAVES OF THE SALOON

The saloon business cannot exist without slaves. You may smile at that statement, but it is absolutely true. Is not the man who is addicted to the drink habit a slave? There are 1,000,000 such slaves in the United States. They are slaves of the saloon. They go out and work a week or a month, draw their pay, go into the saloon, and hand the saloon keeper their money for something which ruins their own lives. Is not this slavery? Has there ever been in the history of the world a worse system of slavery? It is quite natural, of course, that the slaveholder should not care to liberate these slaves.—

Source 2

The neighbourhood was rundown, so was the old saloon, so were the men going in and out. He went home and put on the shabbiest outfit (of clothes) he owned. He followed another man wearing working clothes into the saloon, wiping his face with a dirty handkerchief. He asked for a beer.
The bartender grinned, 'Would you like a lollipop on the side?' The other customers, many with drinks in front of them, began to laugh. Izzy joined in the laughter.
'I'm a stranger,' he said, 'and don't know the ropes nowadays in strange places. I'll buy a pint of whisky – if it's not too expensive.'
The bartender produced the pint. Izzy showed his badge and made his first arrest as a Prohibition agent.
(Thomas M Coffey, writing in 1976, describes how Izzy Einstein, a famous Prohibition agent, made his first arrest.)

Source 3

(i) I'm no Eyetalian. I was born in New York thirty-one years ago.
(ii) If people didn't want beer and wouldn't drink it, a fellow would be crazy going round trying to sell it.
I help the public. You can't cure thirst by law. They call me a bootlegger. Yes. It's bootleg while it's on the trucks, but when your host hands it to you on a silver plate it's hospitality.
(Two statements made by Al Capone to a reporter in 1930.)

Source 4

A photograph, taken in the 1920s, of a man making alcohol in his own home.

Source 5

A set of statistics, published in 1926, by the Association Against the Prohibition Amendment.

PROHIBITION, THE PROOF
WHAT AMERICANS DRANK, 1910–17

	Gallons Average per Year	Price per Gallon	Estimated Retail Cost
Spirits	142,121,000	$5	$710,605,000
Wines	56,316,000	$4	$225,264,000
Beers, Ale, (etc.)	1,924,552,000	$1	$1,924,552,000
Total	2,122,989,000		$2,860,441,000

A GUESS AT WHAT AMERICANS DRINK NOW, 1926

	Gallons Average per Year	Price per Gallon	Estimated Retail Cost
Spirits:			
From industrial alcohol	105,000,000	$20	$2,100,000,000
Smuggled whiskey	1,660,000	$24	$39,840,000
Moonshine	178,540,000	$4	$714,600,000
	285,206,000		$2,854,000,000
Homemade wine	75,000,000	$4	$300,000,000

1   Read Source 3.
      (a)   Who was Al Capone?   **(1)**
      (b)   Why might he deny being Italian?   **(1)**
2   Read Source 2.
      What does this source suggest about:
      (a)   the public's respect for the Prohibition laws?   **(1)**
      (b)   the work done by a Prohibition agent?   **(1)**
3   Look at Source 1.
      What evidence is there that this poster was used for
      propaganda? Explain your answer fully.   **(6)**
4   Do these statistics give a reliable view of the effects of
      Prohibition? Explain your answer fully.   **(8)**
5   Look at all the sources.
      'Prohibition was a good idea in theory but a bad one in
      practice.' Do these sources show this view to be true?
      Explain your answer fully.   **(12)**

3 The Great Crash and Depression

If economics is a science, the way in which governments run their economies is an experiment. In October 1929 began a huge economic crisis which had long-term and devastating effects on the lives of everyone in America, Europe and Asia. In October 1929 occurred the *Wall Street Crash*. What caused the crash, what did it mean, and, more important, what were its consequences?

The Cause of the Crash

Americans had been buying shares as industry boomed throughout the 1920s. This money was used to build new factories and to buy raw materials and machinery. Industrialists, merchants and builders relied on the sale of shares to pay for expanding and running their businesses. Many Americans, either as individuals or as firms, took out loans from the bank to pay for these shares, or promised to pay the money for them later. This was fine so long as prices rose, but when prices fell and loans had to be repaid, many Americans did not have the money to pay their debts.

The Meaning of the Crash

The crash occurred when there was a sharp and continuing drop in the price of shares (see Figure 10.5). Hugh Brogan, a university historian, tells us about the second week of the crash:

Figure 10.5   Share prices of leading American companies

	US Steel	General Electric	Radio Corporation of America
1928	138	128	94
3.9.29	279	296	505
24.10.29 a.m.	205	315	68
24.10.29 noon	193	283	44
1930	182	75	48
1931	145	50	24
1932	48	21	9
1933	24	12	4

Source 10H

Sunday was the day of rest: on Monday the slide began again. Nine million shares were traded; by the end of the day the price of shares had gone down by $14,000,000,000 altogether since the middle of the previous week. The selling had been sharpest at the end of the trading day. Next day, 'Black Tuesday', collapse was total: 650,000 shares in US Steel, bluest of 'blue chips', the most respectable of 'securities', were dumped on the market in the first three minutes. The Stock Exchange reacted like a zoo where all the animals had gone mad. The superintendent later recalled how the brokers [the men buying and selling shares] 'roared like a lot of lions and tigers. They hollered and screamed, they clawed at one another's collars.'

And they sold and sold and sold. Radio collapsed, General Electric collapsed, Tinker Roller Bearing and Anaconda Copper collapsed. It was as if the whole fabric of modern business, industrial America was unravelling. Montgomery Ward, the great mail-order firm, collapsed. The bankers' consortium [a group of bankers] of the week before was quite unable to stem the torrent. Woolworth collapsed. Men rushed screaming from the floor into the street. 'I'm sold out ! Sold out! Out!' Trinity Church on Wall Street was packed with desperate men of all creeds [beliefs/religions] in search of comfort.

    By the time the exchange closed at 3 p.m. 16,383,700 shares had been sold at a loss of $10,000,000,000 – 'twice the amount of currency in circulation in the entire country at the time'. And, simultaneously, panic had been wrecking all the other stock exchanges – in San Francisco, Los Angeles, Chicago. A great part of a generation's savings had been wiped out. The rest were to go in the long slow slide that went on until 1932, when US Steel which had stood at $262 a share in 1929 stood at $22 . . .

(H. Brogan, *The Pelican History of the United States*, Pelican Books, 1985)

The Consequences of the Crash

The demands for repayment of loans taken out by individual share-buyers and firms, and the failure to sell new shares, meant that money dried up for the running

Source 10I   The Crash!

Source   Purnell History of the English Speaking Peoples, p. 1250

of factories, trading and business. American banks also demanded back the money they had lent European countries and businesses, so the Depression hit Europe just as hard as America. The crash in the price of shares wiped out much of the value of many people's life savings, and the failure of a bank could mean that they lost everything, (Source 10I).

In both America and Europe, many firms were forced to close down and make their workers redundant, (Figure 10.6). A vicious circle developed: with factories shutting and no pay packets to take home, demand for goods fell; falling demands meant lower output and fewer jobs; fewer jobs meant even less demand. Unemployment soared (Figure 10.7). Franklin Roosevelt, later President of the USA, visited a sweater factory which employed about 150 people. He heard that:

Figure 10.6 USA business failures (bankruptcies) per 10,000 businesses

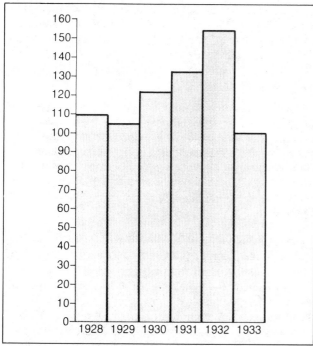

Source Jon Nichol, John Fines and Chris Macdonald *eds.*, *History Resource Summer 1987, Volume 1, Issue 1*, Pergamon Educational Productions, p. 66–2.

Figure 10.7 Unemployment, 1930–40

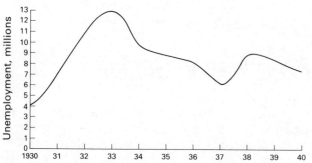

Source Jon Nichol, John Fines and Chris Macdonald *eds.*, *History Resource Summer 1987, Volume 1, Issue 1*, Pergamon Educational Productions, p. 65–1.

Source 10J

The wholesale houses began to give smaller orders than usual because the retailers ordered one or two sweaters where they used to order a dozen at a time. The owner had to close down the mill for longer periods between orders and lay off about half of the employees. The wholesalers asked if he could make a cheaper sweater. He tried to. He got small orders for the cheaper sweater, but that did not bring enough work.

The employer was a local man and his employees were his friends. They begged him to do something, for there was no other work in the neighbourhood. Their savings were exhausted and they had to have work. [He looks for orders.] Finally he found a jobber who said, 'We just got an order for 5000 sweaters to sell at two dollars apiece. Can you fill it.' The employer gasped, 'How could I? You know that doesn't touch the cost.' [He takes the job, having to use the cheapest possible wool thread.] The owner went home and called the people of the mill together, and put it to them. He would give up any profit, he said, and it would give them a few weeks' work at wages he hated to mention . . . The jobber had told him, he said, there were two other firms ready to take the order.

(Frances Perkins, *The Roosevelt I Knew*)

Factories closed, farms turned back into the wilderness, world trade ground to a halt, millions were unemployed. The collapse in trade meant that poor countries, relying on the sale of raw materials to America and Europe, were very badly hit.

THE IMPACT OF THE DEPRESSION

The Great Crash had a profound impact upon all Americans. Between 1929 and 1932, 5,000 banks went out of business. The sale of new cars crashed from around 4.5 million in 1929 to about 1 million in 1932. Just think of how much work goes into building a car, from the smelting of the iron and steel, to the making of electrical wires and bulbs, right down to the final coat of paint. All industry slumped, and as industry slumped unemployment soared. Unemployment was very high in certain industries: for example, in the clothmaking industry 40% of the workers lost their jobs (see Source 10J). Some cities had far more people out of work than others: in Chicago starving women scavenged through the city's rubbish tips looking for scraps of food. The Depression hit certain groups harder than others – the poor, black immigrants were the first to be laid off, and unemployment in the black ghettoes of the cities was as high as 70%. Farmers were among the worst-off – by 1932 farm output had dropped by 70%. Farmers slaughtered animals they could neither sell nor afford to feed, and crops were left to rot in the fields. Many farmers left their farms and moved west to California, hoping to start a new life.

Unemployment

What did it mean to be out of work in America in the early 1930s? No job meant no income, for Hoover refused to introduce state payments to the unemployed. The Gas and Electric Companies cut off the gas and electricity, so cold, darkness and hunger went hand in hand. The Churches and charities kept the unemployed from dying from hunger. If you have no income, you starve, and unemployed Americans were forced to join breadlines for free bread and soup from the 'soup kitchens'. Unable to pay the rent or their mortgages, unemployed families were out on the streets begging. Soon shanty towns of shacks built from cardboard, corrugated iron and spare wood and timber sprang up in every town and city; these were known as *Hoovervilles*. Starving mobs were ready to take the law into their own hands:

Source 10K

Eleven hundred men standing in a Salvation Army bread line on March 19, 1930, near the Bowery Hotel in Manhattan descended upon two trucks delivering baked goods to the hotel. Jelly rolls, cookies, rolls and bread were flung into the street, with the hungry jobless chasing after them. By 1932 organised looting of food was a nation-wide phenomenon. Helen Hall, a Philadelphia social worker, told a Senate committee that many families sent their children out to steal from wholesale markets, to snatch milk for babies, to lift articles from pushcarts to exchange for food.
(I. Bernstein, *The Lean Years*, 1969)

By 1932 the problem of poverty seemed to be a permanent one:

Source 10L

This study of the human cost of unemployment reveals that a new class of poor and dependents is rapidly rising among the ranks of young, sturdy, ambitious labourers, mechanics and professionals. Unemployment and loss of income have ravaged numerous homes. Idleness destroys not only purchasing power, lowering the standards of living, but also destroys efficiency and finally breaks the spirit.
(From the report of the California State Unemployment Commission, 1932)

Hoover and the Great Crash

In 1928 Hoover had stood for election as President. In his successful campaign he said:

Source 10M

We in America today are nearer to the financial triumph over poverty than ever before in the history of our land. The poor man is vanishing from among us. Under the Republican system, our industrial output has increased as never before, and our wages have grown steadily in buying power. Our workers with their average weekly wages can today buy two or even three times more bread and butter than any wage earner in Europe. At one time we demanded for our workers a full dinner pail (a bucket). We have now gone far beyond that . . . Today we demand a larger comfort and greater participation in life and leisure.

The Great Crash took Hoover by surprise, and he took steps to try and solve the crisis. Hoover set up a government agency to lend money to banks and to house owners who could not pay their mortgages. A government scheme helped farmers borrow the money they needed to run their farms, so their animals no longer starved to death. The year 1930 saw a slight improvement in the economy, and Hoover expected the problem to sort itself out through the working of natural economic laws. His belief in a policy of no government action, *(laissez-faire)* claimed that lower prices would mean more demand, more demand would mean more jobs, and the economy would improve quickly. The 1930 hopes for economic recovery were soon dashed; things got much worse, with more factories closing and unemployment soaring. At the same time, in 1930 America raised her trade barriers against imports. The *Smoot–Hawley Tariff* slashed imports, and foreign governments retaliated. However, in 1931 Hoover ordered that foreign countries need not pay their debts that year, to try and encourage them to use the money to support their own industry and buy American goods. This had little impact: from 1929 to 1933 America's foreign trade fell by two-thirds, making the Depression much worse. Even crime felt the cold wind of recession; in New York the police reckoned that the number of speakeasies dropped by two-thirds.

Hoover showed little patience with those out of work. Although he was prepared to help starving animals, he refused to support starving Americans. Typical was his treatment of the *Bonus Marchers* in June 1932. These veterans of the First World War had come to the city with their families to demand from the government the bonus it had promised to pay them. Instead of giving them help, Hoover sent armed troops in tanks to use tear-gas against the Bonus Marchers. The troops tore down the Bonus Marchers' Hooverville near to the White House and drove the marchers out of Washington.

The 1932 Election

In the 1932 Presidential election Hoover faced an opponent, *Franklin Roosevelt*, with a totally different approach to the problem of the Depression. Roosevelt promised government help for the millions of unemployed:

Source 10N

Millions of our citizens cherish the hope that their old standards of living and thought have not gone forever. Those millions cannot and shall not hope in vain. I pledge you, I pledge myself, to a New Deal for the American People. This is more than a political campaign; it is a call to arms. Give me your help, not to win votes alone, but to win in this crusade to restore America . . . I am waging war against Destruction, Delay, Deceit and Despair.

In 1928 Roosevelt had become Governor of New York. Through his *Temporary Relief Administration* (TERA) he had provided help for the unemployed. Roosevelt's success in New York in tackling the Depression made him the natural candidate for the Democratic Party for the 1932 Presidential election. Roosevelt won the 1932 election with ease, Hoover only taking six states. In the four months before Roosevelt took office the Depression worsened, with a huge increase in the number of banks being forced to close. On the day Roosevelt took office, 4 March 1933, the great banks of New York and Chicago refused to open. The closing-down of America's banks seemed near, and with it the final collapse of the American economy. What was Roosevelt going to do?

Examination Guidance

Questions will either be on the Great Crash and its impact, or link the Great Crash to the preceding period of the 1920s (Section 2 above) or to the subsequent New Deal (Section 4 above). Questions can also be linked to the outline paper dealing with the Depression as a world-wide phenomenon (see Chapter 3, Section 1).

ACTIVITY 70a

Targets

Recall, concepts of cause, change and consequence,

empathy (i.e. looking at events from the viewpoint of people in the past).

Question Guide

This is a short-paragraph/essay activity; in answering the questions, follow the suggestions outlined on pages 15–16.

Activity

1. What was the Wall Street Crash of 1929? **(4)**
2. What impact did the crash have? **(4)**
3. What impact did the Smoot-Hawley Tariff have? **(4)**
4. Discuss how the Great Crash might have affected the following:
   (a) the owner of a New York sweater factory **(3)**
   (b) an unemployed veteran of the First World War whose Washington factory closed down in 1930 **(3)**
   (c) a retired couple living on the income from their shares **(3)**
   (d) a poor farmer living in the Tennessee Valley. **(3)**

ACTIVITY 70b

Target

The evaluation of sources.

Question Guide

This question asks you to use your knowledge about the possible evidence upon which sources might be based. For handling such source questions, see pages 12–14, 16–18.

Activity

On what historical evidence do you think each of the sources listed below might have been based?
(a) Source 10H **(4)**
(b) Source 10J **(4)**
(c) Source 10K **(4)**
(d) Source 10L **(4)**
(e) Figure 10.7 **(4)**

ACTIVITY 70c

Target

The evaluation of sources.

Question Guide

This is the LEAG June 1988 question on the Depression. To help you answer the question note that:

Source 1 is Source 10M in the text above
Source 2 is Source 10K in the text above
Source 3 is Source 10L in the text above

The questions test recall, conceptual knowledge, and the handling of sources, the extraction of information and the drawing of conclusions from them, the comparison of sources, assessment of their nature and value as historical sources. Question (e) is a general one about sources in the period.

Activity

North America

5 Study Sources 1, 2, 3, 4 and 5, which refer to the USA during the late 1920s and early 1930s, and then answer questions (a) to (e) which follow.

Source 1

We in America today are nearer to the financial triumph over poverty than ever before in the history of our land. The poor man is vanishing from among us. Under the Republican system, our industrial output has increased as never before, and our wages have grown steadily in buying power. Our workers with their average weekly wages can today buy two or even three times more bread and butter than any wage earner in Europe. At one time we demanded for our workers a full dinner pail. We have now gone far beyond that . . . Today we demand a larger comfort and greater participation in life and leisure.
(from a speech by Herbert Hoover, 1928)

Source 2

Eleven hundred men standing in a Salvation Army bread line on March 19, 1930, near the Bowery Hotel in Manhattan descended upon two trucks delivering baked goods to the hotel. Jelly rolls, cookies, rolls, and bread were flung into the street, with the hungry jobless chasing after them . . . By 1932 organized looting of food was a nation-wide phenomenon. Helen Hall, a Philadelphia social worker, told a Senate committee that many families sent their children out to steal from wholesale markets, to snatch milk for babies, to lift articles from pushcarts to exchange for food.
(from *The Lean Years*, by I. Bernstein, 1969)

Source 3

This study of the human cost of unemployment reveals that a new class of poor and dependents is rapidly rising among the ranks of young, sturdy, ambitious labourers, mechanics and professionals . . . Unemployment and loss of income have ravaged numerous homes. Idleness destroys not only purchasing power, lowering the standards of living, but also destroys efficiency and finally breaks the spirit.
(from the report of the California State Unemployment Commission 1932)

Source 4 (a cartoon published in March 1933)

Source 5

It is wholly wrong to call the measures that we have taken Government control of farming, industry and transportation. It is rather a partnership between Government and farming and industry and transportation, not partnership in profits, for the profits still go to the citizens, but rather a partnership in planning, and a partnership to see that the plans are carried out.

(from a speech by President Roosevelt)

(a)   Study Sources 1, 2 and 3. To what extent do Sources 2 and 3 suggest that the views expressed in Source 1 were mistaken?   **(4)**

(b)   Which of Sources 2 or 3 is likely to be (i) more reliable and (ii) more useful to someone studying the USA? Give reasons for your answer.   **(4)**

(c)   'Hoover believed in laissez-faire (leaving things alone); Roosevelt believed in government control.' Do Sources 1, 4 and 5 support this statement? Refer in detail to the sources in support of your answer.   **(6)**

(d)   Would you describe the cartoonist in Source 4 as a supporter of Roosevelt? Refer in detail to the cartoon in support of your answer.   **(2)**

(e)   (i)   Identify **two** other kinds of primary evidence that you might consult in studying US economic and social history during the late 1920s and early 1930s?   **(2)**

      (ii) What would be the strengths and weaknesses of **one** of these other kinds of primary evidence for someone studying US history during this period?   **(2)**

4 The New Deal

In March 1933 Americans faced a huge crisis. A quarter of the people were out of work, farmers were on the breadline, with farm prices falling by two-thirds since 1930, and industry was making only 40% of what it could produce. Banks, on the brink of closing, were desperately demanding the repayment of loans and mortgages, forcing even more Americans out of business. To cope with this Depression, President Roosevelt had no carefully worked-out plans, no blueprint which he would force upon the American people. Instead he offered hope and aimed to boost confidence; as he said, 'The only thing that we have to fear is fear itself.' Roosevelt believed that the American economic system of capitalism was sound at heart; all it needed was a strong lead from government.

Once in office, Roosevelt began a whirlwind of activity, his hundred days, summed up in the slogan *'Relief, Recovery and Reform'*. Relief was needed to provide food to stop the poor from starving to death and to give them clothes and housing. Recovery was needed to get industry and farming back on their feet. Reform would prevent another Depression. Straightaway Roosevelt faced one major problem abroad and four major problems at home:

1.   the collapse of foreign trade
2.   the collapse of the banking and financial system
3.   widespread poverty and unemployment
4.   the depression in industry
5.   the dreadful state of farming.

Roosevelt's first hundred days set the tone for the New Deal, and set up many of its key agencies (see Figure 10.8). These agencies are often known by their initials, and during the New Deal a number changed their names, which can cause confusion. Much of the agencies' work overlapped, and serious problems were created by rivalries between the heads of the agencies who backed similar ideas and plans. It would be wrong to think that there was a simple, neat plan sitting on the shelf ready to solve the problems of the Depression. Indeed, during the first hundred days even President Roosevelt and members of his cabinet did not know what plans and schemes were being thought up! Before looking at what Roosevelt did at home, we shall examine the one major failure of the New Deal, its handling of the crisis in world trade.

Figure 10.8   The New Deal

1933

Bank Holiday declared. Banking Acts passed to put banks on a sound footing, with federal support or guarantees for their depositors.

Reconstruction Finance Corporation (RFC) channelled government funds to support the work of the New Deal.

Federal Emergency Relief Administration (FERA) provided relief for the poor and money for farmers, and, through the *Civil Works Administration* (CWA), set millions to work on small-scale schemes such as building roads, schools and hospitals.

Civilian Conservation Corps (CCC) set young people to work on conservation projects.

National Industrial Recovery Act set up the *National Recovery Administration* (NRA) to lay down codes for working relations between bosses and workers, and provided work through major public schemes handled by the *Public Works Administration* (PWA). The NRA's sign was the blue eagle.

Tennessee Valley Authority (TVA) established to build power dams and supply water to irrigate the Tennessee Valley.

Farmers' Relief Act and the *Agricultural Adjustment Act* set up the *Agricultural Adjustment Administration* (AAA), which provided the basis for the recovery of American farming from the depths of the Depression.

London Economic Conference failed to solve the problem of trade barriers.

1934

Trade Agreements Act. Roosevelt could fix tariffs to get international trade moving again.

Securities Exchange Commission controlled trading in stocks and shares to make sure that the Great Crash could not happen again.

1935

Works Progress Administration (WPA) replaced the CWA. Provided work for hundreds of thousands of people like artists and actors on small-scale jobs.

The Banking Act – tidying-up measures to control banking system.

Social Security Act made possible state pensions and unemployment and sickness pay based on worker and employer payments.

The Labour Relations Act (the Wagner Act) put into law the structure of drawing up industrial codes.

1938

Fair Labour Standards Act laid down forty-hour week, banned child labour and fixed minimum wages.

THE COLLAPSE OF FOREIGN TRADE

Attempts to deal with the collapse of foreign trade were the least successful aspect of the New Deal. Putting trade back on the same footing as in 1929 would have been a major way of restoring the health of banking, commerce, trade, industry and farming. Roosevelt was faced with a world in which countries were building trade barriers against their old trading partners and cutting off their farmers and industrialists from vital markets for their goods. An attempt to break down trade barriers was missed at the *London Economic Conference* of 1933. Roosevelt refused to allow America to take a lead in dealing with the problems of world trade, and tariffs remained at their high level. Although in 1934 Congress passed a *Trade Agreements Act* which let Roosevelt fix tariffs freely, America had failed to deal with the international trading problem, which would have done so much to help solve the problems of the Depression. We can now enquire into how Roosevelt coped with the Depression at home.

THE REFORM OF THE BANKING AND FINANCIAL SYSTEM

If the owners of the shops near your school and local factories could not get money out of a bank, or borrow from one, what do you think would happen to the running of their businesses? This was the nightmare which faced all Americans when Roosevelt took office on 3 March 1933, when it seemed that there might be a total shutdown of all banks. Roosevelt feared that millions of people would rush to draw their savings from the banks – a move which would force the banks out of business. Roosevelt, with the backing of Congress (the American parliament), was given the powers to declare a bank holiday, that is to close all the banks for a short time. Then Roosevelt would re-open those banks which had the backing of the government. No one knows whether this was legal or not, but he did it all the same. With the banks shut, there was no money. Alistair Cooke, a famous commentator on American life, tells us: *'It was the day the money stopped; literally, you had to cadge a meal, live on the tab in places that knew you, pay with a cheque for a cab ride and once – I remember – for a shoeshine'* (Alistair Cooke, *America*, BBC, 1973).

Roosevelt used the radio to give the first of many *fireside chats* to the American people, in which he told them that all banks that opened now had the support of the government, so their money was safe. The fireside chat was a great success. Roosevelt talked directly to the people of America in warm, clear, simple language, more like a friend than a President. When over 5,000 banks re-opened for business after the closure, the banking crisis was over. More money was put into the banks than was taken out.

In the longer term Roosevelt had to make sure that a Wall Street Crash never occurred again. In 1934 he set up the *Securities Exchange Commission* to control the stock market. Among other measures, the SEC made any purchaser of shares put up half of the money straightaway. This stopped gambling in shares with borrowed money.

Finance was at the heart of the New Deal. Roosevelt used an old body, the *Reconstruction Finance Corporation*, to provide the financial backing which the reformed banking system needed. Under Jesse Jones, a Texan businessman full of drive and energy, the RFC funnelled cash into key areas of the New Deal:

Source 10O

Through its Commodity Credit Corporation it financed the operations of the Triple A [the programme to rescue farming]. Through the Export–Import Bank it tried to revive foreign trade. Through the Electric Home and Farm Authority it stimulated the market for electricity of which the TVA [Tennessee Valley Authority] was becoming a major supplier. In co-operation with the Federal Housing Administration it helped real-estate dealers find customers and first-time house-buyers find mortgages. In short, all the other New Deal agencies discovered, to their delight, the RFC . . . was a bottomless source of cash which was always on tap.
(H. Brogan, *The Pelican History of the United States of America*, Pelican Books, 1985)

The *Banking Act* of 1935 tidied up the banking reforms, and set up the banking system which exists today. These measures also meant that if people were unable to repay loans and mortgages, the banks would no longer seize their goods and houses. Americans no longer feared that they would be thrown out of their houses if they lost their jobs.

WIDESPREAD POVERTY AND UNEMPLOYMENT

The poor needed money for food, clothing and housing. Relief came from the *Federal Emergency Relief Administration (FERA)*. Harry Hopkins, Roosevelt's personal choice to head FERA, gave it driving, imaginative, creative leadership. What did Hopkins do? First, he distributed over 500 million dollars to the States to provide support for the unemployed – money for food, clothes and housing. FERA gave farmers money for tools, seed, livestock and fertiliser. Relief was an immediate solution, but Hopkins pressed for longer-term measures. Next, he set the people to work. Hopkins knew that the winter of 1933 would see millions more out of work, and he believed that the only way out of this looming crisis was a major public works programme. Hopkins went to see Roosevelt for lunch.

Source 10P

'Let's see,' said Roosevelt. 'Four million people – that means roughly four hundred million dollars.' He thought this could be provided from the Public Works fund. [Hopkins got his team of workers together.] They worked most of Saturday night and Sunday in the Hotel Powhatan and drew up the plans for the Civil Works Administration which put the four million people to work in the first thirty days of its existence and, in less than four months, inaugurated 180,000 work projects and spent $933 millions.
(R. E. Sherwood, *Roosevelt and Hopkins*, Harper, 1948).

The *Civil Works Administration (CWA)* set millions to work on schemes such as building roads, schools and hospitals:

Source 10Q

[*Fortune* magazine gave an example of CWA's work: 'In Bay City, Michigan, an underwear manufacturing concern went bankrupt, and the closing of its plant threw some 250 workers on relief. Whereupon the State Relief Administration rented the plant, reopened it, and put the 250 workers back at their jobs on a subsistence level to make enough underwear to give every relief family in the state two sets for the winter.'
. . . its achievement in three and a half months was a

memorable one . . . 40,000 schools built or improved;
12,000,000 feet of sewer pipe laid; 469 airports built; 529 more
improved, 255,000 miles of road built or improved; 50,000
teachers employed to teach adults or to keep open rural
country schools which must otherwise have been closed;
3,700 playgrounds and athletic fields built or improved . . .
(R. E. Sherwood, *Roosevelt and Hopkins*, Harper, 1948)

At the same time Roosevelt pushed through his own pet
relief measure, the *Civilian Conservation Corps (CCC)* for
giving young people the chance to take part in conservation projects in the countryside. While on their six-
month spell at the CCC, young men were paid 30 dollars
a week, 25 of which were sent home, and provided with
food, clothes and somewhere to live.

Source 10R

. . . by July 1 [1933] three hundred thousand young men were
planting trees, tackling soil erosion, and building up against
floods instead of hitch-hiking along the highways or lodging on
the sidewalks. Camps of two hundred were formed all over the
country.
(Compton Mackenzie, *Mr Roosevelt*, Harrap, 1943)

From 1933 to 1941 some 2.5 million young men worked
for the CCC.

In 1935 the *Works Progress Administration (WPA)*
replaced the CWA. Hopkins was once more in charge,
this time with a 5,000 million-dollar budget. Roosevelt
said that this major government programme of public
works would solve the huge problem of providing work
for up to 5 million unemployed:

Source 10S

Work must be found for able-bodied but destitute workers.
I am not willing that the vitality of our people be further sapped
by the giving of cash, of market baskets, of a few hours of
weekly work cutting grass, raking leaves or picking up papers
in the public parks. We must preserve not only the bodies of
the unemployed from destruction, but also their self-respect,
their self-reliance and courage and determination.

Hopkins also provided work for artists and actors, and for
local groups of musicians. Artists were paid the standard
$15 a week to paint murals in public buildings. Frances
Perkins, Roosevelt's Secretary for Labour (1933–45)
gives an insight into the work of the WPA:

Source 10T

An almost deaf, elderly lawyer, a Harvard graduate, unable to
find clients, got a WPA job as assistant caretaker at a small
seaside park. He did double the work anyone could have
expected of him. He made little extra plantings, arranged
charming paths and walks, acted as guide to visitors,
supervised children's play, and made himself useful and
agreeable to the whole community. I had occasion to see him
from time to time and he would always ask me to take a
message to the President – a message of gratitude for a job
which paid him fifteen dollars a week and kept him from
starving to death. It was an honourable occupation that made
him feel useful and not like a derelict he would say with tears in
his eyes.
(Frances Perkins, *The Roosevelt I Knew*)

The final Hopkins measure was the *Social Security Act* of
1935. Payments from workers and employers aimed to

provide pensions for old age and relief from poverty
during times of unemployment. Limited in scope, the
Social Security Act was the first step in America on the
road to the kind of social welfare which British and
German workers enjoyed.

The work of Hopkins overlapped with that of the
National Recovery Administration (NRA), whose job was to
put industry back on its feet.

THE DEPRESSION IN INDUSTRY

To cope with the plight of industry Roosevelt passed in
1933 the *National Industrial Recovery Act*, setting up the
NRA. The NRA was in two parts, the first dealing with
relations between industrialists and the trade unions, the
other setting up a public works programme.

Industrialists agreed to allow workers to form trade
unions in return for the government ending laws against
industries fixing their prices. Each industry agreed to
work with the National Recovery Administration to agree
an industry code to fix the hours of work, wages and
conditions for men, women and children. The eight-hour
day and agreed minimum wages became general. Codes
were agreed for hundreds of industries, including the key
ones of cotton, steel and coal. Child labour ended in
coal-mines and cotton factories, and even Henry Ford,
hater of trade unions, agreed to follow the code for the
car industry. Firms which agreed to a code were allowed
to use the symbol of the NRA, a blue eagle. By June 1934
hourly wages had risen by one-third, total per-head
income was up by 14%, while prices had risen by only
7%. The blue eagle, through public parades and
Roosevelt's fireside chats, became a symbol of national
recovery. Serious problems arose about the codes being
enforced; many owners failed to carry out the agreements.

In 1935 the courts said that the NRA was illegal. So,
Roosevelt passed a new act, the *Labor Relations Act*
(known as the *Wagner Act* after its author), which
restored and strengthened the rights of the trade unions.
To enforce these trade union rights the Wagner Act set up
a *National Labor Relations Board*, which enforced the rights
of trade unions. With the backing of the law, union
membership grew from the 2,250,000 of 1933 to the
c. 14,000,000 of 1945. The final major law protecting the
workers was the *Fair Labor Standards Act* of 1938, which
pushed through the forty-hour week, banned child
labour and fixed minimum wages for many industries.

The second part of the National Recovery Administration was the *Public Works Administration (PWA)*, which
had $3,300,000 to spend on major public projects like
dams, bridges, government buildings and highways.
Frances Perkins, at the heart of the PWA as Roosevelt's
Secretary of Labour (1933–45), tells us:

Source 10U

Large housing projects were among the first approved, slum
clearance in particular. No type of public works better
illustrates the opportunity to put large numbers of people to
work both on the site and in the supply and transportation of
materials and to make, at the same time, proud and worthy
contributions to the community. River control projects having
for their purpose prevention of floods, development of
irrigation, and prevention of soil erosion, were also among the
early undertakings approved. Schools, health and hospital

centres, where those facilities were lacking, as well as sound, well-planned highway projects, also received early approval. (Frances Perkins, *The Roosevelt I Knew*)

THE DREADFUL STATE OF FARMING

Farming was in a ghastly way by 1933. Problems of the 1920s, with the tariff war cutting America off from her foreign markets and causing falling prices, became much worse in 1929. The Great Crash and Depression saw a collapse of markets for farm produce INSIDE America. Factories no longer needed as much raw materials from the farms, and sales of food also fell. Farmers saw their annual incomes fall by two-thirds – from an average of $900 to one of $300. At the same time the price of factory goods only dropped by one-third, so in real terms the farmers were worse off. Source 10V gives clues as to the impact of the Depression on farmers. You should read John Steinbeck's famous novel *The Grapes of Wrath* to get a feel of what the Depression in farming was really like.

Source 10V

Roosevelt asked *Henry Wallace*, an expert on new farming methods and farmers' problems, to work out a plan to save the farmers from ruin. Wallace rushed through the *Farmers' Relief Act* and the *Agricultural Adjustment Act* of 1933 which set up the *Agricultural Adjustment Administration (AAA)*. Wallace knew that farm prices were the key, and in order to push up farm prices, farm output would have to be cut. Farmers were paid for ploughing up their fields, killing their animals and

Figure 10.9   The Tennessee Valley Authority, 1933

Source   Martin Gilbert, *American History Atlas*, Weidenfeld & Nicolson, p. 82

cutting down on the amount of land they would have sown. The farmers in an area had to decide among themselves how many pigs or sheep were to die, how much land they would plough and what crops they would grow. Nature also helped Wallace: in 1934 and 1935 a drought hit the great wheat-bowl of America, and blew away much of the topsoil in red dust storms. Drought meant a drop in output, and a drop in output meant an increase in prices. Farmers' incomes doubled by 1937, and farmers were able to put money into new machines, fences, ditches, stock, seed and farm buildings.

Agricultural Adjustment Administration

This forced farmers to work as a team. Once organised they became a great political power, a quarter of all voters. Government was forced to buy up farmers' extra produce and store it, in order to keep prices up. With government money being paid to acres and not individuals, it was the big, rich farmers who did well out of the AAA. Many poor farmers with small farms were still badly off.

The AAA was a great success, although in 1936 the American Supreme Court declared that the original act was illegal. However, the government passed new laws which allowed the AAA to go on much as before – a pattern which has lasted down to the present day.

The Tennessee Valley Authority (TVA)

Recovery aimed to put American farming, banking, industry and trade back on a firm footing. One of the most spectacular schemes which sums up the aims of the New Deal was the Tennessee Valley Authority. The TVA saw Roosevelt's government use extensive powers to deal with the problem of a ruined farming area in the Tennessee Valley (see Figure 10.9). The region suffered

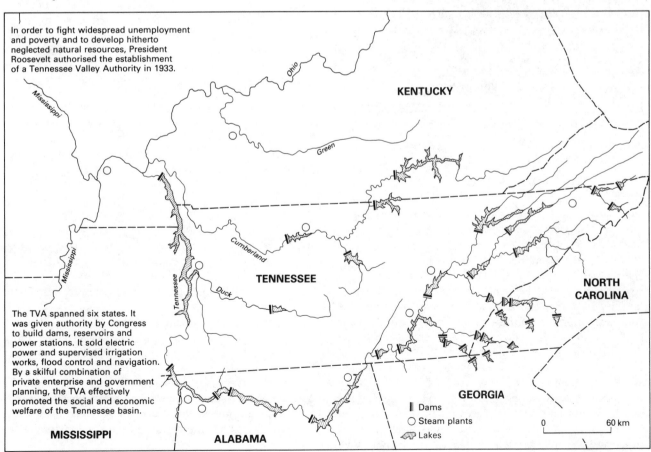

from soil erosion and drought, and needed to harness the power of the Tennessee River to generate electricity and distribute water for irrigation. In 1933 the New Deal established the TVA. The TVA built a string of dams which made electricity, controlled floods, provided water for irrigation and canalised the rivers for trading barges. The scheme provided thousands of jobs building the dams, power-lines and power-stations and running them. The TVA trained thousands of farmers in methods of soil-conservation and new ways of farming. Electricity from the dams not only reached thousands of poor farms and homes, but also meant that there was cheap power for new industries moving into the area.

Source 10W   The new judges

Source   Scott Harrison, *The USA*, Oxford University Press, p. 9

The Supreme Court

In America the Supreme Court has the power to say that laws which Congress passes may be illegal if they go against the rules laid down by the American Constitution. By 1935 the New Deal faced a major problem. The American Supreme Court said that a number of the New Deal measures were not legal. For example, it had declared that both the NRA and the AAA were illegal. Roosevelt asked Congress to pass a law which would allow him to appoint six new judges (Source 10W). There was a huge outcry against Roosevelt's plans, and he had to withdraw them. The measures of the New Deal had upset many old-style businessmen and bankers, both supporters of the Republican party and conservative

members of his own Democratic party. They accused Roosevelt of following plans similar to those of Hitler and Mussolini in Europe. The crisis over the Supreme Court gave them the excuse to mount a fierce attack on Roosevelt. However, with the death of a number of judges who had opposed him, the appointment of new judges who backed the New Deal and a change in attitude by others, after 1936 Roosevelt had little trouble with the Supreme Court.

The New Deal, 1937–41

Roosevelt was swept back into power in the 1936 Presidential election with a huge majority. By 1937 American farming and industry seemed to be recovering well, but Roosevelt had never really understood the key idea about using government spending to end the Depression. When J. M. Keynes, the British economist who showed how government spending could end the Depression, talked to Roosevelt, he used mathematical ideas which Roosevelt could not follow. Keynes failed to explain his ideas simply, as he did to Frances Perkins, Roosevelt's Secretary for Labor:

Source 10X

Keynes pointed out once that a dollar spent on relief by the government was a dollar given to the grocer, by the grocer to the wholesaler, and by the wholesaler to the farmer in payment of supplies. With one dollar paid out for relief or public works or anything else, you have created four dollars worth of national income. (Frances Perkins, *The Roosevelt I Knew*)

Instead of increasing government spending, Roosevelt feared that too much spending would lead to a rise in prices, *inflation*. So, in 1937 he slashed New Deal projects, and there was a 2 million rise in unemployment by Christmas, from 8 to 10 million. In 1938 Roosevelt was forced to restore the cuts, and America again began to lift out of Depression. The later part of the New Deal is sometimes called the *Second New Deal*.

The New Deal – Success of Failure?

A very hard question, with no right or wrong answer. Think about the following points, and make up your own mind:

Success?

1. *The emergency measures of 1933,* particularly banking. What would have happened if Roosevelt had not taken the emergency measures of 1933?
2. *FERA.* The poor and starving received immediate relief.
3. *Farming.* The Farmers' Relief Act helped solve immediate problems, and the AAA put farming back on a sound footing. The TVA was a great success
4. *Industry/economy.* The major and minor public works schemes, support for industry, the codes for the running of industry made between bosses and workers, all these laid the basis for long-term prosperity.

5. *Democracy, the constitution and American capitalism.* The New Deal saved all of these from change and even revolution – the story of Germany, Italy and Russia showed what might have happened. Roosevelt showed what could be done when the President worked with Congress to push through national measures, and he laid down a pattern for running America which has lasted down to the present day.

Failure?

1. *He only scratched at the surface of the Depression* – unemployment stayed at a very high level, industry remained depressed throughout. He failed in 1937/8 to realise that the level of government spending was far too low, and plunged America back into the depths of recession. As Alistair Cooke claims:

Source 10Y

Yet Roosevelt came in on a promise to do something that has balked [defeated] governments of every ideological brand [point of view] before and since – to guarantee full employment in peacetime. He didn't make it. In 1938 there were still ten million unemployed. In the next four years the number did indeed shrink – it went out of sight – but this was not Roosevelt's doing but Hitler's. Because the stacks of the steel mills barely began to belch smoke again until the first war orders came in from the British and the French.
(Alistair Cooke, *America*, BBC, 1973)

2. *International trade.* He failed to tackle the key problem of international trade, without which the economy was unable to recover.
3. *The Supreme Court.* This showed a crucial failure to cope with a serious problem, the way in which a court could block measures upon which a government was elected to office. The Supreme Court had the power to say that laws which the President and Congress had passed were against the Constitution, that is illegal.

Examination Guidance

New Deal questions can ask you to look at the whole of the New Deal and see how successful it was, or to look at its various periods or at aspects of it. The questions will also be linked into the pattern your Examination Group follows, with emphasis upon the handling of sources.

Activity 71 is taken from the June 1988 MEG examination. The Question Guide contains the Group's level of response answers, which give a clear idea of what is required for you to succeed.

ACTIVITY 71a

Targets

Recall, sources – comprehending, extracting, interpreting and evaluating information, comparing sources, detection of gaps and bias, reaching conclusions based upon sources.

Question Guide

Question 1 is recall based upon existing knowledge. Question 2 asks you to interpret the photograph and use your knowledge about Roosevelt being a cripple. Question 3 asks you to interpret the statistics, to relate them to your knowledge of the New Deal, and to judge how effective its measures were. Thus the figures give some idea of the impact of the New Deal measures of 1933–5, with the drop in unemployment from the 1933 peak to the 1937 level, but show that the failure of Roosevelt to carry on the same level of government spending in 1937 led to the dramatic rise in the figures for 1938. Question 4 looks at the idea of bias. You should mention the problem of bias in relation to both cartoons and photographs, and point out that both kinds of source can reflect the views of their producer, i.e. a photographer can create a picture to show what he wants the viewer to think as much as a cartoonist drawing a cartoon can. For Question 5 you should draw your answer from all the different sources, making sure that in each case you mention points which relate to the question. For example, for Source 1 you could suggest that this shows the way in which Roosevelt was able to inspire confidence in working people.

Activity

Source 1

A photograph showing Roosevelt meeting electors in 1932.

Source 2

From Roosevelt's Inaugural Address, March 1933.

Let me first of all state that my firm belief is that the only thing we have to fear is fear itself.

This nation asks for action, and action now. Our primary task is to put people to work. It can be achieved in part by the government itself creating jobs and through this to stimulate and reorganise the use of our natural resources.

I shall ask Congress for power to wage war against the emergency.

Source 3

A newspaper cartoon comments on Roosevelt's New Deal policies.

Source 4

Two of Roosevelt's advisers comment on the New Deal. Both are writing thirty years later.

(i)   It is important to recognize in looking at the history of the 1930s that the most influential people then knew much less about national development than is known today. Progress had to be made by experiment.

Franklin Delano Roosevelt was the kind of man to lead this kind of breakthrough. He had tremendous energy and courage, and the people drew hope from him. He was willing to experiment, and most of his experiments succeeded.

Written by David Cushman Coyle

(ii)   The first New Deal brought about important changes in American life. At the time it was necessary, especially for farming. Left to itself farming was in a state of chaos. There was no need to reorganize industry. We needed to make farmers prosperous to provide a market for industrial products.

The second New Deal was entirely different. I changed my opinion of Roosevelt then. He followed no particular policy. Our economy began to slide downhill after that, until 1940.

Written by Raymond Moby

Source 5

Table showing the numbers of unemployed in the USA at the beginning of each year in the 1930s. The numbers are showing millions of unemployed.

Year	Unemployed
1930	4.3
1931	8.0
1932	12.0
1933	12.8
1934	11.3
1935	10.6
1936	9.0
1937	7.7
1938	10.4
1939	9.5

1.   Read Sources 2 and 4.
      Explain the following terms:
      (i)   Inaugural Address;   **(1)**
      (ii)   second New Deal.   **(1)**

2.   Look at Source 1.
      Using the source and your own knowledge, explain why photographers, in 1932, always showed Roosevelt's smiling face and broad shoulders but not a full length portrait.   **(2)**

3.   Study Source 5.
      In what ways can these statistics be useful to an historian of the USA in the 1930s?   **(6)**

4.   Look at Sources 1 and 3.
      'The photograph in Source 1 is more reliable than the cartoon in Source 3, because the cartoon is biased.' Do you agree with this statement? Explain your answer fully, referring to the sources.   **(8)**

5.   'The USA was able to overcome the great depression only because of the leadership given by F.D. Roosevelt.' Do these sources show this view to be true? Explain your answer fully.   **(12)**

Total (30 marks)

CHINA, 1919–80

Examination Guide

China appears on the syllabuses of all four of the main Examining Groups, in two places; for full details, see pages 3–5 above.

It plays a part in the coverage of international relations, in particular the 1930s through Japan's invasion of Manchuria and attack on China, and post-1945 developments. It also appears as one of a group of topics or studies in depth which centres have to choose from. The relationship of China to other syllabus topics is shown in the table. For LEAG, it is one of two topics, chosen from a list of ten topics for Paper 2. For MEG, it is one of two topics chosen from a list of nine topics for study in detail; for NEA, one of three topics, chosen from a list of three in Sub-Section A of the Paper 2 theme **Governments in Action**; for SEG, it is one of two topics taken from a list of seven for Paper 2, allowing for the study of topics in depth.

Group	%	Number of topics	Coverage
LEAG	15	1 of 5 studied from a list of 20	1918–76
MEG	15	1 of 2 studied from a list of 9	1949–81
NEA	10	1 of 1 studied from a list of 3	1920–81
SEG	15	1 of 2 studied from a list of 7	1934–68

Find from past papers all the questions asked on China. Be careful to look at the general sections on international relations, which will often contain specific China-linked questions, particularly in relation to the Cold War and the superpowers.

QUESTION PATTERNS

The question pattern is more fully dealt with on pages 12–19 above. If you cannot get hold of the last three years' examination papers, or the specimen papers, make sure that you are well prepared to cover the topics listed in the **Topic Guide**.

Topic Guide

1   **Introduction**
2   **The War Lords, 1919–27**
3   **The Guomindang (Kuomintang) and the Communists, 1927–37**
4   **China and Japan, 1937–45, and the Communist Victory, 1946–9**
5   **The Communist Regime, 1949–56**
6   **The Great Leap Forward – Communisation**
7   **The Cultural Revolution**
8   **The Struggle for Power**

1 Introduction

The war is over – the Isle of Wight has been granted to Portugal, Wales is in the hands of the French, the Germans control Scotland, while the Danes occupy East

Anglia and the Norwegians Cumbria. Such was the impact of the European powers and Japan upon China in the late nineteenth and early twentieth centuries (Figure 11.1), confirmed in 1919 by the Versailles Settlement.

Before the nineteenth century China had been a proud and independent empire, under the rule of its Manchu emperor and his officials or *mandarins*. Mandarins were powerful civil servants who had passed a series of ancient examinations. Foreigners were treated with total contempt; a mandarin wrote to the emperor in 1839, *'The English barbarians are an unimportant and loathsome race, trusting to their strong ships and large guns.'* The Europeans wanted to trade with China; they were very keen to sell opium to the Chinese in return for tea and silks. The Chinese refused these demands, so the European powers trusted to their 'strong ships and large guns' to defeat the Chinese in a series of *Opium Wars*. The Westerners forced the Chinese to open their ports to Western trade and hand over lands. European trade flourished, and factories were built (Figure 11.1). In 1900 the Manchu ruler, the Empress, *Tzu Hsi*, turned a peasant rising, the *Boxer Rebellion*, against the Europeans.

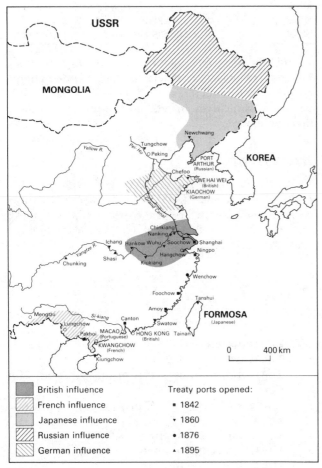

Figure 11.1 Colonial impact on China
Source   John Robottom, *Modern China*, Longman, p. 34.

THE BOXER REBELLION

The Boxers besieged the Europeans in the capital, Peking. The major world powers, led by Britain, Germany, Japan and the USA, sent a 40,000-strong army to the aid of the besieged, and the Boxers were routed and slaughtered. In 1901 the Empress signed a treaty under which the

Boxers' leaders were beheaded; this in effect gave the Europeans and Japanese control over China (Figure 11.1).

Within China, Westernised businessmen, lawyers, teachers and academics were sick of the Empress and her court. One of these Westernised politicians, *Sun Yat-sen*, educated as a doctor, founded a revolutionary party in 1905, later to become the *Guomindang (Kuomintang)*. Sun's party was based upon three principles:

1. the principle of national freedom and independence
2. the principle of democracy – votes for all, free elections and a parliament
3. the principle of land for all, and control over capital.

THE 1911 REVOLUTION

Sun headed a growing movement to topple the Empress, and in 1911 a revolution broke out in Wuhan, headed by Sun's supporters. Sun, in exile, rushed back to China and took over the revolt's leadership. The revolution of 1911 suceeded in overthrowing the Manchus. But Sun had little real power, as he had to rely upon the central government army commander, *Yuan Shi-kai*. In 1912 the Manchus were forced from the throne, and China became a republic, with Yuan Shi-kai as the new President. In 1913, after elections in which Sun's party, the Guomindang, won most seats, Yuan seized power. Yuan had hundreds of the Guomindang leaders murdered; others fled, including Sun. Yuan's death in 1916 meant the end of any attempts at strong, central government. From 1916 onwards China was really in the hands of local army commanders, the *War Lords*, who fought for control over the country.

THE FIRST WORLD WAR

During the First World War (1914–18), China declared its support for the Allies. The Japanese, one of the Allies, had invaded and occupied the German Chinese colony of Shandong (Shantung). With peace in 1918, Sun Yat-sen had hoped that China was going to be as well treated at the Paris Peace Conference (see pages 27–30 above) as the new, emerging countries of Eastern Europe. Sun was in for a rude shock.

Examination Guidance

Activity 72 aims to build up the factual knowledge you will need to make sense of the rest of your work on China.

ACTIVITY 72

Target

Recall.

Question Guide

This kind of short-sentence question will soon be dropped – but it is a good way of learning the topic for revision purposes. Make sure you have one, clear, learnable fact to answer each question. The final question is different – it forces you to think hard about the problem.

Activity

Write a sentence on each of the following, and a paragraph on the final question:

(a)   Who ruled China before 1911?

(b)   What was a mandarin?

(c)   What were the Opium Wars?

(d)   What was their result?

(e)   Who was Tzu Hsi?

(f)   What did she hope the Boxers would do?

(g)   What happened in 1901?

(h)   Who was Sun Yat-sen?

(i)   What did he hope his three principles would bring about?

(j)   What happened in 1911?

(k)   What happened in 1912?

(l)   What happened in 1913?

(m)   Who were the War Lords?

(n)   Why was Sun Yat-sen hopeful about China's treatment at Versailles? (*Clue*: Woodrow Wilson)

2 The War Lords, 1919–27

CHINA AND THE VERSAILLES SETTLEMENT

Have you ever been bitterly disappointed when something that you had set your heart on failed to happen? Sun Yat-sen and his colleagues felt like that in 1919 when the Versailles Settlement was announced. They had hoped that under Wilson's Fourteen Points (see page 28 above) China would win back all the lands she had been forced to hand over to Germany. The Japanese had different ideas, and under their *21 Demands* of 1915 they demanded that the German's Chinese colony, Shandong (Shantung) should be theirs as a reward for backing the Allies. As the Japanese were one of the five main Allied powers, the Chinese protests were completely ignored.

The Results of Versailles

Versailles tended to confirm the worst fears of China's educated classes. There was an outburst of fury in Peking in May, the *4 May Movement*, when news arrived that Shandong had been given to the Japanese.

What was to be the answer? On the one hand there was support for Sun Yat-sen's Guomindang, on the other, new ideas came from Europe, in particular Russia after the Bolsheviks seized power in 1917 (Chapter 8). Mao Zedong (Mao Tse-tung) was searching for new ideas in 1919, and wrote:

Source 11A

In all areas we demand freedom. Freedom to think, freedom in politics, economic freedom, freedom in how men and women live together and freedom in education; all these are going to burst from the dark seething pit where they have been kept, and demand to look at the blue sky.
(*The First Union of the Popular Masses*, 1919)

Both the Guomindang and Mao Zedong turned to Moscow for help. During this period from 1919, China was a total shambles, with constant wars between rival War Lords. Peasants were robbed and murdered, towns sacked and looted. The autobiography of Pu Yi, the last of the Manchu emperors, gives some idea of the chaos. Don't try and make sense of the passage, just read it to get some idea of what was happening!

Source 11B

The battle of Chaoyang in September 1924 was the beginning of the second Chihli-Fentien war. At first Wu Pei-fu's Chihli army was on top, but when Wu Pei-fu was attacking the forces of the Fengtien commander Chang Tso-lin at Shanhaikuan in October his subordinate Feng Yu-hsiang deserted him, marched his troops back to Peking and issued a peace telegram. Under the combined pressure of Feng Yu-hiang and Chang Tso-lin, Wu Pei-yu's troops on the Shanhaikuan front collapsed and Wu himself fled . . .

Feng had put Tsao Kung [the president of the Republic who had bought the votes for his election] under house arrest and dissolved the 'piglet parliament'.

The palace guard was disarmed by Feng's National Army and moved out of the city. Feng's troops also took over their barracks and their posts at the Gate of the Divine Valour. I looked at Coal Hill through a telescope from the Imperial Gardens and saw that it was swarming with soldiers whose uniforms were different from those of the palace guard. The household department sent them tea and food which they accepted.
(*Emperor to Citizen: The Autobiography of Pu Yi*, Oxford University Press, 1987, pp. 144–5)

With the War Lords in control of the government in Peking, Sun Yat-sen had set up his own Guomindang government in the southern city of Guangzhou (Canton). Here he began to build up his own forces, and he sent his leading general Chiang Kaishek (Chiang Kai-shek) to Moscow for training and help. The communist Russian government gave the Guomindang arms, money and advisers, for by this time the Guomindang had linked up with the newly formed Chinese communist party in the struggle against the War Lords. In 1925 Sun died, and Chiang Kaishek became the Guomindang leader.

The year 1926 saw Chiang mount a fierce campaign against the War Lords, the *Northern Campaign* (Figure 11.2). With the backing of the peasants, and communist support in the towns and cities, Chiang soon routed the War Lords, and controlled most of southern China. Shanghai was by now falling into communist hands. The

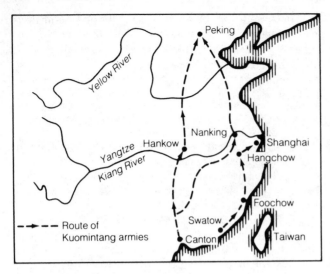

Figure 11.2 The Northern Campaign

Source   Michael Denning, *China 1900–49*, Edward Arnold, p. 16.

alliance of the communists in the towns and cities and Chiang in the countryside suggested that they would soon control all of China. But in 1927 Chiang turned on his allies, the communists.

Examination Guidance

Activity 73 is based upon the LEAG and NEA question pattern.

ACTIVITY 73

Targets

Recall, comprehension, sources – extraction of information.

Question Guide

The activity requires you to use the information in the section to try and answer the questions posed. Notice that some of the questions do not need you to use the sources.

Activity

Study Sources 11A and 11B and answer the questions which follow:

1.   Suggest why Source 11A was published in 1919.
2.   Who was Mao Zedong?
3.   Explain in your own words the reference to 'the dark seething pit'.
4.   Show how the history of China in the 1920s reflects 'demands to look at the blue sky'.
5.   What kind of person was Feng?
6.   Who was Tsao Kung, and what does Source 11B suggest about how he had gained power?
7.   How did the Guomindang try to deal with the problem of the War Lords?

3 The Guomindang (Kuomintang) and the Communists, 1927–37

THE CHINESE COMMUNIST PARTY

The history of communism in China is closely linked to the story of Mao Zedong (Mao Tse-tung). Mao became a teacher in 1918, and after the bitter blow of the Versailles Settlement in 1919 (see Section 2 above) he turned to communism. What was the appeal of communist ideas, as laid out in the writings of Karl Marx and Lenin? In 1919 Lenin had already been ruler of Russia for two years, following the successful Russian Revolution. What did Mao believe in?

COMMUNIST BELIEFS AND GOALS

1.   The history of society is a struggle between classes over the control of wealth. History passes through three stages:
Stage 1. In *feudal society*, landowners struggle against a new *class* of *capitalists*, whose wealth comes from industry.
Stage 2. In *capitalist society*, the capitalists (the bourgeoisie) struggle against *the workers* (the proletariat) who produce the wealth.
Stage 3. In *communist society*, the *workers* own all the wealth. All are equal and live at peace with one another.
2.   The peasants and workers should rule the country and run their own affairs.
3.   Money and wealth should be shared out equally: 'From each according to their means, to each according to their needs.' That is, give what you can, take what you need.
4.   The state should own all land, industry and businesses.
5.   All countries are equal.
6.   All countries should join together in an international body.
7.   *Revolution* will bring about the overthrow of the capitalists.
8.   A *communist party* will bring about the revolution. The party will carry out the wishes of the workers.

THE COMMUNIST PARTY, 1921–7

In 1921 Mao helped found the *Chinese Communist Party (CCP)* and became one of its several leaders. Mao backed Sun Yat-sen's party, the Guomindang, and its three main policies:

1.   *nationalism* – China free from the foreigners.
2.   *democracy* – a Chinese parliament
3.   *land* – land to be given to the peasants.

The Guomindang backed the Bolsheviks in the Russian Revolution and shared many of their ideas. By 1923 Lenin was training Guomindang officers and sending the party money and arms. The CCP and the Guomindang became allies.

In the 1920s the CCP grew in strength, with its appeal to peasants and factory workers to seize the land and strike for better wages. In particular, it built up its strength in the cities of Guangzhou (Canton) and Shanghai. In 1926–7 the CCP played a part in Chiang Kaishek's attack on the War Lords by organizing strikes and rising against the War Lords, as in Shanghai in March 1927.

THE GUOMINDANG AND THE COMMUNIST PARTY, 1927

Chiang believed that industry and the land should remain in the hands of capitalists and landlords – beliefs opposite to those of Mao. Towards the end of his 1926–7 campaign, Chiang turned on his ally, the CCP. In April 1927 Chiang's troops murdered thousands of communists in Shanghai after using them to gain control over the city. During the autumn a communist peasant rising in Hunan was crushed, and in December 1927 the communists seized control of Canton. Bloody fighting followed, in which the communists were defeated and massacred. They wore red scarves, whose dye ran when moist:

Source 11C

Execution squads patrolled the streets, reported Vice-Consul Hinke (US) [the American government representative], and on finding a suspect, they questioned him, examined his neck for the tell-tale red. If found, they ordered the victim to open his mouth, thrust a revolver into it, and another coolie [worker] came to the end of his Communist venture . . .
(R. C. North, *Chinese Communism*, Weidenfeld & Nicolson)

By 1928 Mao and the communists seemed to have been smashed. Mao was one of several communist leaders, and he and his followers took refuge in Jiangxi (Kiangsi) to rebuild their part of the party, the Jiangxi (Kiangsi) Soviet. Meanwhile the Guomindang ruled China, having taken Peking in 1928.

THE GUOMINDANG (KUOMINTANG) GOVERNMENT

Although Chiang ruled the provinces of lowland China, War Lords still controlled the mountainous provinces in the west. Chiang ruled through bankers, army officers and landlords, many of them corrupt. Guomindang land reforms came to nothing. Within China, the Guomindang relied on landlords to control the countryside. The peasants remained in grinding poverty and often had to sell their wives and children to landlords or businessmen. In both the countryside and the cities the soldiers of the Guomindang were free to rob, rape and wreck as they pleased. Elizabeth Lewis, who lived in China at the time, tells us in a novel what happened to a Chinese boy, Yung Fu. Yung Fu, a peasant lad, has found a job in a city. Walking down a street, he sees a crowd, and goes to see what is happening:

Source 11D

[He] found himself almost alone with a half-dozen soldiers. In their midst was a load-coolie [labourer], his back pressed to the wall, his breast pinned by the muzzle of a rifle. His face was ashen as he attempted to reason with his persecutors.

One of the soldiers interrupted him. 'I will count ten', he said. 'If by that time you still refuse to carry our bedding –' he smiled cruelly.

'I dare not, Honourable Military', wailed the coolie. 'I am late with my load for my master. If you do not let me hurry on, he will give me less than my due in payment, and already my family starves for lack of food.'

Yung Fu's gaze shifted from the miserable man to the paving. There were several bundles of bedding belonging to the soldiers, and close by sat two round baskets filled with rice, on the top of which rested the coolie's carrying pole and ropes.

'One, two, three, four, five', counted the soldier.

The coolie's face was contorted with fear. 'Sirs', he begged.

'Six, seven, eight, nine, ten!'

'Sirs, what will you do – '. There was a deafening report and the load-bearer's last protest died away in a faint scream. He slid silently to the ground.

Stricken with horror, Yung Fu stared at the bundle of reddening rags that only a few seconds earlier had been a man intent on earning food for himself and family.
(Elizabeth Foreman Lewis, *Yung Fu of the Upper Yangtze*, Harrap, 1934, pp. 47–8)

The soldiers stole the rice, and forced Yung Fu to carry it to the barracks.

Chiang Kaishek and the Guomindang government faced hard times. In 1931 the Japanese invaded and captured the province of Manchuria (see Chapter 3, Section 2), and in 1932 they attacked Shanghai, from where they were forced to retreat because of the fierceness of the Chinese resistance. The Guomindang government was also in debt to foreign countries and open to bribes from foreign businesses and industrialists, who controlled China's trade and owned most of her factories.

THE JIANGXI (KIANGSI) SOVIET AND THE GUOMINDANG, 1928–37

After the Guomindang attacks on the Communists, Mao took refuge in Jiangxi, and set up a soviet, a communist government of peasants and workers, a worker state. The Jiangxi Soviet was only one of several independent communist organisations. In Jiangxi the Chinese communist party gave land to both the poorest and the middling peasants, schools were set up, and a *Red Army* was founded to fight against the Guomindang. Mao forced his Red Army members to obey the *Six Principles*, which said that they should:

Source 11E

1. put back the doors on houses, and tidy up mattresses, when they left
2. be polite, help people
3. give back everything borrowed, even a needle
4. pay for everything they bought
5. pay for all broken things, even a chopstick
6. not help themselves to things from empty houses.

The Jiangxi Soviet took land from the landlords, and gave some to the peasants for their own private plots. The Red Army grew quickly, and soon the communists ruled Jiangxi province.

The Soviet was a threat to Chiang and the Guomindang. So, from December 1930 to July 1931 the Guomindang carried out three 'extermination campaigns' against the Jiangxi and other communists. During these they captured and shot Mao's wife. In 1932 the communists declared war on the Japanese, but still the Guomindang pressed on with their attacks on the communist forces, known as the Red Army. By 1934 the Guomindang forces had cut off the Jiangxi Soviet from outside help and surrounded it with a series of forts linked by barbed wire and trenches. What were the communists to do?

THE LONG MARCH

In 1934 the Jiangxi Soviet decided to break through the Guomindang lines and set up a new soviet in northern China, where there was a communist base. The breakout of the Red Army led to the famous *Long March* (Figure 11.3). The communists had finally agreed that Mao should lead them. Mao's army marched 6,000 miles and lost some nine out of every ten of its members from illness and constant attacks from Guomindang armies. They marched over mountains, through swamps and across rivers. At each stage of the Long March, the Guomindang forces and bombers attacked. At the end of May, the Red Army's path was blocked at the Tatu River. A suicide unit stormed the bridge. Agnes Smedley, who was with the Red Army, takes up the story:

Source 11F

Platoon commander Ma Ti-chiu stepped out, grasped one of the chains and began swinging, hand over hand, towards the north bank . . . and after him the men. As they swung along, Red Army machine guns laid down a protective screen of fire, and the Engineering Corps began bringing up tree trunks and

laying the bridge flooring . . . Ma Ta-chiu was the first to be shot into the wild torrent below. [The men reach the bridge floor, which the Guomindang has set on fire.] They came and crouched on the planks, releasing their hand grenades and unbuckling their swords. They ran through the flames and threw their hand grenades in the midst of the enemy.
(A. Smedley, *The Great Road*, Calder, 1958)

The march ended with the communists reaching the safety of Yanan (Yenan). Around 10,000 of the original 100,000 on the Long March had survived. In 1935 Mao, now leader of the communist party, set up a new soviet at Yanan in Shaanxi (Shensi) province. At Yanan he preached a new kind of communist revolution, based upon the peasantry owning the land. At the same time he continued the struggle against the Japanese, who had invaded northern China from their base in Manchuria.

Examination Guidance

Activity 74, like Activity 73, is based upon the LEAG and NEA question pattern.

ACTIVITY 74

Targets

Recall, comprehension; locate, comprehend and extract information from historical sources.

Figure 11.3 The Long March
Source   C. K. Macdonald, *Modern China*, Basil Blackwell, p. 25.

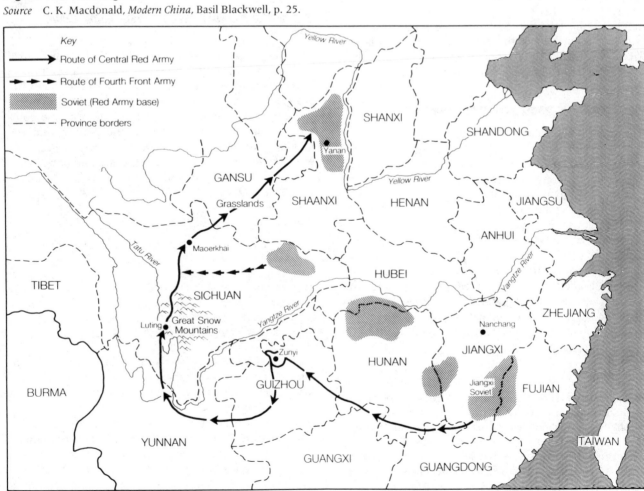

Question Guide

The activity involves using the information in the section to answer the questions listed. Notice that some of the questions do not need you to use the source.

In your answer to Questions 1(a), you should mention two points of detail, not just make general comments; for 1 (b), be precise in picking out the points from Source 11D which are in contrast to those in Source 11E, i.e. robbery, lack of politeness; for 1(c), use your general knowledge of what Mao was fighting for and how the Six Principles would help him achieve his ends.

The main points for Question 2(a) are distance between communist bases and distance travelled, encirclement, problems of terrain, plus knowledge of how the Guomindang army operated. For Question 2(b), you should note the distinctive qualities shown.

Activity

Study Sources 11D and 11E and Figure 11.3 and answer the questions which follow:

1.   (a)   Explain in your own words the attitude of the author of Source 11E towards the peasantry and workers.   **(2)**

     (b)   Show how this attitude is different from that shown by the Guomindang soldiers in Source 11D   **(2)**

     (c)   For what reasons did Mao insist that the Red Army soldiers obeyed the Six Principles (Source 11E)?   **(3)**

2.   (a)   What does Figure 11.3 suggest about the problems which faced Mao and the Red Army in 1931–5?   **(3)**

     (b)   What does Source 11E suggest about how the Red Army fought on the Long March?   **(4)**

3.   Describe and explain how the communist party survived from 1927 to 1937.   **(6)**

4 China and Japan, 1937–45, and the Communist Victory, 1946–9

THE GUOMINDANG AND COMMUNIST ALLIANCE – THE SIAN CRISIS

December 1936. A freezing winter night in Sian, northern China. Soldiers rush into the hotel entrance, shoot the troops on guard and rush up the stairs. A man hears the shooting in his bedroom, hurries down the fire-escape and runs up a hill. As he stands hiding in the bushes, shivering in his silk pyjamas, he hears the enemy soldiers approach. The man surrenders, and demands that they shoot him as well. Instead, they ask him to lead the Chinese army against the Japanese, not the communists.

The man in pyjamas is Chiang Kaishek, and he has been kidnapped by the forces of the commander of his northern army. Chiang is in Sian to discuss with his northern generals how to fight the communists and the Japanese. Chiang Kaishek had failed to defeat the com-

munists, and had used his forces against them instead of the Japanese. More and more he ruled like a military dictator, and not the heir of Sun Yet-sen. Sun's three principles had been ignored in Guomindang China.

Chiang is forced to accept the northern army's *Eight Demands* which means that he has to ally with Mao and the communists.

The alliance just came in the nick of time, for in July 1937 the Japanese invaded the rest of China after the *Marco Polo Bridge* incident, a clash between Japanese and Chinese troops which the Japanese used as an excuse to invade. Despite massive help from the Russians for the Guomindang, the Japanese forces quickly overran northern China, taking Nanking and Shanghai by December 1937 and the rest of northern China by 1939 (Figure 11.4). The Japanese bombed, killed, burned, robbed, raped and tortured, murdering hundreds of thousands of Chinese, including doctors and nurses. Any Chinese soldier who fell into Japanese hands was bayonetted to death. By 1939 huge areas of China were in Japanese hands.

The defeat of the Guomindang armies meant that the communist forces became the main buffer to the Chinese. In 1940, in the *Hundred Regiments Offensive*, the communist army aimed to cut off the occupying Japanese forces from one another, and then mop each one up in turn. The Japanese reacted against the Chinese people with murderous fury in their 'Kill All. Loot All. Burn All.' campaign – laying waste both the town and countryside, and using the Chinese people as slave labour.

Figure 11.4 Japan's invasion of China between 1937–9
Source   James Green, *China*, Oxford University Press, p. 29.

THE GUOMINDANG AND THE COMMUNIST SPLIT

In 1941 fighting broke out between the Guomindang and the communists. The communists now fought on, largely alone, against the Japanese. They organised the Chinese peasants and the Red Army to fight behind the Japanese lines (Sources 11F and 11G), using the tactics of guerrilla warfare. At the same time they set up peasant schools, split up the landlords' land among the villagers and founded peasant associations to run the villages.

Source 11G

Tactics of the Red Army

1. Partisans [fighters] must not fight any losing battles . . .
2. Surprise is the main offensive tactic of the well-led partisan group. Static warfare must be avoided. The partisan brigade has no auxiliary [extra] force, no rear, no line of supplies and communications except that of the enemy.
3. A careful and detailed plan of attack, and especially of retreat, must be worked out before any engagement is offered or accepted. The ability to move more freely than the enemy is vital.
4. In the development of partisan warfare the greatest attention must be paid to the landlords' private troops, the first, the last and most determined line of defence for the landlords.
5. In attacking the enemy's main force, always outnumber it. However, a surprise attack by a smaller force against an enemy weak point can also bring a victory.
6. Be flexible in attack.
7. The tactics of distracting, tricking, diverting, ambushing, false attacks and irritation must be mastered.
8. Partisans must attack the weakest point of the enemy.
9. The enemy must not locate the partisans' main force.
   (Adapted from: Edgar Snow, *Red Star over China*, Gollancz, 1968, pp. 275–6)

The struggle against the Japanese lasted until the end of the Second World War in 1945. The communists controlled most of the countryside in northern China, bottling up the Japanese in the towns and cities (Figure 11.5).

THE COMMUNIST VICTORY, 1946–9

During the war the Americans had provided both the Guomindang and the communist Red Army with supplies. In 1945 the Guomindang armies were some 3 million strong; the Red Army had a million soldiers. The Americans insisted that towns and cities were handed over to the Guomindang. By 1946 the scene was set for another war between the Guomindang and the communists.

The Red Army was in good shape to defeat the Guomindang in 1945. It was well led and had a plentiful supply of weapons. During the war against the Japanese it had not been defeated, and in fighting against the hated enemy it had gained control over most of the villages of occupied China. It had shown the peasants that life was better under the communists than under the Guomindang. The failure of Chiang to destroy the communists in the early 1930s suggested that he had little chance now.

The Americans sent General Marshall to China to try and get an agreement between the Guomindang, the nationalists and the communists. The mission failed, and in 1946 a struggle began for the control of Manchuria. After the war the Russians had occupied Manchuria, and before they withdrew the Guomindang occupied the main towns and cities and built strong points along the railway lines. The communists already had control of the countryside. From 1947 to 1948 the Red Army, under its general Lin Biao, cut off the nationalist forces, defeated them in a series of battles and gained control over the major cities of Changshun and Shenyang (Figure 11.5). The Guomindang forces were routed, and the Red Army marched into Beijing (Peking) in January 1949. By now it was known as the *People's Liberation Army*, the *PLA*. In 1949 the PLA swept south, and the remains of the nationalist forces, some 300,000 troops, fled to Taiwan.

Figure 11.5 The Red Army gaining control
Source   Michael Denning, *China 1900–49*, Edward Arnold, p. 27.

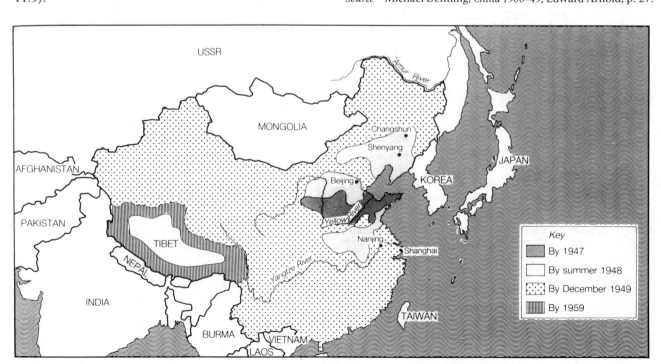

Examination Guidance

Activity 75 is taken from the LEAG 1989 specimen paper.

ACTIVITY 75

Question Guide

The activity involves using the information in the previous sections to answer the detailed questions. It is a thirty-five minute short answers question.

1.   (a)   Why did the Kuomintang and Communists both receive a great deal of support from Chinese people in the years 1917–27?
     (b)   With reference to the 1920s and 1930s, describe and explain the reasons for the split between the Kuomintang and the Communists.
     (c)   What were the causes of the Communist victory over the Kuomintang?

5 The Communist Regime, 1949–56

Source 11H

To win nationwide victory is only the first step in a long march of ten thousand years. Even if this step is worthy of pride, it is comparatively tiny; what will be more worthy of pride is yet to come. After several decades, the victory of the Chinese people's democratic revolution, viewed in retrospect, will seem like only a brief prologue to a long drama. A drama begins with a prologue, but the prologue is not the climax. The Chinese revolution is great, but the road after the revolution will be longer, the work greater and harder.
(Mao Zedong (Mao Tse-tung), 5 March 1949)

MAO ZEDONG'S GOALS AND PROBLEMS

What were the goals of Mao and the communists, and what problems did they face? Mao wanted to bring about communism (see Section 3 above). This meant that all business, commerce, industry and land were to be under the control of the state. In time Mao wanted China to be a classless society and a member of an international brotherhood of nations.

The new China would be formed in the shape of the Jiangxi Soviet – and the men and women who had helped build up the Soviet after the Long March were to run China until today.

MAO'S PROBLEMS

Winning a war is one thing, winning the peace something totally different. Mao faced huge problems in October 1949:

(a)   During the fighting in 1937–45 most of China's industry had been wrecked. After 1945 the Russians had stripped China's industrial heartland, Manchuria, of its machinery to rebuild Russia's shattered industry. The removed machinery was worth some 2 billion dollars.

(b)   Trade and industry had been run by foreigners, who now left the country. They took with them their knowledge of how to manage businesses and factories.

(c)   Money was valueless; inflation was massive.

(d)   Unemployment in towns was high, and in the countryside food was scarce.

(e)   China's population was growing by 15 million a year.

(f)   The landlords and their backers still owned the land.

How did Mao go about building up his communist society, and dealing with the problems he faced?

THE PARTY

The communist party played a key role. Mao decided that four groups of people could belong: the flag of China has a star for each group:

1.   tiny private businesses making wealth – the 'petty bourgeoisie'
2.   larger private businesses making wealth – the 'national bourgeoisie'
3.   the peasants
4.   the industrial working class.

Landlords and capitalists were banned from the party. Because the party had been based in the countryside, big efforts were made to recruit factory workers as party members. The party doubled in size in 1949–50.

Every village, street, factory, team of peasant workers, student body, group of writers was encouraged to have its own party group.

THE WORKING OF THE GOVERNMENT

How was government supposed to work? The party developed policy in the name of the people. It knew the wishes of the people through the *Party Congresses*. Policy was carried out by the Government through the *Councils*.

The Party was organised at four levels, with Congresses of elected party members at each level:

The Party	*The Government*
● local branches	● local councils
● suburb of a town/city or village congresses	● county councils
● county or town/city congresses	● provincial councils
● provincial congresses	● state council
● national congress	

The congresses told the party the views of the people. The party made policy. At each level the government councils carried out party policy.

INFLATION

The government managed to make sure that prices became stable, instead of these being runaway inflation. All private banks were shut, and a government bank was opened instead. Only it could issue money.

EDUCATION

Education was to play a vital role in the building of Modern China. In 1949 only one person in ten could read and write. To solve the problem in the countryside, towns and cities, each local government area or township built its own school. Trained teachers taught members of the township to be teachers as well. By 1956 one in four Chinese had been taught the basics of literacy – reading and writing.

INDUSTRY, 1949–53

The communist government seized control of all the big business, industry, trading and banking which had been in the hands of the Guomindang and foreigners – some 75% of the total. They left the rest of business and industry in the hands of the 'national bourgeoisie' and the 'petty bourgeoisie'. Owners of small workshops, factories and shops were allowed to make larger profits.

Then, in 1952, the government turned on the petty and national bourgeoisie in the *Five Antis Campaign*. The government tried to wipe out:

1.   bribery
2.   the avoiding of taxes
3.   fraud
4.   stealing of government property
5.   stealing of government economic secrets.

So fierce were the attacks on owners of private businesses that over 100 a day died in Shanghai at the height of the Five Antis Campaign in January and February 1952.

From then on businesses were placed under the joint control of the owners and government officials.

From 1949 to 1952 China began to put her heavy industry back on its feet. In 1950 Mao got the backing of the Soviet Union, which promised to invest 300 million dollars a year in China for the next five years, send 10,000 technical helpers to China and take 8,000 Chinese for training in Russia.

The First Five-Year Plan, 1953–7

With Russian help, and following the Russian model, in 1953 China launched its Second Five-Year Plan. This aimed to turn China from a peasant into an industrial economy. The goals were to boost heavy industry and transport.

Heavy Industry

New centres of heavy industry, like Wushan, were built from mining coal, producing iron and steel, and manufacturing heavy industrial goods like chemicals, lorries and tractors and machinery for electrical plants and other factories. The Plan had 694 major projects, the most vital 156 being Russian-aided. Targets were set for workers, bonuses were paid and those who had achieved their targets were set up as models for other workers to follow – the Stakhanovite pattern of Russia (see page 165 above).

It was claimed that all industrial output doubled, while petrol and electricity tripled and cement and iron and steel increased fourfold (Figure 11.6).

Figure 11.6 Increases in output during the Second Five-Year Plan
Source   Official Chinese Government figures

Product	1952	1957 (planned)	1957 (achieved)
Coal (million tons)	63.5	113	124
Pig-iron (million tons)	1.9	4.7	5.86
Steel (million tons)	1.35	4.12	5.24
Chemical Fertilizer (thousand tons)	194	570	740
Machine-tools (pieces)	13734	37192	80000 (1958)
Crude oil (million tons)	0.44	2	1.42
Cement (million tons)	2.6	6	4.65
Electric Power (thousand million kilowatt)	7.26	15.9	19.1

By the end of the plan nearly all industry was in the government's hands. But consumer goods like clothes were in short supply – in 1954 cotton cloth had to be rationed because of shortages, a bit like rationing coal in Newcastle.

Transport

The Chinese rebuilt and expanded their rail and road networks, for efficient transport plays a vital part in the building of any modern economy. Railways were pushed into western China, and major roads, bridges and cuttings made. One of the most impressive was the *Yangtze River Bridge*, over four miles long, with a double railway track and a road, opened in 1954. Over 5,000 miles of new railways were built (Figure 11.7).

LAND REFORM

China was a country of peasants, and the communists had swept into power with their backing. Mao believed

Figure 11.7 New Railways built in Western China

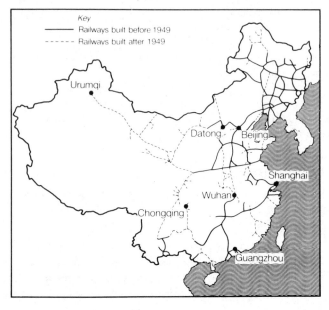

that eventually all private farming should disappear and the land should be farmed by huge state-owned communes. To bring this about would take time.

During 1950–6 land reform passed through three stages. It is vital to remember that areas in the north were much quicker to impose the changes than those in the south – indeed, the Yanan Soviet had reached Stage 2 by 1949:

- *Stage 1.* The village lands would be divided up among the peasants, each peasant family having its own plot of land.
- *Stage 2.* The peasants would pool their lands in *collectives* like the Soviet Union's kolkhozes (see pages 162–165 above).
- *Stage 3.* The collectives would combine in huge *communes.*

In 1950 the government passed its *Farming (Agrarian) Reform Law.* The country was split up into *hsiangs* or townships. There were 250,000 hsiangs, with about 1,500 people in each. In each hsiang, the government officials set up a *peasant association* to carry out the reforms:

(a) All debts were cancelled and rents were slashed.
(b) Rich landlords, who owned 80% of the land, were accused of crimes against the peasants. They were tried in public.
(c) After their trials they were executed or beaten up. Some 2 million were killed.
(d) The landlords' land was shared out amongst the rest of the peasants. Note that this included rich peasants, who already owned large plots of land.

By 1952 farm output had soared, and Mao was ready to introduce *collectivisation.*

Collectivisation

Mao wanted to avoid the problem of rich peasants controlling the land – a new, peasant class of kulaks (see pages 159, 163 above). Communism meant a classless society in which the community owned all the wealth. So, in 1952 he took the first steps towards collectivisation, again beginning in the north of the country:

1. *Mutual Aid Teams* (MATs) were set up in the townships or hsiangs. Each MAT had an average of seven families. They kept the ownership of their land, but pooled their labour, the animals for pulling the ploughs and doing the heavy farm work, and their heavy machinery.
2. *Agricultural Production Co-operatives* (APCs). Now Mao was ready to set up co-operatives, formed from several MATs with about eighty families. Each APC merged its lands, and ploughed up the boundaries between them. The APC farmed the land, using the APC members' animals and farm machinery.

   The members of the MATs and the APCs were paid on the basis of the amount of land and the animals and machinery they had put into the joint venture – in other words, profit-sharing.
3. *Collectivisation.* The next step, introduced widely in 1955, was to combine several APCs of between 200 and 300 families in collectives. The collective

owned the land and paid the members' wages – no longer did families own their own land, nor were profits shared among the families according to the amount of land, animals and machinery worked by the APC.

What did collectivisation mean in reality?

Imagine you are in a house in Lung Gong commune, twenty miles from Canton (Source 11I). Lung Gong is a village of 4,500 people, about 900 families. It is split up into fourteen production teams, each of which runs its own fields. You have been helping the villagers with the harvest (Source 11K). One of your group takes up the story:

Source 11I

We visitors sat at one side of the little kitchen, the team leaders sat facing us – all on tiny wooden stools, except our host who sat on the low brick fuel enclosure by the great cooking pot. We would like to know something about the history of your village since Liberation (1949).

Here is a record of what you were told:

Source 11J

Land Reform. In 1952 we carried out land reform. We had no very big landlords. The worst was a man who made money dealing in opium, and lending money at high interest rates to the peasants. He did not have more than 15 acres of land. In dealing with the rich landlords several things were taken into account – how much land they owned, how much they exploited the peasants, whether they worked the land themselves, and so on. In 1953 we solved many problems

Source 11K A commune in the Hunan Province

Source Camera Press

connected with our land reform. In 1954 we began to form mutual aid teams so we would carry out our work better. Co-operatives began to be formed in 1955. At first only the poor and lower middle peasants joined, but later the other peasants realised the benefits and came in too. We had three co-ops in the village, and in 1956 these were joined together to form one advanced co-op (where income is solely paid according to work and rent is no longer paid for land, nor for hire of animals and equipment).

The co-operatives. The majority of us were eager to form co-operatives and work collectively for two reasons: our small plots of land were awkward to work, so by joining together we could organise the work better and have more manpower for building dikes and dams for irrigation. After land reform, we all worked individually and very soon some got richer and others poorer. Mothers with several children found it hard to live better.

CHINA'S PROGRESS, 1949–56

By 1956 China seemed to have put the problems of the period of civil war behind it. According to an American government report of 1967:

Source 11L

. . . in a remarkable short time the new government had:
suppressed banditry
restored the battered railroad system to operation
repaired and extended the badly neglected system of dikes
replaced the graft-ridden bureaucratic system of local government with apparently incorruptible communist cadres
introduced a stable currency and enforced a nationwide tax system
begun an extensive programme of public health and sanitation
provided a tolerably even distribution of available food and clothing.

6 The Great Leap Forward – Communisation

THE HUNDRED FLOWERS CAMPAIGN

By 1957 China seemed to be making good progress, but a problem was the growth of a new class of business managers and technical experts. Often these technicians, mainly engineers and scientists, were not party members. The technicians thought of themselves as being superior to the ignorant party members, many of whom were peasants and factory workers. Indeed, the technicians felt they were part of the old Chinese class of intellectuals, many of whom became mandarins. This new class of technicians, the people who ran the country's industry and science, was a threat to the party. How could they be converted to the ideas of communism, and become good party members?

Mao decided that debate and argument were the best way, so that the experts would be won over to his ideas. In February 1957 he announced that there should be a nationwide debate over the Party: 'Let a hundred flowers bloom and a hundred schools of thought compete.' So began the great debate, which soon turned into a raging, powerful series of attacks upon party officials for being incompetent, selfish, corrupt and too keen to carry out

communist ideas. The attacks were so bitter, fierce and widespread that Mao decided the debate had got out of control, and so called it off in the middle of 1957. *Chou En-lai*, the country's Prime Minister, clearly saw the threat of the split between the technicians and the Party, when he said in June 1957 that the technicians were:

Source 11M

. . . attempting to drive our country from the path of socialism to the path of capitalism.

THE GREAT LEAP FORWARD

After the Hundred Flowers Campaign, Mao decided that the communist revolution needed another big push forward. The countryside was failing to produce the grain needed to feed China's growing town population and provide the raw materials for China's expanding industries. Despite the spending of huge amounts of money on farming, during the First Five-Year Plan (1953–7), state income from farming had not grown. To deal with the problem, a *Second Five-Year Plan* was introduced in 1958. In the countryside its aim was to make the countryside truly communist and boost farming output by 35% by 1962. The industrial target was just as demanding: China was to double output in five years and so overtake Britain. The countryside was to play a big part in the growth of industry, with the building of factories in the villages. Behind the Second Five-Year Plan was Mao's idea of turning the countryside into a number of huge factories to produce food, the peasants being the factories' machinery. Giant gangs of peasant labour would build dams, dykes, irrigation works and buildings. The use of labour in this way meant the sweeping-away of the collectives and the joining of them together into mammoth communes.

How did things turn out in practice?

COMMUNISATION – THE MOVEMENT'S PROGRESS

Figure 11.8   Communisation Timetable
1958
April. The first commune was set up in Henan (Hunan) province. Named the 'Sputnik' commune after Russia's satellite, the world's first, the commune was made up of 40,000 people.
August. Henan's 38,500 co-operatives had been merged into 1,400 communes. Government calls for spread of communes to all China.
December. Communes introduced throughout China.
1959
By now 24,000 communes had replaced 750,000 co-operatives. Average of 5,000 households in each commune.
1961
Number of communes increased to over 70,000, with about 2,000 households in each commune. Each commune was run by a local party township council (see Section 5 above). The communes' township councils in turn were under the control of their county councils.

Commune Organisation

The commune had three layers of organisation – *commune*, *brigade* and *team*. The commune leaders organised

Figure 11.9

Year	Million metric tonnes of grain
1957	185
1960	150
1961	162
1962	174
1963	183

Source   Official Chinese Government figures

the brigades. The brigades were the same as the APCs (the old co-operatives made up from about 80 families) – around 600 people, usually drawn from a single village. Each brigade was formed from teams of about 200 people. The big difference was that brigades could be joined up to work on joint projects and used throughout the commune. The commune was an attempt to break down the old Chinese pattern of village life. Communes set up communal kitchens, eating halls, nurseries and kindergartens.

Communes and Industry

Each county council which ran the local communes was in charge of the growth of industry. The Great Leap Forward saw a huge boom in the growth of industry within the communes. All across China, communes built their own furnaces, cement works and factories.

COMMUNISATION IN ACTION

What did communisation mean to China's peasants? Let us carry on the story of Lung Gong commune (see Section 5 above) the village twenty miles from Guangzhou of 4,500 people in about 900 families:

Source 11N

The commune. We formed our commune in the winter of 1958 from twenty co-operatives with a population of 60,000. The commune was found to be too big to administer properly so it was divided into two in 1961. Our Shang Yang ('Facing Sun') Commune is divided into twelve production brigades. Our brigade has 14 production teams. (These form farms which organise their own work and share out the income.)

You go on to ask: 'What do you think has been the main advantage for the poor peasants since Liberation?'

Source 11O

Before Liberation none of our daughters got educated. We had one primary school with 200 students for two villages, and most of the students were from landlord or rich peasant homes. Our boys, at most, got one or two years' schooling. Now our village has a primary school with 900 students. We have 25 teachers – half from the village, half from outside. Before Liberation many of our people were beggars. Not full-time beggars, but they begged when they could not get work as farm labourers.

The commune has built an irrigation system. Before:

Source 11P

Most years the land was water-logged in the summer and suffered drought in the autumn. If there was no rain for three days, we had to get water from the wells. They were from three to ten metres deep and we ladled the water out in little buckets. (Everyone laughed when the size of the bucket was indicated by fetching a small basket from the corner). A man couldn't irrigate as much as one mou* in a day. We had an old saying: 'Three fairly good harvests in ten years.'

Commune Life

What was life like in a commune in 1967? Imagine that you are going to work on a commune in Changsha to help with the harvest:

Source 11Q

Changsha village itself lies about twenty miles north of Guangzhou (Canton). The village is in the flood plain of the Pearl River where the plain meets the hills. A large river runs at one side of the commune's lands. Changsha village's population of 1,300 is divided into four teams, which together form a brigade. The brigade is one of eighteen making up the commune, whose headquarters are at the town of Zhonglotan, about a mile away, numbering a total of 20,000 people. The brigade owns a brickworks, employing fifty people, and raises geese. It also runs the lichee-drying plant, the primary school, the clinic and some shops. The teams organise farm work . . . Our team – Number 2, of 80 families and some 300 people – owns a pigsty of about a dozen pens and a threshing machine. The families raise fish, duck and geese.

Our Number 2 team has seventy acres of paddy, which in 1966 produced 160 tons of grain . . . The team had 40 acres of peanuts, and gathered 25 tons in 1966. The previous year was a poor one for lichees, but 1967 proved outstanding, with 18 tons.

Most families raise one pig, and the team pigsty must have raised at least one pig per family. Apart from their rice, peanut oil for cooking and a little fat pork . . . nearly all the peasants' food and tobacco are grown on their own individual plots or, as in the case of eggs and chickens, at home. Family plots were fixed at 35 square yards per person. In Changsha the main crops on the plots seemed to be peanuts, sweet potatoes, beans and cabbage, as well as tobacco. Other crops grown were aubergines, all kinds of marrow, melon and cucumbers, onions and leeks. They were intensely planted and with a twelve-month growing season . . . were very productive.

All income, apart from that from individual plots or the home, is worked out on the basis of work points, which have a money value. The handout of rice, although paid for, is based on the number of mouths to feed.

You are asked to help with the harvest. A typical day in your life runs:

Source 11R

We gathered at 6 a.m., after washing at the well and sweeping out our rooms. We recited several quotations from Chairman Mao, and set off for the lichee orchards. The team member who was responsible for this orchard explained the job and showed us how to pick the fruit, and away we went, picking lichees. After we had enough for several basketfuls, we settled in the shade of a tree to strip the fruit from the branches. [It rains; you go to a nearby cottage and strip the fruit from the branches.]

In the afternoon we went to another orchard, which was near the brick kiln. A group of middle-aged women were working with us. They were very lively, and chatted away gaily as they

*An area of land.

worked, sitting up in the trees picking off the bunches of fruit. Since our timetable was to work until 5.30, we usually started to clear up at about 5 o'clock.

You are staying with the Fong family:

Source 11S

The home consisted of a covered entrance leading to a tiny patio about four yards square, a kitchen on one side of the entrance way containing a huge iron cooking vessel fitted like an old fashioned English wash boiler, a bedroom opposite the kitchen, and finally a third room with no wall on one side which was open to the patio. There were no windows, nor a chimney for the kitchen.

Mrs Fong was a first-grade worker, which means she was employed on work which is rewarded at the top rate, such as caring for the pigs, and was capable of carrying a full load (perhaps 150 lbs!) on her carrying pole. She was also the team's representative on a county advisory committee. Mr Fong was greatly trusted in the village and had been given the job of looking after the team's store. The 22-year-old son was on a tractor drivers' course, in anticipation of the arrival of a tractor that had been ordered by the brigade. Ai-ling, the 20-year-old daughter, was like her mum, very conscientious and capable. She was leader of a shock team of young women, and was being trained by the present man to take over the job of political instructor of the team.

THE GREAT LEAP FORWARD – SUCCESS OR FAILURE?

At first it seemed that communisation was a great success. In 1958 China had its largest-ever harvest, with grain output at twice the level of 1948. The output of iron doubled in 1959 from the 1958 figure, mainly from backyard furnaces. The success was short-lived. Millions of peasants hated working for wages; they preferred the old village ways. The party members often had little idea of how to run farms and factories. Farm output dropped sharply in 1959, and from 1960 to 1962 there was a widespread famine, in which millions died. Bad weather, bringing floods in some places and drought in others, caused the famine, but forced communisation also played a big part. The story of industry was just as bad. Most of the iron produced was useless. Industrial output in 1961 was 25% of the claimed level of 1959. In 1960, because of a fierce row between Mao and Russia's leaders, all Russia's technicians went home. Even worse, they took with them the blueprints of the factories and dams they were building.

In the longer term, the Great Leap Forward had some important results. The mobilising of the commune brigades into huge workforces building dams, canals, irrigation schemes and waterworks meant that Chinese farming had much more effective control over flooding and water supplies than before. In the villages, the building of small-scale power plants had a major impact: during 1957–64 the consumption of electricity in the countryside went up 23 times.

The setting-up of commune factories and machine shops provided a firm basis for commune self-reliance. The communes, as they had evolved by 1960, were based on natural local economic units of around twenty villages and a small town, and they were an excellent way of running China's countryside. The impact of the Great Leap Forward in the long term can be seen from the figures for farming output, Figure 11.9.

Examination Guidance

The establishment of the communes is another likely examination topic. The questions will probably be made up of from two to six separate sources, which you either have to relate to what you know already, or use to extract information from. Activity 76a is based upon an NEA question, Activity 76b on ideas in all board papers.

ACTIVITY 76a

Targets

Comprehension, recall, synthesis, handling evidence.

Question Guide

Questions 1–3 are simple recall ones; they merely want to know what you can remember about the setting-up of the collectives and the communes. Questions 4 and 5 are completely different: Question 4 requires you to think of the nature of the source, and its origin, while Question 5 asks you to apply what you know about looking for bias in the way a piece uses language and is structured. Questions 6 and 7 call upon what you know already; but in answering Question 7 make sure that you go through the source to find evidence to support what you know about changes in Chinese agrarian life in the 1950s and 1960s.

Activity

Study Sources 11R and 11S and then answer the questions.

1. Suggest a likely date for the scene shown in Source 11R, and give a reason for your choice.
2. What is the name given to the group of people who are working together?
3. What organisation does this group belong to, and when would it have been set up?
4. In what ways might Source 11R be a piece of political propaganda?
5. What suggests that the author of Source 11S is in favour of the way in which Changsha is now run?
6. Why might the government have wanted to have reorganised Changsha village along the lines outlined in Source 11Q?
7. Using your own knowledge, and the evidence in Sources 11Q, 11R and 11S, outline the main changes which might have happened to Changsha in the 1950s and 1960s.

ACTIVITY 76b

Targets

Recall, synthesis, comprehension.

Question Guide

This is an exercise in extracting information from a source. Remember to write in clear simple sentences which contain information about each of the topics.

Activity

Using your own knowledge and Sources 11Q–11S, write three sentences about Changsha, using the following headings:

- commune organisation
- commune headquarters – Zhonglotan
- the brigades
- Changsha village
- village land, property
- production teams
- Fong family.

7 The Cultural Revolution

CHINA'S NEW ECONOMIC POLICY, 1961–3

By 1961 Mao Zedung (Mao Tse-tung) had abandoned the extremes of the commune movement – his government's greatest need was to get farming back on to the same footing as four years earlier so as to feed China's people. In 1960 China began to import huge quantities of grain from Australia and Canada. To encourage the peasants, from 1961 the party allowed families to run their own family plots and sell any spare goods, vegetables, grain or cows in free markets. The old village pattern of farming was re-established, but the pattern of commune organisation, with smaller communes, was retained. In this, about twenty villages surrounded a small town and provided a normal, natural economic unit.

By 1964 it was no longer necessary to import grain from abroad to feed China's people. In the towns and cities the factory workers were encouraged to work for bonuses and prizes – the move was away from labouring solely for the state. Mao was following a similar approach to that of Lenin in Russia in the 1920s – the New Economic Policy (see page 159 above). But would this in turn wreck his plans for a communist society of social equals?

MAO AND COMMUNISM – THE MID-1960s

By the mid-1960s Mao was growing worried about the way China was going. Was she to take the road of pure communism, with equality and everyone sharing what was communally produced, or was he going to allow new classes of peasant farmers and factory managers to emerge who were mainly interested in making money? This seemed to be the route along which Khrushchev's Russia (see page 164) was moving. From 1963–6 there was a fierce debate within the Chinese party's Central Committee, the body which made policy, as to the best path to socialism. Mao was under pressure because the Great Leap Forward had not been a great success – the recovery of China from 1961 could be put down to China's NEP. Opposing Mao were powerful Party Leaders like Deng Xiaoping, later the country's leader, and Liu Shaoqi (Liu Shao-chi), official head of the government as the country's President. They backed the Chinese NEP. Mao pressed for a return to the ideas of pure communism. In May 1965 he won a victory, when the army, under the defence minister, Lin Biao (Lin-piao), abol-

ished all ranks. The soldiers were given a copy of Mao's quotations to read, the famous *Little Red Book*. Despite this, in September 1965 Mao was outvoted within the party's ruling body, its Central Committee. What was he to do?

THE CULTURAL REVOLUTION

Mao's second great fear was that pre-1949, middle-class, bourgeois ideas were being handed on to the young of China through their teachers, both in school and at universities. In 1966 he began a campaign to attack them. In June 1966 the lecturers and administrators of Peking University were attacked through a series of huge wall posters. Peking University was run by a friend of Deng. In July, aged 72, Mao went for his famous nine-mile swim in the Yangtze River to show how fit and strong he was.

Then, during August 1966, Mao declared war on China's right-wing leaders like Deng and their backers in the party, the party members who ran the communes, towns, cities and provinces. Mao appealed for help to the young, mainly students, factory workers and peasants. At a giant rally in Peking, Mao laid down his plan for the struggle against his enemies in his *Sixteen Points*, which he had got the Central Committee of the Chinese communist party to back. In it he outlined how to carry out his slogan, *Struggle, Criticise and Reform*. The first of the Sixteen Points reads:

Source 11T

At present our goal is to struggle against and overthrow those people in charge who are taking the capitalist road. We reject and attack the beliefs, values and bourgeois [middle-class] thinking of middle-class and other authorities. We will transform education, literature and art and all other things which do not fit in to the socialist economic system.

To help him, Mao set up the *Red Guards*. Mao had the support of his wife, Jian Qing (Gian Ching), who became the Red Guard's leader. By the autumn, Mao had addressed eight meetings in Peking, which some 11 million Red Guards attended. They carried Mao's message to the rest of China. You might have been a Red Guard. Most students were. What would this mean? An eye witness tells us that members were:

Source 11U

. . . children of workers, poor peasants, revolutionaries. As well as adopting the working style of 'hard work and simple living' of the People's Liberation Army, they also copied its uniform of khaki drab, peaked cap, gym shoes and Sam Browne belts. Red arm bands proclaimed [showed] their identity.

On 18 August 1966, Chairman Mao spoke to 1 million Red Guards at a rally in Peking. Similar rallies were held throughout China (Source 11V). In the communes, factories, schools and universities the Red Guards attacked all those they felt were enemies of the revolution. Huge posters were used to attack their opponents. Three words summed up *The Cultural Revolution*: 'struggle', 'criticise', 'reform'. *Struggle Meetings* were held, where the Red Guards accused their victims of crimes against Chairman Mao and socialism. One such meeting was at Zhongda University, Canton:

Source 11V   Red Guard Rally

Source 11W

(President Li, who ran the University, faced his enemies.]
The student with the hand microphone stepped forward and shouted, 'Down with Li, the top party person taking the capitalist road!' (Li was brought into the hall.) One of the students pushed him in the back from time to time as he walked, which made him stumble a little. People who had been sitting went up and raised their fists at him and shouted, 'Down with Li! Down with Li!' . . . Several people shouted, 'Bow your head, bow your head!' and one of the students pushed his head down further.

The meeting hurled abuse at Li, claiming he had failed to carry out Chaiman Mao's plans to attack communist party members as well as middle-class teachers and lecturers. Li's accuser claimed:

'Li used the militia to suppress the students. All the reports he made at the beginning of the movement showed his policy of directing the spearhead at many in order to protect a handful. He protected leaders at all levels. Since the beginning of the movement about three hundred teachers have been criticised. Over a hundred in the Physics department have been mentioned in posters. Li said that it was all right and that the department was doing quite well.'

Li was led out of the hall, the chant of the Red Guards ringing in his ears:
Long Live the Great Proletarian Cultural Revolution! Overthrow the top party person in authority taking the capitalist road!
Long live the proletarian [workers'] dictatorship!
Long live the Chinese communist party!
Long live our great leader, great Chairman, Comrade Mao!

Li was lucky. He lived. Others were unlucky. Gangs of Red Guards killed over 1 million people. Schools and universities were closed. Books were burned, churches and temples wrecked. The Red Guards and their masters forced millions branded as class enemies to go and live as peasants in the communes or as workers in China's factories. My sister-in-law worked for a year in China in 1985–6. One of her fellow-teachers had spent ten years cleaning out a factory's toilets. If you had been at school in China then, your teachers might well have been forced to go and work as farm labourers or factory workers. Many spent over a decade doing manual labour, cut off from friends, books and the jobs they loved. Buried alive.

Mao let his Red Guards loose on every one. Deng Xiaoping, later China's ruler, has a crippled son, who lives in a wheelchair. In 1968 some Red Guards threw

him out of the window of a tall building. Deng's son never walked again. Deng himself was forced to go and work as a waiter. Liu Shaoqi (Liu Shao-chi) was thrown into jail, where he later died. Fighting broke out in places. In Nanking in January 1967, over fifty died and hundreds were wounded. Law and order broke down in many provinces, and there was even fighting between Red Guards. To replace the old party machinery, Mao set up local revolutionary committees of Red Guards and revolutionary workers, army representatives and members of the old party and government bodies.

The struggle lasted into 1968, by which time the Red Guards had wrecked the old Chinese communist party. Fighting and chaos continued. Who was now to run the communes, factories, hospitals, schools and universities? Mao was forced to call in the army to restore order and get China back to work. Another method of dealing with the Red Guards was to send some 18 million of them to the countryside to work alongside the peasants.

THE IMPACT OF THE CULTURAL REVOLUTION

The Cultural Revolution resulted in:

- the wrecking of the Chinese education system. The closing of schools, colleges and universities meant that a whole Chinese generation lost their chance of education.
- bitterness among China's educated classes. The way they were treated left a lasting hatred of extreme communism. Victims of the Cultural Revolution began to return to their old jobs ten years later.
- fall in industrial output.
- the party struggle. On Mao's death his enemies in the party regained control (see Section 8 below).

Examination Guidance

The Cultural Revolution is very popular with the examination setters. You must learn up its detail. Activity 77a is taken from the MEG November 1988 Paper 2 China question: Activity 77b is based on the sources used in Section 7 above.

ACTIVITY 77a

Targets

Sources – interpretation and evaluation, use of sources as evidence.

Question Guide

This requires a careful reading-through of the sources, and the extraction of the necessary information. Also refer to pages 16–19 above on how to deal with questions asking about the use of sources as historical evidence.

Look carefully at Sources 1-5. Then answer **all** the questions.

Source 1

A British newspaper reporter describes a visit to the East Flower People's Commune, 1958.

The commune is about 30 miles north of Canton, in the heart of lush green paddies. It is not a bad place from which to survey the Chinese Revolution, because people's communes are the hub of it all. This commune covers 130 square miles, has a population of nearly 57,000 and is divided into 319 production teams.

Like all other communes, the East Flower has its own hospital and local clinics, its own radio station, schools, factories producing farming machines, its own coalmines and, perhaps most impressive of all, its own hydro-electricity wrung from dams constructed by peasants scratching stones from the ground.

Everyone is expected to do his or her stint with a commune. The Chairman has said that it is necessary for everyone to realise what work in the countryside really means and how important it is for China's development.

Source 2

Official statistics showing the growth of communes.

Development of the communes

1953	End of April	Mid-September	End of September	End of December
Number of communes	8,730	16,787	26,425	26,578
Number of families in communes	37,780,000	81,220,000	121,000,000	123,250,000
Percentage of peasant farms in communes	30.4	65.3	98	99.1
Average number of families per commune	4,238	4,781	4,614	4,637

Source 3

Extracts from letters sent by Chinese peasants in the late 1950s to relatives living outside China.

(i)   All property has to be state-owned, all houses and furniture turn into government property. They do what they like. No one has any rights at all.

(ii) People fight each other to get to the rice barrels first, but there is never enough.

(iii) Nor are there vegetables available, not to mention fish and meat. Only sick people with certificates are permitted to buy.

Source 4

A Western writer describes a visit to a commune by P'eng Teh-huai, who was the Minister of Defence at that time. He lost his post in 1959, after criticizing 'The Great Leap Forward'.

I found a large pile of crops lying on the ground apparently abandoned. After a lengthy search an old peasant was found who explained that all able-bodied people were busy trying to set a record for steel production. I exclaimed, 'Hasn't anyone of you given a thought to what you will eat next year if you don't bring in the crops? You're never going to be able to eat steel.' The old peasant nodded vigorously in agreement, but added pointedly, 'True enough. Who would disagree with that. But who can stand up against the wind?'

Source 5

Changes introduced in the 1980s, described by an American historian.

Families now signed contracts with the collective organisations that owned the land, by which the family promised to achieve a certain level of production, and would be rewarded handsomely if they exceeded the contract level. Some were even allowed simply to take any production above the contract level and sell it, for their own benefit, in local markets.

1.   Read Source 4.
     Why would peasants be trying to set a record in steel production at the time of the Great Leap Forward?   **(2)**
2.   Read Source 5.
     Why did these changes have to wait until the 1980s?   **(2)**
3.   Read Source 2.
     In what ways can these statistics be useful to the historian of modern China?   **(6)**
4.   Read Sources 1 and 3.
     Which of these two Sources is likely to be more reliable? Explain your answer fully, referring to the sources.   **(8)**
5.   Khrushchev is reported to have commented about communes in 1958, 'They are old-fashioned. They just don't work.' Do these sources show that view to be true? Explain your answer fully.   **(12)**

Total marks **(30)**

ACTIVITY 77b

Targets

Sources – interpretation and evaluation, use of sources as evidence.

Question Guide

Activity 77b did not have its own mark scheme, but we can base one on the mark schemes for other MEG questions. Note the kind of knowledge that the examiners are looking for, and make sure that you have mastered the content of Section 7 above before going into the examination. The mark scheme is organised in terms of levels (see pages 18–19 above).

Activity

Communism in China since 1949

Look carefully at **Sources 1–5,** which are related to the Cultural Revolution. Then answer all the questions.

Source 1

The line Khrushchev pursues is not true Communism. Guided by this line, not only have the old middle-class elements run wild but new middle-class elements have appeared in large numbers among the leadership of the Soviet Party and government, the managers of state industries and collective farms.

(The Central Committee of the Chinese Communist Party attacks Khrushchev's Phoney Communism, in 1963.)

Source 2

A poster published during the Cultural Revolution attacks Khrushchev and Liu Shao-chi.

Source 3

One of the most striking aspects of the Communist Party in China today is its continued reliance upon mass campaigns to carry out its policies.

They do have some advantages. They enable China's leaders to concentrate their efforts on clear targets, and to encourage the people to work hard. However, they often result in the neglect of other tasks; they will result in the misuse of the little skilled talent the country has; they encourage political disputes; they are disruptive to the country as a whole.

(In 1967, an American observer discusses the 'mass campaigns' in China.)

Source 4

(i) An English teacher writes about the Red Guards during the Cultural Revolution.

The Red Guards have changed the face of the countryside, helping to paint slogans on the walls, such as 'Long Live Chairman Mao'. We also saw them working in the fields or sitting with the villagers deep in study with their red book of quotations.

(ii) Red Guards and peasants in the fields.

Source 5

To tell the truth, I have no respect for the bookworms who have done nothing useful. I dislike them intensely. During the busy summer hoeing time, I just could not give up my task on the farm and hide myself in a small room to study. That would have been very selfish. I would have been guilty of being unworthy of the revolutionary cause which concerns both the peasants and myself.

(A Chinese student's view of examinations, written on an examination paper soon after the Cultural Revolution.)

1. Look at Source 4.
   Explain the following terms:
   (a)   Red Guards;   **(1)**
   (b)   their red book.   **(1)**
2. Read Source 3.
   Give an example of a 'mass campaign' organised by the Chinese government.   **(2)**
3. Read Source 5.
   In what ways can this source be useful to the historian of Communist China?   **(6)**
4. Look at Sources 2 and 4.
   'The photograph used in Source D is more reliable than the poster used in Source B, because the poster is simply political propaganda.' Do you agree with this statement? Explain your answer fully, referring to the sources.   **(8)**
5. 'The Cultural Revolution was concerned with the rivalry between China and the Soviet Union, not about events in China itself.' Do these sources prove this statement? Explain your answer fully.   **(12)**

Total marks **(30)**

Mark scheme

Question 1. Target: Recall
Level 1. One sentence saying who they were, and what was their Red Book.   **(1 mark each)**
Question 2 Targets: Recall. Selection
Level 1. The Cultural Revolution.   **(1)**
Level 2. Need for some detail here such as the date, who was involved, how it was carried out in the provinces. Note that if you had written on the commune movement, you should also get full marks.   **(2)**
Question 3 Targets: Historical Sources – use of as evidence.
Level 1. Simple statement, i.e. gives the view of a Red Guard.   **(1–2)**

Level 2. Gives an indication of the views of the Red Guards towards learning and the role of teaching in society. It also indicates that students are identifying with the peasants, and that they expect to enjoy work on the farm, as part of a Red Guards' life.   **(3–4)**
Level 3. Source gives an official view of the Cultural Revolution. The student is representing the opinions of Mao – the fact that an examination paper is a record of what the student thinks would confirm this. The document is perhaps worthless as evidence of what the student really thinks – it takes the form of propaganda.   **(5–6)**
Question 4. Targets: Detection of bias, inconsistencies
Level 1. Acceptance of the question. A photograph is more useful than a poster because it shows things as they were.   **(1–2)**

Level 2. Deals with the meaning of the word 'propaganda'. Suggests that both sources might be of equal value. Looks at the nature of each source – who made it and why. Links the source to the historical context.   **(3–5)**
Level 3. Level 2, plus detailed analysis of the sources, and an account of the use of wall posters and photographs as means of spreading government ideas.   **(6–8)**
Question 5. Targets: Interpretation and evaluation of historical sources, and their use as evidence.
Level 1. Agrees strongly with one of the opinions in the question, and produces a single piece of evidence to support the argument.   **(1–3)**
Level 2. Produces evidence from two or more sources to back up one or other opinion. Limited reference to the historical context.   **(4–6)**

Level 3. Sketches in the historical background, with an account of Sino-Soviet differences. Produces an argument which draws on the sources to support the views being expressed.

(7–9)

Level 4. As with Level 3, but produces points of detail from the sources to back the views being expressed, e.g. using Source D to support the opinion that the views of Mao on communism were the main element within the Cultural Revolution, with both a quotation and a photograph to show that the Red Guards were working and studying the *Little Red Book* at the same time.

ACTIVITY 77c

Targets

Interpretation and evaluation of historical sources, and their use as evidence.

Question Guide

This requires a careful reading through of the sources, and the extraction of the necessary information. Also refer to section 1.00 on how to deal with questions asking about the use of sources as historical evidence.

Activity

With reference to Source 11W write up to three sentences about each of these points:

(a) What might have happened to the 100 teachers criticised in the Physics department?
(b) How might the Red Guards have treated the militia?
(c) What might the meeting suggest should happen to Li?
(d) What might have happened to teaching in the university?
(e) How might the Cultural Revolution have affected the running of: a commune, a factory, a school, a bank?
(f) What evidence is there of bias in the source?

8 The Struggle for Power

MAO'S DEATH

The Cultural Revolution ended in 1969, with the rout of Mao's enemies. Mao's wife, Jiang Qung (Chiang Ching) played a large part in the government, while the Defence Minister Lin Biao (Lin Piao) seemed set to be the next leader. However, fierce rows still split the leaders – in 1971 Lin Biao died in an air crash in Mongolia. Mao claimed he was fleeing to Russia after trying to kill him (Mao)! Mao called back Deng Xiaoping to be one of the country's rulers, and a fierce struggle broke out between Deng and Jiang Qing. Jiang led a group known as the *Gang of Four*, and she wanted to push on with the ideas behind the Cultural Revolution. What she and her enemies fought about is included in Activity 77. Deng backed plans 1, 2, 7, 8, 9; Jiang policies were 3, 4, 5, 6, 10. Throughout reading about this war to the death for control over China, remember that it was basically a quarrel between the small group of survivors of the Long March.

To keep the peace, one of this small group of China's rulers, *Zhou Enlai* (Chou En-lai), took the leading role. In 1975 the Central Committee backed Zhou's *Four Modernisations* policy – to modernise industry, defence, farming and science. But Chou's role as peacemaker ended when he died in January 1976. April saw Deng being thrown out of office, and his enemy *Hua Guofeng* (Hua Kuo-feng) being made Prime Minister. The Gang of Four had triumphed. Their joy was short-lived, for in September 1976 Mao died.

A fierce struggle for power broke out within the Central Committee between Deng's backers and the Gang of Four. October 1976 witnessed the arrest of the Gang of Four. Deng came back into the government in 1977. The Gang of Four were tried on TV in 1981. Deng accused Mao's wife, Jiang, of being foul and evil beyond belief – can you think why? She was found guilty, and exiled to the countryside to work as a peasant. Today in Yanan her name has been removed from the monuments and the caves where Mao and the communist party leaders lived after the Long March.

Deng carried on the Four Modernisations policy and pushed through a series of plans to make China a more efficient country – his own version of the New Economic Policy. In farming, the communes were broken down into family units. Each unit, after paying a fixed amount to the government, can sell the rest of what it grows and makes in the open market place and share out the profits. Today China has around 50,000 free markets. Industry is also run along profit-making lines, and links with foreign countries and companies are encouraged. In 1988 Japan and China signed a 3 billion dollar agreement for Japan to invest in Chinese industry. China seemed set on a path of modernisation and reform. The events of 1989, with the massacre of thousands of students and civilians in Tiananmen Square, brought the reform movement to a crunching halt. Who knows what the future will bring? History suggests that it will be a surprise package!!

Examination Guidance

Questions are most likely to be set on the Gang of Four, the triumph of Deng and the Four Modernisations programme. The Activity asks you to sort out the differences between Deng and Jiang Qing.

ACTIVITY 78

Target

Comprehension.

Question Guide

This requires you to think carefully about what you know of Deng's and Jiang's policies, and then to see how the policies group together.

Activity

Place the policies below under what you think is the correct heading, Deng's policies/Jiang's policies. Explain why you chose the different lists of policies.

(a) The communes have failed because the peasants have no interest in working for wages. They would prefer to work on their own family and village land as in the past.

(b) China needs a modern army to fight its enemies. It should buy weapons from wherever it can and modernise the training of its soldiers and officers.

(c) The only way to make sure that output from the land goes up is to have jointly owned and run farming. The old system of private plots failed.

(d) China can rely on its mass, peasant army to fight any enemy. The old ways were good enough to fight the Japanese to a standstill and halt the Americans in Korea. China does not need a small, highly trained and expensively equipped modern army.

(e) The party is the only way in which communism can be spread to the masses. It must keep full control over all aspects of Chinese life.

(f) An equal society means that pay is based upon what people need. There should not be any special pay for special work.

(g) China is dropping further and further behind in industry, it needs to introduce the profit motive and give each factory and works control over what it makes and how it runs its affairs. Technical knowledge must be bought from the West and Japan.

(h) The party must withdraw from running the peasants' farming, industry and business. It is holding things back because political ideas are lousy for running business.

(i) For China to survive, she needs to encourage her most able and skilled. This will require extra pay and bonuses for those who make the biggest contribution.

(j) In industry China has made huge strides since 1949. The thoughts of Chairman Mao have triumphed, so why leave a path which has been so successful? Communist countries who have borrowed from the West are in a terrible mess – bankrupt, with industry which is no better off than before.

Deng's policies	Jiang's policies

INDEX

Macmillan Work Out Series

For GCSE examinations

Accounting
Biology
Business Studies
Chemistry
Computer Studies
English Key Stage 4
French (cassette and pack available)
Geography
German (cassette and pack available)
Modern World History
Human Biology
Core Maths Key Stage 4
Revise Mathematics to further level
Physics
Religious Studies
Science
Social and Economic History
Spanish (cassette and pack available)
Statistics

For A Level examinations

Accounting
Biology
Business Studies
Chemistry
Economics
English
French (cassette and pack available)
Mathematics
Physics
Psychology
Sociology
Statistics